# WEB OF DEBT

The Shocking Truth
About Our Money System--
The Sleight of Hand
That Has Trapped Us in Debt
and How We Can Break Free

ELLEN HODGSON BROWN, J.D.

Third Millennium Press
Baton Rouge, Louisiana

Cover art by David Dees
www.deesillustration.com

Library of Congress Control Number 2007904766
Includes bibliographic references, glossary and index.
Subject headings:

Banks and banking -- United States.
Business and investing -- Finance.
Developing countries -- Economic policy.
Economics -- Debt and deficits, inflation.
Federal Reserve banks -- History.
Financial crises -- United States.
Imperialism --History -- 20th century.
Greenbacks -- History.
Money and monetary policy.
United States -- Economic policy.

Published by Third Millennium Press
Baton Rouge, Louisiana
www.webofdebt.com
800-891-0390

ISBN 978-0-9795608-0-4

# CONTENTS

*To my grandmother Ella Mae Hodgson,*
*who died in difficult circumstances*
*during the Great Depression;*
*and to my parents Al and Genny Hodgson,*
*who lived through it.*

# ACKNOWLEDGMENTS

This book has been heavily shaped by the feedback of many astute friends, who have puzzled over the concepts and helped me to make them easy to understand; and of a number of experts who have helped me to understand them myself. Georgia Wooldridge helped with structural design with an architect's eye. Bob Silverstein looked at the material with a sharp agent's eye. Gene Harter and Lance Haddix reviewed it from a banker's perspective. My children Jeff and Jamie Brown challenged it as graduate students in economics. Paul Hodgson gave the libertarian perspective. Lawrence Bologna and Don Bruce did detailed editings. Duane Thorin brought a fresh critical approach to the material; and Toni Decker, who purports to know nothing about banking, spotted issues Alan Greenspan might have missed. Valuable insights were also added by Nancy Batchelder, Eddy Taylor, Richard Miles, Bruce Baumrucker, Paul Hunt, Bob Poteat, Nancy O'Hara, Tom Nead and Bonnie Lange. Among the experts, Ed Griffin, Ben Gisin, and Reed Simpson clarified the mysteries of "fractional reserve" banking; Sergio Lub, Tom Greco, Carol Brouillet and Bernard Lietaer illuminated community currency concepts; and Stephen Zarlenga expounded on the Greenback solution. Cordell Svengalis was responsible for formatting, Charles Montgomery experimented with graphics, and David Dees translated the theme into a visually arresting cover. Cliff Brown made this book possible. Acknowledgment is also due to all those diligent researchers who uncovered the puzzle pieces assembled here, who are liberally cited and quoted in the following pages. Thanks.

## Author's Note

Somebody once said works of art are never finished, just relinquished to the world. This research is a work in progress, begun when I was a law student in the 1970s but was limited to the material available in the library and in journals. With the explosion of information in the Internet Age, the missing pieces have fallen into place; but while I have been five years assembling them, I still find errors, quotes that turn out to be apocryphal, and things needing to be updated. I have heavily footnoted my sources and quoted extensively, in hopes of aiding the next generation of researchers who might be inspired to carry on the pursuit.

Ellen Brown, July 2007

# FOREWORD
## by
## REED SIMPSON, M.Sc.,
## Banker and Developer

I have been a banker for most of my career, and I can report that even most bankers are not aware of what goes on behind closed doors at the top of their field. Bankers tend to their own corner of the banking business, without seeing the big picture or the ramifications of the whole system they are helping to perpetuate. I am more familiar than most with the issues raised in Ellen Brown's book <u>Web of Debt</u>, and I still found it to be an eye-opener, a remarkable window into what is really going on.

The process by which money comes into existence is thoroughly misunderstood, and for good reason: it has been the focus of a highly sophisticated and long-term disinformation campaign that permeates academia, media, and publishing. The complexity of the subject has been intentionally exploited to keep its mysteries hidden. Henry Ford said it best: *"It is well that the people of the nation do not understand our banking and monetary system, for if they did, I believe there would be a revolution before tomorrow morning."*

In banking schools and universities, I was drilled in the technology of money and banking, clearing houses, the Federal Reserve System, money creation through the multiplier effect, and the peculiar role of the commercial banker as the guardian of the public treasure. This idealized vision contrasted sharply with what I saw as I worked in the U.S. banking sector. Although there are many financially sound banks that follow the highest ethical standards, corruption is also rampant that flies in the face of the stated ethical objectives of the American Bankers Association and the guidelines of the FDIC, the Comptroller of the Currency, and other regulators. This tendency is particularly evident in the large money center banks, in one of which I worked.

In my experience, in fact, the chief source of bank robbery is not masked men looting tellers' cash tills but the blatant abuse of the extension of credit by white collar criminals. A common practice is for loan officers to ignore the long-term risk of loans and approve those loan transactions with the highest fees and interest paid immediately – income which can be distributed to the principal executives of the bank. Such distribution is buried within the bank's owner/manager compensation and is distributed to the principal owners as dividends and stock options. That helps explain why, in my home state of Kansas, a major bank in Topeka was run into bankruptcy after its chairman entered into a development and construction loan involving a mortgaged 5,000 acre residential development tract in the "exurbs" far outside of Houston, Texas. The development included curbs, gutters, pavement, street lighting, water, sewer, electricity – everything but homes and families! If the loan had been metered out in small phases to match market absorption, the chairman of that once-fine institution would not have been able to disburse to himself and his friends the enormous up-front loan fees and interest owing to that specific transaction, or to the many loans he made just like it. During the 1980s, developers from across the country beat a path to sleepy Topeka and other areas sporting similar financial institutions, just to have a chance to dance with these corrupt lenders. The managers and developers got rich, leaving the banks' shareholders and the taxpayers to pay the bill.

These are just individual instances of corruption, but they indicate a mind-set to exploit and a system that can be exploited. Ellen Brown's book focuses on a more fundamental fraud in the banking system – the creation and control of money itself by private bankers, in a *debt-money* system that returns a steady profit in the form of interest to the debt-money producers, saddling the nation with a growing mountain of unnecessary and impossible-to-repay debt. The fact that money creation is nearly everywhere a private affair is largely unknown today, but the issue is not new. The control of the money system by private interests was known to many of our earlier leaders, as  shown in a number of quotes reprinted in this book, including these:

> *The real truth of the matter is, as you and I know, that a financial element in the large centers has owned the Government ever since the days of Andrew Jackson.*
>
> *-- President Franklin Delano Roosevelt, November 23, 1933, in a letter to Colonel Edward Mandell House*

*Some people think the Federal Reserve Banks are U.S. government institutions. They are not . . . they are private credit monopolies which prey upon the people of the U.S. for the benefit of themselves and their foreign and domestic swindlers, and rich and predatory money lenders. The sack of the United States by the Fed is the greatest crime in history. Every effort has been made by the Fed to conceal its powers, but the truth is the Fed has usurped the government. It controls everything here and it controls all our foreign relations. It makes and breaks governments at will.*

-- *Congressman Charles McFadden, Chairman, House Banking and Currency Committee, June 10, 1932*

Web of Debt gives a blow by blow account of how a network of private bankers has taken over the creation and control of the international money system and what they are doing with that control. Credible evidence is presented of a world power elite intent on gaining absolute control over the planet and its natural resources, including its subservient "human resources" or "human capital." The lifeblood of this power elite is money, and its weapon is fear. The whole of civilization and all of its systems hang on this fulcrum of the money power. In private hands, where it is now, it can be used to enslave nations and ensure perpetual wars and bondage. Internationally, the banksters and their governmental partners use these fraudulent economic tools to weaken or defeat opponents without a shot being fired. Witness the recent East Asian financial crisis of 1997 and the Russian ruble collapse of 1998. Economic means have long been used to spark wars, as a pretext and prelude for the money power to stock and restock the armaments and infrastructure of both sides.

Brown's book is thus about more than just monetary theory and reform. By exposing the present unsustainable situation, it is a first step toward loosening the malign grip on the world held by a very small but powerful financial faction. The book can serve to spark an open dialogue concerning the most important topic of our monetary system, one that is practically off limits today in conventional economic circles due to intimidation and fear of the consequences an honest discourse might bring. Brown is not afraid of stepping on the black patent leather wingtips of the money power and their academic economist servants. Her book is a raised clenched fist of defiance and truth smashing through their finely spun web of disinformation, distortion, deceit, and boldfaced lies concerning money, banking, and economics. It exposes the covert financial enemy that has gotten inside the gates of our Troy, making it our first line of defense against the unrestricted asymmetrical warfare which is presently directed against the people of America and the world.

This book not only exposes the problem but outlines a sound solution for the ever-increasing debt and other monetary woes of the nation and the world. It shows that ending the debt-money fractional reserve banking system and returning to an honest debt-free monetary system could provide Americans with a future that is prosperous beyond our imagining. An editorial directed against Lincoln's debt-free Greenbacks, ascribed to <u>The London Times</u>, said it all:

> *If that mischievous financial policy which had its origin in the North American Republic during the late war in that country, should become indurated down to a fixture, then that Government will furnish its own money without cost. It will pay off its debts and be without debt. It will become prosperous beyond precedent in the history of the civilized governments of the world. The brains and wealth of all countries will go to North America. That government must be destroyed or it will destroy every monarchy on the globe.*

-- REED SIMPSON, M.Sc., Overland Park, Kansas
American Bankers Association Graduate School of Banking
London School of Economics, Graduate School of Economics
University of Kansas Graduate School of Architecture

-- November 2006

# Introduction

# CAPTURED BY THE DEBT SPIDER

*Through a network of anonymous financial spider webbing only a handful of global King Bankers own and control it all. . . . Everybody, people, enterprise, State and foreign countries, all have become slaves chained to the Banker's credit ropes.*

*-- Hans Schicht, "The Death of Banking" (February 2005)*[1]

President Andrew Jackson called the banking cartel "a hydra-headed monster eating the flesh of the common man." New York Mayor John Hylan, writing in the 1920s, called it a "giant octopus" that "seizes in its long and powerful tentacles our executive officers, our legislative bodies, our schools, our courts, our newspapers, and every agency created for the public protection." The debt spider has devoured farms, homes and whole countries that have become trapped in its web.

In "The Death of Banking," financial commentator Hans Schicht states that he had an opportunity in his career to observe the wizards of finance as an insider at close range. Their game, he says, has gotten so centralized and concentrated that the greater part of U.S. banking and enterprise is now under the control of a small inner circle of men. He calls the game "spider webbing." Its rules include:

- Making any concentration of wealth invisible.
- Exercising control through "leverage" – mergers, takeovers, chain share holdings where one company holds shares of other companies, conditions annexed to loans, and so forth.
- Exercising tight personal management and control, with a minimum of insiders and front-men who themselves have only partial knowledge of the game.

Dr. Carroll Quigley was a writer and professor of history at Georgetown University, where he was President Bill Clinton's mentor. Professor Quigley wrote from personal knowledge of an elite clique of global financiers bent on controlling the world. Their aim, he said, was "nothing less than to create a world system of financial control in private hands able to dominate the political system of each country and the economy of the world as a whole." This system was "to be controlled in a feudalist fashion by the central banks of the world acting in concert, by secret agreements."[2] He called this clique simply the "international bankers." Their essence was not race, religion or nationality but was just a passion for control over other humans. The key to their success was that *they would control and manipulate the money system of a nation while letting it appear to be controlled by the government.*

The international bankers have succeeded in doing more than just controlling the money supply. Today they actually *create* the money supply, while making it appear to be created by the government. This devious scheme was revealed by Sir Josiah Stamp, director of the Bank of England and the second richest man in Britain in the 1920s. Speaking at the University of Texas in 1927, he dropped this bombshell:

> *The modern banking system manufactures money out of nothing.* The process is perhaps the most astounding piece of sleight of hand that was ever invented. Banking was conceived in inequity and born in sin . . . . *Bankers own the earth.* Take it away from them but leave them the power to create money, and, with a flick of a pen, they will create enough money to buy it back again. . . . Take this great power away from them and all great fortunes like mine will disappear, for then this would be a better and happier world to live in. . . . But, *if you want to continue to be the slaves of bankers and pay the cost of your own slavery, then let bankers continue to create money and control credit.*[3]

Professor Henry C. K. Liu is an economist who graduated from Harvard and chaired a graduate department at UCLA before becoming an investment adviser for developing countries. He calls the current monetary scheme a "cruel hoax." When we wake up to that fact, he says, our entire economic world view will need to be reordered, "just as physics was subject to reordering when man's world view changed with the realization that the earth is not stationary nor is it the center of the universe."[4] The hoax is that there is virtually no "real" money in the system, only debts. Except for coins, which are issued by the government and make up only about one one-thousandth of the money supply, *the entire U.S. money supply now consists of debt to private banks, for money they created with accounting entries on their books.* It is all done by sleight of hand; and like a magician's trick, we have to see it many times before we realize what is going on. But when we do, it changes everything. All of history has to be rewritten.

The following chapters track the web of deceit that has engulfed us in debt, and present a simple solution that could make the country solvent once again. It is not a new solution but dates back to the Constitution: the power to create money needs to be returned to the government and the people it represents. The federal debt could be paid, income taxes could be eliminated, and social programs could be expanded; and this could all be done *without* imposing austerity measures on the people or sparking runaway inflation. Utopian as that may sound, it represents the thinking of some of America's brightest and best, historical and contemporary, including Abraham Lincoln, Thomas Jefferson and Benjamin Franklin. Among other arresting facts explored in this book are that:

- The "Federal" Reserve is not actually federal. It is a private corporation owned by a consortium of very large multinational banks. (Chapter 13.)
- Except for coins, the government does not create money. Dollar bills (Federal Reserve Notes) are created by the private Federal Reserve, which *lends* them to the government. (Chapter 2.)
- Tangible currency (coins and dollar bills) together make up less than 3 percent of the U.S. money supply. The other 97 percent exists only as data entries on computer screens, and *all* of this money was created by banks in the form of loans. (Chapters 2 and 17.)
- The money that banks lend is not recycled from pre-existing deposits. It is new money, which did not exist until it was lent. (Chapters 17 and 18.)
- Thirty percent of the money created by banks with accounting entries is *invested for their own accounts*. (Chapter 18.)
- The American banking system, which at one time extended productive loans to agriculture and industry, has today become a giant betting machine. An estimated *$370 trillion* are now riding on complex high-risk bets known as derivatives — 28 times the $13 trillion annual output of the entire U.S. economy. These bets are funded by big U.S. banks and are made largely with borrowed money created on a computer screen. Derivatives can be and have been used to manipulate markets, loot businesses, and destroy competitor economies. (Chapters 20 and 32.)
- The U.S. federal debt has not been paid off since the days of Andrew Jackson. Only the interest gets paid, while the principal portion

continues to grow. (Chapter 2.)

- The federal income tax was instituted specifically to coerce taxpayers to pay the interest due to the banks on the federal debt. If the money supply had been created by the government rather than borrowed from banks that created it, the income tax would have been unnecessary. (Chapters 13 and 43.)
- The interest alone on the federal debt will soon be more than the taxpayers can afford to pay. When we can't pay, the Federal Reserve's debt-based dollar system must collapse. (Chapter 29.)
- Contrary to popular belief, creeping inflation is not caused by the government irresponsibly printing dollars. It is caused by banks expanding the money supply with loans. (Chapter 10.)
- Most of the runaway inflation seen in "banana republics" has been caused, not by national governments over-printing money, but by global institutional speculators attacking local currencies and devaluing them on international markets. (Chapter 25.)
- The same sort of speculative devaluation could happen to the U.S. dollar if international investors were to abandon it as a global "reserve" currency, something they are now threatening to do in retaliation for what they perceive to be American economic imperialism. (Chapters 29 and 37.)
- There is a way out of this morass. The early American colonists found it, and so did Abraham Lincoln and some other national leaders: the government can take back the money-issuing power from the banks. (Chapters 8 and 24.)

The bankers' Federal Reserve Notes and the government's coins represent two separate money systems that have been competing for dominance throughout recorded history. At one time, the right to issue money was the sovereign right of the king; but that right got usurped by private moneylenders. Today the sovereigns are the people, and the coins that make up less than one one-thousandth of the money supply are all that are left of our sovereign money. Many nations have successfully issued their own money, at least for a time; but the bankers' debt-money has generally infiltrated the system and taken over in the end. These concepts are so foreign to what we have been taught that it can be hard to wrap our minds around them, but the facts have been substantiated by many reliable authorities. To cite a few –

Robert H. Hemphill, Credit Manager of the Federal Reserve Bank of Atlanta, wrote in 1934:

> We are completely dependent on the commercial Banks. *Someone has to borrow every dollar we have in circulation, cash or credit.* If the Banks create ample synthetic money we are prosperous; if not, we starve. *We are absolutely without a permanent money system.* When one gets a complete grasp of the picture, the tragic absurdity of our hopeless position is almost incredible, but there it is. *It is the most important subject intelligent persons can investigate and reflect upon.*[5]

Graham Towers, Governor of the Bank of Canada from 1935 to 1955, acknowledged:

> Banks create money. That is what they are for. . . . The manufacturing process to make money consists of making an entry in a book. That is all. . . . *Each and every time a Bank makes a loan . . . new Bank credit is created -- brand new money.*[6]

Robert B. Anderson, Secretary of the Treasury under Eisenhower, said in an interview reported in the August 31, 1959 issue of U.S. News and World Report:

> [W]hen a bank makes a loan, it simply adds to the borrower's deposit account in the bank by the amount of the loan. *The money is not taken from anyone else's deposit; it was not previously paid in to the bank by anyone. It's new money, created by the bank for the use of the borrower.*

Michel Chossudovsky, Professor of Economics at the University of Ottawa, wrote during the Asian currency crisis of 1998:

> [P]rivately held money reserves in the hands of "institutional speculators" far exceed the limited capabilities of the World's central banks. The latter acting individually or collectively are no longer able to fight the tide of speculative activity. *Monetary policy is in the hands of private creditors who have the ability to freeze State budgets, paralyse the payments process, thwart the regular disbursement of wages to millions of workers (as in the former Soviet Union) and precipitate the collapse of production and social programmes.*[7]

Today, Federal Reserve Notes and U.S. dollar loans dominate the economy of the world; but this international currency is *not* money issued by the American people or their government. It is money created and lent by a private cartel of international bankers, and this cartel has the United States itself hopelessly entangled in a web of debt. By 2006, combined personal, corporate and federal debt in the United States had reached a staggering 44 trillion dollars – four times the collective national income, or $147,312 for every man, woman and child in the country.[8] The United States is legally bankrupt, defined in the dictionary as being unable to pay one's debts, being insolvent, or having liabilities in excess of a reasonable market value of assets held. By October 2006, the debt of the U.S. government had hit a breathtaking $8.5 trillion. Local, state and national governments are all so heavily in debt that they have been forced to sell off public assets to satisfy creditors. Crowded schools, crowded roads, and cutbacks in public transportation are eroding the quality of American life. A 2005 report by the American Society of Civil Engineers gave the nation's infrastructure an overall grade of D, including its roads, bridges, drinking water systems and other public works. "Americans are spending more time stuck in traffic and less time at home with their families," said the group's president. "We need to establish a comprehensive, long-term infrastructure plan."[9] We need to but we can't, because government at every level is broke.

If governments everywhere are in debt, who are they in debt to? The answer is that they are in debt *to private banks*. The "cruel hoax" is that governments are in debt for money created on a computer screen, money they could have created themselves.

## Money in the Land of Oz

The vast power acquired through this sleight of hand by a small clique of men pulling the strings of government behind the scenes evokes images from <u>The Wizard of Oz</u>, a classic American fairytale that has become a rich source of imagery for financial commentators. In a 2002 article titled "Who Controls the Federal Reserve System?", Victor Thorn wrote:

> In essence, money has become nothing more than illusion -- an electronic figure or amount on a computer screen. . . . As time goes on, we have an increasing tendency toward being sucked into this Wizard of Oz vortex of unreality [by] magician-priests that use the illusion of money as their control device.[12]

Christopher Mark wrote in a series called "The Grand Deception":

> Welcome to the world of the International Banker, who like the famous film, <u>The Wizard of Oz</u>, stands behind the curtain of

orchestrated national and international policymakers and so-called elected leaders.[10]

The late Murray Rothbard, an economist of the classical Austrian School, wrote:

> Money and banking have been made to appear as mysterious and arcane processes that must be guided and operated by a technocratic elite. They are nothing of the sort. In money, even more than the rest of our affairs, we have been tricked by a malignant Wizard of Oz.[11]

James Galbraith wrote in The New American Prospect:

> We are left . . . with the thought that the Federal Reserve Board does not know what it is doing. This is the "Wizard of Oz" theory, in which we pull away the curtains only to find an old man with a wrinkled face, playing with lights and loudspeakers.[13]

The analogies to The Wizard of Oz work for a reason. According to later commentators, the tale was actually written as a monetary allegory, at a time when the "money question" was a key issue in American politics. In the 1890s, politicians were still hotly debating who should create the nation's money and what it should consist of. Should it be created by the government, with full accountability to the people? Or should it be created by private banks behind closed doors, for the banks' own private ends?

William Jennings Bryan, the Populist candidate for President in 1896 and again in 1900, mounted the last serious challenge to the right of private bankers to create the national money supply. According to the commentators, Bryan was represented in Frank Baum's 1900 book The Wonderful Wizard of Oz by the Cowardly Lion. The Lion finally proved he was the King of Beasts by decapitating a giant spider that was terrorizing everyone in the forest. The giant spider Bryan challenged at the turn of the twentieth century was the Morgan/Rockefeller banking cartel, which was bent on usurping the power to create the nation's money from the people and their representative government.

Before World War I, two opposing systems of political economy competed for dominance in the United States. One operated out of Wall Street, the New York financial district that came to be the symbol of American finance. Its most important address was 23 Wall Street, known as the "House of Morgan." J. P. Morgan was an agent of powerful British banking interests. The Wizards of Wall Street and the Old World bankers pulling their strings sought to establish a national currency that was based on the "gold standard," one created privately by the financial elite who controlled the gold. The other system dated back to Benjamin Franklin and operated out of Philadelphia, the country's first capital, where the Constitutional Convention was held and Franklin's "Society for Political Inquiries" planned the industrialization and public works that would free the new republic from economic slavery to England.[14] The Philadelphia faction favored a bank on the model established in provincial Pennsylvania, where a state loan office issued and lent money, collected the interest, and returned it to the provincial government *to be used in place of taxes*. President Abraham Lincoln returned to the colonial system of government-issued money during the Civil War; but he was assassinated, and the bankers reclaimed control of the money machine. The silent coup of the Wall Street faction culminated with the passage of the Federal Reserve Act in 1913, something they achieved by misleading Bryan and other wary Congressmen into thinking the Federal Reserve was actually federal.

Today the debate over who should create the national money supply is rarely heard, mainly because few people even realize it is an issue. Politicians and economists, along with everybody else, simply assume that money is created by the government, and that the "inflation" everybody complains about is caused by an out-of-control government running the dollar printing presses. The puppeteers working the money machine were more visible in the 1890s than they are today, largely because they had not yet succeeded in buying up the media and cornering public opinion.

Economics is a dry and forbidding subject that has been made intentionally complex by banking interests intent on concealing what is really going on. It is a subject that sorely needs lightening up, with imagery, metaphors, characters and a plot; so before we get into the ponderous details of the modern system of money-based-on-debt, we'll take an excursion back to a simpler time, when the money issues were more obvious and were still a burning topic of discussion. The plot line for The Wizard of Oz has been traced to the first-ever march on Washington, led by an obscure Ohio businessman who sought to persuade Congress to return to Lincoln's system of government-issued money in 1894. Besides sparking a century of protest marches and the country's most famous fairytale, this little-known visionary and the band of unemployed men he led may actually have had the solution to the whole money problem, then and now . . . .

# Section I

## THE YELLOW BRICK ROAD: FROM GOLD TO FEDERAL RESERVE NOTES

*"Did you bring your broomstick?"*
*"No, I'm afraid I didn't."*
*"Then you'll have to walk. . . . It's always best to start at the beginning . . . all you do is follow the Yellow Brick Road."*

-- *The Wizard of Oz* (1939 film)

# Chapter 1
# LESSONS FROM
# THE WIZARD OF OZ

*"The great Oz has spoken! Pay no attention to that man behind the curtain! I am the great and powerful Wizard of Oz!"*

In refreshing contrast to the impenetrable writings of economists, the classic fairytale The Wizard of Oz has delighted young and old for over a century. It was first published by L. Frank Baum as The Wonderful Wizard of Oz in 1900. In 1939, it was made into a hit Hollywood movie starring Judy Garland, and later it was made into the popular stage play The Wiz. Few of the millions who have enjoyed this charming tale have suspected that its imagery was drawn from that most obscure and tedious of subjects, banking and finance. Fewer still have suspected that the real-life folk heroes who inspired its plot may have had the answer to the financial crisis facing the country today!

The economic allusions in Baum's tale were first observed in 1964 by a schoolteacher named Henry Littlefield, who called the story "a parable on Populism," referring to the People's Party movement challenging the banking monopoly in the late nineteenth century.[1] Other analysts later picked up the theme. Economist Hugh Rockoff, writing in the Journal of Political Economy in 1990, called the story a "monetary allegory."[2] Professor Tim Ziaukas, writing in 1998, stated:

> "The Wizard of Oz" . . . was written at a time when American society was consumed by the debate over the "financial question," that is, the creation and circulation of money. . . . The characters of "The Wizard of Oz" represented those deeply involved in the debate: the Scarecrow as the farmers, the Tin Woodman as the industrial workers, the Lion as silver advocate

William Jennings Bryan and Dorothy as the archetypal American girl.[3]

The Germans established the national fairytale tradition with Grimm's Fairy Tales, a collection of popular folklore gathered by the Brothers Grimm specifically to reflect German populist traditions and national values.[4] Baum's tale did the same thing for the American populist (or people's) tradition. The Wizard of Oz has been called "the first truly American fairytale."[5] It was all about people power, manifesting your dreams, finding what you wanted in your own backyard. According to Littlefield, the march of Dorothy and her friends to the Emerald City to petition the Wizard of Oz for help was patterned after the 1894 march from Ohio to Washington of an "Industrial Army" led by Jacob Coxey, urging Congress to return to the system of debt-free government-issued Grenbacks initiated by Abraham Lincoln. The march of Coxey's Army on Washington began a long tradition of people taking to the streets in peaceful protest when there seemed no other way to voice their appeals. As Lawrence Goodwin, author of The Populist Moment, described the nineteenth century movement to change the money system:

> [T]here was once a time in history when people acted. . . . [F]armers were trapped in debt. They were the most oppressed of Americans, they experimented with cooperative purchasing and marketing, they tried to find their own way out of the strangle hold of debt to merchants, but none of this could work if they couldn't get capital. So they had to turn to politics, and they had to organize themselves into a party. . . . [T]he populists didn't just organize a political party, they made a movement. They had picnics and parties and newsletters and classes and courses, and they taught themselves, and they taught each other, and they became a group of people with a sense of purpose, a group of people with courage, a group of people with dignity.[6]

Like the Populists, Dorothy and her troop discovered that they had the power to solve their own problems and achieve their own dreams. The Scarecrow in search of a brain, the Tin Man in search of a heart, the Lion in search of courage actually had what they wanted all along. When the Wizard's false magic proved powerless, the Wicked Witch was vanquished by a defenseless young girl and her little dog. When the Wizard disappeared in his hot air balloon, the unlettered Scarecrow took over as leader of Oz.

The Wizard of Oz came to embody the American dream and the American national spirit. In the United States, the land of abundance, all you had to do was to realize your potential and manifest it. That was one of the tale's morals, but it also contained a darker one, a message for which its imagery has become a familiar metaphor: that there are invisible puppeteers pulling the strings of the puppets we see on the stage, in a show that is largely illusion.

## The March on Washington
## That Inspired the March on Oz

The 1890s were plagued by an economic depression that was nearly as severe as the Great Depression of the 1930s. The farmers lived like serfs to the bankers, having mortgaged their farms, their equipment, and sometimes even the seeds they needed for planting. They were charged so much by a railroad cartel for shipping their products to market that they could have more costs and debts than profits. The farmers were as ignorant as the Scarecrow of banking policies; while in the cities, unemployed factory workers were as frozen as the Tin Woodman from the lack of a free-flowing supply of money to "oil" the wheels of industry. In the early 1890s, unemployment had reached 20 percent. The crime rate soared, families were torn apart, racial tensions boiled. The nation was in chaos. Radical party politics thrived.

In every presidential election between 1872 and 1896, there was a third national party running on a platform of financial reform. Typically organized under the auspices of labor or farmer organizations, these were parties of the people rather than the banks. They included the Populist Party, the Greenback and Greenback Labor Parties, the Labor Reform Party, the Antimonopolist Party, and the Union Labor Party. They advocated expanding the national currency to meet the needs of trade, reform of the banking system, and democratic control of the financial system.[7]

Money reform advocates today tend to argue that the solution to the country's financial woes is to return to the "gold standard," which required that paper money be backed by a certain weight of gold bullion. But to the farmers and laborers who were suffering under its yoke in the 1890s, the gold standard was the problem. They had been there and done it and knew it didn't work. William Jennings Bryan called the bankers' private gold-based money a "cross of gold." There was simply not enough gold available to finance the needs of an expanding economy. The bankers made loans in notes backed by gold and required repayment in notes backed by gold; but the bankers controlled the gold, and its price was subject to manipulation by speculators. Gold's price had increased over the course of the century, while the prices laborers got for their wares had dropped. People short of gold had to borrow from the bankers, who periodically contracted the money supply by calling in loans and raising interest rates. The result was "tight" money – insufficient money to go around. Like in a game of musical chairs, the people who came up short wound up losing their homes to the banks.

The solution of Jacob Coxey and his Industrial Army of destitute unemployed men was to augment the money supply with government-issued United States Notes. Popularly called "Greenbacks," these federal dollars were first issued by President Lincoln when he was faced with usurious interest rates in the 1860s. Lincoln had foiled the bankers by funding the government with U.S. Notes that did not accrue interest and did not have to be paid back to the banks. The same sort of debt-free paper money had financed a long period of colonial abundance in the eighteenth century, until King George forbade the colonies from issuing their own currency. The money supply had then shrunk, precipitating a depression that led to the American Revolution.

To remedy the tight-money problem that resulted when the Greenbacks were halted after Lincoln's assassination, Coxey proposed that Congress should increase the money supply with a further $500 million in Greenbacks. This new money would be used to redeem the federal debt and to stimulate the economy by putting the unemployed to work on public projects.[8] The bankers countered that allowing the government to issue money would be dangerously inflationary. What they failed to reveal was that their own paper banknotes were themselves highly inflationary, since the same gold was "lent" many times over, effectively counterfeiting it; and when the bankers lent their paper money to the government, the government wound up heavily in debt for something it could have created itself. But those facts were buried in confusing rhetoric, and the bankers' "gold standard" won the day.

## The Silver Slippers: The Populist Solution
## to the Money Question

The Greenback Party was later absorbed into the Populist Party, which took up the cause against tight money in the 1890s. Like the Greenbackers, the Populists argued that money should be issued by the government rather than by private banks. William Jennings Bryan, the Populists' loquacious leader, gave such a stirring speech at the Democratic convention that he won the Democratic nomination for President in 1896. Outgoing President Grover Cleveland was also a Democrat, but he was an agent of J. P. Morgan and the Wall Street banking interests. Cleveland favored money that was issued by the banks, and he backed the bankers' gold standard. Bryan was opposed to both. He argued in his winning nomination speech:

> We say in our platform that *we believe that the right to coin money and issue money is a function of government.* . . . Those who are opposed to this proposition tell us that the issue of paper money is a function of the bank and that the government ought to go out of the banking business. I stand with Jefferson . . . and tell them, as he did, that *the issue of money is a function of the government and that the banks should go out of the governing business.* . . . [W]hen we have restored the money of the Constitution, all other necessary reforms will be possible, and . . . until that is done there is no reform that can be accomplished.

He concluded with these famous lines:

> You shall not press down upon the brow of labor this crown of thorns, you shall not crucify mankind upon a cross of gold.[9]

Since the Greenbackers' push for government-issued paper money had failed, Bryan and the "Silverites" proposed solving the liquidity problem in another way. The money supply could be supplemented with coins made of silver, a precious metal that was cheaper and more readily available than gold. Silver was considered to be "the money of the Constitution." The Constitution only referred to the "dollar," but the dollar was understood to be a reference to the Spanish milled silver dollar coin then in common use. The slogan of the Silverites was "16 to 1": 16 ounces of silver would be the monetary equivalent of 1 ounce of gold. Ounces is abbreviated oz, hence "Oz." The Wizard of the Gold Ounce (Oz) in Washington was identified by later commentators as Marcus Hanna, the power behind the Republican Party, who controlled the mechanisms of finance in the administration of President William McKinley.[10] (Karl Rove, political adviser to President George Bush Jr., reportedly took Hanna for a role model.[11])

Frank Baum, the journalist who turned the politics of his day into The Wonderful Wizard of Oz, marched with the Populist Party in support of Bryan in 1896. He is said to have had a deep distrust of big-city financiers. But when his dry goods business failed, he bought a Republican newspaper, which had to have a Republican message to retain its readership.[12] That may have been why the Populist message was so deeply buried in symbolism in his famous fairytale. Like Lewis Carroll, who began his career writing uninspiring tracts about mathematics and politics and wound up satirizing Victorian society in Alice's Adventures in Wonderland, Baum was able to suggest in a children's story what he could not say in his editorials. His book contained many subtle allusions to the political and financial issues of the day. The story's inspirational message was a product of the times as well. Commentators trace it to the theosophical movement, of which Baum was an active member.[13] Newly-imported from India, it held that reality is a construct of the mind. What you want is already yours; you need only to believe it, to "realize" it or "make it real."

Looking at the plot of this familiar fairytale, then, through the lens of the contemporary movements that inspired it . . . .

## An Allegory of Money, Politics and Believing in Yourself

The story begins on a barren Kansas farm, where Dorothy lives with a very sober aunt and uncle who "never laughed" (the 1890s depression that hit the farmers particularly hard). A cyclone comes up, carrying Dorothy and the house into the magical world of Oz (the American dream that might have been). The house lands on the Wicked Witch of the East (the Wall Street bankers and their man Grover Cleveland), who has kept the Munchkins (the farmers and factory workers) in bondage for many years.

For killing the Wicked Witch, Dorothy is awarded magic silver slippers (the Populist silver solution to the money crisis) by the Good Witch of the North (the North was then a Populist stronghold). In the 1939 film, the silver slippers would be transformed into ruby slippers to show off the cinema's new technicolor abilities; but the monetary imagery Baum suggested was lost. The silver shoes had the magic power to solve Dorothy's dilemma, just as the Silverites thought that expanding the money supply with silver coins would solve the problems facing the farmers.

Dorothy wanted to get back to Kansas but was unaware of the power of the slippers on her feet, so she set out to the Emerald City to seek help from the Wizard of Oz (the apparently all-powerful President, whose strings were actually pulled by financiers concealed behind a curtain).

"The road to the City of Emeralds is paved with yellow brick," she was told, "so you cannot miss it." Baum's contemporary audience, wrote Professor Ziaukas, could not miss it either, as an allusion to the gold standard that was then a hot topic of debate.[14] Like the Emerald City and the Great and Powerful Oz himself, the yellow brick road would turn out to be an illusion. In the end, what would carry Dorothy home were *silver* slippers.

On her journey down the yellow brick road, Dorothy was first joined by the Scarecrow in search of a brain (the naive but intelligent farmer kept in the dark about the government's financial policies), and then by the Tin Woodman in search of a heart (the factory worker frozen by unemployment and dehumanized by mechanization). Littlefield commented:

> The Tin Woodman . . . had been put under a spell by the Witch of the East. Once an independent and hard working human being, the Woodman found that each time he swung his axe it chopped off a different part of his body. Knowing no other trade he "worked harder than ever," for luckily in Oz tinsmiths can repair such things. Soon the Woodman was all tin. In this way Eastern witchcraft dehumanized a simple laborer so that the faster and better he worked the more quickly he became a kind of machine. Here is a Populist view of evil Eastern influences on honest labor which could hardly be more pointed.

The Eastern witchcraft that had caused the Woodman to chop off parts of his own body reflected the dark magic of the Wall Street bankers, whose "gold standard" allowed less money into the system than was collectively owed to the banks, causing the assets of the laboring classes to be systematically devoured by debt.

The fourth petitioner to join the march on Oz was the Lion in search of courage. According to Littlefield, he represented the orator Bryan himself, whose roar was mighty like the king of the forest but who lacked political power. Bryan was branded a coward by his opponents because he was a pacifist and anti-imperialist at a time of American expansion in Asia. The Lion became entranced and fell asleep in the Witch's poppy field, suggesting Bryan's tendency to get side-tracked with issues of American imperialism stemming from the Opium Wars. Since Bryan led the "Populist" or "People's" Party, the Lion also represented the people, collectively powerful but entranced and unaware of their strength.

In the Emerald City, the people were required to wear green-colored glasses attached by a gold buckle, suggesting green paper money shackled to the gold standard. To get to her room in the Emerald Palace, Dorothy had to go through 7 passages and up 3 flights of stairs, an allusion to the "Crime of '73," the congressional Act that changed the money system from bimetallism (paper notes backed by both gold and silver) to an exclusive gold standard. The Crime of '73 proved to all Populists that Congress and the bankers were in collusion.[15]

Dorothy and her troop presented their requests to the Wizard, who demanded that they first vanquish the Wicked Witch of the West, representing the McKinley/Rockefeller faction in Ohio (then considered a Western state). The financial powers of the day were the Morgan/Wall Street/Cleveland faction in the East (the Wicked Witch of the East) and this Rockefeller-backed contingent from Ohio, the state of McKinley, Hanna, and Rockefeller's Standard Oil cartel. Hanna was an industrialist who was a high school friend of John D. Rockefeller and had the financial backing of the oil giant.[16]

Dorothy and her friends learned that the Witch of the West had enslaved the Yellow Winkies and the Winged Monkeys (an allusion to the Chinese immigrants working on the Union-Pacific railroad, the native Americans banished from the northern woods, and the Filipinos denied independence by McKinley). Dorothy destroyed the Witch by melting her with a bucket of water, suggesting the rain that would reverse the drought, and the financial liquidity that the Populist solution would bring to the land. As one nineteenth century commentator put it, "Money and debt are as opposite in nature as fire and water; money extinguishes debt as water extinguishes fire."[17]

When Dorothy and her troop got lost in the forest, she was told to call the Winged Monkeys by using a Golden Cap she had found in the Witch's cupboard. When the Winged Monkeys came, their leader explained that they were once a free and happy people; but they were now "three times the slaves of the owner of the Golden Cap, whosoever he may be" (the bankers and their gold standard). When the Golden

Cap fell into the hands of the Wicked Witch of the West, the Witch had made them enslave the Winkies and drive Oz himself from the Land of the West.

Dorothy used the power of the Cap to have her band of pilgrims flown to the Emerald City, where they discovered that the "Wizard" was only a smoke and mirrors illusion operated by a little man behind a curtain. A dispossessed Nebraska man himself, he admitted to being a "humbug" without real power. "One of my greatest fears was the Witches," he said, "for while I had no magical powers at all I soon found out that the Witches were really able to do wonderful things."

If the Wizard and his puppet were Marcus Hanna and William McKinley, who were the Witches they feared? Behind the Wall Street bankers were powerful British financiers, who funded the Confederates in the Civil War and had been trying to divide and conquer America economically for over a century. Patriotic Americans had regarded the British as the enemy ever since the American Revolution. McKinley was a protectionist who favored high tariffs to keep these marauding British free-traders out. When he was assassinated in 1901, no conspiracy was proved; but some suspicious commentators saw the invisible hand of British high finance at work.[18]

The Wizard lacked magical powers but was a very good psychologist, who showed the petitioners that they had the power to solve their own problems and manifest their own dreams. The Scarecrow just needed a paper diploma to realize he had a brain. For the Tin Woodman, it was a silk heart; for the Lion, an elixir for courage. The Wizard offered to take Dorothy back to Kansas in his hot air balloon, but the balloon took off before she could get on board. Dorothy and her friends then set out to find Glinda the Good Witch of the South, who they were told could help Dorothy find her way home.

On the way they faced various challenges, including a great spider that ate everything in its path and kept everyone unsafe as long as it was alive. The Lion (the Populist leader Bryan) welcomed this chance to test his new-found courage and prove he was indeed the King of Beasts. He decapitated the mighty spider with his paw, just as Bryan would have toppled the banking cartel if he had won the Presidency.

The group finally reached Glinda, who revealed that Dorothy too had the magic tokens she needed all along: the Silver Shoes on her feet would take her home. But first, said Glinda, Dorothy must give up the Golden Cap (the bankers' restrictive gold standard that had enslaved the people).

The moral also worked for the nation itself. The economy was deep in depression, but the country's farmlands were still fertile and its factories were ready to roll. Its entranced people merely lacked the paper tokens called "money" that would facilitate production and trade. The people had been deluded into a belief in scarcity by defining their wealth in terms of a scarce commodity, gold. The country's true wealth consisted of its goods and services, its resources and the creativity of its people. Like the Tin Woodman in need of oil, all it needed was a monetary medium that would allow this wealth to flow freely, circulating from the government to the people and back again, without being perpetually drained into the private coffers of the bankers.

## Sequel to Oz

The Populists did not achieve their goals, but they did prove that a third party could influence national politics and generate legislation. Although Bryan the Lion failed to stop the bankers, Dorothy's prototype Jacob Coxey was still on the march. In a plot twist that would be considered contrived if it were fiction, he reappeared on the scene in the 1930s to run against Franklin D. Roosevelt for President, at a time when the "money question" had again become a burning issue. In one five-year period, over 2,000 schemes for monetary reform were advanced. Needless to say, Coxey lost the election; but he claimed that his Greenback proposal was the model for the "New Deal," Roosevelt's plan for putting the unemployed to work on government projects to pull the country out of the Depression. The difference was that Coxey's plan would have been funded with debt-free currency issued by the government, on Lincoln's Greenback model. Roosevelt funded the New Deal with borrowed money, indebting the country to a banking cartel that was surreptitiously creating the money out of thin air, just as the government itself would have been doing under Coxey's plan without accruing a crippling debt to the banks.

After World War II, the money question faded into obscurity. Today, writes British economist Michael Rowbotham, "The surest way to ruin a promising career in economics, whether professional or academic, is to venture into the 'cranks and crackpots' world of suggestions for reform of the financial system."[19] Yet the claims of these cranks and crackpots have consistently proven to be correct. The U.S. debt burden has mushroomed out of control, until just the interest on the federal debt now threatens to be a greater tax burden than the taxpayers can afford. The gold standard precipitated the problem, but unbuckling the dollar from gold did not solve it. Rather, it caused worse financial ills. Expanding the money supply with increasing amounts of "easy" bank credit just put increasing amounts of money in the bankers' pockets, while consumers sank further into debt. The problem proved to be something more fundamental: it was in *who* extended the nation's credit. As long as the money supply was created as a debt owed back to private banks with interest, the nation's wealth would continue to be drained off into private vaults, leaving scarcity in its wake.

Today's monetary allegory goes something like this: the dollar is a national resource that belongs to the people. It was an original invention of the early American colonists, a new form of paper currency backed by the "full faith and credit" of the people. But a private banking cartel has taken over its issuance, turning debt into money and demanding that it be paid back with interest. Taxes and a crushing federal debt have been imposed by a financial ruling class that keeps the people entranced and enslaved. In the happy storybook ending to the tale, the power to create money is returned to the people, and abundance returns to the land. But before we get there, the Yellow Brick Road takes us through the twists and turns of history and the writings and insights of a wealth of key players. We're off to see the Wizard . . . .

# Chapter 2

# BEHIND THE CURTAIN:
# THE FEDERAL RESERVE
# AND THE FEDERAL DEBT

*"Orders are — nobody can see the Great Oz! Not nobody — not nohow! . . . He's in conference with himself on account of this trouble with the Witch. And even if he wasn't you wouldn't have been able to see him anyway on account of nobody has — not even us in the Palace!"*

*- The Wizard of Oz,*
*"The Guardian of the Gates"*

The Federal Reserve did not yet exist when Frank Baum wrote The Wonderful Wizard of Oz, but the book's image of an all-too-human wizard acting behind a curtain of secrecy has been a favorite metaphor for the Fed's illustrious Chairman, who has been called the world's most powerful banker. Unlike the U.S. President, who must worry about re-election every four years and can serve only two terms, the head of the Fed can be reappointed indefinitely and answers to no one. Alan Greenspan served for more than eighteen years under four Presidents before he retired. In a 2001 article titled "Greenspan: Financial Wizard of Oz," journalist Paul Sperry wrote of that long-standing Chairman:

> You may think that congress – and therefore the people – can control him. But all lawmakers can do is call him to testify periodically . . . . The hearings are an exercise in futility, not accountability, because Greenspan just obfuscates till everyone is bored silly. You may think that the press can pin him down. In fact, we have no access to him. No press conferences or

interviews are allowed. The high priest is untouchable in his
marble temple here on Constitution Avenue.[1]

Sperry quoted another Fed-watcher, who remarked:

Here's this guy, projecting this huge brain, and everyone's in
awe of him. But pull back the curtain and there's just this little
man frantically pulling at levers to maintain the image of an
intellectual giant.[2]

Why must the Federal Reserve act behind a curtain of secrecy,
independent of congressional oversight and control? Supposedly this
is necessary so that it can take actions that are in the best interests of
the economy although they might be unpopular with voters. But as
Wright Patman, Chairman of the House Banking and Currency Committee, pointed out in the 1960s, Congress makes decisions every day
that are unpopular, including raising taxes, cutting programs, and
increasing expenditures; yet it does so after open debate, in the democratic way. Why can't the Fed's Chairman, who doesn't even have to
worry about re-election, lay his cards on the table in the same way?

The Wizard of Oz could no doubt have answered that question:
the whole money game is sleight of hand, and it depends on deception
to work.

## A Game of Smoke and Mirrors

Illusion surrounding the Federal Reserve begins with its name. The
Federal Reserve is not actually federal, and it keeps no reserves — at
least, not in the sense most people think. No gold or silver backs its
Federal Reserve notes (our dollar bills). A booklet published by the
Federal Reserve Bank of New York states:

Currency cannot be redeemed, or exchanged, for Treasury gold
or any other asset used as backing. The question of just what
assets "back" Federal Reserve notes has little but bookkeeping
significance.[3]

Although the Federal Reserve is commonly called the "Fed," confusing it with the U.S. government, it is actually a private corporation.[4] It is so private that its stock is not even traded on the stock
exchange. The government doesn't own it. You and I can't own it. It
is owned by a consortium of private banks, the biggest of which are
Citibank and J. P. Morgan Chase Company. These two mega-banks
are the financial cornerstones of the empires built by J. P. Morgan and

John D. Rockefeller, the "Robber Barons" who orchestrated the Federal Reserve Act in 1913. (More on this in Chapter 13.)

As for keeping "reserves," Wright Patman decided to see for himself. Having heard that Federal Reserve Banks hold large amounts of cash, he visited two regional Federal Reserve banks, where he was led into vaults and shown great piles of government securities (I.O.U.s representing debt).[i] When he asked to see their cash, the bank officials seemed confused. He repeated the request, only to be shown some ledgers and bank checks. Patman wrote:

> The cash, in truth, does not exist and never has existed. What we call "cash reserves" are simply bookkeeping credits entered upon the ledgers of the Federal Reserve Banks. These credits are created by the Federal Reserve Banks and then passed along through the banking system.[5]

Where did the Federal Reserve get the money to acquire all the government bonds in its vaults? Patman answered his own rhetorical question:

> *It doesn't get money, it creates it.* When the Federal Reserve writes a check for a government bond *it does exactly what any bank does, it creates money, it created money purely and simply by writing a check.* [When] the recipient of the check wants cash, then the Federal Reserve can oblige him by printing the cash — Federal Reserve notes — which the check receiver's commercial bank can hand over to him. *The Federal Reserve, in short, is a total money-making machine.*[6]

### Turning Debt Into Money

Although the Federal Reserve is indispensable to the bankers' money-making machine, the dollar bills it creates represent only a very small portion of the money supply. Most money today is created *neither* by the government *nor* by the Federal Reserve but by *private commercial banks*. The "money supply" is defined as the entire quantity of bills, coins, loans, credit, and other liquid instruments in a country's economy.

---

[i] A "security" is a type of transferable interest representing financial value. The securities composing the federal debt consist of U.S. Treasury bills (or T-bills -- securities which mature in a year or less), Treasury notes (which mature in two to ten years), and Treasury bonds (which mature in ten years or longer).

"Liquid" instruments are those that are easily convertible into cash. The American money supply is officially divided into M1, M2, and M3. Only M1 is what we usually think of as money – coins, dollar bills, and the money in our checking accounts. M2 is M1 plus savings accounts, money market funds, and other individual or "small" time deposits. (The "money market" is the trade in short-term, low-risk securities, such as certificates of deposit and U.S. Treasury notes.) M3 is M1 and M2 plus institutional and other larger time deposits (including institutional money market funds) and eurodollars (American dollars circulating abroad).

In 2005, M1 (coins, dollar bills and checking account deposits) tallied in at $1.4 trillion. Federal Reserve Notes in circulation came to $758 billion, but about 70 percent of those circulated overseas, bringing the figure down to $227.5 billion in use in the United States.[7] The U.S. Mint reported that in September 2004, circulating collections of coins came to only $993 million, or just under $1 billion.[8] M3 (the largest measure of the money supply) was $9.7 trillion in 2005.[9] Thus coins made up only about one one-thousandth of the total money supply (M3), and tangible currency in the form of coins and Federal Reserves Notes (dollar bills) together made up only about 2.4 percent of it. *The other 97.6 percent magically appeared from somewhere else.* This was the money Wright Patman said was created by banks when they make loans.

The mechanics of money creation were explained in a revealing booklet published by the Chicago Federal Reserve in the 1960s, called "Modern Money Mechanics: A Workbook on Bank Reserves and Deposit Expansion."[10] The booklet is a gold mine of insider information and will be explored at length later, but here are some highlights. It begins, "The purpose of this booklet is to describe the basic process of money creation in a 'fractional reserve' banking system. . . . *The actual process of money creation takes place primarily in banks*." The Chicago Fed states:

> [Banks] *do not really pay out loans from the money they receive as deposits. If they did this, no additional money would be created.* What they do when they make loans is to accept promissory notes in exchange for credits to the borrowers' transaction accounts.

The booklet explains that money creation is done by "building up" deposits, and that this is done by making loans. Contrary to popular belief, then, loans *become* deposits rather than the reverse.

The Chicago Fed stated:

> [B]anks can build up deposits by increasing loans and investments so long as they keep enough currency on hand to redeem whatever amounts the holders of deposits want to convert into currency. This unique attribute of the banking business was discovered many centuries ago. It started with goldsmiths . . . .

The "unique attribute" the goldsmiths discovered was that they could issue and lend paper receipts for the same gold many times over, so long as they kept enough gold in "reserve" for any depositors who might come for their money. This sleight of hand was what came to be known as "fractional reserve" banking.

## The Shell Game of the Goldsmiths Becomes "Fractional Reserve" Banking

In seventeenth century Europe, trade was conducted primarily in gold and silver coins. Coins were durable and had value in themselves, but they were hard to transport in bulk and could be stolen if not kept under lock and key. Many people therefore deposited their coins with the goldsmiths, who had the strongest safes in town. The goldsmiths issued convenient paper receipts that could be traded in place of the bulkier coins they represented. These receipts were also used when people who needed coins came to the goldsmiths for loans. The mischief began when the goldsmiths noticed that only about 10 to 20 percent of their receipts came back to be redeemed in gold at any one time. They could safely "lend" the gold in their strongboxes at interest several times over, as long as they kept 10 to 20 percent of the value of their outstanding loans in gold to meet the demand. They thus created "paper money" (receipts for loans of gold) worth several times the gold they actually held. They typically issued notes and made loans in amounts that were four to five times their actual supply of gold. At an interest rate of 20 percent, the same gold lent five times over produced a 100 percent return every year – on gold the goldsmiths did not actually own and could not legally lend at all! If they were careful not to overextend this "credit," the goldsmiths could thus become quite wealthy without producing anything of value themselves. Since more money was owed back than the townspeople as a whole possessed, the wealth of the town and eventually of the country was siphoned into the vaults of these goldsmiths-turned-bankers, while the people fell progressively into their debt.[11]

If a landlord had rented the same house to five people at one time and pocketed the money, he would quickly have been jailed for fraud. But the goldsmiths had devised a system in which they traded, not things of value, but paper receipts for them. The system was called "fractional reserve" banking because the gold held in reserve was a mere fraction of the banknotes it supported. In 1934, Elgin Groseclose, Director of the Institute for International Monetary Research, would wryly observe:

> A warehouseman, taking goods deposited with him and devoting them to his own profit, either by use or by loan to another, is guilty of a tort, a conversion of goods for which he is liable in civil, if not in criminal, law. By a casuistry which is now elevated into an economic principle, but which has no defenders outside the realm of banking, a warehouseman who deals in money is subject to a diviner law: the banker is free to use for his private interest and profit the money left in trust. . . . He may even go further. *He may create fictitious deposits on his books, which shall rank equally and ratably with actual deposits in any division of assets in case of liquidation.*[12]

A *tort* is a wrongdoing for which a civil action may be brought for damages. *Conversion* is treating someone else's property as one's own. Another tort that has been applied to this sleight of hand is *fraud*, defined in Black's Law Dictionary as "a false representation of a matter of fact, whether by words or by conduct, by false or misleading allegations, or by concealment of that which should have been disclosed, which deceives and is intended to deceive another so that he shall act upon it to his legal injury." That was the term used by the court in a landmark Minnesota lawsuit in 1969 . . . .

## Taking It to Court

First National Bank of Montgomery vs. Daly was a courtroom drama worthy of a movie script. Defendant Jerome Daly opposed the bank's foreclosure on his $14,000 home mortgage loan on the ground that there was no consideration for the loan. "Consideration" ("the thing exchanged") is an essential element of a contract. Daly, an attorney representing himself, argued that the bank had put up no real money for his loan.

The courtroom proceedings were recorded by Associate Justice Bill Drexler, whose chief role, he said, was to keep order in a highly charged courtroom where the attorneys were threatening a fist fight. Drexler hadn't given much credence to the theory of the defense, until Mr. Morgan, the bank's president, took the stand. To everyone's surprise, Morgan admitted that the bank routinely created money "out of thin air" for its loans, and that this was standard banking practice.

"*It sounds like fraud to me,*" intoned Presiding Justice Martin Mahoney amid nods from the jurors. In his court memorandum, Justice Mahoney stated:

> Plaintiff admitted that it, in combination with the Federal Reserve Bank of Minneapolis, . . . *did create the entire $14,000.00 in money and credit upon its own books by bookkeeping entry.* That this was the consideration used to support the Note dated May 8, 1964 and the Mortgage of the same date. The money and credit first came into existence when they created it. *Mr. Morgan admitted that no United States Law or Statute existed which gave him the right to do this. A lawful consideration must exist and be tendered to support the Note.*

The court rejected the bank's claim for foreclosure, and the defendant kept his house. To Daly, the implications were enormous. If bankers were indeed extending credit *without* consideration – without backing their loans with money they actually had in their vaults and were entitled to lend – a decision declaring their loans void could topple the power base of the world. He wrote in a local news article:

> This decision, which is legally sound, has the effect of declaring all private mortgages on real and personal property, and all U.S. and State bonds held by the Federal Reserve, National and State banks to be null and void. This amounts to an emancipation of this Nation from personal, national and state debt purportedly owed to this banking system. Every American owes it to himself . . . to study this decision very carefully . . . for *upon it hangs the question of freedom or slavery.*[13]

Needless to say, the decision failed to change prevailing practice, although it was never overruled. As for Justice Mahoney, he took the rash step of threatening to prosecute and expose the bank. He died less than six months after the Daly trial, in a mysterious accident that appeared to involve poisoning.[14] Since that time, a number of defendants have attempted to avoid loan defaults using the defense Daly raised; but they have met with only limited success. As one judge said off the record, using a familiar <u>Wizard of Oz</u> metaphor:

> If I let you do that – you and everyone else – it would bring the whole system down. . . . I cannot let you go behind the bar of the bank. . . . *We are not going behind that curtain!*[15]

In an informative website called <u>Money: What It Is, How It Works</u>, William Hummel writes that banks today account for only about 20 percent of total credit market debt. The rest is advanced by non-bank financial institutions, including finance companies, pension funds, mutual funds, insurance companies, and securities dealers. These institutions merely recycle pre-existing funds, either by borrowing at a low interest rate and lending at a higher rate or by pooling the money of investors and lending it to borrowers. In other words, they do what most people think *banks* do: they borrow low and lend high, pocketing the "spread" as their profit. Hummel explains that what banks do is something quite different:

> Banks are not ordinary intermediaries. Like non-banks, they also borrow, but *they do not lend the deposits they acquire. They lend by crediting the borrower's account with a new deposit* . . . . The accounts of other depositors remain intact and their deposits fully available for withdrawal. *Thus a bank loan increases the total of bank deposits, which means an increase in the money supply.*[16]

If the money supply is being increased, money is being created by sleight of hand. What Elgin Groseclose called the "diviner law" of the bankers allows them to magically pull money out of an empty hat.

## The "Impossible Contract"

Failure of consideration and fraud are not the only possible grounds on which the bankers' fractional reserve loans might be challenged in court. In theory, at least, they could also be challenged because they are collectively impossible to perform. Under state civil codes, a contract that is impossible to perform is void.[17] The impossibility in this case arises because the banks create the principal but not the interest needed to pay back their loans. The debtors scramble to find the interest somewhere else, but there is never enough money to go around. Like in a grand game of musical chairs, when the music stops somebody has to default. In an 1850 treatise called <u>The Importance of Usury Laws</u>, a writer named John Whipple did the math. He wrote:

If 5 English pennies . . . had been [lent] at 5 per cent compound interest from the beginning of the Christian era until the present time (say 1850), it would amount in gold of standard fineness to 32,366,648,157 spheres of gold each eight thousand miles in diameter, or as large as the earth.[18]

Thirty-two billion earth-sized spheres! Such is the nature of compound interest. It "compounds" in a parabolic curve that is virtually flat at first but goes nearly vertical after 100 years. Debts don't usually grow to these extremes because most loans are for 30 years or less, when the curve remains relatively flat. But the premise still applies: in a system in which money comes into existence only by borrowing at interest, the system as a whole is always short of funds, and *somebody has to default.*

Bernard Lietaer helped design the single currency system (the Euro) as a European central banker and has authored several books on monetary reform. He explains the interest problem like this:

> When a bank provides you with a $100,000 mortgage, it creates only the principal, which you spend and which then circulates in the economy. The bank expects you to pay back $200,000 over the next 20 years, but it doesn't create the second $100,000 — the interest. Instead, the bank sends you out into the tough world to battle against everybody else to bring back the second $100,000.

He concludes:

> [G]reed and competition are not a result of immutable human temperament . . . . *[G]reed and fear of scarcity are in fact being continuously created and amplified as a direct result of the kind of money we are using.* . . . [W]e can produce more than enough food to feed everybody, and there is definitely enough work for everybody in the world, but there is clearly not enough money to pay for it all. *The scarcity is in our national currencies. In fact, the job of central banks is to create and maintain that currency scarcity. The direct consequence is that we have to fight with each other in order to survive.*[19]

## The Money Supply and the Federal Debt

In hearings before the House Committee on Banking and Currency in 1941, Wright Patman asked Marriner Eccles, then Governor of the Federal Reserve Board, how the Federal Reserve got the money to buy government bonds.

"We created it," Eccles replied.

"Out of what?"

"Out of the right to issue credit money."

"And there is nothing behind it, is there, except our government's credit?"

"That is what our money system is," Eccles replied. *"If there were no debts in our money system, there wouldn't be any money."*[20]

That explains why the federal debt never gets paid off. It hasn't been paid off since the presidency of Andrew Jackson nearly two centuries ago. In all but five fiscal years since 1961 (1969 and 1998 through 2001), in fact, the government has *exceeded* its projected budget, *adding* to the national debt.[21] Economist John Kenneth Galbraith wrote in 1975:

> In numerous years following the [civil] war, the Federal Government ran a heavy surplus. [But] it could not pay off its debt, retire its securities, because to do so meant there would be no bonds to back the national bank notes. *To pay off the debt was to destroy the money supply.*[22]

The federal debt has been the basis of the U.S. money supply ever since the Civil War, when the National Banking Act authorized private banks to issue their own banknotes backed by government bonds deposited with the U.S. Treasury. (This complicated bit of chicanery is explored in Chapter 9.)

When President Clinton announced "the largest budget surplus in history" in 2000, and President Bush predicted a $5.6 trillion surplus by the end of the decade, many people got the impression that the federal debt had been paid off; but this was another illusion. Not only did the $5.6 trillion budget "surplus" never materialize (it was just an optimistic estimate projected over a ten-year period based on an anticipated surplus for the year 2001 that never materialized), but *it entirely ignored the principal owing on the federal debt.* Like the deluded consumer who makes the minimum monthly interest payment on his credit card bill and calls his credit limit "cash on hand," politicians who speak of "balancing the budget" include in their calculations *only* the interest on the national debt. By 2000, when President Clinton announced the largest-ever budget surplus, the federal debt had actually topped $5 trillion; and by October 2005, when the largest-ever projected surplus had turned into the largest-ever budget deficit, the federal debt had mushroomed to $8 trillion. M3 was $9.7 trillion the same year, not much more. It is hardly an exaggeration to say that *the money supply is the federal debt and cannot exist without it.* Commercial loans alone cannot sustain the money supply because they zero out when they get paid back. In order to keep money in the system, *some* major player has to incur substantial debt that *never* gets paid back; and this role is played by the federal government.

That is one reason the federal debt can't be paid off, but today there is an even more compelling reason: the debt has simply grown too large. To get some sense of the magnitude of an 8-plus trillion dollar debt, if you took 7 trillion steps you could walk to the planet Pluto, which is a mere 4 billion miles away.[23] If the government were to pay $100 *every second*, in 317 years it would have paid off only one trillion dollars of debt. And that's just for the principal. If interest were added at the rate of only 1 percent compounded annually, the debt could *never* be paid off in this way, because the debt would grow faster than it was being repaid.[24] Paying an $8 trillion debt off in a lump sum through taxation, on the other hand, would require increasing the tax bill by more than $100,000 for every family of four, a non-starter for most families.[25]

In the 1980s, policymakers openly declared that "deficits don't matter." The government could engage in "deficit spending" and simply allow the debt to grow. This policy continues to be cited with approval by policymakers today.[26] The truth is that *nobody even expects the debt to be paid off*, because it *can't* be paid off – at least, it can't while money is created as a debt to private banks. The government doesn't have to pay the principal so long as it keeps "servicing" the debt by paying the interest. But according to David M. Walker, Director of the U.S. General Accounting Office and Comptroller General of the United States, *just the interest tab will soon be more than the taxpayers can afford to pay.* When the government can't pay the interest, it will have to renege on the debt, and the economy will collapse.[27]

How did we get into this boiling cauldron, and how can we get out of it? The utopian vision of the early American colonists involved a money system that was quite different from what we have today. To understand what we lost and how we lost it, we'll need to journey back down the Yellow Brick Road to eighteenth century America . . .

# Chapter 3
# EXPERIMENTS IN UTOPIA:
# COLONIAL PAPER MONEY
# AS LEGAL TENDER

*Dorothy and her friends were at first dazzled by the brilliancy of the wonderful City. The streets were lined with beautiful houses all built of green marble and studded everywhere with sparkling emeralds. They walked over a pavement of the same green marble, and where the blocks were joined together were rows of emeralds, set closely, and glittering in the brightness of the sun. . . . Everyone seemed happy and contented and prosperous.*

– *The Wonderful Wizard of Oz,*
"The Emerald City of Oz"

Frank Baum's vision of a magical city shimmering in the sun captured the utopian American dream. Walt Disney would later pick up the vision with his castles in the clouds, the happily-ever-after endings to romantic Hollywood fairytales. Baum, who was Irish, may have been thinking of the Emerald Isle, the sacred land of Ireland. The Emerald City also suggested the millennial visions of the Biblical New Jerusalem and the "New Atlantis," the name Sir Francis Bacon gave to the New World.

The American colonies were an experiment in utopia. In an uncharted territory, you could design new systems and make new rules. Paper money was already in use in England, but it had fallen into the hands of private bankers who were using it for private profit at the expense of the people. In the American version of this new medium of exchange, paper money was issued and lent by provincial governments, and the proceeds were used for the benefit of the people. The colonists' new paper money financed a period of prosperity that was considered remarkable for isolated colonies lacking their own silver and gold. By 1750, Benjamin Franklin was able to write of New England:

> There was abundance in the Colonies, and peace was reigning on every border. It was difficult, and even impossible, to find a happier and more prosperous nation on all the surface of the globe. Comfort was prevailing in every home. The people, in general, kept the highest moral standards, and education was widely spread.

## Money as Credit

The distinction of being the first local government to issue its own paper money went to the province of Massachusetts. The year was 1691, three years before the charter of the Bank of England. Jason Goodwin, who tells the story in his 2003 book <u>Greenback</u>, writes that Massachusetts' buccaneer governor had led a daring assault on Quebec in an attempt to drive the French out of Canada; but the assault had failed. Militiamen and widows needed to be paid. The local merchants were approached but had declined, saying they had other demands on their money.

The idea of a paper currency had been suggested in 1650, in an anonymous British pamphlet titled "The Key to Wealth, or, a New Way for Improving of Trade: Lawfull, Easie, Safe and Effectual." The paper currency proposed by the pamphleteer, however, was modeled on the receipts issued by London goldsmiths and silversmiths for the precious metals left in their vaults for safekeeping. The problem for the colonies was that they were short of silver and gold. They had to use foreign coins to conduct trade; and since they imported more than they exported, the coins were continually being drained off to England and other countries, leaving the colonists without enough money for their own internal needs. The Massachusetts Assembly therefore proposed a new kind of paper money, a "bill of credit" representing the government's "bond" or I.O.U. – its promise to pay tomorrow on a debt incurred today. The paper money of Massachusetts was backed only by the "full faith and credit" of the government.[1]

Other colonies then followed suit with their own issues of paper money. Some were considered government I.O.U.s, redeemable later in "hard" currency (silver or gold). Other issues were "legal tender" in themselves. *Legal tender* is money that must legally be accepted in the payment of debts. It is "as good as gold" in trade, without bearing debt or an obligation to redeem the notes in some other form of money later.[2]

When confidence in the new paper money waned, Cotton Mather, who was then the most famous minister in New England, came to its defense. He argued:

> Is a Bond or Bill-of-Exchange for £1000, other than paper? And yet is it not as valuable as so much Silver or Gold, supposing the security of Payment is sufficient? Now what is the security of your Paper-money less than the Credit of the whole Country?[3]

Mather had redefined money. What it represented was not a sum of gold or silver. It was credit: "the credit of the whole country."

## The Father of Paper Money

Benjamin Franklin was such an enthusiast for the new medium of exchange that he has been called "the father of paper money." Unlike Cotton Mather, who went to Harvard at the age of 12, Franklin was self-taught. He learned his trade on the job, and his trade happened to be printing. In 1729, he wrote and printed a pamphlet called "A Modest Enquiry into the Nature and Necessity of a Paper-Currency," which was circulated throughout the colonies. It became very popular, earning him contracts to print paper money for New Jersey, Pennsylvania, and Delaware.[4]

Franklin wrote his pamphlet after observing the remarkable effects that paper currency had had in stimulating the economy in his home province of Pennsylvania. He said, "Experience, more prevalent than all the logic in the World, has fully convinced us all, that [paper money] has been, and is now of the greatest advantages to the country." Paper currency secured against future tax revenues, he said, turned prosperity tomorrow into ready money today. The government did not need gold to issue this currency, and it did not need to go into debt to the banks. In America, the land of opportunity, this ready money would allow even the poor to get ahead. Franklin wrote, "Many that understand . . . Business very well, but have not a Stock sufficient of their own, will be encouraged to borrow Money; to trade with, when they have it at a moderate interest." He also said, "The riches of a country are to be valued by the quantity of labor its inhabitants are able to purchase and not by the quantity of gold and silver they possess."

When gold was the medium of exchange, money determined production rather than production determining the money supply. When gold was plentiful, things got produced. When it was scarce, men were out of work and people knew want. The virtue of government-issued paper scrip was that it could grow along with productivity, allowing potential wealth to become real wealth. The government could pay for services with paper receipts that were basically community credits. In this way, *the community actually created supply and demand at the same time.* The farmer would not farm, the teacher would not teach, the miner would not mine, unless the funds were available to compensate them for their labors. Paper "scrip" underwrote the production of goods and services that would not otherwise have been on the market. Anything for which there was a buyer and a producer could be produced and traded. If A had what B wanted, B had what C wanted, and C had what A wanted, they could all get together and trade. They did not need the moneylenders' gold, which could be hoarded, manipulated, or lent only at usurious interest rates.

## Representation Without Taxation

The new paper money did more than make the colonies independent of the British bankers and their gold. *It actually allowed the colonists to finance their local governments without taxing the people.* This development is traced in a 2002 article called "Representation Without Taxation" by Alvin Rabushka, a senior fellow at the Hoover Institution at Stanford University. He writes that there were two main ways the colonies issued paper money. Most colonies used both, in varying proportions. One was a direct issue of notes, usually called "bills of credit" or "treasury notes." These were I.O.U.s of the government backed by specific future taxes. However, the payback was deferred well into the future, and sometimes the funds never got returned to the treasury at all. Like in a bathtub without a drain, the money supply kept increasing without a means of recycling it back to its source; but at least the funds were not owed back to private foreign lenders, and no interest was due on them. They were just credits issued and spent into the economy on goods and services.

The recycling problem was solved when a second method of issue was devised. Colonial assemblies discovered that provincial loan offices could generate a steady stream of revenue in the form of interest *by taking on the lending functions of banks.* A government loan office called a "land bank" would issue paper money and lend it to residents (usually farmers) at low rates of interest. The loans were secured by mortgages on real property, silver plate, and other hard assets. Franklin wrote, "Bills issued upon Land are in Effect Coined Land." New money issued and lent to borrowers came back to the loan office on a regular payment schedule, preventing the money supply from over-inflating and keeping the values of paper loan-office bills stable in terms of English sterling. The interest paid on the loans also went into the public coffers, funding the government. Colonies relying on this method of issuing paper money thus wound up with more stable currencies than those relying heavily on new issues of bills of credit.

The most successful loan offices were in the middle colonies – Pennsylvania, Delaware, New York and New Jersey. The model that earned the admiration of all was the loan office established in Pennsylvania in 1723. The Pennsylvania plan showed that it was quite possible for the government to issue new money in place of taxes *without* inflating prices. From 1723 until the French and Indian War in the 1750s, *the provincial government collected no taxes at all.* The loan office was the province's chief source of revenue, supplemented by import duties on liquor. During this period, Pennsylvania wholesale prices remained stable. The currency depreciated by 21 percent against English sterling, but Rabushka shows that this was due to external trade relations rather than to changes in the quantity of currency in circulation.[5]

Before the loan office came to the rescue, Pennsylvania had been losing both business and residents due to a lack of available currency. The loan office injected new money into the economy, and it allowed people who had been forced to borrow from private bankers at 8 percent interest to refinance their debts at the 5 percent rate offered by the provincial government. Franklin said that this money system was the reason that Pennsylvania "has so greatly increased in inhabitants," having replaced "the inconvenient method of barter" and given "new life to business [and] promoted greatly the settlement of new lands (by lending small sums to beginners on easy interest)." When he was asked by the directors of the Bank of England why the colonies were so prosperous, he replied that they issued paper money "in proper proportions to the demands of trade and industry." The secret was in not issuing too much, and in recycling the money back to the government in the form of principal and interest on government-issued loans.

The paper currencies of the New England colonies – Massachusetts, Rhode Island, Connecticut and New Hampshire – were less successful than those of the middle colonies, mainly because they failed to limit their issues to these "proper proportions," or to recycle the money back to the government. The paper money of the New England colonies helped to finance development and growth that would not otherwise have occurred, but the currencies did not maintain their value, because bills of credit were issued in far greater quantities than the provincial governments ever hoped to redeem. Because the money was pumped into the economy without flowing back to the government, the currency depreciated and price inflation resulted.

## King George Steps In

Rapid depreciation of the New England bills eventually threatened the investments of British merchants and financiers who were doing business with the colonies, who leaned on Parliament to prohibit the practice. In 1751, King George II enacted a ban on the issue of all new paper money in the New England colonies, forcing the colonists to borrow instead from the British bankers. This ban was continued under King George III, who succeeded his father in 1752.

In 1764, Franklin went to London to petition Parliament to lift the ban. When he arrived, he was surprised to find rampant unemployment and poverty among the British working classes. "The streets are covered with beggars and tramps," he observed. When he asked why, he was told the country had too many workers. The rich were already overburdened with taxes and could not pay more to relieve the poverty of the working classes. Franklin was then asked how the American colonies managed to collect enough money to support their poor houses. He is quoted as replying:

> We have no poor houses in the Colonies; and if we had some, there would be nobody to put in them, since *there is, in the Colonies, not a single unemployed person, neither beggars nor tramps.*[6]

His English listeners had trouble believing this, since when their poor houses and jails had become too cluttered, the English had actually shipped their poor to the Colonies. When the directors of the Bank of England asked what was responsible for the booming economy of the young colonies, Franklin reportedly replied:

That is simple. In the colonies we issue our own money. It is called Colonial Scrip. We issue it to pay the government's approved expenses and charities. We make sure it is issued in proper proportions to make the goods pass easily from the producers to the consumers. . . . In this manner, creating for ourselves our own paper money, we control its purchasing power, and *we have no interest to pay to no one.* You see, a legitimate government can both spend and lend money into circulation, while banks can only lend significant amounts of their promissory bank notes, for they can neither give away nor spend but a tiny fraction of the money the people need. Thus, when your bankers here in England place money in circulation, there is always a debt principal to be returned and usury to be paid. The result is that you have always too little credit in circulation to give the workers full employment. *You do not have too many workers, you have too little money in circulation, and that which circulates, all bears the endless burden of unpayable debt and usury.*[7]

Banks were limited to *lending* money into the economy; and since more money was always owed back in principal and interest (or "usury") than was lent in the original loans, there was never enough money in circulation to pay the interest and still keep workers fully employed. The *government*, on the other hand, had *two* ways of getting money into the economy: it could both *lend* and *spend* the money into circulation. *It could spend enough new money to cover the interest due on the money it lent*, keeping the money supply in "proper proportion" and preventing the "impossible contract" problem — the problem of having more money owed back on loans than was created in the loans themselves.

After extolling the benefits of colonial scrip to the citizens of Pennsylvania, Franklin reportedly told his listeners, "New York and New Jersey have also increased greatly during the same period, with the use of paper money; so that it does not appear to be of the ruinous nature ascribed to it." Jason Goodwin observes that it was a tricky argument to make. The colonists had been stressing to the mother country how poor they were — so poor, they were forced to print paper money for lack of precious metals. Franklin's report demonstrated to Parliament and the British bankers that the pretext for allowing paper money had been removed. The point of having colonies was not, after all, to bolster the colonies' economies. It was to provide raw materials at decent rates to the mother country. In 1764, the Bank of England used its influence on Parliament to get a Currency Act passed that made it illegal for any of the colonies to print their own money.[8] The colonists were forced to pay all future taxes to Britain in silver or gold. Anyone lacking in those precious metals had to borrow them at interest from the banks.

Only a year later, Franklin said, the streets of the colonies were filled with unemployed beggars, just as they were in England. The money supply had suddenly been reduced by half, leaving insufficient funds to pay for the goods and services these workers could have provided. He maintained that it was "the poverty caused by the bad influence of the English bankers on the Parliament which has caused in the colonies hatred of the English and . . . the Revolutionary War." This, he said, was the real reason for the Revolution: "The colonies would gladly have borne the little tax on tea and other matters had it not been that England took away from the colonies their money, which created unemployment and dissatisfaction." John Twells, an English historian, confirmed this view of the Revolution, writing:

> In a bad hour, the British Parliament took away from America its representative money, forbade any further issue of bills of credit, these bills ceasing to be legal tender, and ordered that all taxes should be paid in coins. Consider now the consequences: this restriction of the medium of exchange paralyzed all the industrial energies of the people. Ruin took place in these once flourishing Colonies; most rigorous distress visited every family and every business, discontent became desperation, and reached a point, to use the words of Dr. Johnson, when human nature rises up and asserts its rights.[9]

Alexander Hamilton, the nation's first Treasury Secretary, said that paper money had composed three-fourths of the total money supply before the American Revolution. When the colonists could not issue their own currency, the money supply had suddenly shrunk, leaving widespread unemployment, hunger and poverty in its wake. Unlike in the Great Depression of the 1930s, people in the 1770s were keenly aware of who was responsible for their distress. One day they were trading freely with their own paper money. The next day it was gone, banned by order of a king an ocean away, who demanded tribute in the coin of the British bankers. The outraged populace ignored the ban and went back to issuing their own paper money. In

The Lost Science of Money, Stephen Zarlenga quotes historian Alexander Del Mar, who wrote in 1895:

[T]he creation and circulation of bills of credit by revolutionary assemblies . . . coming as they did upon the heels of the strenuous efforts made by the Crown to suppress paper money in America [were] acts of defiance so contemptuous and insulting to the Crown that forgiveness was thereafter impossible . . . [T]here was but one course for the Crown to pursue and that was to suppress and punish these acts of rebellion . . . . *Thus the Bills of Credit of this era, which ignorance and prejudice have attempted to belittle into the mere instruments of a reckless financial policy were really the standards of the Revolution. They were more than this: they were the Revolution itself!*[10]

## The Cornerstone of the Revolution

Like Massachusetts nearly a century earlier, the colonies suddenly found themselves at war and without the means to pay for it. The first act of the new Continental Congress was to issue its own paper scrip, popularly called the Continental. Most of the Continentals were issued as I.O.U.s or debts of the revolutionary government, to be redeemed in coinage later.[11] Eventually, 200 million dollars in Continental scrip were issued. By the end of the war, the scrip had been devalued so much that it was essentially worthless; but it still evoked the wonder and admiration of foreign observers, because it allowed the colonists to do something that had never been done before. They succeeded in financing a war against a major power, with virtually no "hard" currency of their own, *without taxing the people.* Franklin wrote from England during the war, "the whole is a mystery even to the politicians, how we could pay with paper that had no previously fixed fund appropriated specifically to redeem it. *This currency as we manage it is a wonderful machine.*" Thomas Paine called it a "corner stone" of the Revolution:

Every stone in the Bridge, that has carried us over, seems to have claim upon our esteem. But this was a corner stone, and its usefulness cannot be forgotten.[12]

The Continental's usefulness was forgotten, however, with a little help from the Motherland . . . .

## Economic Warfare: The Bankers Counterattack

The British engaged in a form of economic warfare that would be used again by the bankers in the nineteenth century against Lincoln's Greenbacks and in the twentieth century against a variety of other currencies: they attacked their competitor's currency and drove down its value. In the 1770s, when paper money was easy to duplicate, its value could be diluted by physically flooding the market with counterfeit money. In modern times, as we'll see later, the same effect is achieved by another form of counterfeiting known as the "short sale." During the Revolution, Continentals were shipped in by the boatload and could be purchased in any amount, essentially for the cost of the paper on which they were printed. Thomas Jefferson estimated that counterfeiting added $200 million to the money supply, effectively doubling it; and later historians thought that this figure was low. Zarlenga quotes nineteenth century historian J. W. Schuckers, who wrote, "The English Government which seems to have a mania for counterfeiting the paper money of its enemies entered into competition with private criminals."

The Continental was battered but remained viable. Schuckers quoted a confidential letter from an English general to his superiors, stating that "the experiments suggested by your Lordships have been tried, no assistance that could be drawn from the power of gold or the arts of counterfeiting have been left untried; *but still the currency . . . has not failed.*"[13]

The beating that did take down the Continental was from speculators -- mostly northeastern bankers, stockbrokers and businessmen -- who bought up the revolutionary currency at a fraction of its value after convincing people it would be worthless after the war. The Continental had to compete with other currencies, rendering it vulnerable to speculative attack in the same way that foreign currencies left to "float" in international markets are today. (More on this in Chapters 21 and 22.) The Continental had to compete with the States' paper notes and the British bankers' gold and silver coins. Gold and silver were regarded as far more valuable than the paper promises of a revolutionary government that might not prevail, and the States' paper notes had the taxation power to back them. The problem might have been avoided by making the Continental the sole official currency, but the Continental Congress did not yet have the power to enforce that sort of order. It had no courts, no police, and no authority to collect taxes to redeem the notes or contract the money supply. The colonies had just rebelled against taxation by the British and were not ready to commit to that burden from the new Congress.[14] Speculators took advantage of these weaknesses by trading Continentals at a deeper and deeper discount until they became virtually worthless, giving rise to the expression "not worth a Continental."

# Chapter 4
# HOW THE GOVERNMENT WAS PERSUADED TO BORROW ITS OWN MONEY

*The Witch happened to look into the child's eyes and saw how simple the soul behind them was, and that the little girl did not know of the wonderful power the Silver Shoes gave her. So the Wicked Witch laughed to herself, and thought, "I can still make her my slave, for she does not know how to use her power."*

– *The Wonderful Wizard of Oz,*
*"The Search for the Wicked Witch"*

Just as Dorothy did not know the power of the silver shoes on her feet, so the new country's leaders failed to recognize the power of the government-issued paper money Tom Paine had called "a cornerstone of the Revolution." The economic subservience King George could not achieve by force was achieved by the British bankers by stealth, by persuading the American people that they needed the bankers' paper money instead of their own.

President John Adams is quoted as saying, "There are two ways to conquer and enslave a nation. One is by the sword. The other is by debt." Sheldon Emry, expanding on this concept two centuries later, observed that conquest by the sword has the disadvantage that the conquered are likely to rebel. Continual force is required to keep them at bay. Conquest by debt can occur so silently and insidiously that the conquered don't even realize they have new masters. On the surface, nothing has changed. The country is merely under new management. "Tribute" is collected in the form of debts and taxes, which the people believe they are paying for their own good. "Their captors," wrote Emry, "become their 'benefactors' and 'protectors.'. . . Without realizing it, they are conquered, and the instruments of their own society are used to transfer their wealth to their captors and make the conquest complete."[1]

Colonies in the seventeenth and eighteenth centuries all had the same purpose – to enhance the economy of the mother country. That was how the mother country saw it, but the American colonists had long opposed any plan that would systematically drain their money supply off to England. The British had considered the idea of a land bank as far back as 1754, as a way to provide a circulating medium of exchange for the colonies; but the idea was rejected by the colonists when they learned that the interest the bank generated would be subject to appropriation by the King.[2] It was only after the American Revolution that British bankers and their Wall Street vassals succeeded in pulling this feat off by stealth, by acquiring a controlling interest in the stock of the new United States Bank.

The first step in that silent conquest was to discredit the paper scrip issued by the revolutionary government and the States. By the end of the Revolution, that step was achieved. Rampant counterfeiting and speculation had so thoroughly collapsed the value of the Continental that the new country's leaders were completely disillusioned with what they called "unfunded paper." At the Constitutional Convention, Alexander Hamilton, Washington's new Secretary of the Treasury, summed up the majority view when he said:

> To emit an unfunded paper as the sign of value ought not to continue a formal part of the Constitution, nor ever hereafter to be employed; being, in its nature, repugnant with abuses and liable to be made the engine of imposition and fraud.[3]

The Founding Fathers were so disillusioned with paper money that they simply omitted it from the Constitution. Congress was given the power only to "coin money, regulate the value thereof," and "to borrow money on the credit of the United States . . . ." An enormous loophole was thus left in the law. Creating and issuing money had long been considered the prerogative of governments, but the Constitution failed to define exactly what "money" was. Was "to coin money" an eighteenth-century way of saying "to create money"? Did this include creating paper money? If not, who *did* have the power to create paper money? Congress was authorized to "borrow" money, but did that include borrowing paper money or just gold? The presumption was that the paper notes borrowed from the bankers were "secured" by a sum of silver or gold; but in the illusory world of finance, then as now, things were not always as they seemed . . . .

## The Bankers' Paper Money Comes in
## Through the Back Door

While the Founding Fathers were pledging their faith in gold and silver as the only "sound" money, those metals were quickly proving inadequate to fund the new country's expanding economy. The national war debt had reached $42 million, with no silver or gold coins available to pay it off. The debt might have been avoided if the government had funded the war with Continental scrip that was stamped "legal tender," making it "money" in itself; but the revolutionary government and the States had issued a major portion of their paper money as promissory notes payable after the war. The notes represented debts, and the debt had now come due. The bearers expected to get their gold, and the gold was not to be had. There was also an insufficient supply of money for conducting trade. Tightening the money supply by limiting it to coins had quickly precipitated another depression. In 1786, a farmers' rebellion broke out in Massachusetts, led by Daniel Shays. Farmers brandishing pitchforks complained of going heavily into debt when paper money was plentiful. When it was no longer available and debts had to be repaid in the much scarcer "hard" coin of the British bankers, some farmers lost their farms. The rebellion was defused, but visions of anarchy solidified the sense of an urgent need for both a strong central government and an expandable money supply.

The solution of Treasury Secretary Hamilton was to "monetize"[i] the national debt by turning it into a source of money for the country.[4] He proposed that a national bank be authorized to print up banknotes and swap them for the government's bonds.[5] The government would pay regular interest on the debt, using import duties and money from the sale of public land. Opponents said that acknowledging the government's debt at face value would unfairly reward the speculators who had bought up the country's I.O.U.s for a pittance from the soldiers, farmers and small businessmen who had actually earned them; but Hamilton argued that the speculators had earned this windfall for their "faith in the country." He thought the government needed to enlist the support of the speculators, or they would do to the new country's money what they had done to the Continental. Vernon

---

[i]　To *monetize* means to convert government debt from securities evidencing debt (bills, bonds and notes) into currency that can be used to purchase goods and services.

Parrington, a historian writing in the 1920s, said:

> In developing his policies as Secretary of the Treasury, [Hamilton] applied his favorite principle, that government and property must join in a close working alliance. *It was notorious that during the Revolution men of wealth had forced down the continental currency for speculative purposes;* was it not as certain that they would support an issue in which they were interested? The private resources of wealthy citizens would thus become an asset of government, for the bank would link "the interest of the State in an intimate connection with those of the rich individuals belonging to it."[6]

Hamilton thought that the way to keep wealthy speculators from destroying the new national bank was to give them a financial stake in it. His proposal would do this and dispose of the government's crippling debts at the same time, by allowing creditors to trade their government bonds or I.O.U.s for stock in the new bank. Jefferson, Hamilton's chief political opponent, feared that giving private wealthy citizens an ownership interest in the bank would link their interests *too* closely with it. The government would be turned into an oligarchy, a government by the rich at war with the working classes. A bank owned by private stockholders, whose driving motive was profit, would be less likely to be responsive to the needs of the public than one that was owned by the public and subject to public oversight. Stockholders of a private bank would make their financial decisions behind closed doors, without public knowledge or control. But Hamilton's plan had other strategic advantages, and it won the day. Besides neatly disposing of a crippling federal debt and winning over the "men of wealth," it secured the loyalty of the individual States by making their debts, too, exchangeable for stock in the new Bank. The move was controversial; but by stabilizing the States' shaky finances, Hamilton got them on board, thwarting the plans of the pro-British faction that hoped to split the States and establish a Northern Confederacy.[7]

## Promoting the General Welfare:
## The American System Versus the British System

Hamilton's goal was first and foremost a strong federal government. He was the chief author of <u>The Federalist Papers</u>, which helped to get the votes necessary to ratify the Constitution and formed the basis for much of it. The Preamble to the Constitution made promoting the general welfare a guiding principle of the new Republic. Hamilton's plan for achieving this ideal was to nurture the country's fledgling industries with protective measures such as tariffs (taxes placed on imports or exports) and easy credit provided through a national bank. Production and the money to finance it would all be kept "in house," independent of foreign financiers.

Senator Henry Clay later called this the "American system" to distinguish it from the "British system" of "free trade."[ii] Clay was a student of Matthew Carey, a well-known printer and publisher who had been tutored by Benjamin Franklin. What Clay called the "British system" was rooted in the dog-eat-dog world of Thomas Hobbes, John Locke and Scottish economist Adam Smith. Smith maintained in his 1776 book <u>The Wealth of Nations</u> that if every man pursued his own greed, all would automatically come out right, as if by some "invisible hand." Proponents of the American system rejected this *laissez-faire* approach in favor of guiding and protecting the young country with a system of rules and regulations. They felt that if the economy were left to the free market, big monopolies would gobble up small entrepreneurs; foreign bankers and industrialists could exploit the country's labor and materials; and competition would force prices down, ensuring subjugation to British imperial interests.

The British model assumed that one man's gain could occur only through another's loss. The goal was to reach the top of the heap by climbing on competitors and driving them down. In the American vision of the "Common Wealth," all men would rise together by leavening the whole heap at once. A Republic of sovereign States would work together for their mutual benefit, improving their collective lot by promoting production, science, industry and trade, raising the standard of living and the technological practice of all by cooperative effort.[8] It was an idealistic reflection of the American dream, which assumed the best in people and in human potential. You did not need to exploit foreign lands and people in pursuit of "free trade." Like Dorothy in <u>The Wizard of Oz</u>, you could find your heart's desire in your own backyard. That was the vision, but in the sort of negotiated compromise that has long characterized politics, it got lost somewhere in the details.

---

[ii] The term "free trade" is used to mean trade between nations unrestricted by such things as import duties and trade quotas. Critics say that in more developed nations, it results in jobs being "exported" abroad, while in less developed nations, workers and the environment are exploited by foreign financiers.

## Hamilton Charters a Bank

Hamilton argued that to promote the General Welfare, the country needed a monetary system that was independent of foreign masters; and for that, it needed its own federal central bank. The bank would handle the government's enormous war debt and create a standard form of currency. Jefferson remained suspicious of Hamilton and his schemes, but Jefferson also felt strongly that the new country's capital city should be in the South, in his home state of Virginia. Hamilton (who did not care where the capital was) agreed on the location of the national capital in exchange for Jefferson's agreement on the bank.

When Hamilton called for a tax on whiskey to pay the interest on the government's securities, however, he went too far. Jefferson's supporters were furious. In the type of political compromise still popular today, President Washington proposed moving the capital even closer to Mt. Vernon. In 1789, Congress passed Hamilton's bill; but the President still had to sign it. Washington was concerned about the continued opposition of Jefferson and the Virginians, who thought the bill was unconstitutional. The public would have to use the bank, but the bank would not have to serve the public. Hamilton assured the President that to protect the public, the bank would be required to retain a percentage of gold in "reserve" so that it could redeem its paper notes in gold or silver on demand. Hamilton was eloquent; and in 1791, Washington signed the bill into law.

The new banking scheme was hailed as a brilliant solution to the nation's economic straits, one that disposed of an oppressive national debt, stabilized the economy, funded the government's budget, and created confidence in the new paper dollars. If the new Congress had simply printed its own paper money, speculators would have challenged the currency's worth and driven down its value, just as they had during the Revolution. To maintain public confidence in the national currency and establish its stability, the new Republic needed the *illusion* that its dollars were backed by the bankers' gold, and Hamilton's bank successfully met that challenge. It got the country up and running, but it left the bank largely in private hands, where it could still be manipulated for private greed. Worse, the government ended up in debt for money it could have generated itself.

## How the Government Wound Up
## Borrowing Its Own Bonds

The charter for the new bank fixed its total initial capitalization at ten million dollars. Eight million were to come from private stockholders and two million from the government. But the government did not actually have two million dollars, so the bank (now a chartered lending institution) lent the government the money at interest. The bank, of course, did not have the money either. The whole thing was sleight of hand.[9]

The rest of the bank's shares were sold to the public, who bought some in hard cash and some in government securities (the I.O.U.s that had been issued by the revolutionary government and the States). The government had to pay six percent interest annually on all the securities now held by the bank – those exchanged for the "loan" of the government's own money, plus the bonds accepted by the bank from the public. The bank's shareholders were supposed to pay one-fourth the cost of their shares in gold; but only the first installment was actually paid in hard money, totaling $675,000. The rest was paid in paper banknotes. Some came from the Bank of Boston and the Bank of New York; but most of this paper money was issued by the new U.S. Bank itself and lent back to its new shareholders, through the magic of "fractional reserve" lending.

Within five years, the government had borrowed $8.2 million from the bank. The additional money was obviously created out of thin air, just as it would have been if the government had printed the money itself; but the government now owed principal and interest back to the bank. To reduce its debt to the bank, the government was eventually forced to sell its shares, largely to British financiers. To his credit, Hamilton is reported to have opposed these sales.[10] But the sales went through, and the first Bank of the United States wound up largely under foreign ownership and control.

## When Political Duels Were Deadly

Hamilton was widely acclaimed as a brilliant writer, orator and thinker; but to Jefferson he remained a diabolical schemer, a British stooge pursuing a political agenda for his own ends. The first Bank of the United States was modeled on the Bank of England, the same private bank against which the colonists had just rebelled. Years later,

Jefferson would say that Hamilton had tricked him into approving the bank's charter. Jefferson had always suspected Hamilton of monarchical sympathies, and his schemes all seemed tainted with corruption. Jefferson would go so far as to tell Washington he thought Hamilton was a dangerous traitor.[10] He complained to Madison about Hamilton's bookkeeping:

> I do not at all wonder at the condition in which the finances of the United States are found. Hamilton's object from the beginning was to throw them into forms which should be utterly indecipherable.[11]

Hamilton, for his part, thought little better of Jefferson. The feud between the two Founding Fathers resulted in the two-party system. Hamilton's party, the Federalists, favored a strong central government funded by a centralized federal banking system. Jefferson's party, the Democratic Republicans or simply Republicans, favored State and individual rights. Jefferson's party was responsible for passing the Bill of Rights.[12]

Hamilton had worked with Aaron Burr in New York City to establish the Manhattan Company, which would eventually become the Chase Manhattan Bank. But Hamilton broke with Burr and the Boston Federalists when he learned that they were plotting to split the northern States from the Union. Hamilton's first loyalty was to the Republic. Burr and his faction were working closely with British allies, who would later try to break up the Union by backing the Confederacy in the Civil War. Hamilton swung his support to Jefferson against Burr in the presidential election of 1800, and other patriotic Federalists did the same. The Federalist Party ceased to be a major national party after the War of 1812, when the Boston Federalists sided with England, which lost.[13]

In 1801, Jefferson became President with Hamilton's support; and Burr became Vice President. In 1804, when Burr sought the governorship of New York, he was again defeated largely through Hamilton's opposition. In the course of the campaign, Hamilton accused Burr in a newspaper article of being "a dangerous man" who "ought not to be trusted with the reins of government." When Hamilton refused to apologize, Burr challenged him to a duel; and at the age of 49, Hamilton was dead.

Hamilton remains a controversial figure, but he earned his place in history. He succeeded in stabilizing the shaky new economy and getting the country on its feet, and his notions of "monetizing" debt and "federalizing" the banking system were major innovations. He restored the country's credit, gave it a national currency, made it economically independent, and incorporated strong federal provisions into the Constitution that would protect and nurture the young country according to a uniquely American system founded on "promoting the General Welfare."

Those were his positive contributions, but Hamilton also left a darker legacy. Lurking behind the curtain in his new national bank, a privileged class of financial middlemen were now legally entitled to siphon off a perpetual tribute in the form of interest; and because they controlled the money spigots, they could fund their own affiliated businesses with easy credit, squeezing out competitors and perpetuating the same class divisions that the "American system" was supposed to have circumvented. The money power had been delivered into private hands; and they were largely foreign hands, the same interests that had sought to keep America in a colonial state, subservient to an elite class of oligarchical financiers.

Who were these foreign financiers, and how had they come to acquire so much leverage? The Yellow Brick Road takes us much farther back into history, back to when the concept of "usury" was first devised . . . .

# Chapter 5
# FROM MATRIARCHIES OF ABUNDANCE TO PATRIARCHIES OF DEBT

*"I'm melting! My world! My world! Who would have thought a little girl like you could destroy my beautiful wickedness!"*

*– The Wicked Witch of the West to Dorothy*

When Frank Baum made his witch-vanquishing hero a defenseless young girl, he probably wasn't thinking about the gender ramifications of economic systems; but Bernard Lietaer has given the subject serious thought. In <u>The Mystery of Money</u>, he traces the development of two competing monetary schemes, one based on shared abundance, the other based on scarcity, greed and debt. The former characterized the matriarchal societies of antiquity. The latter characterized the warlike patriarchal societies that forcibly displaced them.[1] The issue wasn't really one of gender, of course, since every society is composed half of each. The struggle was between two archetypal world views. What Lietaer called the matriarchal and patriarchal systems, Henry Clay called the American and British systems – cooperative abundance versus competitive greed. But that classification isn't really accurate either, or fair to the British people, since their own economic conquerors also came from somewhere else, and the British succeeded in withstanding the moneylenders' advances for hundreds of years. Lietaer traces this archetypal struggle back much farther, to the cradle of Western civilization in ancient Sumer.

## When Money Could Grow

Located where Iraq is today, Sumer was a matriarchal agrarian economy with a financial system based on abundance and shared wealth. One of the oldest known bronze coins was the Sumerian shekel, dating from 3,200 B.C. It was inscribed with the likeness of the Goddess Inanna-Ishtar, who bestowed kingship in Sumer and was the goddess of fertility, life and death. Inanna wore the horns of a cow, the sacred animal that personified the Great Mother everywhere in ancient myth. Hathor, the Egyptian equivalent, had cow ears and a human face and was the goddess of love, fertility and abundance. Her horn was the "cornucopeia" from which poured the earth's plenty. Isis, an even more powerful Egyptian mother figure, was portrayed wearing the horns of a cow with the sun disc between them. In India, the cow goddess was Kali, for whom cows are sacred to this day. Cows were also associated with money, since they were an early medium of exchange. The Sumerian word for "interest" was the same as the word for "calf." It was natural to repay advances of cattle with an extra calf, because the unit of exchange itself multiplied over the loan period. This was also true for grain, for which the temples served as storehouses. Grain advanced over the growing period was repaid with extra grain after the harvest, in gratitude to God for multiplying the community's abundance.

The temples were public institutions that also served welfare functions, including the support of widows, orphans, the elderly and infirm. Temples were endowed with land to provide food for their dependent labor, and resources such as herds of sheep to provide wool for their workshops. They operated autonomously, supporting themselves not through taxation but by renting lands and workshops and charging interest on loans. Goods were advanced to traders, who returned the value of the goods plus interest. The temples also acted as central banks. Sacrificial coins inscribed "debt to the Gods" were paid to farmers in acknowledgment that wheat taxes had been contributed to the temple. These coins were also lent to borrowers. When interest was paid on the loans, it went back to the temple to fund the community's economic and social programs and to cover losses from bad loans.[2]

It was only after the Indo-European invasions of the second millennium B.C. that moneylending became the private enterprise of the infamous moneychangers. The Goddess Inanna was superseded as the source of supreme kingship by the male god Enlil of Nippur, and the matriarchal system of shared communal abundance was forcibly displaced by a militant patriarchal system. The cornucopia of the Horned Goddess became the bull horns of the Thunder God, representing masculine power, virility and force.[3]

In the temple system, the community extended credit and received the money back with interest. In the system that displaced it, interest on debts went into private vaults to build the private fortunes of the moneychangers. Interest was thus transformed from a source of income for the community into a tool for impoverishing and enslaving people and nations. Unlike corn and cows, the gold the moneylenders lent was inorganic. It did not "grow," so there was never enough to cover the additional interest charges added to loans. When there was insufficient money in circulation to cover operating expenses, farmers had to borrow until harvest time; and the odd man out in the musical chairs of finding eleven coins to repay ten wound up in debtor's prison. Historically, most slavery originated from debt.[4]

## The Proscription Against Usury

"Usury" is now defined as charging "excess" interest, but originally it meant merely charging a fee or interest for the use of money. Usury was forbidden in the Christian Bible, and anti-usury laws were strictly enforced by the Catholic Church until the end of the Middle Ages. But in Jewish scriptures, which were later joined to the Christian books as the "Old Testament," usury was forbidden only between "brothers." Charging interest to foreigners was allowed and even encouraged.[i] The "moneychangers" thus came to be associated with the Jews, but they were not actually the Jewish people. In fact the Jewish people may have suffered more than any other people from the moneychangers' schemes, which were responsible for much anti-semitism.[5]

In the informative documentary video The Money Masters, Bill Still and Patrick Carmack point out that when Jesus threw the moneychangers out of the temple, it was actually to protect the Jewish people. Half-shekels, the only pure silver coins of assured weight

---

[i]    See Deuteronomy (New World Translation) -- 15:6 [Y]ou will certainly lend on pledge to many nations, whereas you yourself will not borrow; and you must dominate over many nations, whereas over you they will not dominate. 23:19 You must not make your brother pay interest . . . . 23:20 You may make a foreigner pay interest, but your brother you must not make pay interest.

without the image of a pagan Emperor on them, were the only coins considered acceptable for paying the Temple tax, a tribute to God. But half-shekels were scarce, and the moneychangers had cornered the market for them. Like the modern banking cartel, they had monopolized the medium of exchange and were exacting a charge for its use.[6]

Despite the injunctions in the New Testament, there were times when the king needed money. In the Middle Ages, England was short of gold, which had left during the Crusades. In 1087, when King William (Rufus) needed gold to do business with the French, he therefore admitted the moneylenders on condition that the interest be demanded in gold and that half be paid to the king. But the moneylenders eventually became so wealthy at the expense of the people that the Church, with promptings from the Pope, prohibited them from taking interest; and in 1290, when they had lost their usefulness to the king, most Jews were again expelled from the country. This pattern, in which Jews as a people have been persecuted for the profiteering of a few and have been used as scapegoats to divert attention from the activities of the rulers, has been repeated over the centuries.

## Money as a Simple Tally of Accounts

Meanwhile, England faced the problem of what to use for money in a country short of gold. The coinage system was commodity-based. It assumed that "money" was something having value in itself (gold or silver), which was bartered or traded for goods or services of equal value. But Aristotle had a different view of money. He maintained:

> Money exists not by nature but by law. [It acts] as a measure [that] makes goods commensurate and equates them. . . . There must then be a unit, and that fixed by agreement.[7]

Money was a mere *fiat* of the law. *Fiat* means "let it be done" in Latin. "Fiat money" is money that is legal tender by government decree. It is simply a "tally," something representing units of value that can be traded in the marketplace, a receipt for goods or services that can legally be tendered for other goods or services. In Mandarin China, where paper money was invented in the ninth century, this sort of *fiat* currency funded a long and prosperous empire. Fiat money was also used successfully in medieval England, but in England it was made of wood.

The English tally system originated with King Henry I, son of William the Conqueror, who took the throne in 1100 A.D. The printing press had not yet been invented, and taxes were paid directly with goods produced by the land. Under King Henry's innovative system, payment was recorded with a piece of wood that had been notched and split in half. One half was kept by the government and the other by the recipient. To confirm payment, the two halves were matched to make sure they "tallied." Since no stick splits in an even manner, and since the notches tallying the sums were cut right through both pieces of wood, the method was virtually foolproof against forgery. The tally system has been called the earliest form of bookkeeping. According to historian M. T. Clanchy in <u>From Memory to Written Record, England 1066-1307</u>:

> Tallies were . . . a sophisticated and practical record of numbers. They were more convenient to keep and store than parchments, less complex to make, and no easier to forge.[8]

Clanchy notes that only a few hundred tallies survive, but millions were made. Tallies were used by the government not only as receipts for the payment of taxes but to pay soldiers for their service, farmers for their wheat, and laborers for their labor. At tax time, the treasurer accepted the tallies in payment of taxes. By the thirteenth century, the financial market for tallies was sufficiently sophisticated that they could be bought, sold, or discounted. Tallies were used by individuals and institutions to register debts, record fines, collect rents, and enter payments for services rendered. In the 1500s, King Henry VIII gave them the force of a national currency when he ordered that tallies *must* be used to evidence the payment of taxes.[9] That meant everyone had to have them. In <u>War Cycles, Peace Cycles</u>, Richard Hoskins writes that by the end of the seventeenth century, about 14 million pounds' worth of tally-money was in circulation.[10] Stephen Zarlenga cites a historian named Spufford, who said that English coinage had never exceeded half a million pounds up to that time.[11] The tally system was thus not a minor monetary experiment, as some commentators have suggested. Indeed, during most of the Middle Ages, tallies may have made up the bulk of the English money supply. The tally system was in use for more than five centuries before the usury bankers' gold-based paper money scheme took root, helping to fund a long era of leisure and abundance that flowered into the Renaissance.

## A Revisionist View of the Middle Ages

Modern schoolbooks generally portray the Middle Ages as a time of poverty, backwardness, and economic slavery, from which the people were freed only by the Industrial Revolution; but reliable early historians painted a quite different picture. Thorold Rogers, a nineteenth century Oxford historian, wrote that in the Middle Ages, "*a labourer could provide all the necessities for his family for a year by working 14 weeks.*" Fourteen weeks is only a quarter of a year! The rest of the time, some men worked for themselves; some studied; some fished. Some helped to build the cathedrals that appeared all over Germany, France and England during the period, massive works of art that were built mainly with volunteer labor. Some used their leisure to visit these shrines. One hundred thousand pilgrims had the wealth and leisure to visit Canterbury and other shrines yearly. William Cobbett, author of the definitive History of the Reformation, wrote that Winchester Cathedral "was made when there were no poor rates; when every labouring man in England was clothed in good woollen cloth; and when all had plenty of meat and bread . . . ." Money was available for inventions and art, supporting the Michelangelos, Rembrandts, Shakespeares, and Newtons of the period.[12]

The Renaissance is usually thought of as the flowering of the age; but the university system, representative government in a Parliament, the English common law system, and the foundations of a great literary and spiritual movement were all in place by the thirteenth century, and education was advanced and widespread. As one scholar of the era observes:

> We are very prone to consider that it is only in our time that anything like popular education has come into existence. As a matter of fact, however, the education afforded to the people in the little towns of the Middle Ages, represents an ideal of educational uplift for the masses such as has never been even distantly approached in succeeding centuries. The Thirteenth Century developed the greatest set of technical schools that the world has ever known. . . . These medieval towns, . . . during the course of the building of their cathedrals, of their public buildings and various magnificent edifices of royalty and for the nobility, succeeded in accomplishing such artistic results that the world has ever since held them in admiration.[13]

The common people had leisure, education, art, and economic security. According to <u>The Catholic Encyclopedia</u>:

> Economic historians like Rogers and Gibbins declare that during the best period of the Middle Ages – say, from the thirteenth to the fifteenth century, inclusive – there was no such grinding and hopeless poverty, no such chronic semi-starvation in any class, as exists to-day among large classes in the great cities . . . . In the Middle Ages there was no class resembling our proletariat, which has no security, no definite place, no certain claim upon any organization or institution in the socio-economic organism.[14]

Richard Hoskins attributes this long period of prosperity to the absence of usurious lending practices.[15] Rather than having to borrow the moneylenders' gold, the people relied largely on interest-free tallies. Unlike gold, wooden tallies could not become scarce; and unlike paper money, they could not be counterfeited or multiplied by sleight of hand. They were simply a unit of measure, a tally of goods and services exchanged. The tally system avoided both the depressions resulting from a scarcity of gold and the inflations resulting from printing paper money out of all proportion to the goods and services available for sale. Since they came into existence *along with* goods and services, supply and demand increased together, and prices remained stable. The tally system provided an organic form of money that expanded naturally as trade expanded and contracted naturally as taxes were paid. Bankers did not have to meet behind closed doors to set interest rates and manipulate markets to keep the money supply in balance. It balanced the way a checkbook balances, as a matter of simple math. The system of government-issued tallies kept the British economy stable and thriving until the mid-seventeenth century, when Oliver Cromwell, the "Pretender," needed money to fund a revolt against the Tudor monarchy . . . .

# Chapter 6
# PULLING THE STRINGS
# OF THE KING:
# THE MONEYLENDERS
# TAKE ENGLAND

> *"Oz is a Great Wizard, and can take any form he wishes. . . . But who the real Oz is, when he is in his own form, no living person can tell."*
>
> – *The Wonderful Wizard of Oz,*
> *"The Guardian of the Gates"*

The image of puppet and puppeteer has long been a popular metaphor for describing the Money Power pulling the strings of government. Benjamin Disraeli, British Prime Minister from 1868 to 1880, said, "The world is governed by very different personages from what is imagined by those who are not behind the scenes." Nathan Rothschild, who controlled the Bank of England after 1820, notoriously declared:

> I care not what puppet is placed upon the throne of England to rule the Empire on which the sun never sets. *The man who controls Britain's money supply controls the British Empire, and I control the British money supply.*

In the documentary The Money Masters, narrator Bill Still uses the puppet metaphor to describe the transfer of power from the royal line of English Stuarts to the German royal House of Hanover in the eighteenth century:

> England was to trade masters: an unpopular King James II for a hidden cabal of Money Changers pulling the strings of their

usurper, King William III, from behind the scenes. This symbiotic relationship between the Money Changers and the higher British aristocracy continues to this day. The monarch has no real power but serves as a useful shield for the Money Changers who rule the City . . . . In its 20 June 1934 issue, <u>New Britain</u> magazine of London cited a devastating assertion by former British Prime Minister David Lloyd George, that *"Britain is the slave of an international financial bloc."*[1]

Where did these international financiers come from, and how did they achieve their enormous power? The moneylenders had been evicted not only from England but from other European countries. They had regrouped in Holland, where they plotted their return; but the English kings and queens staunchly resisted their advances. The king did not need to borrow money when he had the sovereign right to issue it himself. For a brief period in the 1500s, King Henry VIII relaxed the laws concerning usury when he broke away from the Catholic Church; but when Queen Mary took the throne, she tightened the laws again. The result was to seriously contract the money supply, but Queen Elizabeth I (Mary's half-sister) was determined to avoid the usury trap. She solved the problem by supplementing the money supply with metal coins issued by the public treasury.[2]

The coins were made of metal, but their value came from the stamp of the sovereign on them. This was established as a matter of legal precedent in 1600, when Queen Elizabeth issued relatively worthless base metal coins as legal tender in Ireland. All other coins were annulled and had to be returned to the mints. When the action was challenged in the highest court of the land, the court ruled that it was the sovereign's sole prerogative to create the money of the realm. What she declared to be money was money, and *it was treason for anyone else to create it.* Stephen Zarlenga writes that this decision was so detested by the merchant classes, the goldsmiths, and later the British East India Company that they worked incessantly to destroy it. He quotes Alexander Del Mar, who wrote in 1895:

> This was done by undermining the Crown and then passing the free coinage act of 1666, opening the way for the foreign element to establish a new Monarch, and to reconstitute the money prerogative in the hands of a specific group of financiers – not elected, not representing society, and in large part not even English.[3]

Britain thrived with government-issued currency (tallies and coins) until the king's sovereign authority was eroded by Cromwell's "Glorious Revolution" in the mid-seventeenth century. The middle classes (the traders, manufacturers and small farmers) sided with Parliament under Cromwell, who was a Puritan Protestant. The nobles and gentry sided with the King -- Charles I, son of James I, who followed the Church of England, the English Catholic Church. The Protestants were more lenient than the Catholics toward usury and toward the Dutch moneylenders who practiced it. The moneylenders agreed to provide the funds to back Parliament, on condition that they be allowed back into England and that the loans be guaranteed. That meant the permanent removal of King Charles, who would have repudiated the loans had he gotten back into power. Charles' recapture, trial, and execution were duly arranged and carried out to secure the loans.[4]

After Cromwell's death, Charles' son Charles II was invited to return; but Parliament had no intention of granting him the sovereign power over the money supply enjoyed by his predecessors. When the king needed a standing army, Parliament refused to vote the funds, forcing him to borrow instead from the English goldsmiths at usurious interest rates. The final blow to the royal prerogative was the Free Coinage Act of 1666, which allowed anyone to bring gold or silver to the mint to have it stamped into coins. The power to issue money, which had for centuries been the sole right of the king, had been transferred into private hands. Bankers now had the power to cause inflations and depressions at will by issuing or withholding their gold coins.[5]

None of the earlier English kings or queens would have agreed to charter a private central bank that had the power to create money and lend it to the government, since they could issue money themselves and had no need for loans. But King William III, who followed Charles II, was a Dutchman and a tool of the powerful Wisselbank of Amsterdam . . . .

## A Dutch-bred King Charters the Bank of England
## on Behalf of Foreign Moneylenders

The man who would become King William III began his career as a Dutch aristocrat. He was elevated to Captain General of the Dutch Forces and then to Prince William of Orange with the backing of Dutch moneylenders. His marriage was arranged to Princess Mary of York, eldest daughter of the English Duke of York; and they were married in 1677. When the Duke, who was next in line to be King of England, died in 1689, William and Mary became King and Queen of England.

William was soon at war with Louis XIV of France. To finance his war, he borrowed 1.2 million pounds in gold from a group of moneylenders, whose names were to be kept secret. The money was raised by a novel device that is still used by governments today: *the lenders would issue a permanent loan on which interest would be paid but the principal portion of the loan would not be repaid.*[6] The loan also came with other strings attached. They included:

(1) The lenders were to be granted a charter to establish a Bank of England, which would be given a monopoly to issue banknotes that would circulate as the national paper currency.

(2) The bank would create banknotes out of nothing, with only a fraction of them backed by coin.

(3) Banknotes created and lent to the government would be backed mainly by government I.O.U.s, which would serve as "reserves" for creating additional loans to private parties.

(4) The lenders would be allowed to consolidate the national debt on their loan to the government and to secure its payment by direct taxation of the people.[7]

Called "the Mother of Central Banks," the Bank of England was chartered in 1694 to William Paterson, a Scotsman who had previously lived in Amsterdam.[8] A circular distributed to attract subscribers to the Bank's initial stock offering said, "*The Bank hath benefit of interest on all moneys which it, the Bank, creates out of nothing.*"[9] The negotiation of additional loans caused England's national debt to go from 1.2 million pounds in 1694 to 16 million pounds in 1698. The lenders not only reaped huge profits, but the indebtedness gave them substantial political leverage.

The Bank's charter gave the force of law to the "fractional reserve" banking scheme that put control of the country's money in a privately owned company. The central bank had the legal right to create paper money out of nothing and lend it to the government at interest, something it did by trading its own paper notes for paper bonds representing the government's promise to pay principal and interest back to the Bank -- the same device used by the U.S. Federal Reserve and other central banks today.

## The Tally System Goes the Way of the Witches

After the Bank of England began issuing paper banknotes in the 1690s, the government followed suit by issuing paper tallies against future tax revenues. Paper was easily negotiable, making the paper tallies competitive with private banknote money. For the next century, banknotes and tallies circulated interchangeably; but they were not mutually compatible means of exchange. The bankers' paper money expanded when credit expanded and contracted when loans were canceled or "called," producing cycles of "tight" money and depression alternating with "easy" money and inflation. Yet these notes *appeared* to be more sound than the government's tallies because of their gold backing. They appeared to be sound until a bank's customers got suspicious and all demanded their gold at the same time, when there would be a run on the bank and it would have to close its doors because it did not have enough gold to go around. Meanwhile, the government tallies were permanent money that remained stable and fixed. They made the bankers' paper money look bad, and they had to go.

The tallies had to go for another reason. King William's right to the throne was disputed, and the Dutch moneylenders who backed him could be evicted if the Catholics got back in and forbade moneylending again. To make sure that did not happen, the moneylenders used their new influence to discount the tallies as money and get their own banknotes legalized as the money of the realm. The tallies were called "unfunded" debt, while the Bank of England's paper notes were euphemistically labeled "funded" debt. Modern economic historians call this shift a "Financial Revolution." According to a scholarly article published at Harvard University in 2002, "Tallies and departmental bills were issued to creditors in anticipation of annual tax revenues but were not tied to any specific revenue streams; hence they were 'unfunded.'" When debt was "funded," on the other hand, "Parliament set aside specific revenues to meet interest payments, a feature that further enhanced confidence in lending to the government."

What seems to have been overlooked is that until the mid-seventeenth century, the tallies did not *need* to be "funded" through taxes, since *they were not debts.* They were *receipts* for goods and services, which could be used by the bearers in the *payment* of taxes. It was because the tallies were accepted and sometimes even required in the payment of taxes that they retained a stable value as money. Before Cromwell's Revolution, *the king did not need to borrow because he could issue metal coins or wooden tallies at will to pay his bills.* The Harvard authors presented a chart showing that in 1693, 100 percent of the government's debt was "unfunded" (or paid in government tallies). "By the 1720s," they wrote, "over 90 percent of all government borrowing was long term and funded. This, in a nutshell, was the Financial Revolution."[10] *In a nutshell, the "Financial Revolution" transferred the right to issue money from the government to private bankers.*

In the end, the tallies met the same fate as the witches – death by fire. The medieval "witches" were mainly village healers, whose natural herbs and potions competed with the male-dominated medical profession and papal church. According to some modern estimates, nine million women were executed as witches for practicing natural herbal medicine and "occult" religion.[11] The tallies were similarly the money of the people, which competed with the money of the usury bankers. In 1834, after the passage of certain monetary reform acts, the tally sticks went up in flames in a huge bonfire started in a stove in the House of Lords. In an ironic twist, the fire quickly got out of control, and wound up burning down both the Palace of Westminster and the Houses of Parliament. It was symbolic of the end of an equitable era of trade, with the transfer of power from the government to the Bank.[12]

### John Law Proposes a National Paper Money Supply

Popular acceptance of the bankers' privately-issued money scheme is credited to the son of a Scottish goldsmith named John Law, who has been called "the father of finance." Law published a series of pamphlets in 1705 on trade, money and banking, in which he claimed to have found the true "Philosopher's Stone," referring to a mythical device used by medieval alchemists to turn base material into gold. Paper could be converted into gold, Law said, through the alchemy of paper money. He proposed the creation of a national paper money supply consisting of banknotes redeemable in "specie" (hard currency in the form of gold or silver coins), which would be officially recognized as money. Paper money could be expanded indefinitely and was much cheaper to make than coins. To get public confidence, he suggested that a certain fraction of gold should be kept on hand for the few people who actually wanted to redeem their notes. The goldsmiths had already established through trial and error that specie could support about ten times its value in paper notes. Thus a bank holding $10 in gold could safely print and lend about $100 in paper money.[13] This was the "secret" that the Chicago Federal Reserve said was discovered by the goldsmiths: a bank could lend about ten times as much money as it actually had, because a trusting public, assuming their money was safely in the bank, would not come to collect more than about 10 percent of it at any one time. (See Chapter 2.)

Law planned to open a National Bank in Scotland on the model of the Bank of England; but William Paterson, who held the charter for the Bank of England, had the plan halted in the Scottish Parliament. Law then emigrated to France. He had another reason for leaving the country. Notorious for escapades of all sorts, he had gotten into a duel over a woman, which he had won; but he had wound up with a murder conviction in England.

In France, he was able to put his banking theories into practice when the French chose him to head the "Banque Generale" in 1716. Like the Bank of England, it was a private bank chartered by the government for the purpose of creating money in the form of paper notes. It was also in France that Law implemented his most notorious "Ponzi scheme."[i] The "Mississippi bubble" involved the exchange of a significant portion of French government debt for shares in a company that had a monopoly on trade with French Louisiana. The venture was called a "bubble" because most of the company's shares were bought on credit. In a huge speculative run, the shares went from about 500 French *livres* in 1719 to 10,000 *livres* by February 1720. They dropped back to 500 *livres* in September 1721. When the mania

---

[i] A *Ponzi scheme* is a form of pyramid scheme in which investors are paid with the money of later investors. Charles Ponzi was an engaging Boston ex-convict who defrauded investors out of $6 million in the 1920s, in a scheme in which he promised them a 400 percent return on redeemed postal reply coupons. For a while, he paid earlier investors with the money of later investors; but eventually he just collected without repaying. The scheme earned him ten years in jail.

ended, the investors were completely broke; and Law was again on the run.

The Mississippi bubble was short-lived because it was recognized as a sham as soon as more investors demanded payment than there were funds to pay them. Law's more enduring Ponzi scheme was the one that escaped detection, the "Philosopher's Stone" by which a national money supply could be created from government debt that had been "monetized" or turned into paper money by private bankers. *The reason this sleight of hand never got detected was that the central bank never demanded the return of its principal.* If the bankers had demanded the money back, the government would have had to levy taxes, rousing the people and revealing what was up the wizard's sleeve. But the wily bankers just continued to roll over the debt and collect the interest, on a very lucrative investment that paid (and continues to pay) like a slot machine year after year.

This scheme became the basis of the banking system known as "central banking," which remains in use today. A private central bank is chartered as the nation's primary bank and lends exclusively to the national government. It lends the central bank's own notes (printed paper money), which the government swaps for bonds (its promises to pay) and circulates as a national currency. The government's debt is never paid off but is just rolled over from year to year, becoming the basis of the national money supply. Until the twentieth century, banks followed the model of the goldsmiths and literally printed their own supply of notes against their own gold reserves. These were then multiplied many times over on the "fractional reserve" system. The bank's own name was printed on the notes, which were lent to the public and the government. Today, federal governments have taken over the printing; but in most countries the notes are still drawn on private central banks. In the United States, they are printed by the U.S. Bureau of Engraving and Printing at the request of the Federal Reserve, which "buys" them for the cost of printing them and calls them "Federal Reserve Notes."[14] But today there is no gold on "reserve" for which the notes can be redeemed. Like the illusory ghosts in the Haunted House at Disneyland, the dollar is the fractal of a hologram, the reflection of a debt for something that does not exist.

## The Tallies Leave Their Mark

The tallies were wiped off the books and fell down the memory hole, but they left their mark on the modern financial system. The word "stock," meaning a financial certificate, comes from the Middle English for the tally stick. Much of the stock in the Bank of England was originally purchased with tally sticks. The holder of the stock was said to be the "stockholder," who owned "bank stock." One of the original stockholders purchased his shares with a stick representing £25,000, an enormous sum at the time. A substantial share of what would become the world's richest and most powerful corporation was thus bought with a stick of wood! According to legend, the location of Wall Street, the New York financial district, was chosen because of the presence of a chestnut tree enormous enough to supply tally sticks for the emerging American stock market.

Stock issuance was developed during the Middle Ages as a way of financing businesses when usury and interest-bearing loans were forbidden. In medieval Europe, banks run by municipal or local governments helped finance ventures by issuing shares of stock in them. These municipal banks were large, powerful, efficient operations that fought the moneylenders' private usury banks tooth and nail. The usury banks prevailed in Europe only when the revolutionary government of France was forced to borrow from the international bankers to finance the French Revolution (1789-1799), putting the government heavily in their debt.

In the United States, the usury banks fought for control for two centuries before the Federal Reserve Act established their private monopoly in 1913. Today, the U.S. banking system is not a topic of much debate; but in the nineteenth century, the fight for and against the Bank of the United States defined American politics. And that brings us back to Jefferson and his suspicions of foreign meddling . . .

# Chapter 7
# WHILE CONGRESS DOZES
# IN THE POPPY FIELDS:
# JEFFERSON AND JACKSON
# SOUND THE ALARM

*The Scarecrow and the Tin Woodman, not being made of flesh, were not troubled by the scent of the flowers. "Run fast," said the Scarecrow to the Lion. "Get out of this deadly flower bed as soon as you can. We will bring the little girl with us, but if you should fall asleep you are too big to be carried."*

– *The Wonderful Wizard of Oz,*
"The Deadly Poppy Field"

The foreign moneylenders who had conquered Britain set the same debt traps in America, and they did it by the same means: they provoked a series of wars. British financiers funded the opposition to the American War for Independence, the War of 1812, and both sides of the American Civil War. In each case, war led to inflation, heavy government debt, and the chartering of a private "Bank of the United States" to fund the debt, delivering the power to create money to private interests. In each case, opposition to the bank was opposed by a few alert leaders. Opposition to the First U.S. Bank was led by Thomas Jefferson, the country's second President; while opposition to the Second U.S. Bank was led by Andrew Jackson, the country's seventh President. The two leaders did not have much else in common -- Jefferson was of the landed gentry, while Jackson was called the "roughshod President" -- but they shared a deep suspicion of any private arrangement for issuing the national currency. Both were particularly concerned that the nation's banking system had fallen into foreign hands. Jefferson is quoted as saying:

> If the American people ever allow the banks to control the issuance of their currency, first by inflation and then by deflation, the banks and corporations that will grow up around them will deprive the people of all property, until their children will wake up homeless on the continent their fathers occupied.

A similar wakeup call is attributed to Jackson, who told Congress in 1829:

> If the American people only understood the rank injustice of our money and banking system, there would be a revolution before morning.

Jefferson was instrumental in Congress's refusal to renew the charter of the first U.S. Bank in 1811. When the Bank was liquidated, Jefferson's suspicions were confirmed: 18,000 of the Bank's 25,000 shares were owned by foreigners, mostly English and Dutch. The foreign domination the Revolution had been fought to eliminate had crept back in through the country's private banking system. Congressman Desha of Kentucky, speaking in the House of Representatives, declared that "this accumulation of foreign capital was one of the engines for overturning civil liberty," and that he had "no doubt King George III was a principal stockholder."[1]

When Congress later renewed the Bank's charter, Andrew Jackson vetoed it. He too expressed concern that a major portion of the Bank's shareholders were foreigners. He said in his veto bill:

> Is there no danger to our liberty and independence in a bank that in its nature has so little to bind it to our country? . . . Of the course which would be pursued by a bank almost wholly owned by the subjects of a foreign power, . . . there can be no doubt. . . Controlling our currency, receiving our public monies, and holding thousands of our citizens in dependence, *it would be more formidable and dangerous than a naval and military power of the enemy.*

Who were these "subjects of a foreign power" who owned the bank? In The History of the Great American Fortunes, published in 1936, Gustavus Myers pointed to the formidable British banking dynasty the House of Rothschild. Myers wrote:

> Under the surface, the Rothschilds long had a powerful influence in dictating American financial laws. The law records show that they were the power in the old Bank of the United States.[2]

## Return of the King's Bankers

Like the German Hanoverian kings, the Rothschild banking empire was British only in the sense that it had been in England a long time. Its roots were actually in Germany. The House of Rothschild was founded in Frankfurt in the mid-eighteenth century, when a moneylender named Mayer Amschel Bauer changed his name to Amschel Rothschild and fathered ten children. His five sons were sent to the major capitals of Europe to open branches of the family banking business. Nathan, the most astute of these sons, went to London, where he opened the family branch called N. M. Rothschild & Sons. Nathan's brothers managed N. M. Rothschild's branches in Paris, Vienna, Berlin and Naples.

The family fortunes got a major boost in 1815, when Nathan pulled off the mother of all insider trades. He led British investors to believe that the Duke of Wellington had lost to Napoleon at the Battle of Waterloo. In a matter of hours, British government bond prices plummeted. Nathan, who had advance information, then swiftly bought up the entire market in government bonds, acquiring a dominant holding in England's debt for pennies on the pound. Over the course of the nineteenth century, N. M. Rothschild would become the biggest bank in the world, and the five brothers would come to control most of the foreign-loan business of Europe. "Let me issue and control a nation's money," Nathan Rothschild boasted in 1838, "and I care not who writes its laws."[3]

In 1811, when the U.S. Congress declined to renew the charter of the first U.S. Bank, Nathan Rothschild already possessed substantial political clout in England and was lending money to the U.S. government and certain States. "Either the application for renewal of the Charter is granted," he is reported to have threatened, "or the United States will find itself in a most disastrous war."[4] The charter was not granted, and the United States did find itself in another war with England, the War of 1812.

War again led to inflation and heavy government debt. This and an inability to collect taxes were the reasons given for chartering the Second Bank of the United States as a private national bank. The twenty-year charter was signed by President James Madison in 1816. It authorized the Bank and its branches to issue the nation's money in the form of bank notes, again shifting the power to create the national money supply into private hands.

## Jefferson Realizes Too Late the Need for a National Paper Currency Issued by the Government

Jefferson was out of town when the Constitution was drafted, serving as America's minister to France during the dramatic period leading up to the French Revolution. But even if he had been there, he would probably have gone along with the majority and voted to omit paper money from the Constitution. After watching the national debt mushroom, he wrote to John Tyler in 1878, "I wish it were possible to obtain a single amendment to our constitution . . . taking from the federal government the power to borrow money. *I now deny their power of making paper money or anything else a legal tender.*"[5]

It would be several decades before Jefferson realized that the villain was not paper money itself. It was private debt masquerading as paper money, a private debt owed to bankers who were merely "pretending to have money." Jefferson wrote to Treasury Secretary Gallatin in 1815:

> The treasury, lacking confidence in the country, delivered itself bound hand and foot to *bold and bankrupt adventurers and bankers pretending to have money, whom it could have crushed at any moment.*

Jefferson wrote to John Eppes in 1813, "*Although we have so foolishly allowed the field of circulating medium to be filched from us by private individuals, I think we may recover it . . . . The states should be asked to transfer the right of issuing paper money to Congress, in perpetuity.*" He told Eppes, "the nation may continue to issue its bills [paper notes] as far as its needs require and the limits of circulation allow. Those limits are understood at present to be 200 millions of dollars."[6]

Writing to Gallatin in 1803, Jefferson said of the private national bank, "This institution is one of the most deadly hostility against the principles of our Constitution . . . . [S]uppose a series of emergencies should occur . . . . [A]n institution like this . . . in a critical moment might overthrow the government." He asked, "Could we start toward independently *using our own money to form our own bank?*"

The Constitution gave Congress the power only to "coin money," but Jefferson argued that Constitutions could be amended. He wrote to Samuel Kercheval in 1816:

> Some men look at constitutions with sanctimonious reverence, and deem them like the ark of the Covenant, too sacred to be touched. They ascribe to the men of the preceding age a wisdom

more than human, and suppose what they did to be beyond amendment . . . [L]aws and institutions must go hand in hand with the progress of the human mind. . . . [A]s that becomes more developed, more enlightened, as new discoveries are made, institutions must advance also, to keep pace with the times. . . . We might as well require a man to wear still the coat which fitted him when a boy as civilized society to remain forever under the regimen of their barbarous ancestors.[7]

When Congress was deliberating on a Second U.S. Bank, Senator John Calhoun proposed a plan for a truly "national" bank along the lines suggested by Jefferson. A wholly government-owned national bank could issue the nation's own credit directly, without having to borrow from a private bank that issued it. This plan was later endorsed by Senator Henry Clay, but it would be several more decades before the Civil War would provide the pretext for Abraham Lincoln to authorize Congress to issue its own money. The Second U.S. Bank chartered in 1816 was 80 percent privately owned.[8]

## Jackson Battles the Hydra-headed Monster

Andrew Jackson was a hero of the War of 1812 and a leader with enormous popular appeal. He was the first of the "unlettered Scarecrows" to reach the White House, to be followed by the even mightier Abraham Lincoln (who actually looked like a Scarecrow). Jackson received an honorary degree from Harvard College in 1833, but it was over the objection of Harvard alumnus John Quincy Adams, who called him "a barbarian who could not write a sentence of grammar and hardly could spell his own name." Perhaps, but "Old Hickory" truly believed in the will of the democratic majority, and he spoke to the common people in a way they could understand.

After the Federalists ceased to be a major national party, the Democratic-Republicans dominated the political scene alone for a time. In 1824, four candidates ran for President as Democratic-Republicans from different States: Andrew Jackson, John Quincy Adams, William Crawford, and Henry Clay. Jackson easily won the popular vote, but he did not have enough electoral votes to win the Presidency, so the matter went to the House of Representatives, where Clay threw his support to Adams, who won. But popular sentiment remained with Jackson, who won by a wide margin against Adams in the election of 1828. Jackson believed in a strong Presidency and a strong union. He stood up to the bankers on the matter of the bank, which he viewed as operating mainly for the upper classes at the expense of working people. He warned in 1829:

> The bold efforts the present bank has made to control the government are but premonitions of the fate that awaits the American people should they be deluded into a perpetuation of this institution or the establishment of another like it.

Whether Congress itself had the right to issue paper money, Jackson argued, was not clear; but "If Congress has the right under the Constitution to issue paper money, *it was given them to be used by themselves, not to be delegated to individuals or to corporations.*" His grim premonitions about the Bank appeared to be confirmed, when mismanagement under its first president led to financial disaster, depression, bankruptcies, and unemployment. But the Bank began to flourish under its second president, Nicholas Biddle, who petitioned Congress for a renewal of its charter in 1832. Jackson, who was then up for re-election, expressed his views to this bid in no uncertain terms. "You are a den of vipers and thieves," he railed at a delegation of bankers discussing the Bank Renewal Bill. "I intend to rout you out, and by the eternal God, I will rout you out." He called the bank "a hydra-headed monster eating the flesh of the common man." He swore to do battle with the monster and to slay it or be slain by it.[9]

In the 1832 election, Jackson ran on the Democratic Party ticket against Henry Clay, whose party was now called the National Republican Party. Its members considered themselves "nationalists" because they saw the country as a nation rather than a loose confederation of States, and because they promoted strong nation-building measures such as the construction of inter-state roads. Clay advocated a strongly protectionist platform that kept productivity and financing within the country, allowing it to grow up "in its own backyard," free from economic attack from abroad. It was Clay who first called this approach the "American system" to distinguish it from the "British system" of "free trade." The British system was supported by Jackson and opposed by Clay, who thought it would open the country to exploitation by foreign financiers and industrialists. To prevent that, Clay advocated a tariff favoring domestic industry, congressionally-financed national improvements, and a national bank.

More than three million dollars were poured into Clay's campaign, then a huge sum; but Jackson again won by a landslide. He had the vote of the people but not of Congress, which proceeded to pass the

Bank Renewal Bill. Jackson as promptly vetoed it. Showing how eloquent the self-taught could be, he said in his veto bill:

> There are no necessary evils in government. Its evils exist only in its abuses. If it would confine itself to equal protection, and, as Heaven does its rains, shower its favor alike on the high and the low, the rich and the poor, it would be an unqualified blessing. In the act before me there seems to be a wide and unnecessary departure from these just principles. Many of our rich men have not been content with equal protection and equal benefits, but have besought us to make them richer by act of Congress. . . . If we can not at once, in justice to interests vested under improvident legislation, make our Government what it ought to be, we can at least take a stand against all new grants of monopolies and exclusive privileges, against any prostitution of our Government to the advancement of the few at the expense of the many . . . .

Jackson succeeded in vetoing the bill, but he knew that his battle with the Bank was just beginning. "The hydra of corruption is only scotched, not dead," he exclaimed. Boldly taking the hydra by the horns, he ordered his new Treasury Secretary to start transferring the government's deposits from the Second U.S. Bank into state banks. When the Secretary refused, Jackson fired him and appointed another. When that Secretary refused, Jackson appointed a third. When the third Secretary proceeded to do as he was told, Jackson was triumphant. "I have it chained," he said of the banking monster. "I am ready with screws to draw every tooth and then the stumps." But Biddle and his Bank were indeed only scotched, not dead. Biddle used his influence to get the Senate to reject the new Secretary's nomination. Then he threatened to cause a national depression if the Bank were not rechartered. Biddle openly declared:

> *Nothing but widespread suffering will produce any effect on Congress.* . . . Our only safety is in pursuing a steady course of firm [monetary] restriction – and I have no doubt that such a course will ultimately lead to restoration of the currency and the recharter of the Bank.

Biddle proceeded to make good on his threat by sharply contracting the money supply. Old loans were called in and new ones were refused. A financial panic ensued, followed by a deep economic depression. Biddle blamed it all on Jackson, and the newspapers picked up the charge. Jackson was officially censured by a Senate resolution.

The tide turned, however, when the Governor of the Pennsylvania (where the Bank was located) came out in support of the President and strongly critical of the Bank; and Biddle was caught boasting in public about the Bank's plan to crash the economy. In April 1834, the House of Representatives voted 134 to 82 against re-chartering the Bank, and a special committee was established to investigate whether it had caused the crash.[10]

In January 1835, in what may have been his finest hour, Jackson paid off the final installment on the national debt. He had succeeded in doing something that had never been done before and has not been done since: he reduced the national debt to zero and accumulated a surplus.[i] The following year, the charter for the Second Bank of the United States expired; and Biddle was later arrested and charged with fraud. He was tried and acquitted, but he died while tied up in civil suits.

Jackson had beaten the Bank. His personal secretary, Nicholas Trist, called it "the crowning glory of A.J.'s life and the most important service he has ever rendered his country." The Boston Post compared it to Jesus throwing the moneychangers out of the Temple. But Jackson, like Jesus, found that taking on the moneychangers was risky business. "The Bank is trying to kill me," he said, "but I will kill it!" He was the victim of an assassination attempt, but both the assassin's shots missed.[11]

Abraham Lincoln would not be so lucky.

---

[i] Recall that President Clinton's balancing of the budget did not include paying off the national debt, which stood at $5 trillion in 2000.

# Chapter 8
# SCARECROW WITH A BRAIN:
# LINCOLN FOILS THE BANKERS

*"With the thoughts you'd be thinkin',*
*"You could be another Lincoln,*
*"If you only had a brain . . . ."*

*– Dorothy to the Scarecrow (1939 film)*

L ike the Scarecrow who wound up ruling Oz, Abraham
Lincoln went from hayseed to the top of his class by sheer
native wit and determination, epitomizing the American dream. Following in the footsteps of Andrew Jackson, he rose from the back-
woods to the Presidency without ever going to college. Lincoln's
mother could barely read. Like Jackson, Lincoln risked life and limb
battling the Money Power; but the two Presidents had quite different
ideas about how it should be done. Jackson had captured the popular
imagination by playing on the distrust of big banks and foreign bankers; but in throwing out the national bank and its foreign controllers,
he had thrown out Hamilton's baby with the bath water, leaving the
banks in unregulated chaos. There was now no national currency.
Banks printed their own notes and simply had to be trusted to redeem
them in specie (or gold bullion). When trust faltered, there would be a
run on the bank and the bank would generally wind up closing its
doors. Bank-fed speculation had collapsed much of the factory system; and federal support for road, canal and railway construction
was halted, halting the pioneer settlement of the West along with it.

Lincoln was only 24 when he joined the fight as an Illinois state
legislator to continue the pioneering internal improvements begun by
Henry Clay and the National Republicans. The National Republicans
were now called "Whigs" after the British Whigs, the party in opposition to the King. Jackson had taken such unprecedented powers to

himself that he had come to be called "King Andrew," making the American opposition party Whigs by extension. The "Illinois Improvement Program" centered on construction of the Illinois-Michigan canal and a 3,000-mile railroad system. The result was an unbroken transportation line from the Hudson River to the Great Lakes and the Mississippi River. Lincoln also joined the movement to restore the country's financial, industrial and political independence by restoring a national bank and a national currency.[1]

When the Whig Party disintegrated over the question of slavery, Lincoln joined the Republican Party, which was created in 1854 to oppose the expansion of slavery into Kansas. It opposed the political control exerted by southern slave owners over the national government; maintained that free-market labor was superior to slavery; promised free homesteads to farmers; and advanced a progressive vision emphasizing higher education, banking, railroads, industry and cities.[2] Lincoln became the first Republican candidate to be elected President.

Both Jackson and Lincoln were targets of assassination attempts, but for Lincoln they started before he was even inaugurated. He had to deal with treason, insurrection, and national bankruptcy within the first days of taking office. Considering the powerful forces arrayed against him, his achievements in the next four years were nothing short of phenomenal. His government built and equipped the largest army in the world, smashed the British-financed insurrection, abolished slavery, and freed four million slaves. Along the way, the country managed to become the greatest industrial giant the world had ever seen. The steel industry was launched, a continental railroad system was created, the Department of Agriculture was established, a new era of farm machinery and cheap tools was promoted, a system of free higher education was established through the Land Grant College System, land development was encouraged by passage of a Homestead Act granting ownership privileges to settlers, major government support was provided to all branches of science, the Bureau of Mines was organized, governments in the Western territories were established, the judicial system was reorganized, labor productivity increased by 50 to 75 percent, and standardization and mass production was promoted worldwide.

How was all this accomplished, with a Treasury that was completely broke and a Congress that hadn't been paid themselves? As Benjamin Franklin might have said, "That is simple." Lincoln tapped into the same cornerstone that had gotten the impoverished colonists through the American Revolution and a long period of internal development before that: the government issued its own paper *fiat* money. National control was reestablished over banking, and the economy was jump-started with a 600 percent increase in government spending and cheap credit directed at production.[3] A century later, Franklin Roosevelt would use the same techniques to pull the country through the Great Depression; but Roosevelt's New Deal would be financed with borrowed money. Lincoln's government used a system of payment that was closer to the medieval tally. Officially called United States Notes, these nineteenth century tallies were popularly called "Greenbacks" because they were printed on the back with green ink (a feature the dollar retains today). They were basically just receipts acknowledging work done or goods delivered, which could be traded in the community for an equivalent value of goods or services. The Greenbacks represented man-hours rather than borrowed gold. Lincoln is quoted as saying, *"The wages of men should be recognized as more important than the wages of money."* Over 400 million Greenback dollars were printed and used to pay soldiers and government employees, and to buy supplies for the war.

The Greenback system was not actually Lincoln's idea, but when pressure grew in Congress for the plan, he was quick to endorse it. The South had seceded from the Union soon after his election in 1860. To fund the War between the States, the Eastern banks had offered a loan package that was little short of extortion – $150 million advanced at interest rates of 24 to 36 percent. Lincoln knew the loan would be impossible to pay off.[4] He took the revolutionary approach because he had no other real choice. The government could either print its own money or succumb to debt slavery to the bankers.

## The Wizard Behind Lincoln's Curtain

Lincoln's economic advisor was Henry Carey, the son of Matthew Carey, the printer and publisher mentioned earlier who was tutored by Benjamin Franklin and had tutored Henry Clay. Clay was the leader of the Philadelphia-based political faction propounding the "American system" of economics. In the 1920s, historian Vernon Parrington called Henry Carey "our first professional economist." Thomas DiLorenzo, a modern libertarian writer, calls him "Lincoln's (and the Republican Party's) economic guru." Carey was known around the world during the Civil War and its aftermath, and his writings were translated into many European and Asian languages.

According to Parrington, Carey began his career as a classical *laissez-faire* economist of the British school; but he came to believe that American industrial development was being held back by a false financial policy imposed by foreign financiers. To recognize only gold bullion as money gave the bankers who controlled the gold a lock on the money supply and the economy. The price of gold was established in a world market, and the flow of bullion was always toward the great financial centers that were already glutted with it. To throw the world's money into a common pool that drained into these financial capitals was to make poorer countries the servants of these hubs. Since negative trade balances were settled in gold, gold followed the balance of trade; and until America could build up an adequate domestic economy, its gold would continue to drain off, leaving too little money for its internal needs.

Carey came to consider "free trade" and the "gold standard" to be twin financial weapons forged by England for its own economic conquest. His solution to the gold drain was for the government to create an independent national currency that was non-exportable, one that would remain at home to do the country's own work. He advocated a currency founded on "national credit," something he defined as "a national system based entirely on the credit of the government with the people, not liable to interference from abroad." Like the wooden tally, this paper money would simply be a unit of account that tallied work performed and goods delivered. Carey also supported expanding the monetary base with silver.[5]

Carey's theories were an elaboration of the "American system" propounded by Henry Clay and the National Republican Party. Their platform was to nurture local growth and development using local raw materials and local money, freeing the country from dependence on foreign financing. Where Jackson's Democratic Party endorsed "free trade," the National Republican Party sought another sort of freedom, the right to be free from exploitation by powerful foreign financiers and industrialists. Free traders wanted freedom *from* government. Protectionists looked *to* the government to keep them free from foreign marauders. Clay's protectionist platform included:

- Government regulation of banking and credit to deter speculation and encourage economic development;

- Government support for the development of science, public education, and national infrastructure;[i]
- Regulation of privately-held infrastructure to ensure it met the nation's needs;
- A program of government-sponsored railroads, and scientific and other aid to small farmers;
- Taxation and tariffs to protect and promote productive domestic activity; and
- Rejection of class wars, exploitation and slavery, physical or economic, in favor of a "Harmony of Interests" between capital and labor.[6]

Lincoln also endorsed these goals. He eliminated slavery, established a national bank, and implemented and funded national education, national transportation, and federal development of business and farming. He also set very high tariffs. He made this common-sense observation:

> I don't know much about the tariff, but I know this much: When we buy manufactured goods abroad we get the goods and the foreigner gets the money. When we buy the manufactured goods at home, we get both the goods and the money.

## The Legal Tender Acts and the Legal Tender Cases

The Greenback system undergirded Lincoln's program of domestic development by providing a much-needed *national* paper money supply. After Jackson had closed the central bank, the only paper money in circulation were the banknotes issued privately by individual state banks; and they were basically just private promises to pay later in hard currency (gold or silver). The Greenbacks, on the other hand, *were* currency. They were "legal tender" in themselves, money that did not have to be repaid later but was "as good as gold" in trade. Like metal coins, the Greenbacks were permanent money that could continue to circulate in their own right. The Legal Tender Acts of 1862 and 1863 made all the "coins and currency" issued by the U.S.

---

[i] *Infrastructure* is defined as "the set of interconnected structural elements that provide the framework for supporting the entire structure." In a country, it consists of the basic facilities needed for the country's functioning, providing a public framework under which private enterprise can operate safely and efficiently.

Government "legal tender for all debts, public and private." Government-issued paper notes were made a legal substitute for gold and silver, even for the payment of pre-existing debts.

In the twentieth century, the Legal Tender Statute (31 U.S.C. Section 5103) applied this definition of "legal tender" to Federal Reserve Notes, but it was a distortion of the intent of the original Acts. The Legal Tender Acts made only currency *issued by the United States Government* legal tender. Federal Reserve Notes were issued by the Federal Reserve, a private banking corporation. However, that rather obvious discrepancy was slipped past the American people with the smoke-and-mirrors illusion that the Federal Reserve was actually federal.

## Did the Greenbacks Cause Price Inflation?

Lincoln's Greenback program has been blamed for the price inflation occurring during the Civil War, but according to Irwin Unger in The Greenback Era (1964): "It is now clear that inflation would have occurred even without the Greenback issue."[7] War is always an inflationary venture. What forced prices up during the Civil War was actually a severe shortage of goods. Zarlenga quotes historian J. G. Randall, who observed in 1937:

> *The threat of inflation was more effectively curbed during the Civil War than during the First World War.* Indeed as John K. Galbraith has observed, "it is remarkable that without rationing, price controls, or central banking, [Treasury Secretary] Chase could have managed the federal economy so well during the Civil War."[8]

If Lincoln had not issued the extra money he needed to fund the war in the form of Greenbacks, he would have had to issue more bonds. Either alternative would have inflated the money supply, since the banks that bought the government's bonds were also short of gold. They could only have paid for them with their own newly-issued banknotes; and the bond option would have plunged the government further into debt. As Thomas Edison reasonably observed in an interview reported in The New York Times in 1921:

> If the Nation can issue a dollar bond it can issue a dollar bill. The element that makes the bond good makes the bill good also. The difference between the bond and the bill is that the bond

lets the money broker collect twice the amount of the bond and an additional 20%. Whereas the currency, the honest sort provided by the Constitution pays nobody but those who contribute in some useful way. It is absurd to say our Country can issue bonds and cannot issue currency. *Both are promises to pay, but one fattens the usurer and the other helps the People.*

The Greenbacks did lose value as against gold during the war, but this was to be expected, since gold was a more established currency that people naturally preferred. Again the problem for the Greenback was that it had to compete with other forms of currency. People remained suspicious of paper money, and the Greenback was not accepted for everything. Particularly, it could not be used for the government's interest payments on its outstanding bonds. By December 1865, the Greenback was still worth 68 cents to one gold dollar, not bad under the circumstances. Meanwhile, the Confederates' paper notes had become devalued so much that they were worthless. The Confederacy had made the mistake of issuing fiat money that was *not* legal tender but was only a bond or promise to pay after the War. As the defeat of the Confederacy became more and more certain, its currency's value plummeted.[9]

In 1972, the United States Treasury Department was asked to compute the amount of interest that would have been paid if the $400 million in Greenbacks had been borrowed from the banks instead. According to the Treasury Department's calculations, in his short tenure Lincoln saved the government a total of $4 billion in interest, just by avoiding this $400 million loan.[10]

# Chapter 9
# LINCOLN LOSES THE BATTLE
# WITH THE MASTERS
# OF EUROPEAN FINANCE

*"When she knows you are in the country of the Winkies she will find you, and make you all her slaves."*

*"Perhaps not," said the Scarecrow, "for we mean to destroy her."*

*"Oh, that is different," said the Guardian of the Gates. "No one has ever destroyed her before, so I naturally thought she would make slaves of you, as she has of the rest. But take care. She is wicked and fierce, and may not allow you to destroy her."*

– <u>The Wonderful Wizard of Oz,</u>
<br>"The Search for the Wicked Witch"

The Confederacy was not the only power that was bent on destroying Lincoln's Union government. Lurking behind the curtain pulling the strings of war were powerful foreign financiers. Otto von Bismarck, Chancellor of Germany in the second half of the nineteenth century, called these puppeteers "the masters of European finance." He wrote:

> I know of absolute certainty, that the division of the United States into federations of equal force was decided long before the Civil War by the high financial powers of Europe. These bankers were afraid that the United States, if they remained in one block and as one nation, would attain economic and financial independence, which would upset their financial domination over Europe and the world. Of course, in the "inner circle" of Finance, the voice of the Rothschilds prevailed. They saw an opportunity for prodigious booty if they could substitute two feeble democracies, burdened with debt to the financiers, . . . in place of a vigorous Republic sufficient unto herself. Therefore,

they sent their emissaries into the field to exploit the question of slavery and to drive a wedge between the two parts of the Union. . . . *The rupture between the North and the South became inevitable; the masters of European finance employed all their forces to bring it about and to turn it to their advantage.*[1]

The European bankers wanted a war that would return the United States to its colonial status, but they were not necessarily interested in preserving slavery. Slavery just meant that the owners had to feed and care for their workers. The bankers preferred "the European plan" – *capital could exploit labor by controlling the money supply, while letting the laborers feed themselves.* In July 1862, this ploy was revealed in a notorious document called the Hazard Circular, which was circulated by British banking interests among their American banking counterparts. It said:

> Slavery is likely to be abolished by the war power and chattel slavery destroyed. This, I and my European friends are glad of, for *slavery is but the owning of labor and carries with it the care of the laborers, while the European plan, led by England, is that capital shall control labor by controlling wages. This can be done by controlling the money.* The great debt that capitalists will see to it is made out of the war, must be used as a means to control the volume of money. To accomplish this, *the bonds must be used as a banking basis. . . . It will not do to allow the greenback, as it is called, to circulate as money any length of time, as we cannot control that.*[2]

The system the bankers wanted to preserve was what Henry Clay and Henry Carey had called the "British system," with its twin weapons of "free trade" and the "gold standard" keeping the less industrialized countries in a colonial state, supplying raw materials to Britain's factories. The American South had already been subjugated in this way. The bankers had now set their sights on the North, to be reeled in with usurious war loans; but Lincoln had refused to take the bait. The threat the new Greenback system posed to the bankers' game was reflected in an article attributed to an unidentified editorialist writing in <u>The London Times</u> in 1865. It warned:

> [I]f that mischievous financial policy, which had its origin in the North American Republic, should become indurated down to a fixture, then *that Government will furnish its own money without cost.* It will pay off debts and be without a debt. It will have all the money necessary to carry on its commerce. It will become

prosperous beyond precedent in the history of the civilized governments of the world. The brains and the wealth of all countries will go to North America. *That government must be destroyed, or it will destroy every monarchy on the globe.*[3]

Bismarck wrote in 1876, "The Government and the nation escaped the plots of the foreign financiers. They understood at once, that the United States would escape their grip. The death of Lincoln was resolved upon." Lincoln was assassinated in 1865.

## The Worm in the Apple: The National Banking Act of 1863-64

The European financiers had failed to trap Lincoln's government with usurious war loans, but they achieved their ends by other means. While one faction in Congress was busy getting the Greenbacks issued to fund the war, another faction was preparing a National Banking Act that would deliver a monopoly over the power to create the nation's money supply to the Wall Street bankers and their European affiliates. The National Banking Act was promoted as establishing safeguards for the new national banking system; but while it was an important first step toward a truly national bank, it was only a compromise with the bankers, and buried in the fine print, it gave them exactly what they wanted. A private communication from a Rothschild investment house in London to an associate banking firm in New York dated June 25, 1863, confided:

> The few who understand the system will either be so interested in its profits or so dependent upon its favors that there will be no opposition from that class while, on the other hand, the great body of people, mentally incapable of comprehending . . . will bear its burdens without complaint.[4]

The Act looked good on its face. It established a Comptroller of the Currency, whose authority was required before a National Banking Association could start business. It laid down regulations covering minimum capitalization, reserve requirements, bad debts, and reporting. The Comptroller could at any time appoint investigators to look into the affairs of any national bank. Every bank director had to be an American citizen, and three-quarters of the directors of a bank had to be residents of the State in which the bank did business. Interest rates were limited by State usury laws; and if no laws were in effect, then to 7 percent.  Banks could not hold real estate for more than five years, except for bank buildings.  National banks were not allowed to circulate notes they printed themselves.  Instead, they had to deposit U.S. bonds with the Treasury in a sum equal to at least one-third of their capital.  They got government-printed notes in return.

So what was the problem?  Although the new national banknotes were technically issued by the Comptroller of the Currency, this was actually just a formality, like the printing of Federal Reserve Notes by the Bureau of Engraving and Printing today.  The currency bore the name of the bank posting the bonds, and it was issued at the bank's request.  In effect, the National Banking Act authorized the bankers to issue and lend their own paper money.  The banks "deposited" bonds with the Treasury, but they still owned the bonds; and they immediately got their money back in the form of their own banknotes.  Topping it off, the National Banking Act effectively removed the competition to these banknotes.  It imposed a heavy tax on the notes of the state-chartered banks, essentially abolishing them.[5] It also curtailed competition from the Greenbacks, which were limited to specific issues while the bankers' notes could be issued at will.  Treasury Secretary Salmon P. Chase and others complained that the bankers were buying up the Greenbacks with their own banknotes.  Zarlenga cites a historian named Dewey, who wrote in 1903:

> The banks were accused of absorbing the government notes as fast as they were issued and of putting out their own notes in substitution, and then at their convenience converting the notes into bonds on which they earned interest [in gold].[6]

The government got what it needed at the time – a loan of substantial sums for the war effort and a sound circulating currency for an expanding economy – but the banks were the real winners.  They not only got to collect interest on money of which they still had the use, but they got powerful leverage over the government as its creditors.  The Act that was supposed to regulate the bankers wound up chartering not one but a whole series of private banks, which all had the power to create the currency of the nation.

The National Banking Act was recommended to Congress by Treasury Secretary Chase, ironically the same official who had sponsored the Greenback program the Act effectively eliminated.  In a popular 1887 book called <u>Seven Financial Conspiracies That Have Enslaved the American People</u>, Sarah Emery wrote that Chase had acquiesced only after several days of meetings and threats of financial coercion by bank delegates. He is quoted as saying later:

> My agency in procuring the passage of the National Bank Act was the greatest financial mistake of my life. It has built up a monopoly that affects every interest in the country. It should be repealed. But before this can be accomplished, the people will be arrayed on one side and the banks on the other in a contest such as we have never seen in this country.[8]

Although Lincoln was assassinated in 1865, it would be another fifty years before the promise of his debt-free Greenbacks were erased from the minds of a people long suspicious of the usury bankers and their gilded paper money. The "Gilded Age" – the period between the Civil War and World War I – was a series of battles over who should issue the country's currency and what it should consist of.

## Skirmishes in the Currency Wars

Chase appeared on the scene again in 1869, this time as Chief Justice of the Supreme Court. He wrote the opinion in Hepburn v. Griswold, 75 U.S. 603, holding the Legal Tender Acts to be unconstitutional. Chase considered the Greenbacks to be a temporary war measure. He wrote that the Constitution prohibits the States from passing "any . . . law impairing the obligation of contracts," and that to compel holders of contracts calling for payment in gold and silver to accept payment in "mere promises to pay dollars" was "an unconstitutional deprivation of property without due process of law."

In 1871, however, with two new justices on the bench, the Supreme Court reversed and found the Legal Tender Acts constitutional. In the Legal Tender cases (Knox v. Lee, 79 U.S. 457, 20 L.Ed. 287; and Juilliard v. Greenman, 110 U.S. 421, 4 S.Ct. 122, 28 L.Ed. 204), the Court declared that Congress has the power "to coin money and regulate its value" with the objects of self-preservation and the achievement of a more perfect union, and that "no obligation of contract can extend to the defeat of legitimate government authority."

In 1873, an Act the Populists would call the "Crime of '73" eliminated the free coinage of silver. Like when King George banned the use of locally-issued paper scrip a century earlier, the result was "tight" money and hard times. A bank panic followed, which hit the western debtor farmers particularly hard.

In 1874, the politically powerful farmers responded by forming the Greenback Party. Their proposed solution to the crisis was for the government to finance the building of roads and public projects with additional debt-free Greenbacks, augmenting the money supply and putting the unemployed to work, returning the country to the sort of full employment and productivity seen in Benjamin Franklin's time. The Greenbacks could also be used to redeem the federal debt. Under the "Ohio Idea," all government bonds not specifying payment in gold or silver would be repaid in Greenbacks.[9] The plan was not adopted, but the Scarecrow had shown he had a brain. The Timid Lion had demonstrated the courage and the collective will to organize and make a difference.

In 1875, a Resumption Act called for redemption by the Treasury of all Greenbacks in "specie." The Greenbacks had to be withdrawn and replaced with hard currency, producing further contraction of the money supply and deeper depression.

In 1878, the Scarecrow and the Tin Woodman joined forces to form the Greenback-Labor Party. They polled over one million votes and elected 14 Representatives to Congress. They failed to get a new issue of Greenbacks, but they had enough political clout to stop further withdrawal of existing Greenbacks from circulation. The Greenbacks then outstanding ($346,681,016 worth) were made a permanent part of the nation's currency.

In 1881, James Garfield became President. He boldly took a stand against the bankers, charging:

> Whosoever controls the volume of money in any country is absolute master of all industry and commerce . . . And when you realize that the entire system is very easily controlled, one way or another, by a few powerful men at the top, you will not have to be told how periods of inflation and depression originate.

President Garfield was murdered not long after releasing this statement, when he was less than four months into his presidency. Depression deepened, leaving masses of unemployed to face poverty and starvation at a time when there was no social security or unemployment insurance to act as a safety net. Produce was left to rot in the fields, because there was no money to pay workers to harvest it or to buy it with when it got to market. The country was facing poverty amidst plenty, because there was insufficient money in circulation to keep the wheels of trade turning. The country sorely needed the sort of liquidity urged by Lincoln, Carey and the

Greenbackers; but the bankers insisted that allowing the government to print its own  money would be dangerously inflationary.  That was their argument, but critics called it "humbuggery" . . . .

# Chapter 10
# THE GREAT HUMBUG:
# THE GOLD STANDARD AND THE
# STRAW MAN OF INFLATION

*"Hush, my dear," he said. "Don't speak so loud, or you will be
overheard – and I should be ruined. I'm supposed to be a Great
Wizard."*

*"And aren't you?" she asked.*

*"Not a bit of it, my dear; I'm just a common man."*

*"You're more than that," said the Scarecrow, in a grieved tone;
"you're a humbug."*

*"Exactly so!" declared the little man, rubbing his hands together as
if it pleased him. "I am a humbug."*

> – The Wonderful Wizard of Oz,
> "The Magic Art of the Great Humbug"

*Humbug* is a word that isn't used much today, but in the
Gilded Age it was a popular term for describing frauds, shams
and con artists. Vernon Parrington, a Pulitzer prize-winning historian
writing in the 1920s, used it to describe the arguments of the bankers
to silence the farmers who were trying to reform the banker-controlled
money system in the 1890s. It was the farmers who particularly felt
the pinch of tight money when the bankers withheld their gold.
Parrington wrote that the farmers "pitted their homespun experience
against the authority of the bankers and the teaching of the schools."
In response to their clear-headed arguments, the bankers defended
with a smokescreen of confusing rhetoric:

> Denunciation took the place of exposition, and hysteria of
> argument; and in this revel of demagoguery the so-called
> educated classes -- lawyers and editors and business men -- were

perhaps the most shameless purveyors of *humbuggery.* Stripped of all hypocrisy the main issue was this: *Should the control of currency issues -- with the delegated power of inflation and deflation -- lie in the hands of private citizens or with the elected representatives of the people?* . . . [But] throughout the years when the subject was debated in every newspaper and on every stump the real issue was rarely presented for consideration. The bankers did not dare to present it, for too much was at stake and once it was clearly understood by a suspicious electorate their case was lost. *Hence the strategy of the money group was to obscure the issue, an end they achieved by dwelling on the single point of inflation* . . . .[1]

## The Quantity Theory of Money

The gold standard and the inflation argument that was used to justify it were based on the classical "quantity theory of money." The foundation of classical monetary theory, it held that inflation is caused by "too much money chasing too few goods." When "demand" (the money available to buy goods) increases faster than "supply" (goods and services), prices are forced up. If the government were allowed to simply issue all the Greenback dollars it needed, the money supply would increase faster than goods and services, and price inflation would result. If paper money were tied to gold, a commodity in limited and fixed supply, the money supply would remain stable and price inflation would be avoided.

A corollary to that theory was the classical maxim that the government should balance its budget at all costs. If it ran short of money, it was supposed to borrow from the bankers rather than print the money it needed, in order to keep from inflating the money supply. The argument was a "straw man" argument – one easily knocked down because it contained a logical fallacy – but the fallacy was not immediately obvious, because the bankers were concealing their hand. The fallacy lay in the assumption that the money the government borrowed from the banks already existed and was merely being recycled. If the bankers themselves were creating the money they lent, the argument collapsed in a heap of straw. The money supply would obviously increase just as much from bank-created money as from government-created money. In either case, it was money pulled out of an empty hat. Money created by the government had the advantage that it would not plunge the taxpayers into debt; and it provided a *permanent* money supply, one not dependent on higher and higher levels of borrowing to stay afloat.

The quantity theory of money contained another logical fallacy, which was pointed out later by British economist John Maynard Keynes. Adding money ("demand") to the economy would drive up prices only if the "supply" side of the equation remained fixed. If new Greenbacks were used to create new goods and services, supply would increase along with demand, and prices would remain stable.[2] When a shoe salesman with many unsold shoes on his shelves suddenly got more customers, he did not raise his prices. He sold more shoes. If he ran out of shoes, he ordered more from the factory, which produced more. If he were to raise his prices, his customers would go to the shop down the street, where shoes were still being sold at the lower price. Adding more money to the economy would inflate prices *only* when the producers ran out of the labor and materials needed to make more goods. Before that, supply and demand would increase together, leaving prices as they were before.

That theoretical revision helps explain such paradoxical data as the "economic mystery" of China. The Chinese have managed to keep the prices of their products low for thousands of years, although their money supply has continually been flooded with the world's gold and silver, and now with the world's dollars, as those currencies have poured in to pay for China's cheap products.[3] The Keynesian explanation is that prices have remained stable because the money has gone into producing more goods, increasing supply along with demand.

While bankers in America were insisting that the government must borrow rather than print the money it needed, the residents of a small island state off the coast of England were quietly conducting a 200-year experiment that would show the bankers' inflation argument to be a humbug.

## The Remarkable Island of Guernsey

The island state of Guernsey is located among the British Channel Islands, about 75 miles south of Great Britain. In 1994, Dr. Bob Blain, Professor of Sociology at Southern Illinois University, wrote of this remarkable island:

In 1816 its sea walls were crumbling, its roads were muddy and only 4 1/2 feet wide. Guernsey's debt was 19,000 pounds. The island's annual income was 3,000 pounds of which 2,400 had to be used to pay interest on its debt. Not surprisingly, people were leaving Guernsey and there was little employment.

Then the government created and loaned new, interest-free state notes worth 6,000 pounds. Some 4,000 pounds were used to start the repairs of the sea walls. In 1820, another 4,500 pounds was issued, again interest-free. In 1821, another 10,000; 1824, 5,000; 1826, 20,000. By 1837, 50,000 pounds had been issued interest free for the primary use of projects like sea walls, roads, the marketplace, churches, and colleges. This sum more than doubled the island's money supply during this thirteen year period, but *there was no inflation*. In the year 1914, as the British restricted the expansion of their money supply due to World War I, the people of Guernsey commenced to issue another 142,000 pounds over the next four years and never looked back. By 1958, over 542,000 pounds had been issued, all without inflation.[4]

Guernsey has an income tax, but the tax is relatively low (a "flat" 20 percent), and it is simple and loophole-free. It has no inheritance tax, no capital gains tax, and *no federal debt*. Commercial banks service private lenders, but the government itself never goes into debt. When it wants to create some public work or service, it just issues the money it needs to pay for the work. The Guernsey government has been issuing its own money for nearly two centuries. During that time, the money supply has mushroomed to about 25 times its original size; yet the economy has not been troubled by price inflation, and it has remained prosperous and stable.[5]

Many other countries have also successfully issued their own money, but Guernsey is one of the few to have stayed under the radar long enough to escape the covert attacks of an international banking cartel bent on monopolizing the money-making market. As we'll see later, governments that have dared to create their own money have generally wound up dealing with a presidential assassination, a coup, a boycott, a war, or a concerted assault on the national currency by international speculators. The American colonists operated successfully on their own sovereign money until British moneylenders leaned on Parliament to halt the practice, prompting the American Revolution. England had a thriving economy that operated on the sovereign money of the king until Oliver Cromwell's "Glorious Revolution," which let the moneylenders inside the gates. After 1700, the right to create money was transferred to the private Bank of England, based on a fraudulent "gold standard" that allowed it to duplicate the gold in its vaults many times over in the form of paper banknotes. Today governments are in the position of the disenfranchised king, having to borrow money created by the banks rather than issuing it themselves.

## The Gold Humbug

In 1863, Eleazar Lord, a New York banker, called the gold standard a humbug. He wrote:

> The so-called specie basis [or gold standard], whenever there is a foreign demand for coin, proves to be a mere fiction, *a practical humbug*; and whenever, by an excess of imports, this pretended basis is exported to pay foreign debts, the bank-notes are withdrawn from circulation or become worthless, the currency for the time is annihilated, prices fall, business is suspended, debts remain unpaid, panic and distress ensue, men in active business fail, bankruptcy, ruin, and disgrace reign.[6]

The requirement that paper banknotes be backed by a certain weight of gold bullion, Lord said, was a fiction. Banks did not have nearly enough gold to "redeem" all the paper money that was supposed to be based on it, and there was no real reason the nation's paper money had to be linked to gold at all. The gold standard just put America at the mercy of the foreign financiers who controlled the gold. When national imports exceeded exports, gold bullion left the country to pay the bill; and when gold stores shrank, the supply of paper money "based" on it shrank as well.

As Vernon Parrington pointed out, the real issue was not *what* money consisted of but *who* created it. Whether the medium of exchange was gold or paper or numbers in a ledger, when it was lent into existence by private lenders and was owed back to them with interest, more money would always be owed back than was created in the first place, spiraling the economy into perpetual debt. A dollar borrowed at 6 percent interest, compounded annually,[i] grows in 100 years to be a debt of $13,781.[7] That is true whether the money takes the form of gold or paper or accounting entries. As noted earlier, the banks lend the dollar into existence but not the additional $13,780 needed to pay the loan off, forcing the public to go further and further into debt in search of the ephemeral interest due on their money-built-on-debt. Merchants continually have to raise their prices to try to cover this interest tab, producing perpetual price inflation. Like the Tin Woodman whose axe was enchanted by the Witch to chop off parts of his own body, the more people work, the less they seem to have left for themselves. They cannot keep up because their money keeps shrinking, as sellers keep raising their prices in a futile attempt to pay off loans that are collectively impossible to repay.

## Challenging Corporate Feudalism

If the Scarecrow in search of a brain represented the unschooled farmers matching wits with the bankers, the Tin Woodman who had chopped out his own heart reflected the plight of the working man exploited by the corporation, which was increasingly replacing the small family business competing in a "free market." In 1886, corporations were given the rights and privileges of "individuals" although they lacked the morality and the conscience of live human beings. Their sole motive was profit, the sort of single-minded devotion to self-interest that in a live human being would be considered pathological. Corporations are feudalistic organizations designed in the structure of a pyramid, with an elite group at the top manipulating masses of workers below. Workers are kept marching in lockstep, passing received orders down from above, out of fear of losing their jobs, their homes and their benefits if they get out of line. At the top of the pyramid is a small group of controllers who alone know what is really going on. Critics have noted that the pyramid with an overseeing eye at the top is also the symbol on the Federal Reserve Note, the privately-issued currency that became the national monetary unit in 1913.

The popular grassroots movements that produced the Greenback and Populist Parties in the 1890s represented the interests of the common man over these corporate and financial oppressors. Although "populism" today tends to be associated with the political left, the word comes from the Latin word simply for the "people." In the nineteenth century, it stood for the "government of the people, by the people, for the people" proclaimed by Abraham Lincoln. According

---

[i] *Compound interest* is interest calculated not only on the initial principal but on the accumulated interest of prior payment periods.

to <u>Wikipedia</u> (an online encyclopedia written collaboratively by volunteers):

> Populism . . . on the whole does not have a strong political identity as either a left-wing or right-wing movement. Populism has taken left-wing, right-wing, and even centrist forms. In recent years, conservative United States politicians have begun adopting populist rhetoric; for example, promising to "get big government off your backs."

Although the oppressor today is seen to be big government, what the nineteenth century Populists were trying to get off their backs was a darker, more malevolent force. They still believed that the principles set forth in the Constitution could be achieved through a democratic government of the people. They saw their antagonist rather as the private money power and the corporations it had spawned, which were threatening to take over the government unless the people intervened. Abraham Lincoln is quoted as saying:

> I see in the near future a crisis approaching that unnerves me and causes me to tremble for the safety of my country. Corporations have been enthroned, an era of corruption in high places will follow, and the money power of the country will endeavor to prolong its reign by working upon the prejudices of the people until the wealth is aggregated in the hands of a few and the Republic is destroyed.[9]

Lincoln may not actually have said this. As with many famous quotations, its authorship is disputed.[10] But whoever said it, the insight was prophetic. In a January 2007 article called "Who Rules America?", Professor James Petras wrote, "Today it is said *2% of the households own 80% of the world's assets.* Within this small elite, a fraction embedded in financial capital owns and controls the bulk of the world's assets and organizes and facilitates further concentration of conglomerates." Professor Petras observed:

> Within the financial ruling class, . . . political leaders come from the public and private equity banks, namely Wall Street -- especially Goldman Sachs, Blackstone, the Carlyle Group and others. They organize and fund both major parties and their electoral campaigns. They pressure, negotiate and draw up the most comprehensive and favorable legislation on global strategies (liberalization and deregulation) and sectoral policies . . . . They pressure the government to "bailout" bankrupt and failed

speculative firms and to balance the budget by lowering social expenditures instead of raising taxes on speculative "windfall" profits.

. . . [T]hese private equity banks are involved in every sector of the economy, in every region of the world economy and increasingly speculate in the conglomerates which are acquired. Much of the investment funds now in the hands of US investment banks, hedge funds and other sectors of the financial ruling class originated in profits extracted from workers in the manufacturing and service sector.[10]

It seems the Tin Man has indeed been stripped of his heart and soul by the Witch of the East, the Wall Street bankers, just as Lincoln, the Greenbackers and the Populists foresaw . . . .

# Section II
# THE BANKERS CAPTURE THE MONEY MACHINE

*The Wicked Witch of the East held all the Munchkins in bondage for many years, making them slave for her night and day.*

– <u>The Wonderful Wizard of Oz</u>,
*"The Council with the Munchkins"*

# Chapter 11
# NO PLACE LIKE HOME:
# FIGHTING FOR THE FAMILY FARM

*"No matter how dreary and gray our homes are, we people of flesh and blood would rather live there than in any other country, be it ever so beautiful. There is no place like home."*

– Dorothy to the Scarecrow,
<u>The Wonderful Wizard of Oz</u>

People today might wonder why Dorothy, who could have stayed and played in the technicolor wonderland of Oz, was so eager to get home to her dreary Kansas farm. But readers could have related to that sentiment in the 1890s, when keeping the family homestead was a key political issue. Home foreclosures and evictions were occurring in record numbers. A document called "The Bankers Manifesto of 1892" suggested that it was all part of a deliberate plan by the bankers to disenfranchise the farmers and laborers of their homes and property. The document's origins are obscure, but its introduction to Congress is attributed to Representative Charles Lindbergh Sr., the father of the famous aviator, who served in Congress between 1903 and 1913. The Manifesto read in part:

> We must proceed with caution and guard every move made, for the lower order of people are already showing signs of restless commotion. . . . The Farmers Alliance and Knights of Labor organizations in the United States should be carefully watched by our trusted men, and we must take immediate steps to control these organizations in our interest or disrupt them. . . . Capital [the bankers and their money] must protect itself in every possible manner through combination [monopoly] and legislation. The courts must be called to our aid, debts must be collected, bonds

and mortgages foreclosed as rapidly as possible. *When through the process of the law, the common people have lost their homes, they will be more tractable and easily governed* through the influence of the strong arm of the government applied to a central power of imperial wealth under the control of the leading financiers. *People without homes will not quarrel with their leaders.*[1]

The Farmers Alliance and Knights of Labor were the Scarecrow and Tin Woodman of Baum's tale. They were a serious force to be reckoned with; they were militant, and they were mad. To split these powerful opponents, the Bankers Manifesto recommended a tactic that is still used today:

> [While] our principal men . . . are engaged in forming an imperialism of the world . . . , the people must be kept in a state of political antagonism. . . . *By thus dividing voters, we can get them to expend their energies in fighting over questions of no importance to us . . . .* Thus, by discrete action, we can secure all that has been so generously planned and successfully accomplished.

The voters, then as now, would be kept pacified with the right to vote for one of two or three candidates, all manipulated by the same puppeteers. As Indian author Arundhati Roy would complain of the election process a century later:

> It's not a real choice, it's an apparent choice, like choosing a brand of detergent. Whether you buy Ivory Snow or Tide, they're both owned by Proctor and Gamble. . . . Those in positions of real power, the bankers, the CEOs, are not vulnerable to the vote, and in any case they fund both sides.[2]

It was this sort of disillusionment with the political process that prompted Howard Zinn, Professor Emeritus in Boston University's history department, to state in 2001:

> For progressive movements, the future does not lie with electoral politics. It lies in street warfare – protest movements and demonstrations, civil disobedience, strikes and boycotts – using all of the power consumers and workers have in direct action against the government and corporations.[3]

The tradition of the street protest dates back to 1894, when Coxey's Army marched from Ohio to Washington D.C. to petition Congress to revive the Greenback system.

## Petitions in Boots

In striking contrast to the rag-tag army he led, "General" Jacob S. Coxey was a wealthy Populist who owned a sand quarry, bred horses, and wore hand-tailored suits. He was in it for the cause, one to which he was so committed that he named his son "Legal Tender." Like Frank Baum, Coxey was a follower of the new theosophical movement that was all the rage in the 1890s. He said his monetary solution had come to him fully formed in a dream.[4] He didn't just dream it but took it right to the Capitol steps, in the sort of can-do spirit that would come to characterize the Populist movement. He called his protest march a "petition in boots."

When Coxey's Army, some 500 strong, entered Washington D.C. and marched down Pennsylvania Avenue, the perceived threat was so great that 1,500 U.S. soldiers were stationed to resist them.[5] Coxey attempted to deliver his speech on the Capitol steps but was prevented by the police. He wound up spending 20 days in jail for trespassing on the grass and for displaying a prohibited "banner" (actually a 3 inch by 2 inch lapel pin).[6] His prepared speech was later entered into the Congressional record by his supporters. It was quite eloquent and moving, revealing the extremity and the despair of a people who had become progressively poorer as the bankers had become richer. Coxey said:

> Up these steps the lobbyists of trusts and corporations have passed unchallenged on their way to committee rooms, access to which we, the representatives of the toiling wealth-producers, have been denied. We stand here to-day in behalf of millions of toilers whose petitions have been buried in committee rooms, whose prayers have been unresponded to, and whose opportunities for honest, remunerative, productive labor have been taken from them by unjust legislation, which protects idlers, speculators, and gamblers: we come to remind the Congress here assembled of the declaration of a United States Senator, "that for a quarter of a century the rich have been growing richer, the poor poorer, and that by the close of the present century *the middle class will have disappeared as the struggle for existence becomes fierce and relentless.*"
>
> . . . We have come here through toil and weary marches, through storms and tempests, over mountains, and amid the

trials of poverty and distress, to lay our grievances at the doors of our National Legislature . . . .We are here to petition for legislation which will furnish employment for every man able and willing to work; for legislation which will bring universal prosperity and emancipate our beloved country from financial bondage to the descendants of King George.

. . . We are engaged in a bitter and cruel war with the enemies of all mankind – a war with hunger, wretchedness, and despair, and we ask Congress to heed our petitions and issue for the nation's good a sufficient volume of the same kind of money which carried the country through one awful war and saved the life of the nation.[7]

Coxey proposed two bills, one primarily to help farmers, the other to help urban laborers. Under his "Good Roads Bill," $500 million would be issued in legal tender notes or Greenbacks to construct the roads particularly needed in rural America. For city dwellers, Coxey proposed a "Noninterest-Bearing Bonds Bill." It would authorize state and local governments to issue noninterest-bearing bonds that would be used to borrow legal tender notes from the federal treasury. The monies raised by these transactions would be used for public projects such as building libraries, schools, utility plants, and marketplaces.[8]

Coxey was thus proposing something quite new and revolutionary: the government would determine the projects it wanted to carry out, then issue the money to pay for them. The country did not need to be limited by the money it already had, money based on gold the bankers controlled. "Money" was simply a receipt for labor and materials, which the government could and should issue itself. If the labor and materials were available, and people wanted the work done, they could all get together and trade, using paper receipts of their own design. It was a manifestation of the theosophical tenet that you can achieve your dreams simply by "realizing" them – by making them real. You can realize the abundance you already have, just by bringing its potential into manifestation.

When Coxey's Army failed to move Congress, other "industrial armies" were inspired to take up the cause. There were over forty in all. Some 1,200 protesters managed to overcome the resistance of the railroad companies, federal marshals, the U.S. Army, and judicial injunctions to arrive in Washington in 1894. One group, called "Hogan's Army," began its march in Montana -- too far to walk to the Capitol, so the protesters commandeered a train. When the U.S. Marshall and his men attempted to stop them, a gun battle resulted in several injuries and one death. The U.S. Army finally seized the train. "Hogan's Heroes" were arrested, and Hogan spent six months in jail.[9]

Over the next century, progressively larger street protests were built on the precedent Coxey's Army had established. In 1913, woman suffragists sponsored a national march on Washington that had federal support. In 1932, approximately 20,000 starving unemployed World War I veterans and their families marched for the "Bonus Bill" drafted by Congressman Wright Patman. The bill sought to give veterans the present value of their bonuses, which had been issued in 1924 but were not to be paid until 1945. When their demands were turned down by President Hoover, the "Bonus Army" camped out in shantytowns called "Hoovervilles" across the Potomac. The camps did not disband until Hoover sent in troops, led by his brightest and best – Douglas MacArthur, Dwight Eisenhower, and George Patton. The veterans were routed and their camps set ablaze, killing three and injuring about a thousand.[10] On April 25, 2004, in the largest-ever protest march recorded up to that date, more than one million people filled the Capitol petitioning for women's rights. The day before that, thousands marched to protest World Bank/IMF policies.[11]

## Popularizing the Money Question

When the Greenback Party failed to achieve monetary reform, many of its members joined the Populist Party. The Populists felt that they rather than the older political parties represented the true American principles of the Founding Fathers, and one fundamental principle they felt had been lost was that creating the national currency was the sole prerogative of the government. The Populists also favored retrieving for the Common Wealth certain public assets that had been usurped by the cartels, including the banks, railroads, telephone, and telegraph; and the public lands that had been given away to private railroad and other corporate monopolies.

The Populist movement of the 1890s represented the last serious challenge to the bankers' monopoly over the right to create the nation's money. In 1895, popular interest in the money question was aroused by a book called Coin's Financial School, which quickly sold a million copies. Written by a Chicago journalist named William Hope Harvey, it expressed the issues in a way that common people could understand. Harvey maintained that the attempt to restrict the coinage of silver was a conspiracy designed to enrich the London-controlled Eastern financiers at the expense of farmers and debtors. He called England "a power that can dictate the money of the world, and thereby create world misery." The "Crime of '73" – the Act limiting the free coinage of silver – took away the silver money of the people and replaced it with the gold of the British bankers. Harvey observed that the United States was then paying England 200 million dollars in gold annually just in interest on its bonds, and that the devaluation of silver as against gold had caused Americans to lose the equivalent of 400 million dollars in property to meet this interest burden.

Coin's Financial School set the stage for William Jennings Bryan's "Cross of Gold" speech, which met with a receptive audience; and Harvey became an important economic adviser to Bryan in his bid for the Presidency. In 1896, Populist supporters and Silverites dominated the Democratic convention. All they needed, said one reporter, was "a Moses." Bryan appeared to fill the bill; but William McKinley, his Republican opponent, had the support of big business, including a $250,000 contribution from Rockefeller's Standard Oil, then an enormous sum. The election was close, but McKinley won; and he won again in 1900.

Although McKinley had the support of big money, he was also a protectionist who favored high tariffs to keep foreign marauders out. He accepted the pro-British Teddy Roosevelt as his Vice President over the vigorous objection of Marcus Hanna, the power behind McKinley's Presidency and the man identified by later commentators as the "Wizard of the Gold Ounce (Oz)." Hanna told McKinley that his chief duty in office was just to stay alive, to save the country from "that madman" Roosevelt. But in 1901, McKinley failed in that endeavor. He was the third President to be assassinated since the Civil War. Although no conspiracy was proved, suspicious commentators noted that the elimination of the protectionist McKinley was highly convenient for pro-British interests. The door had been opened to an Anglo-American alliance backed by powerful financiers on both sides of the Atlantic. This would never have happened in the nineteenth century, when England was still regarded by loyal Americans as the enemy.[13]

According to a historical treatise by Murray Rothbard, politics after McKinley became a struggle between two competing banking giants, the Morgans and the Rockefellers. The parties have sometimes changed hands, but the puppeteers pulling the strings have always been one of these two big-money players.[14] No popular third party candidate has had a real chance of winning, because the bankers, who have the exclusive power to create the national money supply, hold the winning cards.

Teddy Roosevelt called himself a "trustbuster," but while the anti-trust laws were on the books, little harm came to the powerful corporate monopolies called "trusts" during his administration. The trusts and cartels remained the puppeteers with real power, pulling the strings of puppet politicians who were basically bribed to stand back and do nothing, while the powerful conglomerates the antitrust laws were designed to manipulate manipulated the laws. Roosevelt complained in 1906:

> Behind the ostensible government sits enthroned an invisible government owing no allegiance and acknowledging no responsibility to the people. To destroy this invisible government, to befoul the unholy alliance between corrupt business and corrupt politics is the first task of the statesmanship of the day.

# Chapter 12
# TALKING HEADS AND
# INVISIBLE HANDS:
# THE SECRET GOVERNMENT

*"But I don't understand," said Dorothy, in bewilderment. "How was it that you appeared to me as a great Head?"*

*"That was one of my tricks," answered Oz. . . . He pointed to a corner in which lay the great Head, made out of many thicknesses of paper, and with a carefully painted face.*

*"This I hung from the ceiling by a wire," said Oz. "I stood behind the screen and pulled a thread, to make the eyes move and the mouth open."*

– <u>The Wonderful Wizard of Oz,</u>
*"The Discovery of Oz the Terrible"*

The idea of an "invisible hand" controlling the market was first advanced by Scottish economist Adam Smith in <u>The Wealth of Nations</u> in 1776. But Smith's invisible hand was a benign one, a sort of mystical force that would make everything come out right if the market were just left alone. The invisible hand alluded to by later commentators was of a more insidious sort, a hand that wrote the pages of history with its own secret agenda. President Woodrow Wilson, who signed the Federal Reserve Act into law in 1913, said:

> We have come to be one of the worst ruled, one of the most completely controlled governments in the civilized world -- no longer a government of free opinion, no longer a government by . . . a vote of the majority, but a government by the opinion and duress of a small group of dominant men.

Who were these dominant men? Wilson only hinted, saying:

> Some of the biggest men in the United States, in the field of commerce and manufacture, are afraid of something. They know that there is a power somewhere so organized, so subtle, so watchful, so interlocked, so complete, so pervasive, that they had better not speak above their breath when they speak in condemnation of it.[1]

Many other leaders also hinted that the government was controlled by invisible puppeteers. President Franklin D. Roosevelt, Teddy Roosevelt's distant cousin, acknowledged in 1933:

> The real truth of the matter is, as you and I know, that a financial element in the large centers has owned the government since the days of Andrew Jackson. . . . The country is going through a repetition of Jackson's fight with the Bank of the United States – only on a far bigger and broader basis.

Felix Frankfurter, Justice of the Supreme Court, said in 1952:

> The real rulers in Washington are invisible and exercise power from behind the scenes.

Congressman Wright Patman, Chairman of the House Banking and Currency Committee, said in a speech on the House floor in 1967:

> In the U.S. today, we have in effect two governments. We have the duly constituted government, then we have an independent, uncontrolled and uncoordinated government in the Federal Reserve, operating the money powers which are reserved to congress by the Constitution.

Two decades later, Senator Daniel Inouye would testify at the Iran Contra hearings:

> There exists a shadowy Government with its own Air Force, its own Navy, its own fundraising mechanism, and the ability to pursue its own ideas of national interest, free from all checks and balances, and *free from the law itself.*[2]

In 1927, Mayor John Hylan of New York compared the invisible government to a "giant octopus," recalling the "hydra-headed monster" battled by Andrew Jackson. In a speech in the <u>New York Times</u>, Hylan said:

> The warning of Theodore Roosevelt has much timeliness today, for the real menace of our republic is this invisible government which like a giant octopus sprawls its slimy length

over City, State, and nation ... It seizes in its long and powerful tentacles our executive officers, our legislative bodies, our schools, our courts, our newspapers, and every agency created for the public protection.

... [A]t the head of this octopus are the Rockefeller-Standard Oil interest and a small group of powerful banking houses generally referred to as the international bankers. The little coterie of powerful international bankers virtually run the United States government for their own selfish purposes.

They practically control both parties, write political platforms, make catspaws of party leaders, use the leading men of private organizations, and resort to every device to place in nomination for high public office only such candidates as will be amenable to the dictates of corrupt big business. ...

These international bankers and Rockefeller-Standard Oil interests control the majority of the newspapers and magazines in this country. They use the columns of these papers to club into submission or drive out of office public officials who refuse to do the bidding of the powerful corrupt cliques which compose the invisible government.[3]

In 1934, these international bankers and businessmen were labeled the "Robber Barons" by Matthew Josephson in a popular book of the same name.[4] The Robber Barons were an unscrupulous lot, who "lived for market conquest, and plotted takeovers like military strategy." John D. Rockefeller's father was called a snake-oil salesman, flimflam man, bigamist, and marginal criminal – never convicted but often accused, of crimes ranging from horse theft to rape. He once boasted, "I cheat my boys every chance I get, I want to make 'em sharp." Once the Robber Barons had established a monopoly, they would raise prices, drop the quality of service, and engage in unfair trading practices to drive other firms out of business. The abuses of these monopolies became such a national scandal that in 1890, the Sherman Antitrust Act passed both houses of Congress with only one dissenting vote. The problem was enforcing it. In 1888, the entire Commonwealth of Massachusetts had receipts of only $7 million to oversee a Boston railroad monopoly with gross receipts of $40 million.[5]

## Can You Trust a Trust?

"Trusts" are concentrations of wealth in the hands of a few. The name came from the private banks entrusted with the money of depositors. Paper bank notes were called "fiduciary" money (after the Latin word *fide*, meaning to "trust"), because the bankers had to be "trusted" to keep a sum of gold on hand to redeem their paper receipts on demand.[6] These fiduciary banks played a key role in forming the giant trusts of the Gilded Age. The trusts had their own private banks, which were authorized to create and lend money at will. Like in the board game "Monopoly," they used this paper money to buy up competitors and monopolize the game.

Monopoly growth and abuse were at their height in the Gilded Age, the country's greatest period of *laissez faire*.[i] The trusts were so powerful that the trend toward monopolizing industry actually worsened after the Sherman Act was passed. Before 1898, there were an average of 46 major industrial mergers a year. After 1898, the number soared to 531 a year. By 1904, the top 4 percent of American businesses produced 57 percent of America's total industrial production, with a single firm dominating at least 60 percent of production in 50 different industries. Ironically, the trusts became the strongest advocates of federal regulation, since their monopoly power depended on the exclusive rights granted them by the government. By planting their own agents in the federal commissions, they used government regulation to gain greater control over industry, protect themselves from competition, and maintain high prices.

## The Banks and the Rise of Wall Street

There were many Robber Barons, but J. Pierpont Morgan, Andrew Carnegie, and John D. Rockefeller led the pack. Morgan dominated finance, Carnegie dominated steel, and Rockefeller monopolized oil. Carnegie built his business himself, and he loved competition; but Morgan was a different type of capitalist. He didn't build, he bought. He took over other people's businesses, and he hated competition. In 1901, Morgan formed the first billion dollar corporation, U.S. Steel, out of mills he purchased from Carnegie.

---

[i]    French for "let it be" – a policy of deliberate non-intervention in the market.

Rockefeller, too, dealt with competitors by buying them out. His company, Standard Oil, became the greatest of all monopolies and the first major multinational corporation. Before World War I, the financial and business structure of the United States was dominated by Morgan's finance and transportation companies and Rockefeller's Standard Oil; and these conglomerates had close alliances with each other. Through interlocking directorships, they were said to dominate almost the entire economic fabric of the United States.[7]

Other industrialists, seeing the phenomenal success of the Morgan and Rockefeller trusts, dreamt of buying out their competition and forming huge monopolies in the same way. But with the exception of Carnegie, no other capitalists had the money for these predatory practices. Aspiring empire-builders were therefore drawn to Morgan and the other Wall Street bankers in search of funding. Corporations began drifting to New York to be near the big investment houses. By 1895, New York had become the headquarters for America's major corporations and the home of half its millionaires. Morgan's bank at 23 Wall Street, known as the "House of Morgan," was for decades the most important address in American finance. In 1920, a bomb exploded in front of the bank, killing 40 and injuring 400. Later, the nexus of American finance moved to the World Trade Center, the chosen target for another tragic attack in 2001.

Early in the twentieth century, Morgan controlled a Wall Street syndicate that financial writer John Moody called "the greatest financial power in the history of the world." Morgan dominated a hundred corporations with more than $22 billion in assets. In 1913, in a book called Other People's Money and How the Bankers Use It, Supreme Court Justice Louis Brandeis wrote that the greatest threat to the American economy was the "money trust." According to The Wall Street Journal, the "money trust" was just another name for J. Pierpont Morgan, who had founded the world's most powerful bank. Like the Rothschilds in England, Morgan had extraordinary political influence in the United States. Morgan men routinely represented the U.S. government at international monetary meetings, something they continue to do today. Alan Greenspan, longstanding Chairman of the Federal Reserve, was a corporate director for J. P. Morgan before President Ronald Reagan appointed him to that post.[8]

Those fortunate corporations favored with funding from Morgan and the other Wall Street bankers were able to monopolize their industries. But where did the Wall Street banks get the money to underwrite all these mergers and acquisitions? The answer was revealed by Congressman Wright Patman and other close observers: the Robber Barons were pulling money out of an empty hat. Their privately owned banks held the ultimate credit card, a bottomless source of accounting-entry money that could be "lent" to their affiliated corporate mistresses. The funds could then be used to buy out competitors, corner the market in scarce raw materials, make political donations, lobby Congress, and control public opinion.

## Who Pulled the Strings of the Robber Barons?

Rockefeller and Morgan were rivals who competed for power on the political scene, but they both had the support of powerful British financiers. John D. Rockefeller Sr. first made his fortune with some dubious railroad rebate deals during the Civil War. By 1895, he had acquired 95 percent of America's oil refining business. Chase Bank (named after Salmon P. Chase in honor of his role in passing the National Banking Act) was bought by Rockefeller with financing traced to the Rothschilds. The funds came from a New York banking firm called Kuhn, Loeb, & Co., which was then under the control of a German immigrant named Jacob Schiff. Schiff had bought into the partnership with financial backing from the Rothschilds. He later bought out Kuhn and married the eldest daughter of Loeb. The Manhattan Company (the banking firm established by Hamilton and Burr at the turn of the nineteenth century) also came under the control of the Rothschilds through the banking interests of Kuhn, Loeb and the Warburgs, another Rothschild-related Frankfurt banking dynasty. In 1955, Rockefeller's Chase Bank merged with the Manhattan Company to become the Chase Manhattan Bank.[9]

The Morgan family banking interest could be traced back to England in an even more direct way. In the 1850s, Junius Morgan became a partner in what would become Peabody, Morgan, and Company, a London investment business specializing in transactions between Britain and the United States. During the Civil War, the partnership became the chief fiscal agent for the Union. John Pierpont Morgan, Junius' son, later became head of the firm's New York branch, which was named J. P. Morgan & Co. in 1895. J. P. Morgan Jr., John Pierpont's son, then became a partner in the branch in London, where he moved in 1898 to learn the central banking system as dominated by the Bank of England.

Although the Rothschilds were technically rivals of the Peabody/Morgan firm, rumor had it that they had formed a secret alliance. Nathan Rothschild was not well liked, in part because of religious prejudice. Morgan biographer George Wheeler wrote in 1973, "Part of the reality of the day was an ugly resurgence of anti-Semitism. . . . Someone was needed as a cover." August Belmont (born Schoenberg) had played that role for Morgan during the Civil War; but when the Belmont/Rothschild connection became common knowledge, the ploy no longer worked. Wheeler wrote, "Who better than J. Pierpont Morgan, a solid, Protestant exemplar of capitalism able to trace his family back to pre-Revolutionary times?" That could explain why, in the periodic financial crises of the Gilded Age, Morgan's bank always came out on top. In the bank panics of 1873, 1884, 1893, and 1907, while other banks were going under, Morgan's bank always managed to come up with the funds to survive and thrive.[10]

## The Shadow Government

In 1879, Rockefeller turned his company Standard Oil into the new vehicle called a "trust" in order to coordinate all of its production, refining, transportation, and distribution activities. The Rockefeller trust consisted of a network of companies that were wholly or partially owned by Rockefeller, and that invested in each other. The scheme worked until 1882, when Standard Oil was driven out of Ohio due to antitrust investigations. In 1883, Rockefeller's trust moved to New York, where it proceeded to systematically devour independent oil producers and refiners across the country and the world. It was aided in these rapacious practices by illegal railroad rebates from Morgan, who had bought up the railroads with funding from the Rothschild bank. Independent oil refiners, being unable to compete, were forced to sell out at a huge loss or face financial ruin.

By 1890, Rockefeller owned all of the independent oil refiners in the country and had a monopoly on worldwide oil sales. In 1911, the U.S. Supreme Court ruled that the Standard Oil cartel was a "dangerous conspiracy" that must be broken up "for the safety of the Republic." ("Conspiracy" is a legal term meaning an agreement between two or more persons to commit a crime or accomplish a legal purpose through illegal action.) In 1914, Standard Oil was referred to in the Congressional Record as the "shadow government."[11] Following the Court's antitrust order, the Standard Oil monolith was split into 38 new companies, including Exxon, Mobil, Amoco, Chevron, and Arco; but Rockefeller secretly continued to control them by owning a voting majority of their stock.

The invention of the automobile and the gasoline engine gave the Rockefeller/Morgan syndicate a virtual stranglehold on the energy business. Rather than conserving oil and finding alternatives to the inefficient gasoline engine, they encouraged waste and consumption and ruthlessly suppressed competition.[12] International strategist Henry Kissinger would say much later that whoever controlled oil controlled the world. That was true so long as the world was powered by oil, and the oil cartel evidently intended to keep it that way. Early in the twentieth century, energy genius Nikola Tesla was reportedly on the verge of developing "free energy" that would be independent of both fossil fuels and wires.[13] But Tesla had the ill fortune of being funded by J. P. Morgan. When Morgan learned that there would be no way to charge for the new energy, he cut off Tesla's funding and took steps to insure the latter's financial ruin. Tesla wrote in a plaintive letter to Morgan, "I came to you with the greatest invention of all times. I knew you would refuse . . . . What chance have I to land the biggest Wall Street monster with the soul's spider thread?"[14]

# Chapter 13
# WITCHES' COVEN:
# THE JEKYLL ISLAND AFFAIR AND
# THE FEDERAL RESERVE
# ACT OF 1913

*"One of my greatest fears was the Witches, for while I had no magical powers at all I soon found out that the Witches were really able to do wonderful things."*

— The Wonderful Wizard of Oz,
"The Discovery of Oz the Terrible"

If the Wall Street bankers were the Wicked Witches of the Gilded Age, the coven where they conjured up their grandest of schemes was on Jekyll Island, a property off the coast of Georgia owned by J. P. Morgan. The coven was hosted in 1910 by Senator Nelson Aldrich of Rhode Island, a business associate of Morgan and the father-in-law of John D. Rockefeller Jr. The Republican "whip" in the Senate, Aldrich was known as the Wall Street Senator, a spokesman for big business and banking.

Although Aldrich hosted the meeting, credit for masterminding it is attributed to a German immigrant named Paul Warburg, who was a partner of Kuhn, Loeb, the Rothschild's main American banking operation after the Civil War. Other attendees included Benjamin Strong, then head of Morgan's Bankers Trust Company; two other heads of Morgan banks; the Assistant Secretary of the U.S. Treasury; and Frank Vanderlip, president of the National City Bank of New York, then the most powerful New York bank (now called Citibank), which represented William Rockefeller and Kuhn, Loeb. Morgan was the chief driver behind the plan, and the Morgan and Rockefeller factions had long been arch-rivals, but they had come together in this secret rendezvous to devise a banking scheme that would benefit them both. Vanderlip wrote later of the meeting:

> We were instructed to come one at a time and as unobtrusively as possible to the railroad terminal . . . where Senator Aldrich's private car would be in readiness. . . . Discovery, we knew, simply must not happen. . . . If it were to be exposed publicly that our particular group had written a banking bill, that bill would have no chance whatever of passage by Congress . . . [A]lthough the Aldrich Federal Reserve plan was defeated its essential points were contained in the plan that was finally adopted.[1]

Opposition to the plan was led by William Jennings Bryan and Charles Lindbergh Sr., who were strongly against any bill suggesting a central bank or control by Wall Street money. Only a major bank panic had led Congress to even consider such a bill. The panic of 1907 was triggered by rumors that the Knickerbocker Bank and the Trust Company of America were about to become insolvent. Later evidence pointed to the House of Morgan as the source of the rumors. The public, believing the rumors, proceeded to make them come true by staging a run on the banks. Morgan then nobly helped to avert the panic by importing $100 million worth of gold from Europe to stop the bank run. The mesmerized public came to believe that the country needed a central banking system to stop future panics.[2] Robert Owens, a co-author of the Federal Reserve Act, later testified before Congress that the banking industry had conspired to create such financial panics in order to rouse the people to demand "reforms" that served the interests of the financiers.[3] Congressman Lindbergh charged:

> The Money Trust caused the 1907 panic . . . . [T]hose not favorable to the Money Trust could be squeezed out of business and the people frightened into demanding changes in the banking and currency laws which the Money Trust would frame.[4]

The 1907 panic prompted the congressional inquiry headed by Senator Aldrich, and the clandestine Jekyll Island meeting followed. The result was a bill called the Aldrich Plan, but the alert opposition saw through it and soundly defeated it. Bryan said he would not support any bill that resulted in *private* money being issued by *private* banks. Federal Reserve Notes must be *Treasury* currency, issued and guaranteed by the government; and the governing body must be appointed by the President and approved by the Senate.

## Morgan's Man in the White House

Morgan had another problem besides the opposition in Congress. He needed a President willing to sign his bill. William Howard Taft, the President in 1910, was not a Morgan man. McKinley had been succeeded by his Vice President Teddy Roosevelt, who was in the Morgan camp and had been responsible for breaking up Rockefeller's Standard Oil. Taft, who followed Roosevelt, was a Republican from Rockefeller's state of Ohio. He took vengeance on Morgan by filing antitrust suits to break up the two leading Morgan trusts, International Harvester and United States Steel. Taft was a shoo-in for reelection in 1912. To break his hold on the Presidency, Morgan deliberately created a new party, the Progressive or Bull Moose Party, and brought Teddy Roosevelt out of retirement to run as its candidate. Roosevelt took enough votes away from Taft to allow Morgan to get his real candidate, Woodrow Wilson, elected on the Democratic ticket in 1912. Roosevelt walked away realizing he had been duped, and the Progressive Party was liquidated soon afterwards. Wilson was surrounded by Morgan men, including "Colonel" Edward Mandell House, who had his own rooms at the White House. Wilson called House his "alter ego."[5]

To get their bill passed, the Morgan faction changed its name from the Aldrich Bill to the Federal Reserve Act. They brought it three days before Christmas, when Congress was preoccupied with departure for the holidays. The bill was so obscurely worded that no one really understood its provisions. The Aldrich team knew it would not pass without Bryan's support, so in a spirit of apparent compromise, they made a show of acquiescing to his demands. He said happily, "The right of the government to issue money is not surrendered to the banks; the control over the money so issued is not relinquished by the government . . . ." So he thought; but while the national money supply would be *printed* by the U.S. Bureau of Engraving and Printing, it would be issued as an *obligation* or *debt* of the government, owed back to the private Federal Reserve with interest. And while Congress and the President would have some input in appointing the Federal Reserve Board, the Board would work behind closed doors with the regional bankers, without Congressional oversight or control.[6]

The bill passed on December 22, 1913, and President Wilson signed it into law the next day. Later he regretted what he had done. He is reported to have said before he died, "I have unwittingly ruined my country." Bryan was also disillusioned and soon resigned as Secretary of State, in protest over President Wilson's involvement in Europe's war following the suspect sinking of the Lusitania.

The first chairmanship of the Federal Reserve was offered to Paul Warburg, but he declined. Instead he became vice chairman, a position he held until the end of World War I, when he relinquished it to avoid an apparent conflict of interest. He would have had to negotiate with his brother Max Warburg, who was then financial advisor to the Kaiser and Director of the Reichsbank, Germany's private central bank.[7]

## The Incantations of Fedspeak

The Federal Reserve Act of 1913 was a major coup for the international bankers. They had battled for more than a century to establish a private central bank with the exclusive right to "monetize" the government's debt (that is, to print their own money and exchange it for government securities or I.O.U.s). The Act's preamble said that its purposes were "to provide for the establishment of Federal Reserve Banks, to furnish an elastic currency, to afford a means of rediscounting commercial paper, to establish a more effective supervision of banking in the United States, and for other purposes." It was the beginning of Fedspeak, abstract economic language that shrouded the issues in obscurity. "Elastic currency" is credit that can be expanded at will by the banks. "Rediscounting" is a technique by which banks would be allowed to magically multiply funds by re-lending them without waiting for outstanding loans to mature. In plain English, the Federal Reserve Act authorized a private central bank to create money out of nothing, lend it to the government at interest, and control the national money supply, expanding or contracting it at will. Representative Lindbergh called the Act "the worst legislative crime of the ages." He warned:

> [The Federal Reserve Board] can cause the pendulum of a rising and falling market to swing gently back and forth by slight changes in the discount rate, or cause violent fluctuations by greater rate variation, and in either case it will possess inside information as to financial conditions and advance knowledge of the coming change, either up or down.
>
> This is the strangest, most dangerous advantage ever placed in the hands of a special privilege class by any Government that ever existed. . . . *The financial system has been turned over to . . . a purely profiteering group. The system is private, conducted for the*

*sole purpose of obtaining the greatest possible profits from the use of other people's money.*

In 1934, in the throes of the Great Depression, Representative Louis McFadden would go further, stating on the Congressional record:

Some people think that the Federal Reserve Banks are United States Government institutions. *They are private monopolies which prey upon the people of these United States for the benefit of themselves and their foreign customers; foreign and domestic speculators and swindlers; and rich and predatory money lenders.* In that dark crew of financial pirates there are those who would cut a man's throat to get a dollar out of his pocket; there are those who send money into states to buy votes to control our legislatures; there are those who maintain International propaganda for the purpose of deceiving us into granting of new concessions which will permit them to cover up their past misdeeds and set again in motion their gigantic train of crime.

*These twelve private credit monopolies were deceitfully and disloyally foisted upon this Country by the bankers who came here from Europe and repaid us our hospitality by undermining our American institutions.*[8]

## Who Owns the Federal Reserve?

The "Federal" Reserve is actually an independent, privately-owned corporation.[9] It consists of twelve regional Federal Reserve banks owned by many commercial member banks. The amount of Federal Reserve stock held by each member bank is proportional to its size. The Federal Reserve Bank of New York holds the majority of shares in the Federal Reserve System (53 percent). The largest shareholders of the Federal Reserve Bank of New York are the largest commercial banks in the district of New York.

In 1997, the New York Federal Reserve reported that its three largest member banks were Chase Manhattan Bank, Citibank, and Morgan Guaranty Trust Company. In 2000, JP Morgan and Chase Manhattan merged to become JPMorgan Chase Co., a bank holding company with combined assets of $668 billion. That made it the third largest bank holding company in the country, after Citigroup (at $791 billion) and Bank of America (at $679 billion). Bank of America was founded in California in 1904 and remains concentrated in the western and southwestern states. Citigroup is the cornerstone of the Rockefeller empire.

In January 2004, JPMorgan Chase & Co. undertook one of the largest bank mergers in history, when it acquired BankOne for $58 billion. The result was to make this Morgan-empire bank the second-largest U.S. bank, both in terms of assets ($1.1 trillion to Citigroup's nearly $1.2 trillion) and deposits ($490 billion to Bank of America's $552 billion). JPMorgan Chase now issues the most Visas and MasterCards of any bank nationwide and holds the largest share of U.S. credit card balances. In 2003, credit cards surpassed cash and checks as a medium of exchange used in stores.[10] Thus Citibank and JPMorgan Chase Co., the financial cornerstones of the Rockefeller and Morgan empires, are not only the two largest banks in the United States but are the two largest shareholders of the New York Federal Reserve, the branch of the Fed holding a majority of the shares in the Federal Reserve system. The Federal Reserve evidently remains squarely under the control of the Robber Barons who devised it.

The central Federal Reserve Board in Washington was set up to include the Treasury Secretary and Comptroller of the Currency, who were U.S. government officials; but the Board had little control over the 12 regional Federal Reserve Banks, which set most of their own policy. They followed the lead of the New York Federal Reserve Bank, where the Fed's real power was concentrated. Benjamin Strong, one of the Jekyll Island attendees, became the first president of the New York Federal Reserve. Strong had close ties to the financial powers of London and owed his career to the favor of the Morgan bank.[11]

### The Master Spider

A popular rumor has it that the Federal Reserve is owned by a powerful clique of foreign financiers, but this is obviously not true. It is owned by Federal Reserve Banks, which are owned by American commercial banks, which are required by law to make their major shareholders public; and none of these banks is predominantly foreign-owned.[12] But that does not mean that the banking spider is not in control behind the scenes. According to Hans Schicht (the financial insider quoted in the Introduction), the "master spider" has just moved to Wall Street. He says the greater part of U.S. banking and enterprise is now controlled by a very small inner circle of men, perhaps headed by only one man. It is all done behind closed doors, through the game he calls "spider webbing." As noted earlier, the rules of the game include exercising tight personal management and control, with a minimum of insiders and front-men who themselves have only partial knowledge of the game; exercising control through "leverage" (mergers, takeovers, chain share holdings where one company holds shares of other companies, conditions annexed to loans, and so forth); and making any concentration of wealth invisible. The master spider studiously avoids close scrutiny by maintaining anonymity, taking a back seat, and appearing to be a philanthropist.[13]

Before World War II, the reins of international finance were held by the powerful European banking dynasty the House of Rothschild. But during the war, control crossed the Atlantic to their Wall Street affiliates. Schicht says the role of master spider fell to David Rockefeller Sr., grandson on his father's side of John D. Rockefeller Sr. and on his mother's side of Nelson Aldrich, the Senator for whom the precursor to the Federal Reserve Act was named. David Rockefeller was a director of the Council on Foreign Relations from 1949 to 1985 and its chairman from 1970 until 1985, and he founded the Trilateral Commission in 1976. Schicht states that he also convoked the 1944 Bretton Woods Conference, at which the International Monetary Fund and the World Bank were devised; and he was instrumental in founding the elite international club called the "Bilderbergers."[14]

The Council on Foreign Relations (CFR) is an international group set up in 1919 to advise the members' respective governments on international affairs. It has been called the preeminent intermediary between the world of high finance, big oil, corporate elitism, and the U.S. government. The policies it promulgates in its quarterly journal become U.S. government policy.[15]

The Trilateral Commission has been described as an elite group of international bankers, media leaders, scholars and government officials bent on shaping and administering a "new world order," with a central world government held together by economic interdependence.[16] Former presidential candidate Barry Goldwater said of it:

> The Trilateralist Commission is international [and] is intended to be the vehicle for multinational consolidation of commercial and banking interests by seizing control of the political government of the United States. The Trilateralist Commission represents a skillful, coordinated effort to seize control and consolidate the four centers of power — political, monetary, intellectual, and ecclesiastical.

The "Bilderbergers" were described by a June 3, 2004 BBC special as "one of the most controversial and hotly-debated alliances of our times," composed of "an elite coterie of Western thinkers and power-brokers" who have been "accused of fixing the fate of the world behind closed doors." The group has been suspected of steering international policy. Some say it plots world domination.[17] But nobody knows for sure, because its members are sworn to secrecy and the press won't report on its meetings.

## The Information Monopoly

Secrecy has been maintained because the Robber Barons have been able to use their monopoly over money to buy up the major media, educational institutions, and other outlets of public information. While Rockefeller was buying up universities, medical schools, and the Encyclopedia Britannica, Morgan bought up newspapers. In 1917, Congressman Oscar Callaway stated on the Congressional Record:

> In March, 1915, the J.P. Morgan interests, the steel, shipbuilding, and powder interests, and their subsidiary organizations, got together 12 men high up in the newspaper world, and employed them to select the most influential newspapers in the United States and sufficient number of them to control generally the policy of the daily press of the United States. . . . They found it was only necessary to purchase the control of 25 of the greatest papers. The 25 papers were agreed upon; emissaries were sent to purchase the policy, national and international, of these papers; . . . an editor was furnished for each paper to properly supervise and edit information regarding the questions of preparedness, militarism, financial policies, and other things of national and international nature considered vital to the interests of the purchasers [and to suppress] everything in opposition to the wishes of the interests served.[18]

By 1983, according to Dean Ben Bagdikian in the The Media Monopoly, fifty corporations owned half or more of the media business. By 2000, that number was down to six corporations, with directorates interlocked with each other and with major commercial banks.[19] Howard Zinn observes:

[W]hether you have a Republican or a Democrat in power, *the Robber Barons are still there*. . . . Under the Clinton administration, more mergers of huge corporations took place [than] had ever taken place before under any administration. . . . [W]hether you have Republicans or Democrats in power, big business is the most powerful voice in the halls of Congress and in the ears of the President of the United States.[20]

In The Underground History of American Education, published in 2000, educator John Taylor Gatto traces how Rockefeller, Morgan and other members of the financial elite influenced, guided, funded, and at times forced compulsory schooling into the mainstream of American society. They needed three things for their corporate interests to thrive: (1) compliant employees, (2) a guaranteed and dependent population, and (3) a predictable business environment. It was largely to promote these ends, says Gatto, that modern compulsory schooling was established.[21]

## Harnessing the Tax Base

The Robber Barons had succeeded in monopolizing the money spigots, the oil spigots, and the public's access to information; but Morgan wanted more. He wanted to secure the banks' loans to the government with a reliable source of taxes, one that was imposed directly on the incomes of the people.[22] There was just one snag in this plan: a federal income tax had consistently been declared unconstitutional by the U.S. Supreme Court . . . .

# Chapter 14
# HARNESSING THE LION:
# THE FEDERAL INCOME TAX

*With Dorothy hard at work, the Witch thought she would go into the courtyard and harness the Cowardly Lion like a horse. It would amuse her, she was sure, to make him draw her chariot whenever she wished to go to drive.*

– *The Wonderful Wizard of Oz,*
*"The Search for the Wicked Witch"*

If the Cowardly Lion represented the people unaware of their power, the harness that would hitch the Lion to the chariot of the bankers was the federal income tax. Slipping the harness over the Lion's mane was no mean feat. The American people had chafed at the burden of taxes ever since King George III had imposed them on the colonies. The colonists had been taxed for all sorts of consumer goods, from tea to tobacco to legal documents. Taxation without representation led to the revolt of the Boston Tea Party, in which colonists dumped tea into the Boston Harbor rather than pay tax on it.

In designing the Constitution for their new utopia, the Founding Fathers left the federal income tax out. They considered the taxation of private income, the ultimate source of productivity, to be economic folly. To avoid excess taxation, they decided at the Federalist Debates that the States and the new federal government could not impose the same kind of tax at the same time. For example, if the States imposed a property tax, the federal government could not impose one. Congress would be responsible for collecting national taxes from the States, which would collect taxes from their citizens. Direct taxes were to be apportioned according to the population of each State. Income taxes were considered unapportioned direct taxes in violation of this provision of the Constitution.

The absence of an income tax had allowed the economy to grow and its citizens to prosper for over a century. From 1776 to 1913, except for brief periods when the country was at war, the federal government had been successfully funded mainly with customs and excise taxes.[i] In 1812, to fund the War of 1812, the first sales tax was imposed on gold, silverware, jewelry and watches. The first income tax was also imposed that year; but in order to comply with constitutional requirements, it was apportioned among the States, which collected the tax from property owners. In 1817, when the war was over, the new taxes were terminated.[1]

The first national income tax as we know it was imposed in 1862. Again it was to support a war effort, the War between the States. The tax was set at a mere one to three percent of income, and it applied only to those having annual incomes over $800, a category that then included less than one percent of the population. Congress avoided Constitutional apportionment requirements by classifying the new tax as an indirect tax. It was a misapplication of the law, but the tax was not challenged until 1871. The delay allowed a precedent to be established by which Congress could bypass constitutional restrictions by incorrectly classifying taxes.

In 1872, this tax too was repealed. Another income tax was passed in 1894; but no war was in progress to win sympathy for it, and it was immediately struck down by the U.S. Supreme Court. In 1895, in Pollock v. Farmer's Loan & Trust Co., the Court held that general income taxes violate the constitutional guideline that taxes levied directly on the people are to be levied in proportion to the population of each State.

That ruling has never been overruled. Instead, the Wall Street faction decided to make an end run around the Constitution. In 1913, the Sixteenth Amendment was introduced to Congress as a package deal along with the Federal Reserve Act. Both were supported by the Wall Street Senator, Nelson Aldrich. The Amendment provided:

> The Congress shall have power to lay and collect taxes on incomes, from whatever source derived, without apportionment among the several states, and without regard to any census or enumeration.

---

[i]    *Customs* are duties on imported goods. *Excise taxes* are internal taxes imposed on certain non-essential consumer goods.

Wealthy businessmen who had opposed a federal income tax were won over when they learned they could avoid paying the tax themselves by setting up tax-free foundations. The tax affected only incomes over $4,000 a year, a sum that was then well beyond the wages of most Americans. The Amendment was simply worded, the tax return was only one page long, and the entire Tax Code was only 14 pages long. It seemed harmless enough at the time . . . .

## From Little Amendments Mighty Hydras Grow

The Tax Code is now a 17,000-page sieve of obscure legalese, providing enormous loopholes for those who can afford the lobbyists to negotiate them. Corporations with enough clout, such as Enron, have had whole pages devoted to their private interests. Enron paid no taxes for four of the five years from 1996 through 2000, although it was profitable during those years.[2] The tax system has become so complex that tens of millions of taxpayers have to seek professional help to comply with its mandates. At least $250 billion are paid annually for these services, in addition to the $8 billion required to operate the Internal Revenue Service itself. The IRS has 144,000 employees – more than all but the 36 largest U.S. corporations – and it employs more investigators than the FBI and the CIA combined. According to calculations made in 1995, more than five billion hours are spent annually in the effort to comply with federal income tax requirements – close to the total number of hours worked yearly by all the people in all the jobs in the State of Indiana.[3]

The obscure court holdings testing the Tax Code's constitutionality can be as impenetrable as the Code itself. Take, for example, this convoluted single sentence in a tax case titled <u>Brushaber v. Union Pacific Railroad</u>, 240 U.S. 1 (1916):

> [T]he contention that the Amendment treats a tax on income as a direct tax although it is relieved from apportionment and is necessarily therefore not subject to the rule of uniformity as such rule only applies to taxes which are not direct, thus destroying the two great classifications which have been recognized and enforced from the beginning, is also wholly without foundation since the command of the Amendment that all income taxes shall not be subject to apportionment by a consideration of the sources from which the taxed income may be derived, forbids

the application to such taxes of the rule applied in the Pollock Case by which alone such taxes were removed from the great class of excises, duties and imposts subject to the rule of uniformity and were placed under the other or direct class.[4]

The Brushaber case, while not easy to decipher, has been construed as holding that the Sixteenth Amendment does *not* overrule Pollock in declaring general income taxes unconstitutional, and that the Amendment does *not* amend the U.S. Constitution on the question of income taxes. Rather, said the Court, the Sixteenth Amendment applies to excise taxes; it merely clarifies the federal government's existing authority to create excise taxes without apportionment; and it applies only to gains and profits from commercial and investment activities.[5]

## Watering the Hydra

These fine points were of little interest to most people before World War II, since few people were actually affected by the tax; but war again provided the pretext for expanding the law's scope. In 1939, Congress passed the Public Salary tax, taxing the wages of federal employees. In 1940 it passed the Buck Act, authorizing the federal government to tax federal workers living outside Washington D.C. In 1942, Congress passed the Victory Tax under its Constitutional authority to support the country's war efforts. A voluntary tax-withholding program was proposed by President Roosevelt which allowed workers to pay the tax in installments. This program was so successful that the number of taxpayers increased from 3 percent to 62 percent of the U.S. population. In 1944, the Victory Tax and Voluntary Withholding Laws were repealed as required by the U.S. Constitution. But the federal government, without raising the matter before the Court or the voters, continued to collect the income tax, pointing for authority to the Sixteenth Amendment.[6]

Today the federal income tax has acquired the standing of a legitimate tax enforceable by law, despite longstanding rulings by the Supreme Court strictly limiting its constitutional scope. Other taxes have also been added to the list, which currently includes an Accounts Receivable Tax, Building Permit Tax, Capital Gains Tax, CDL License Tax, Cigarette Tax, Corporate Income Tax, Federal Unemployment Tax (FUTA), Food License Tax, Fuel Permit Tax, Gasoline Tax, Inheritance Tax, Inventory Tax, IRS Interest Charges, IRS Penalties, Liquor Tax, Luxury Taxes, Marriage License Tax, Medicare Tax,

Property Tax, Real Estate Tax, Service Charge Taxes, Road Usage Taxes (Truckers), Road and Toll Bridge Taxes, Sales Tax, School Tax, Social Security Tax, State Unemployment Tax (SUTA), Telephone Taxes and Surcharges, Trailer Registration Tax, Utility Taxes, Vehicle License Registration Tax, Vehicle Sales Tax, and Workers Compensation Tax, among others. Estimates are that when the hidden taxes paid by workers all the way up the chain of production are factored in, *over 40 percent of the average citizen's income may be going to taxes.*[7]

## Was the Sixteenth Amendment Properly Ratified?

A variety of challenges to the Tax Code have been prompted by inequities in the system. In 1984, a tax protester named Bill Benson spent a year visiting State capitals, researching whether the Sixteenth Amendment was properly ratified by the States in 1913. He found that of the 38 States allegedly ratifying it, 33 had amended the language to say something other than what was passed, a power States do not possess. He argued that the Amendment was properly ratified by only two States. He attempted unsuccessfully to defend a suit for tax evasion on that ground, and spent some time in jail; but that did not deter later tax protesters from raising the defense. In 1989, the Seventh Circuit Court of Appeals again rejected the argument, not because the court disagreed with the data but because it concluded that when Secretary of State Philander Knox declared the amendment adopted in 1913, he had taken the defects into consideration. Knox's decision, said the Seventh Circuit, "is now beyond review."[8]

## So Who Was Philander Knox?

It comes as no great surprise that Philander Knox was the Robber Barons' man behind the scenes. He was an attorney who became a multi-millionaire as legal counsel to multi-millionaires. He saved Andrew Carnegie from prosecution and civil suit in 1894, when it was shown that Carnegie had defrauded the Navy with inferior armor plate for U.S. warships. Knox saved Carnegie again when the president of the Pennsylvania Railroad testified that Carnegie had regularly received illegal kickbacks from the railroad. Knox also saved his college friend William McKinley from financial ruin, before McKinley won the 1896 presidential race. In 1899, President McKinley offered Knox the post of U.S. Attorney General, but he declined. He was then too busy arranging the largest conglomerate in history, the merger of the railroad, oil, coal, iron and steel interests of Carnegie, J. P. Morgan, Rockefeller, and other Robber Barons into U.S. Steel. After completing the U.S. Steel merger, Knox accepted McKinley's offer, over vigorous opposition. The appointment put him in charge of prosecuting the antitrust laws against the same Robber Barons he had built a career and a personal fortune representing. When the U.S. Steel merger met with public outcry, Knox said he knew nothing and could do nothing, and U.S. Steel emerged unscathed.

When McKinley was assassinated in 1901, Knox continued as Attorney General under Teddy Roosevelt, drafting federal statutes that gave his wealthy and powerful friends even more power and control over interstate commerce. Agents of the conglomerates wound up sitting on the government boards and commissions that set rates and eliminated competition in restraint of trade. Knox was appointed Secretary of State by President Taft in 1909, when Senator Aldrich gave the Sixteenth Amendment a decisive push through Congress. The Amendment was rushed through right before Knox resigned as Secretary of State. That may explain why he was willing to overlook a few irregularities. If he had left the matter to a successor, there was no telling the outcome.[9]

## Do We Need a Federal Income Tax?

In upholding these irregularities against constitutional challenge, courts may have been motivated by a perceived need to preserve a federal income tax that has come to be considered indispensable to funding the government. But is it? A report issued by the Grace Commission during the Reagan Administration concluded that *most federal income tax revenues go just to pay the interest on the government's burgeoning debt.* Indeed, that was the purpose for which the tax was originally designed. When the federal income tax was instituted in 1913, *all* income tax collections were forwarded directly to the Federal Reserve. In fiscal year 2005, the U.S. government spent $352 billion just to service the government's debt. The sum represented more than one-third of individual income tax revenues that year, which totaled $927 billion.[10]

As for the other two-thirds of the individual income tax tab, the Grace Commission concluded that those payments did not go to service necessary government operations either. A cover letter addressed to

President Reagan stated that a third of all income taxes were consumed by waste and inefficiency in the federal government. Another third of any taxes actually paid went to make up for the taxes not paid by tax evaders and the burgeoning underground economy, a phenomenon that had blossomed in direct proportion to tax increases. The report concluded:

> With two-thirds of everyone's personal income taxes wasted or not collected, 100 percent of what is collected is absorbed solely by interest on the Federal debt and by Federal Government contributions to transfer payments. In other words, *all individual income tax revenues are gone before one nickel is spent on the services which taxpayers expect from their Government.*[11]

Even the third going for interest on the federal debt could have been avoided, if Congress had created the money itself on the Franklin/ Lincoln model; but the obscurely-worded Federal Reserve Act had delegated the power to create money to a private banking cartel. Congress, like the sleeping public, had been deceived by the bankers' sleight of hand. The head had thundered and the walls had shook. The wizard's wizardry had worked, at least on the mesmerized majority. Among the few who remained awake was Representative Charles Lindbergh Sr., who warned on the day the Federal Reserve Act was passed:

> This Act establishes the most gigantic trust on earth. When the President signs this bill, the invisible government by the Monetary Power will be legalized. The people may not know it immediately, but the day of reckoning is only a few years removed.

The day of reckoning came sixteen years later.

# Chapter 15

# REAPING THE WHIRLWIND:

# THE GREAT DEPRESSION

*Uncle Henry sat upon the doorstep and looked anxiously at the sky, which was even grayer than usual. . . . From the far north they heard a low wail of the wind, and Uncle Henry and Dorothy could see where the long grass bowed in waves before the coming storm.*

– The Wonderful Wizard of Oz,
"The Cyclone"

The stock market crashed in 1929, precipitating a world wide depression that lasted a decade. Few people remember it today, but we can still get the flavor in the movies. The Great Depression was depicted in the barren black-and-white Kansas drought opening the 1939 film The Wizard of Oz. It was also the setting for It's a Wonderful Life, a classic 1946 film shown on TV every Christmas. The film starred Jimmy Stewart as a beloved small-town banker named George Bailey, who was driven to consider suicide after a "run" on his bank, when the townspeople all demanded their money and he couldn't pay. The promise of the Federal Reserve Act – that it would prevent bank panics by allowing a conglomeration of big banks to come to the rescue of little banks that got caught short-handed – had obviously failed. The Crash of 1929 was the biggest bank run in history.

The problem began in the Roaring Twenties, when the Fed made money plentiful by keeping interest rates low. Money seemed to be plentiful, but what was actually flowing freely was "credit" or "debt." Production was up more than wages were up, so more goods were available than money to pay for them; but people could borrow. By the end of the 1920s, major consumer purchases such as cars and radios (which were then large pieces of furniture that sat on the floor) were bought mainly on credit. Money was so easy to get that people were borrowing just to invest, taking out short-term, low-interest loans that were readily available from the banks.

The stock market held little interest for most people until the Robber Barons started promoting it, after amassing large stock holdings very cheaply themselves. They sold the public on the idea that it was possible to get rich quick by buying stock on "margin" (or on credit). The investor could put a down payment on the stock and pay off the balance after its price went up, reaping a hefty profit. This investment strategy turned the stock market into a speculative pyramid scheme, in which most of the money invested did not actually exist.[1] People would open margin accounts, not because they could not afford to pay 100 percent of the stock price, but because it allowed them to leverage their investments, buying ten times as much stock by paying only a 10 percent down payment.[i] The public went wild over this scheme. In a speculative fever, many people literally "bet the farm." They were taking out loans against everything they owned – homes, farms, life insurance – anything to get the money to get into the market and make more money. Homesteads that had been owned free and clear were mortgaged to the bankers, who fanned the fever by offering favorable credit terms and interest rates.[2] The Federal Reserve made these favorable terms possible by substantially lowering the rediscount rate – the interest rate member banks paid to borrow from the Fed. The Fed thus made it easy for the banks to acquire additional reserves against which they could expand the money supply by many multiples with loans.

## Hands Across the Atlantic

Why would the Fed want to flood the U.S. economy with borrowed money, inflating the money supply? The evidence points to a scheme between Benjamin Strong, then Governor of the Federal Reserve Bank of New York, and Montagu Norman, head of the Bank of England, to deliver control of the financial systems of the world to a small group of private central bankers. Strong was a Morgan man who had a very close relationship with Norman – so close that it was evidently more than just business. In 1928, when Strong had to retire due to illness, Norman wrote intimately, "Whatever is to happen to us – wherever

---

[i]  *Leveraging* means buying securities with borrowed money.

you and I are to live – we cannot now separate and ignore these years. Somehow we must meet and sometimes we must live together . . . ."[4] Professor Carroll Quigley wrote of Norman and Strong:

> In the 1920s, they were determined to use the financial power of Britain and of the United States to force all the major countries of the world to go on the gold standard and to operate it through central banks free from all political control, with all questions of international finance to be settled by agreements by such central banks without interference from governments.[4]

Norman, as head of the Bank of England, was determined to keep the British pound convertible to gold at pre-war levels, although the pound had lost substantial value as against gold during World War I. The result was a major drain on British gold reserves. To keep gold from flowing out of England into the United States, the Federal Reserve, led by Strong, supported the Bank of England by keeping U.S. interest rates low, inflating the U.S. dollar. The higher interest rates in London made it a more attractive place for investors to put their gold, drawing it from the United States to England; but the lower rates in the United States caused an inflation bubble, which soon got out of hand. The meetings between Norman and Strong were very secretive, but the evidence suggests that in February 1929, they concluded that a collapse in the market was inevitable and that the best course was to let it correct "naturally" (naturally with a little help from the Fed). They sent advisory warnings to lists of preferred customers, including wealthy industrialists, politicians, and high foreign officials, telling them to get out of the market. Then the Fed began selling government securities in the open market, reducing the money supply by reducing the reserves available for backing loans. The bank-loan rate was also increased, causing rates on brokers' loans to jump to 20 percent.[5]

The result was a huge liquidity squeeze – a lack of available money. Short-term loans suddenly became available only at much higher interest rates, making buying stock on margin much less attractive. As fewer people bought, stock prices fell, removing the incentive for new buyers to purchase the stocks bought by earlier buyers on margin. Many investors were forced to sell at a loss by "margin calls" (calls by brokers for investors to bring the cash in their margin accounts up to a certain level after the value of their stocks had fallen). The panic was on, as investors rushed to dump their stocks for whatever they could get for them. The stock market crashed overnight. People withdrew their savings from the banks, and foreigners withdrew their gold, further depleting the reserves on which the money stock was built. From 1929 to 1933, the money stock fell by a third, and a third of the nation's banks closed their doors. Strong said privately that the problem could easily be corrected by adding money to the shrinking money supply; but unfortunately for the country, he died suddenly without passing this bit of wisdom on.[6] It was dramatic evidence of the dangers of delegating the power to control the money supply to a single autocratic head of an autonomous agency.

A vicious cyclone of debt wound up dragging all in its path into hunger, poverty and despair. Little money was available to buy goods, so workers got laid off. Small-town bankers like George Bailey were lucky if they escaped bankruptcy, but the big banks made out quite well. Many wealthy insiders also did quite well, quietly pulling out of the stock market just before the crash, then jumping back in when they could buy up companies for pennies on the dollar. While small investors were going under and jumping from windows, the Big Money Boys were accumulating the stocks that had been sold at distressed prices and the real estate that had been mortgaged to buy the stocks. The country's wealth was systematically transferred from the Great American Middle Class to Big Money.

The Homestead Laws were established in the days of Abraham Lincoln to encourage settlers to move onto the land and develop it. The country had been built by these homesteaders, who staked out their plots of land, farmed them, and defended them. That was the basis of capitalism and the American dream, the "level playing field" on which the players all had a fair start and something to work with. The field was level until the country was swept by depression, when homes and farms that had been in the family since the Civil War or the Revolution were sucked up in a cyclone of debt and delivered to the banks and financial elite.

## Austerity for the Poor,
## Welfare for the International Bankers

The Federal Reserve scheme had failed, but Congress did not shut down the shell game and prosecute the perpetrators. Rather, the Federal Deposit Insurance Corporation (FDIC) was instituted, ostensibly to prevent the Great Depression from ever happening again. It would do this by having the federal government provide backup money to cover bank failures, furnishing a form of insurance for the banks at the expense of the taxpayers. The FDIC was prepared to rescue some banks but not all. It was designed to favor rich and powerful banks. Ed Griffin writes in The Creature from Jekyll Island:

> The FDIC has three options when bailing out an insolvent bank. The first is called a *payoff*. It involves simply paying off the insured depositors [those with deposits under $100,000] and then letting the bank fall to the mercy of the liquidators. This is the option usually chosen for small banks with no political clout. The second possibility is called a *sell off*, and it involves making arrangements for a larger bank to assume all the real assets and liabilities of the failing bank. Banking services are uninterrupted and, aside from a change in name, most customers are unaware of the transaction. This option is generally selected for small and medium banks. In both a payoff and a sell off, the FDIC takes over the bad loans of the failed bank and supplies the money to pay back the insured depositors. The third option is called *bailout* . . . . Irvine Sprague, a former director of the FDIC, explains: "In a bailout, the bank does not close, and everyone – insured or not – is fully protected. . . . Such privileged treatment is accorded by FDIC only rarely to an elect few."

The "elect few" are the wealthy and powerful banks that are considered "too big to fail" without doing irreparable harm to the community. In a bailout, the FDIC covers *all* of the bank's deposits, even those over $100,000. Wealthy investors, including wealthy foreign investors, are fully protected. Griffin observes:

> Favoritism toward the large banks is obvious at many levels. . . . [T]he large banks get a whopping free ride when they are bailed out. Their uninsured accounts are paid by FDIC, and the cost of that benefit is passed to the smaller banks and to the taxpayer. This is not an oversight. *Part of the plan at Jekyll Island was to give a competitive edge to the large banks.*[7]

The FDIC shielded the bankers both from losses to themselves and from prosecution for the losses of others. Later, the International Monetary Fund was devised to serve the same backup function when whole countries defaulted. Austerity measures and belt-tightening were imposed on the poor while welfare was provided for the rich, saving the moneyed class from the consequences of their own risky investments.

## The Blame Game

Who was to blame for this decade-long cyclone of debt and devastation? Milton Friedman, professor of economics at the University of Chicago and winner of a Nobel Prize in economics, stated categorically:

> The Federal Reserve definitely caused the Great Depression by contracting the amount of currency in circulation by one-third from 1929 to 1933.

The Honorable Louis T. McFadden, Chairman of the House Banking and Currency Committee, went further. He charged:

> [The depression] was not accidental. It was a carefully contrived occurrence. . . . *The international bankers sought to bring about a condition of despair here so that they might emerge as rulers of us all.*[8]

Representative McFadden could not be accused of partisan politics. He had been elected by the citizens of Pennsylvania on both the Democratic and Republican tickets, and he had served as Chairman of the Banking and Currency Committee for more than ten years, putting him in a position to speak with authority on the vast ramifications of the gigantic private credit monopoly of the Federal Reserve. In 1934, he filed a Petition for Articles of Impeachment against the Federal Reserve Board, charging fraud, conspiracy, unlawful conversion and treason. He told Congress:

> This evil institution has impoverished and ruined the people of these United States, has bankrupted itself, and has practically bankrupted our Government. It has done this through the defects of the law under which it operates, through the maladministration of that law by the Fed and through the corrupt practices of the moneyed vultures who control it.
>
> . . . From the Atlantic to the Pacific, our Country has been ravaged and laid waste by the evil practices of the Fed and the interests which control them. At no time in our history, has the general welfare of the people been at a lower level or the minds of the people so full of despair. . . .
>
> Recently in one of our States, *60,000 dwelling houses and farms were brought under the hammer in a single day.* 71,000 houses and farms in Oakland County, Michigan, were sold and their erstwhile owners dispossessed. The people who have thus been driven out

are the wastage of the Fed. They are the victims of the Fed. *Their children are the new slaves of the auction blocks in the revival of the institution of human slavery.*[9]

A document called "The Bankers Manifesto of 1934" added weight to these charges. An update of "The Bankers Manifesto of 1892," it was reportedly published in The Civil Servants' Yearbook in January 1934 and in The New American in February 1934 and was circulated privately among leading bankers. It read in part:

> Capital must protect itself in every way, through combination [monopoly] and through legislation. Debts must be collected and loans and mortgages foreclosed as soon as possible. When through a process of law, the common people have lost their homes, they will be more tractable and more easily governed by the strong arm of the law applied by the central power of wealth, under control of leading financiers. *People without homes will not quarrel with their leaders.* This is well known among our principal men now engaged in forming an imperialism of capital to govern the world.[10]

That was the sinister view of the Great Depression, but the charitable explanation was that the Fed had simply misjudged. Whatever had happened, the monetary policy of the day had clearly failed. Change was in the wind. Over 2,000 schemes for monetary reform were advanced, and populist organizations again developed large followings.

## Return to Oz: Coxey Runs for President

Nearly four decades after he had led the march on Washington that inspired the march on Oz, Jacob Coxey reappeared on the scene to run on the Farmer-Labor Party ticket for President. Nothing if not persistent, Coxey actually ran for office thirteen times between 1894 and 1936. He was elected only twice, as mayor of Massillon, Ohio, in 1932 and 1933; but he did succeed in winning a majority in the Ohio presidential primary in 1932.[11]

Franklin Roosevelt came from banking and railroad money and had the support of big business along with the general public. He easily won the presidential election. But Coxey maintained that it was his own plan for government-financed public works that was the blueprint for the "New Deal," the program widely credited with pulling the country out of the Depression.[12] It was the same plan

Coxey had proposed in the 1890s: Congress could jump-start the economy by "priming the pump" with various public projects that would put the unemployed to work, using government-issued, debt-free money to pay for the labor and materials. Roosevelt adopted the pump-priming part but not the proposal to finance it with debt-free Greenbacks. Although a bill called the Thomas Amendment was passed during Roosevelt's tenure that authorized new issues of government Greenbacks, no Greenbacks were actually issued under it. Instead, Roosevelt financed the New Deal with deficit spending and tax increases.

In 1944, Coxey was honored for his work by being allowed to deliver a speech on the Capitol steps, with the formal blessing of the Vice President and the Speaker of the House. It was the same speech he had been barred from giving there half a century before. In 1946, at the age of 92, he published a new plan to avoid unemployment and future wars. He died in 1951, at the age of 97.[13]

## Another Aging Populist Returns

Another blast from the past on the presidential campaign trail was William Hope Harvey, author of Coin's Financial School and economic adviser to William Jennings Bryan in the 1890s. Harvey ran for President in 1932 on the Liberty Party ticket. Like Coxey, he was an obscure candidate who was later lost to history; but his insights would prove to be prophetic. Harvey stressed that people who took out loans at a bank were not actually borrowing "money." They were borrowing debt; and the commercial oligarchy to whom it was owed would eventually end up running the country. The workers would live on credit and buy at the company store, becoming wage-slaves who owned nothing of their own.

Harvey considered money to be a direct representation of a man's labor, and usury and debt to be a scheme to put middleman bankers between a man's labor and his property. Even efficient farmers operating on the debt-money system would eventually have some bad years, and they would default on their loans. Every year there would be a certain number of foreclosures and the banks would get the land, which would be sold to the larger farm owners. The country's property would thus gradually become concentrated in fewer and fewer hands. The farms, factories and businesses would wind up owned by a few individuals and corporations that were controlled by the bankers who controlled the money supply. At the heart of the problem, said Harvey, was the Federal Reserve System, which allowed banks to issue debt and pretend it was money. This sleight of hand was what had allowed the bankers to slowly foreclose on the country, moving ownership to the Wall Street banks, brokerage houses and insurance companies. The ultimate culprit was the English banking system, which had infected and corrupted America's banking system. It was the English who had first demonetized silver in 1816, and who had decreased the value of everything else by hoarding gold. Debts to English banks had to be paid in gold, and countries that did not produce gold had to buy it to pay their debts to England. The result was to drive down the value of the goods those countries did produce, indenturing them to the English bankers. In a fictionalized book called A Tale of Two Countries, Harvey wrote of a fat English banker named Baron Rothe, who undertook to corrupt the American economy and government in order to place the reins of the country in the hands of his worldwide banking system.

Harvey's solution was to return the Money Power to the people, something he proposed doing by nationalizing the banks. He would have nationalized other essential industries as well – those that operated on a large scale and produced basic commodities, including public utilities, transportation, and steel. The profits would have gone into the public coffers, replacing taxes, which Harvey thought should be abolished. The Populists of the 1890s had campaigned to expand the money supply by adding silver to the gold that backed paper money, but Harvey now felt that both gold and silver should be de-monetized. The national currency did not need precious metal backing. It could be what Franklin and Lincoln said it was – simply a receipt for labor. Paper money could be backed by government services. Although that is a novel idea today, it has a familiar precedent: the postage stamp is a kind of money redeemable in government services. One postage stamp represents the amount of government labor required to transport one letter from one place to another. Postage stamps are fungible and can be saved or traded.[14]

Although Harvey and Coxey both failed in their political aspirations, both saw elements of their platforms adopted in the New Deal. Roosevelt took the dollar off the gold standard as Harvey had advocated, and he jump-started the economy by putting the unemployed to work as Coxey had advocated. Roosevelt came from banker money and had the support of big business, but he also had a strong streak of the can-do Populist spirit . . . .

# Chapter 16
# OILING THE RUSTED JOINTS OF THE ECONOMY: ROOSEVELT, KEYNES AND THE NEW DEAL

*"What can I do for you?" she inquired softly . . . .*
*"Get an oilcan and oil my joints," he answered. "They are rusted*
*so badly that I cannot move them at all. If I am well oiled I shall soon*
*be all right again."*

– *The Wonderful Wizard of Oz,*
"The Rescue of the Tin Woodman"

In the Great Depression, labor had again rusted into non-productivity due to a lack of available money to oil the wheels of production. In the 1890s, Coxey's plan to "prime the pump" with public projects was an idea ahead of its time; but in the 1930s, Roosevelt actually carried it out. The result was a national infrastructure that has been called a revolutionary model for the world. The Tennessee Valley Authority developed hydroelectric power for farming areas that had never had electricity before. It accomplished flood control and river diversion, provided scientific agriculture, developed new industry, and overcame illiteracy by spreading public education. The Rural Electrification Administration was built, along with tens of thousands of sanitation projects, hospitals, schools, ports and public buildings. Public works programs were launched, employing millions of workers. Revolutionary social programs were also introduced, including Social Security for the aged and disabled, unemployment insurance, and the right of labor to organize. Farm and home foreclosures were stopped, and savings accounts were restored.[1]

Where Roosevelt's plan diverged from Coxey's was in the source of the funds. Rather than issuing the money outright, he borrowed it from the banks. Even that step was considered radical at the time. The dogma of the day was that the government's budget had to be balanced at all costs. The novel idea that the government could operate on borrowed money was urged by John Maynard Keynes, a respected British economist, who said it was a more sensible course than austerely trying to balance the budget when funds were not to be had. In an open letter in The New York Times, Keynes advised Roosevelt that "only the expenditures of public authority" could reverse the Depression. The government had to spend to get money into circulation.

Keynes has been called an elitist, because he was an intellectual with expensive tastes, wealthy friends and banker affiliations; but like Roosevelt, he had a strong streak of the can-do Populist spirit. At a time when conventional economists were gloomy naysayers maintaining that nothing could be done, Keynes was an optimist who thought like the Wizard of Oz. There was no reason to put up with recession, depression and unemployment. Balancing the budget by cutting jobs, at a time when people were already out of work, he thought was economic folly. The way to get the ball rolling again was just to roll up your sleeves and get busy. It could all be paid for on credit!

But Keynes would not go so far as to advocate that the government should issue the money outright. "Increasing the quantity of money is like trying to get fat by buying a larger belt," he said.[2] It was a colorful analogy but a questionable one. The money supply had just shrunk by a third. The emaciated patient needed to be fattened up with a good infusion of liquidity just to replace the money that had been lost.

Keynes started thinking more like the Greenbackers at the end of World War II, when he proposed a debt-free Greenback-style currency called the "Bancor" to serve as the reserves of the International Monetary Fund (the fund established to stabilize global currencies). But by then England's economic power had been exhausted by two world wars, and America called the shots. The Bancor lost out to the U.S. dollar, which would become the world's reserve currency along with gold. (More on this in Section III.)

## Challenging Classical Economic Theory

The Keynesian theory that dominated economic policy after World War II was the one endorsing "deficit spending." The notion that the government could borrow its way to prosperity represented a major departure from classical economic theory. Under the classical "quantity theory of money," there was no need to increase the amount of money in circulation. When the money supply contracted, prices and wages would naturally adjust downward, leaving all as it was before. Murray Rothbard, an economist of the classical Austrian School, put it like this:

> We come to the startling truth that *it doesn't matter what the supply of money is.* Any supply will do as well as any other supply. The free market will simply adjust by changing the purchasing power, or effectiveness, of its [monetary] unit. There is no need whatever for any planned increase in the money supply, for the supply to rise to offset any condition, or to follow any artificial criteria. More money does not supply more capital, is not more productive, does not permit "economic growth."[3]

That was the theory, but in the Great Depression it clearly wasn't working. The country was suffering from crippling unemployment, although people wanted to work, there was work to be done, and there were consumers wanting to purchase the fruits of their productive labors. The farmers' hens were laying, but the eggs never made it to market. The cows were producing milk, but the milk was being dumped on the ground. The apple trees were producing bumper crops, but the growers were leaving them to rot in the orchards. People everywhere were out of work and starving; yet the land was still fertile, the factories were ready to roll, and the raw materials were available to run them. Keynes said that what was needed was the very thing classical economists said would have no effect – an infusion of new money to get the wheels of production turning again.

Roosevelt was slow to go along with Keynes' radical notions, but as the Depression got worse, he decided to give them a try. He told the country in a fireside chat, "We suffer from a failure of consumer demand because of a lack of buying power." When the United States entered World War II, Roosevelt had no choice but to test the limits of the national credit card; and in a dramatic empirical display, the pump-priming theory was proven to work. Unemployment dropped from more than 17 percent to just over 1 percent. The economy grew along with the money supply to double its original size, the fastest growth in U.S. history.[4] The country was pulled out of the Depression by "priming the pump" with liquidity, funding new production that put new wages in consumers' pockets.

Keynes had turned classical theory on its head. The classical assumption was that output ("supply") was fixed and prices were flexible. Increasing "demand" (money) would therefore increase prices. Keynes said that prices tended to be fixed and output to be flexible.[5] When the economy was operating at less than full employment, adding money would not increase prices. It would increase productivity. As long as there were idle resources to draw from, watering a liquidity-starved economy with new money would not produce inflation. It would produce abundance.

And that was how it actually worked, for a while; but adding liquidity by borrowing money into existence did not actually create money. It created debt; and to service the debt, the taxpayers had to pay interest compounded annually. Roosevelt's plan put people to work, putting more money in their pockets; but much of this money was taken out again in the form of taxes, which went largely to pay the burgeoning interest tab. From 1933 to 1940, federal taxes tripled. In the New Deal years, the average annual federal budget deficit was about $3 billion out of an entire federal budget of $6 billion to $9 billion -- a greater percentage even than today, when deficit spending has reached record levels.[6] Wholesale endorsement of Keynesian deficit spending caused the federal debt to balloon from $22 billion in 1933 to *$8 trillion* in 2005, a 364-fold increase in just 72 years. The money supply increased along with the debt. In 1959, when the Fed first began reporting M3, it was a mere $288.8 billion. By February 2004, it had reached $9 trillion.[7] In only 45 years, M3 had multiplied by *over 30 times*.

Prices have gone up in tandem. Many people still remember when ice cream cones and comic books were 25 cents each. Today they are $2.50 or more. What was once a 10 cent cup of coffee is now $1.50 to $2.00. A house that was $30,000 in 1970 is now more than $300,000. In 1970, it could have been bought by a single-breadwinner family. For most families today, both parents have to work outside the home to make the mortgage payments.[8] These parabolic price increases reflect a parabolic increase in the money supply. Where did all this new money come from? No gold was added to the asset base of the country, which went off the gold standard in the 1930s. *All* of this increase came into existence as accounting-entry bank loans. More specifically, it came from government loans, which never get paid back but just get rolled over from year to year. Under the plan of Coxey and the Greenbackers, rather than borrowing from banks that pulled the money out of an empty hat, Uncle Sam could have pulled the money out of his own tall hat and avoided a mushrooming debt.

By 2007, the federal debt was approaching $9 trillion; and little of this borrowed money was going to improve infrastructure or to increase employment. Jobs were being out-sourced abroad, while taxpayers struggled to make the interest payments on the federal debt. Under Coxey's plan, there would have been *no* federal debt and ample Greenback dollars to fund infrastructure and other public projects that would have put the unemployed to work.

## Roosevelt in the Middle

Coxey was not alone in urging the Greenback cure for the economy's ills. Some influential federal officials also thought it was the way to reverse the depression. In a congressional address in 1933, Representative Louis McFadden quoted a Hearst newspaper article by Robert Hemphill, credit manager of the Atlanta Federal Reserve, in which Hemphill argued:

> We are rapidly approaching a situation where the government *must* issue additional currency. It will very soon be the only move remaining. *It should have been the first step in the recovery program.* Immediately upon a revival of the demand that the government increase the supply of currency, we shall again be subjected to a barrage of skillfully designed and cunningly circulated propaganda by means of which a small group of international bankers have been able, for two centuries to frighten the peoples of the civilized world against issuing their own good money in sufficient quantities to carry on their necessary commerce. *By this simple, but amazingly successful device these "money changers" – parasites in a busy world intent on creating and exchanging wealth – have been able to preserve for their private and exclusive right the monopoly of manufacturing an inferior substitute for money which they have hypnotized civilized nations into using, because of their pressing need to exchange goods and services.* We shall never recover on credit. Even if it were obtainable, it is uncertain, unreliable, does not expand in

accordance with demand, and contracts unexpectedly and for causes unrelated to the needs of commerce and industry.

. . . We need in circulation $250.00 per capita in *permanent uncontractible currency*, deposited in depositaries and payable on demand, to sustain the standard of living to which we had arrived in 1927-29, to pay the then prevailing prices, wages and costs; to produce incomes and restore the property values of that period. . . . *In our present situation the issue of additional currency is the only way out.*[9]

Hemphill said the government needed to issue enough new, debt-free currency to replace what had been lost. Congressman Wright Patman went further. The government, he said, needed to take over ownership and operation of the banks. In an address to Congress on March 13, 1933, he asked rhetorically:

Why is it necessary to have Government ownership and operation of banks? Let us go back to the Constitution of the United States and follow it . . . . The Constitution of the United States says that Congress shall coin money and regulate its value. That does not mean . . . that the Congress of the United States, composed of the duly elected representatives of the people, have a right to farm out the great privilege to the banking system, until today a few powerful bankers control the issuance and distribution of money – something that the Constitution of the United States says Congress shall do.[10]

Flanked on the right by the classical laissez-faire economists who said the money supply and the banking scheme should not be tampered with at all, and on the left by the radical reformers who said that the power to create money and perhaps even the banking system itself should be taken over by the government, Roosevelt took the middle road and opted for the Keynesian deficit spending alternative. He expanded the money supply, but he did it without unseating the private banking cartel.

Instead, Roosevelt tried to regulate the bankers. In 1934, the Federal Reserve System was overhauled to provide additional safeguards for the economy and the money supply. The old Federal Reserve Board was dissolved and replaced by a seven-member Board of Governors, appointed by the U.S. President for 14-year terms. The Board was given greatly increased powers, including the power to appoint the presidents of the 12 Federal Reserve Banks. The Open Market Committee was created, with one representative from each Federal

Reserve Bank. It was empowered to inject new money into the economy by using newly-created money to purchase government bonds, and to remove money from the economy by selling government bonds.[11] (More on this in Chapter 19.)

The money supply was better protected by these measures, but the Fed remained a hierarchical citadel, run from the top down. Today, even the commercial banks that own the Federal Reserve Banks do not have ordinary voting rights. The system is subject to the control of a small cartel of appointed banking representatives, who operate behind a curtain of secrecy. The Head of the Fed is always chosen from the private banking sector and remains aligned with its interests. The country that holds democracy out as an ideal is in the anomalous position of having an economic system controlled by an autocratic head who is beyond the reach not only of the public but of the Fed's own shareholders.[12]

## Going for the Gold

In 1933, Roosevelt took another controversial step when he took the dollar off the gold standard. England's pound sterling had gone off the gold standard in 1931, prompting foreigners to turn to the United States for gold at a time when Federal Reserve Notes had to be backed by 40 percent gold reserves. The result was a run on the nation's gold stores that was dangerously shrinking the money supply by shrinking the dollar's gold backing.[13] If everyone holding dollars had been allowed to trade them in for gold, no reserves would have been left to back the dollar, and the money supply would have collapsed completely. To halt that alarming trend, in 1933 Roosevelt pronounced the country officially bankrupt and declared a national emergency. Then, with a wave of the Presidential fiat, he changed the Federal Reserve Note from a promise to pay in gold into legal tender itself, backed only by "the full faith and credit of the United States."

The price of gold was subsequently raised, reducing the value of the dollar so more goods could be sold abroad. But first, all gold coins, gold bullion, and gold certificates held by the public were ordered turned over to the U.S. Treasury, under threat of fines and imprisonment. The point of this exercise was evidently to prevent a windfall to gold owners when the price of gold went up. Private gold owners were paid $20.67 per ounce in paper Federal Reserve money for their confiscated gold. Then the price of gold was raised to $35 per ounce.

The result was an immediate 40 percent devaluation of the paper money the public had just received for their gold. The Federal Reserve also had to turn in its gold, but the Fed was paid in gold certificates (paper money redeemable in gold).

Congressman McFadden was outraged. He argued that private gold stores were not needed to rebuild the national money supply, since the gold backing had just been removed from the dollar. The Fed was still obligated to redeem foreign holdings of Federal Reserve Notes in gold, and raising the price of gold reduced those obligations; but that was the Fed's problem, not the public's.[14] He accused the Federal Reserve Board and its foreign manipulators of deliberately draining the gold from the U.S. Treasury. "Roosevelt did what the International Bankers ordered him to do!", McFadden charged in a 1934 address to Congress. "He is preparing to cancel the war debts by fraud!"

The Fed was legally obligated to redeem its Federal Reserve Notes in gold to the American people, McFadden said. It had defaulted on this obligation by irresponsibly letting its gold reserves be siphoned off by foreigners. The Fed was bankrupt because of its own mis-dealings. He told Congress:

> There was no national emergency here when Franklin D. Roosevelt took office excepting the bankruptcy of the Fed – a bankruptcy which has been going on under cover for several years and which has been concealed from the people so that the people would continue to permit their bank deposits and their bank reserves and their gold and the funds of the United States Treasury to be impounded in these bankrupt institutions.
>
> Under cover, the predatory International Bankers have been stealthily transferring the burden of the Fed debts to the people's Treasury and to the people themselves. They [took] the farms and the homes of the United States to pay for their thievery! That is the only national emergency that there has been here since the depression began.
>
> . . . Roosevelt divorced the currency of the United States from gold, and the United States currency is no longer protected by gold. *It is therefore sheer dishonesty to say that the people's gold is needed to protect the currency.*
>
> . . . Mr. Chairman, I am in favor of compelling the Fed to pay their own debts. *I see no reason why the general public should be forced to pay the gambling debts of the International Bankers.*[15]

## Reining in Wall Street

Although McFadden accused Roosevelt of bowing to the international bankers, FDR was not actually marching to the drummer of his own moneyed class, much to their chagrin. From his first months in office, he implemented tough legislation against the Wall Street looting and corruption that had brought down the stock market and the economy. He took aim at the trusts and monopolies that had returned in force with the *laissez-faire* government of the Roaring Twenties. By 1929, about 1,200 mergers had swallowed up more than 6,000 previously independent companies, leaving only 200 corporations in control of over half of all American industry. FDR reversed this trend with new legislation, reviving the policies initiated by his cousin Teddy.

He also imposed strict regulations on Wall Street. The Glass-Steagall Act was passed, limiting speculation and preventing banks from gambling with money entrusted to them. Regular commercial banks were separated from investment banks dealing with stocks and bonds, in order to prevent bankers from creating stock offerings and then underwriting or selling the offerings by hyping the stock. Banks had to choose to be either commercial banks or investment banks. Commercial banks were prohibited from underwriting most securities, with the exception of government-issued bonds. Speculative abuses were regulated through the Securities Act of 1933 and the Securities Exchange Act of 1934. The Securities and Exchange Commission (SEC) was formed; information requirements to potential investors were established; regulations were promulgated for buying securities on margin (or on credit), and for bank lending for the purchase of stocks and bonds; and restrictions were placed on the suspect practice known as the short sale. (More on this in Chapter 19.)

Needless to say, the Wall Street financiers were not pleased. "They are unanimous in their hatred of me," Roosevelt said defiantly, "and I welcome their hatred!"[16] A clique of big financiers and industrialists was rumored to be so unhappy with the President that they plotted to assassinate him. Major General Smedley Butler testified before Congress that he had been solicited by Morgan banking interests to lead the plot. He said he was told by a Morgan agent that Wall Street was about to cut off credit to the New Deal, and that Roosevelt "has either got to get more money out of us or *he has got to change the method of financing the government, and we are going to see that he does not change that method.*"[17]

Change the method of financing the government to what? Hemphill had urged the government to issue its own Greenback-style currency, and Patman had proposed nationalizing the banks. Greenback-style funding was actually authorized by the Thomas Amendment, which provided that the President could issue $3 billion in new Greenbacks if the Federal Reserve Banks failed to fund $3 billion in government bonds.[18] That authority was never exercised, but the threat was there. The plot to assassinate Roosevelt failed, but according to Smedley, it was only because he had refused to lead it.

As for Congressman McFadden's impeachment action against the Fed, he never got a chance to prove his case. His Congressional investigation was terminated by his sudden death in 1936, under suspicious circumstances. The month he died, the journal Pelley's Weekly reported:

> Now that this sterling American patriot has made the Passing, it can be revealed that not long after his public utterance against the encroaching powers of [the international bankers], it became known among his intimates that he had suffered two attacks against his life. The first attack came in the form of two revolver shots fired at him from ambush as he was alighting from a cab in front of one of the Capital hotels. Fortunately both shots missed him, the bullets burying themselves in the structure of the cab.
>
> He became violently ill after partaking of food at a political banquet at Washington. His life was only saved from what was subsequently announced as poisoning by the presence of a physician friend at the banquet, who at once procured a stomach pump and subjected the Congressman to emergency treatment.[19]

McFadden then died mysteriously of "heart-failure sudden-death," following a bout of "intestinal flue." His petition for Articles of Impeachment against the Federal Reserve Board for fraud, conspiracy, unlawful conversion and treason was never acted upon.

Wright Patman took up the torch where McFadden left off . . . .

# Chapter 17
# WRIGHT PATMAN
# EXPOSES THE MONEY MACHINE

*Toto jumped . . . and tipped over the screen that stood in a corner.
As it fell with a crash they looked that way, and the next moment all
of them were filled with wonder. For they saw, standing in just the spot
the screen had hidden, a little old man, with a bald head and a wrinkled
face, who seemed to be as much surprised as they were. . . .*

*"I am Oz, the Great and Terrible," said the little man, in a
trembling voice.*

– *The Wonderful Wizard of Oz,*
*"The Discovery of Oz the Terrible"*

If Wright Patman had been a character in The Wizard of Oz,
he would probably have been Dorothy's feisty dog Toto, who
nipped fearlessly at the Wicked Witch's heels, saved his mistress by
leaping boldly across a closing drawbridge, and exposed the man behind the curtain pretending to be a Great and Powerful Wizard.
Patman spent nearly fifty years barking at the wicked institutions he
thought were out to get the farmers and small businessmen of his
Texas constituency. They included big business, chain stores, tax-exempt foundations and – most wicked of all – the Federal Reserve Board,
whose restrictive monetary policies he felt placed the interests of Wall
Street above those of Main Street.[1]

Patman was first elected to Congress in 1928 and was re-elected
24 times. He served as Chairman of the House Banking and Currency
Committee from 1963 to 1975 and in Congress until his death in 1976.
He was called an "economic Populist." He inspired a major protest
march on Washington in 1932, the march of unemployed World War
I veterans petitioning for the "Bonus Bill" he wrote. He was the first
to call for the investigation not only of Penn Central (1970) but of
Watergate (1972). One reviewer described him as:

a cranky eccentric, out of place in the increasingly slick and polished world of Washington politics. But therein lay his significance . . . . He used his outsider status to force onto the national agenda issues that few politicians cared or dared to raise.[2]

In his role as Chairman of the House Banking and Currency Committee, Patman penetrated the official Fedspeak to expose what was really going on. After a probing investigation of the Federal Reserve, he charged:

The Open Market Committee of the Federal Reserve System . . . has the power to obtain, and does obtain, the printed money of the United States -- Federal Reserve Notes -- from the Bureau of Engraving and Printing, and exchanges these printed notes, which of course are not interest bearing, for United States government obligations that are interest bearing. After making the exchange, the interest bearing obligations are retained by the 12 Federal Reserve banks and the interest collected annually on these government obligations goes into the funds of the 12 Federal Reserve banks. . . . These funds are expended by the system without an adequate accounting to the Congress.[3]

The Open Market Committee was the group formed in 1934 to take charge of "open market operations," the Fed's buying and selling of government securities (the bills, bonds and notes by which the government borrows money). Then as now, the Open Market Committee acquired Federal Reserve Notes from the Federal Bureau of Engraving and Printing, essentially for the cost of printing them. The average cost today is about 4 cents per bill.[4] Then in deft card-shark fashion, these dollar bills are swapped for an equivalent stack of notes labeled Treasury securities. Turning Treasury securities (or debt) into "money" (Federal Reserve Notes) is called "monetizing" the debt. The government owes this money back to the Fed, although the Fed has advanced nothing but printed paper to earn it. In a revealing treatise called A Primer on Money, Patman concluded:

*The Federal Reserve is a total moneymaking machine.* It can issue money or checks. And it never has a problem of making its checks good because it can obtain the $5 and $10 bills necessary to cover its check simply by asking the Treasury Department's Bureau of Engraving to print them.[5]

This statement was confirmed by Marriner Eccles, then Chairman of the Federal Reserve Board, in testimony before the House Banking and Currency Committee in 1935. Eccles acknowledged:

> In purchasing offerings of Government bonds, the banking system as a whole creates new money, or bank deposits. When the banks buy a billion dollars of Government bonds as they are offered . . . the banks credit the deposit account of the Treasury with a billion dollars. They debit their Government bond account a billion dollars; or *they actually create, by a bookkeeping entry, a billion dollars.*[6]

Economist John Kenneth Galbraith would later comment, "The process by which banks create money is so simple that the mind is repelled." The mind is repelled because the process is sleight of hand. It is also completely foreign to what we have been taught. In a phenomenon called "cognitive dissonance," we can read the words and still doubt whether we have read them right. To make sure that we have, then, here is another credible source --

In 1993, National Geographic Magazine published an article by assistant editor Peter White titled "Do Banks Really Create Money Out of Thin Air?" White began by observing that 92 percent of the money supply consists, not of bills or coins, but of checkbook and other non-tangible money. To find out where this money comes from, he asked a Federal Reserve official, who said that every day, the Federal Reserve Bank of New York buys U.S. government securities from major banks and brokerage houses. That's if the Fed wants to expand the money supply. If it wants to contract the money supply, it sells government securities. White wrote:

> Say today the Fed buys a hundred million dollars in Treasury bills from those big securities dealers, who keep a stock of them to trade with the public. When the Fed pays the dealers, a hundred million dollars will thereby be added to the country's money supply, because the dealers will be credited that amount by their banks, which now have that much more on deposit. But where did the Fed get that hundred million dollars? "We created it," a Fed official tells me. He means that anytime the central bank writes a check, so to speak, it creates money. "It's money that didn't exist before," he says. Is there any limit on that? "No limit. Only the good judgement and the conscience of the responsible Federal Reserve people." And where did they get this vast authority? "It was delegated to them in the Federal

Reserve Act of 1913, based on the Constitution, Article I, Section 8. 'Congress shall have the power . . . to coin money, regulate the value thereof . . . .'"[7]

Andrew Jackson would probably have said "vipers and thieves!" He stressed that the Constitution gives Congress the power only to *coin* money; and if "coining" money means "creating" money, it gives that power *only* to Congress. The Tenth Amendment provides that powers not delegated to the United States or forbidden to the States are reserved to the States or the people. In 1935, the U.S. Supreme Court held that "Congress may not abdicate or transfer to others its legitimate functions." (Schechter Pultry v. U.S., 29 U.S. 495, 55 U.S. 837, 842.)

## The Real Windfall

After relentless agitation by Patman's Committee, the Fed finally agreed to rebate most of the interest it received on its government bonds to the U.S. Treasury. Congressman Jerry Voorhis, another early Fed watchdog, said that the agreement was a tacit admission that the Fed wasn't entitled to interest. It wasn't entitled to interest because its own money wasn't being lent.[8] Fed apologists today argue that since the interest, or most of it, is now rebated to the government, no net advantage has accrued to the Fed.[9] But that argument overlooks a far greater windfall to the banks that are the Fed's owners and real constituents. The bonds that have been acquired essentially for free become the basis of the Fed's "reserves" – the phantom money that is advanced many times over by commercial banks in the form of loans.

We've seen that virtually all money in circulation today has come from government debt that been "monetized" by the Federal Reserve and the banking system.[10] In 2006, M3 (the broadest measure of the money supply) was nearly $10 trillion, while the Treasury securities held by the Federal Reserve came to about $1.1 trillion. That means the money supply has expanded by a factor of about 10 for every dollar of federal debt monetized by the Federal Reserve, and *all of this monetary expansion consists of loans on which the banks have been paid interest.*[11] It is *this* interest, not the interest paid to the Federal Reserve, that is the real windfall to the banks – this and the fact that the banks now have a money-making machine to back them up whenever they get in trouble with their "fractional reserve" lending scheme. The Jekyll Island plan worked beautifully: the bankers succeeded in creating a secret source of unlimited funds that could be tapped into whenever they were caught short-handed. And to make sure their scheme remained a secret, they concealed this money machine in obscure Fedspeak that made the whole subject seem dull and incomprehensible to the uninitiated, and was misleading even to people who thought they understood it.

In <u>The Creature from Jekyll Island</u>, Ed Griffin writes that "modern money is a grand illusion conjured by the magicians of finance and politics." The function of the Federal Reserve, he says, "is *to convert debt into money*. It's just that simple." The mechanism may seem complicated at first, but "it is simple if one remembers that the process is not intended to be logical but to confuse be and deceive." The process by which the Fed converts debt into money begins after the government's bonds are offered to the public at auction. Griffin explains:

> [T]he Fed takes all the government bonds which the public does not buy and writes a check to Congress in exchange for them . . . . *There is no money to back up this check*. These fiat dollars are created on the spot for that purpose. *By calling these bonds "reserves," the Fed then uses them as the base for creating 9 additional dollars for every dollar created for the bonds themselves.* The money created for the bonds is spent by the government, whereas the money created on top of those bonds is the source of all the bank loans made to the nation's businesses and individuals. *The result of this process is the same as creating money on a printing press, but the illusion is based on an accounting trick rather than a printing trick.*[12]

The result is the same with this difference: in the minds of most people, printing press money is created by the government. *The accounting trick that generates 99 percent of the U.S. money supply today is the sleight of hand of private banks.*

## The Magical Multiplying Reserves

The shell game devised by the seventeenth century goldsmiths is now called "fractional reserve" banking. The fraction of a bank's outstanding loans that must be held in "reserve" is called the "reserve requirement" and is set by the Fed. The website of the Federal Reserve Bank of New York (FRBNY) explains:

> Reserve requirements . . . are computed as percentages of
> deposits that banks must hold as vault cash or on deposit at a
> Federal Reserve Bank. . . . As of December 2006, the reserve
> requirement was 10% on transaction deposits, and there were
> zero reserves required for time deposits. . . . If the reserve
> requirement is 10%, for example, a bank that receives a $100
> deposit may lend out $90 of that deposit. If the borrower then
> writes a check to someone who deposits the $90, the bank
> receiving that deposit can lend out $81. As the process
> continues, the banking system can expand the initial deposit of
> $100 into a maximum of $1,000 of money ($100+$90+81+
> $72.90+ . . . =$1,000).[13]

It sounds reasonable enough, but let's have a closer look. First,
some definitions: a *time deposit* is a bank deposit that cannot be withdrawn before a date specified at the time of deposit. *Transaction deposit* is a term used by the Federal Reserve for "checkable" deposits
(deposits on which checks can be drawn) and other accounts that can
be used directly as cash without withdrawal limits or restrictions.
Transaction deposits are also called *demand deposits*: they can be withdrawn on demand at any time without notice. All checking accounts
are demand deposits. Some savings accounts require funds to be kept
on deposit for a minimum length of time, but most savings accounts
also permit unlimited access to funds.[14] As long as enough money is
kept in "reserve" to satisfy depositors who come for their money,
"transaction deposits" can be lent many times over. The 90 percent
the bank lends is redeposited, and 90 percent of that is relent, in a
process that repeats about 20 times, until the $100 becomes $1,000.

But wait. These funds belong to the depositors and must remain
available for their own use. How can the money be available to the
depositor and lent out at the same time? Obviously, it can't. The
money is basically counterfeited in the form of loans. The 10 percent
reserve requirement harkens back to the seventeenth century
goldsmiths, who found through trial and error that depositors
collectively would not come for more than about 10 percent of their
money at one time. The money could therefore be lent 9 times over
without anyone being the wiser. Today the scheme gets obscured
because many banks are involved, but the collective result is the same:
when the banks receive $1 million in deposits, they can "lend" not
just $900,000 (90 percent of $1 million) but *$9 million* in computer-
generated funds. As we'll see shortly, "reserves" are being phased

out, so the multiple is actually higher than that; but to keep it simple, we'll use that figure. Here is a hypothetical case for illustration:

You live in a small town with only one bank. You sell your house for $100,000 and deposit the money into your checking account at the bank. The bank then advances 90 percent of this sum, or $90,000, to Miss White to buy a house from Mr. Black. The bank proceeds to collect from Miss White both the interest and the principal on this loan. Assume the prevailing interest rate is 6.25 percent. Interest at 6.25 percent on $90,000 over the life of a 30-year mortgage comes to $109,490. Miss White thus winds up owing $199,490 in principal and interest on the loan – not to you, whose money it allegedly was in the first place, but to the bank.[i] Legally, Miss White has title to the house; but the bank becomes the effective owner until she pays off her mortgage.

Mr. Black now takes the $90,000 Miss White paid him for his house and deposits it into his checking account at the town bank. The bank adds $90,000 to its reserve balance at its Federal Reserve bank and advances 90 percent of this sum, or $81,000, to Mrs. Green, who wants to buy a house from Mr. Gray. Over 30 years, Mrs. Green owes the bank $81,000 in principal plus $98,541 in interest, or $179,541; and the bank has become the effective owner of another house until the loan is paid off.

Mr. Gray then deposits Mrs. Green's money into his checking account. The process continues until the bank has "lent" $900,000, on which it collects $900,000 in principal and $985,410 in interest, for a total of $1,885,410. The bank has thus created $900,000 out of thin air and has acquired effective ownership of a string of houses, at least temporarily, *all from an initial $100,000 deposit*; and it is owed $985,410 in interest on this loan. The $900,000 principal is extinguished by an entry on the credit side of the ledger when the loans are paid off; but the other half of this conjured $2 million – the interest – remains solidly in the coffers of the bank, and if any of the borrowers should default on their loans, the bank becomes the owner of the mortgaged property.

---

[i]   In practice, you probably wouldn't keep $100,000 in a checking account that paid no interest; you would invest it somewhere. But when the bank makes loans based on its collective checking account deposits, the result is the same: the bank keeps the interest.

Instead of houses, let's try it with the $100 million in Treasury bills bought by the Fed in a single day in the <u>National Geographic</u> example, using $100 million in book-entry money created out of thin air. At a reserve requirement of 10 percent, $100 million can generate $900 million in loans. If the interest rate on these loans is 5 percent, the $900 million will return $45 million the first year in interest to the banks that wrote the loans. At compound interest, then, a $100 million "investment" in money created out of thin air is doubled in about two years!

## To Audit or Abolish?

The Fed reports that 95 percent of its profits are now returned to the U.S. Treasury.[15] But a review of its balance sheet, which is available on the Internet, shows that it reports as profits *only* the interest received from the federal securities it holds as reserves.[16] No mention is made of the much greater windfall afforded to the banks that are the Fed's corporate owners, which use the securities as the "reserves" that get multiplied many times over in the form of loans. The Federal Reserve maintains that it is now audited every year by Price Waterhouse and the Government Accounting Office (GAO), an arm of Congress; but some functions remain off limits to the GAO, including its transactions with foreign central banks and its open market operations (the operations by which it creates money with accounting entities).[17] Thus the Fed's most important – and most highly suspect – functions remain beyond public scrutiny.

Wright Patman proposed cleaning up the books by abolishing the Open Market Committee and nationalizing the Federal Reserve, reclaiming it as a truly *federal* agency under the auspices of Congress. The dollars the Fed created would then be government dollars, issued debt-free without increasing the debt burden of the country. Jerry Voorhis also advocated skipping the middleman and letting the government issue its own money. But neither proposal was passed by Congress. Rather, Patman was removed as head of the House Banking and Currency Committee, after holding that position for twelve years; and Voorhis lost the next California Congressional election to Richard Nixon, after being targeted by an aggressive smear campaign financed by the American Bankers' Association.[18]

## The Illusion of Reserves

At one time, a bank's "reserves" consisted of gold bullion, which was kept in a vault and was used to redeem paper banknotes presented by depositors. The "fractional reserve" banking scheme concealed the fact that there was insufficient gold to redeem all the notes laying claim to it. Today, Federal Reserve Notes cannot be redeemed for anything but more paper notes when the old ones wear out; yet the banks continue to operate on the "fractional reserve" system, lending out many times more money than they actually have on "reserve."

The reserve requirement itself is becoming obsolete. According to a press release issued by the Federal Reserve Board on October 4, 2005, no reserves would be required in 2006 for the first $7.8 million of net transaction accounts. At a zero percent reserve, there is no limit to the number of times deposits can be relent. There is really no limit in any case, as the New York Fed acknowledged on its website. After explaining the exercise in which a $100 deposit becomes $1,000 in loan money, it obliquely conceded:

> In practice, the connection between reserve requirements and money creation is not nearly as strong as the exercise above would suggest. [T]he Federal Reserve operates in a way that permits banks to acquire the reserves they need to meet their requirements from the money market, so long as they are willing to pay the prevailing price (the federal funds rate) for borrowed reserves. Consequently, *reserve requirements currently play a relatively limited role in money creation in the United States.*

It seems that banks can conjure up as much money as they want, whenever they want. If a bank runs out of reserves, it can just borrow them from the Fed, which creates them out of thin air in "open market operations." That is how it seems; and to confirm that we have the facts straight, we'll turn to that most definitive of all sources, the Federal Reserve itself . . . .

# Chapter 18
# A LOOK INSIDE
# THE FED'S PLAYBOOK

*"I guess I should warn you, if I turn out to be particularly clear,
you've probably misunderstood what I've said."*

– *Federal Reserve Chairman Alan Greenspan*
*in a speech to the Economic Club of New York, 1988*

"Modern Money Mechanics" is a revealing Federal Reserve manual that is now out of print, perhaps because it revealed too much; but it is still available on the Internet.[1] It was published in 1963 by the Chicago Federal Reserve, which (as part of the Federal Reserve system) naturally wrote in Fedspeak. Some concentration is therefore needed to decipher it, but the effort rewards the diligent with a gold mine of insider information. The booklet begins, "The actual process of money creation takes place primarily in banks." The process of money creation occurs, it says, "when the proceeds of loans made by the banks are credited to borrowers' accounts." It goes on:

> Of course, [banks] do not really pay out loans from the money they receive as deposits. If they did this, no additional money would be created. What they do when they make loans is to accept promissory notes in exchange for credits to the borrowers' transaction accounts. . . . [T]he deposit credits constitute new additions to the total deposits of the banking system.

The bank's "loans" are not recycled deposits of other customers; they are just "deposit credits" advanced against the borrower's promise to repay. The booklet continues, "banks can build up deposits by increasing loans and investments." They can build up deposits *either* by making loans of accounting-entry funds *or* by investing newly-created deposits for their own accounts. (More on this arresting revelation later.) The Chicago Fed then asks, "*If deposit money can be created so easily, what is to prevent banks from making too much?*" It answers its own question:

> [A bank] must maintain legally required reserves, in the form of vault cash and/or balances at its Federal Reserve Bank, equal to a prescribed percentage of its deposits. . . . [E]ach bank must maintain . . . reserve balances at their Reserve Bank and vault cash which together are equal to its required reserves . . . .

The implication is that the bank's "reserves" are drawn from its depositors' accounts, but a close reading reveals that this is not the case. The required reserves are made up of whatever vault cash the bank has on hand *and* something called "reserve balances maintained at their Reserve Bank." What are these? Under the heading "Where Do Bank Reserves Come From?", the Chicago Fed states:

> Increases or decreases in bank reserves can result from a number of factors discussed later in this booklet. From the standpoint of money creation, however, the essential point is that the reserves of banks are, for the most part, liabilities of the Federal Reserve Banks, and net changes in them are largely determined by actions of the Federal Reserve System. . . . *One of the major responsibilities of the Federal Reserve System is to provide the total amount of reserves consistent with the monetary needs of the economy at reasonably stable prices.*

If the "reserves" had come from the depositors, the Fed would not have the "responsibility" of providing them "at reasonably stable prices." They would already be in the banks' vaults or on their books. Recall what the New York Fed said on its website: "[T]he Federal Reserve operates in a way that permits banks to acquire the reserves they need to meet their requirements from the money market, *so long as they are willing to pay the prevailing price (the federal funds rate) for borrowed reserves.*"

In short, banks don't have to *have* the money they lend before they make loans, because the Fed will "provide" the necessary reserves by making them available at the federal funds rate. The banks borrow from the Fed at a low interest rate and extend credit to their customers at a higher rate. Where the sleight of hand comes in is that *the Fed itself creates the reserves out of thin air.* (More on this shortly.)

That is one bit of sleight of hand. Another is that the loan of newly-created money becomes a *deposit*, which the bank or its fellow banks can then relend many times over, multiplying the money supply and charging interest each time. A source that explains this in easier language than the Fed itself is the informative website by William Hummel cited earlier, called "Money: What It Is, How It Works." He writes:

Banks with adequate capital can and do lend without adequate reserves on hand. If a bank has a creditworthy borrower and a profitable opportunity, *it will issue the loan and then borrow the required reserves in the money market.*[2]

He uses the example of a bank with $100 million in demand deposits and $10 million in reserves – just enough reserves to meet the reserve ratio of 10 percent (the approximate amount needed to pay any depositors who might come for their money). The bank plans to issue new mortgage loans totaling $5 million for a new housing development. Can it do so before it acquires more reserves? Hummel says it can. Why? *Because the bank is allowed to enter the newly-created loan money as a deposit on its books.* The bank's assets and liabilities increase by the same amount, leaving its reserve requirement unaffected. When the borrower spends the money, it is transferred out of the bank into other banks, so the originating bank has to come up with new money to meet its reserve requirement; but it can do this by borrowing the money from the Fed or some other source in the money market. Meanwhile, the banks that got the $5 million now have new deposits against which they too can make new loans. Since they also need to keep only 10 percent in reserve to back these new deposits, they can lend out $4,500,000, increasing the money supply by that amount; and so the process continues.[3]

So let's review: the bank lends money it doesn't have, and this loan of new money becomes a "deposit," balancing its books. When the borrower spends the money, the bank brings its reserves back up to 10 percent by borrowing from the Fed or other sources. As for the Fed itself, it can't run out of reserves either, because that is what "open market operations" are all about. Like Santa Claus, the Fed can't run out of reserves because it *makes* the reserves.

How this is done was explained by the Chicago Fed with the following hypothetical case. If it seems hard to follow or makes no sense, don't worry; it *is* hard to follow and it *doesn't* make sense, except as sleight of hand. The important line is the last one: "These reserves . . . are matched by . . . *deposits that did not exist before.*" The Chicago Fed states:

> How do open market purchases add to bank reserves and deposits? Suppose the Federal Reserve System, through its trading desk at the Federal Reserve Bank of New York, buys $10,000 of Treasury bills from a dealer in U. S. government securities. In today's world of computerized financial transac-

tions, *the Federal Reserve Bank pays for the securities with a "telectronic" check drawn on itself.* Via its "Fedwire" transfer network, the Federal Reserve notifies the dealer's designated bank (Bank A) that payment for the securities should be credited to (deposited in) the dealer's account at Bank A. At the same time, Bank A's reserve account at the Federal Reserve is credited for the amount of the securities purchase. The Federal Reserve System has added $10,000 of securities to its assets, which it has paid for, in effect, by *creating* a liability on itself in the form of bank reserve balances. *These reserves on Bank A's books are matched by $10,000 of the dealer's deposits that did not exist before.*

What happens after that was explained in an article by Murray Rothbard titled "Fractional Reserve Banking," using a hypothetical that again is a bit easier to follow than the Fed's. In his example, $10 million in Treasury bills are bought by the Fed from a securities dealer, who deposits the money in Chase Manhattan Bank. The $10 million are created with accounting entries, increasing the money supply by that sum. But this, says Rothbard, is "only the beginning of the inflationary, counterfeiting process":

> For Chase Manhattan is delighted to get a check on the Fed, and rushes down to deposit it in its own checking account at the Fed, which now increases by $10,000,000. But this checking account constitutes the "reserves" of the banks, which have now increased across the nation by $10,000,000. But this means that Chase Manhattan can create deposits based on these reserves, and that, as checks and reserves seep out to other banks . . . , each one can add its inflationary mite, until the banking system as a whole has increased its demand deposits by $100,000,000, ten times the original purchase of assets by the Fed. *The banking system is allowed to keep reserves amounting to 10 percent of its deposits, which means that the "money multiplier" – the amount of deposits the banks can expand on top of reserves – is 10.* A purchase of assets of $10 million by the Fed has generated very quickly a tenfold, $100,000,000 increase in the money supply of the banking system as a whole. Interestingly, *all economists agree on the mechanics of this process* even though they of course disagree sharply on the moral or economic evaluation of that process.[4]

In order to pull all this off, the Fed has had to alter the meaning of certain words. "Reserves" are not what the word implies – money kept in a safe to pay claimants. Reserves are accounting entries at

Federal Reserve Banks that allow commercial banks to make many times those sums in loans. In an article titled "Money and Myths," Carmen Pirritano writes that a "reserve account" is basically a second set of books kept at the Federal Reserve Bank. Thus in the Chicago Fed's example, the dealer acquired federal securities from the government and tendered them to the Federal Reserve, which "paid" by crediting the dealer's account, causing new money to magically appear as numbers at the dealer's bank. This new "deposit" was then added to the bank's "reserve balance" at its local branch of the Federal Reserve. These reserves were not "real" money kept at the commercial bank for paying depositors. They existed *only* as a liability on the Federal Reserve Bank's books. Pirritano maintains that the reserve accounts kept at the Federal Reserve Bank are just a system for keeping track of how much money commercial banks create. There is no limit to this money expansion, which banks can engage in to whatever extent they can get customers to take out new loans. He observes:

> "The Federal Reserve System Purposes and Functions" states that the Federal Reserve requires that *all* banks (as of 1980) must "hold a certain fraction of their deposits in reserve, either as cash in their vaults or as non-interest-bearing balances at the Federal Reserve." The term "non-interest-bearing balances at the Federal Reserve" means that "Reserve Accounts" are nothing more than bookkeeping tallies representing the portion of the member banks' deposit account balances that may be used as a base to extend new money creation credit. Member banks do *not* physically transfer ("deposit") a percentage of their demand deposit account balances to their Reserve accounts at their Federal Reserve Bank branch. . . . *I believe these "accounts" were designed to further the appearance of a gigantic system of "reserves" mandated by the Federal Reserve System to "force" prudent banking.*[5]

Put less charitably, reserve accounts are a smoke and mirrors accounting trick concealing the fact that banks create the money they lend out of thin air, borrowing any "reserves" they need from the Fed, which also creates the money out of thin air. Disturbing enough, but there is more . . . .

## How Banks Create Their Own Investment Money

The Chicago Fed continues with its example involving Bank A:

> If the process ended here, there would be no "multiple" expansion, i.e., deposits and bank reserves would have changed by the same amount. However, banks are required to maintain reserves equal to only a fraction of their deposits. Reserves in excess of this amount may be used to increase earning assets – *loans and investments.*

Recall that the deposits in Bank A "did not exist" until the Fed conjured them up, something it did by "creating a liability on itself in the form of bank reserve balances." At a 10 percent reserve requirement, 10 percent of these newly-created deposits are kept in "reserve." The other 90 percent are "excess reserves," which "may be used to increase earning assets," including not only "loans" but "investments" that pay a return to the bank.

The Chicago Fed states that if business is active, the banks with excess reserves will probably have opportunities to lend these reserves. But if the banks do not have willing borrowers (indeed, even if they do), they can choose to invest the money. In effect, they are borrowing money created by themselves with accounting entries and investing it for their own accounts. The Chicago Fed states:

> *Deposit expansion can proceed from investments as well as loans.* Suppose that the demand for loans . . . is slack. *These banks would then probably purchase securities.* . . . [Most] likely, these banks would purchase the securities through dealers, *paying for them with checks on themselves or on their reserve accounts.* These checks would be deposited in the sellers' banks. . . . *[T]he net effects on the banking system are identical with those resulting from loan operations.*

The net effect when banks make loans is to expand their deposits, so this must also be the net effect when they invest the money for their own accounts: they expand the level of deposits, or create new money. How much of a bank's allotted "reserve balance" is invested rather than lent? Pirritano cites "Federal Reserve Statistical Release (H.8)," detailing the assets and liabilities of domestic banks, which puts the ratio of loans to investments at 7 to 3. Thus in the hypothetical given by Murray Rothbard, in which $10 million was created by the Fed and was fanned into $100 million as the money passed through the banking system, the $100 million would have created $70 million in loans to customers and *$30 million in investments for the banks.*

## Banks as Traders

Commercial banks have traditionally invested conservatively in government securities, but that is not true of investment banks. The Glass-Steagall Act requiring commercial banking and investment banking to be conducted in separate institutions was repealed in 1999, following assurances that these banking functions would be separated by "Chinese walls" within the organizations.[i] Chinese walls, however, are paper thin, and there are significant differences between commercial and investment banks that make them uneasy partners.[6] Commercial banks have traditionally taken in deposits, issued commercial loans, and otherwise served their customers. Investment banks are not allowed to take in deposits or make commercial loans; they raise money for their clients by overseeing stock issuance and sales. Their more important business today, however, is something called "proprietary trading." An entry by that name in Wikipedia[ii] defines *proprietary trading* as "a term used in investment banking to describe when a bank trades stocks, bonds, options, commodities, or other items *with its own money as opposed to its customers' money, so as to make a profit for itself.*" The entry states:

> Although investment banks are usually defined as businesses which assist other business in raising money in the capital markets (by selling stocks or bonds), *in fact most of the largest investment banks make the majority of their profit from trading activities.*

The potential for conflicts of interest was discussed in a June 2006 article by Emily Thornton in Business Week Online titled "Inside Wall

---

i    "Chinese walls" are defined in Wikipedia as "information barriers implemented in firms to separate and isolate persons within a firm who make investment decisions from persons within a firm who are privy to undisclosed material information which may influence those decisions . . . to safeguard inside information and ensure there is no improper trading."

ii    The reliability of Wikipedia has been questioned, since it is researched by volunteers, but defenders note that inaccurate information is quickly corrected by other researchers; and it is an accessible online encyclopedia that gives information not readily found elsewhere.

Street's Culture of Risk: Investment Banks Are Placing Bigger Bets Than Ever and Beating the Odds – At Least for Now." After discussing the new boom in bank trading, Thornton observed that investment bank wizards have so consistently beaten the odds that "[s]uspicions are rising that bank traders are acting on nonpublic information gleaned from their clients." Trading for the banks' own accounts has been criticized not only for suspected ethical violations but because it exposes the banks to enormous risks. Thornton writes:

> This trading boom, *fueled by cheap money*, is fundamentally different from the ones of the past. When traders last ruled Wall Street, during the mid-'90s, few banks put much of their own balance sheets at risk; most acted mainly as brokers, arranging trades between clients. *Now, virtually all banks are making huge bets with their own assets on many more fronts, and using vast sums of borrowed money to jack up the risk even more.*

Where do these "vast sums of borrowed money" come from? Although investment banks are not allowed to take in deposits or make loans of imaginary money based on "fractional reserves," commercial banks are. Now that the lines between these two forms of banking have become blurred, it is not hard to envision bank traders having ready access to some very favorable loans.

Thornton continues:

> [M]any investment banks now do more trading than all but the biggest hedge funds, those lightly regulated investment pools that almost brought down the financial system in 1998 when one of them, Long-Term Capital Management, blew up. *What's more, banks are jumping into the realm of private equity, spending billions to buy struggling businesses as far afield as China that they hope to turn around and sell at a profit.*

*Equity* is ownership interest in a corporation, and the *equity market* is the stock market. These banks are not just investing in short-term Treasury bills on which they collect a modest interest, as commercial banks have traditionally done. *They are buying whole businesses with borrowed money, and they are doing it not to develop the productive potential of the business but just to reap a quick profit on resale.*

Leading the attack in this lucrative new field, says Thornton, is the very successful investment bank Goldman Sachs, headed until recently by Henry Paulson Jr. Paulson left the firm to become U.S. Treasury Secretary in June 2006, but neither Goldman nor its cronies are showing signs of easing up:

With $25 billion of capital under management, Goldman's private equity arm itself is *one of the largest buyout firms in the world* . . . . All of them are ramping up teams of so-called proprietary traders *who play with the banks' own money.* . . . Banks are paying up, offering some traders $10 million to $20 million a year.[7]

The practice of buying whole corporations in order to bleed them of their profits has been given the less charitable name of "vulture capitalism." Why the term fits was underscored in a January 2006 article by Sean Corrigan called "Speculation in the Late Empire":

When the buy-out merchants and private equity partnerships can borrow what are effectively limitless sums of cheap, tax-advantaged debt with which to buy out corporate shareholders (not all of them willing sellers, remember); when they can then proceed to ruin the target business' balance sheet in a flash, by ordering payment of special dividends and by weighing it down with junk debt, in order to return their funds at the earliest juncture; when their pecuniary motives are mollified by so little pretense of undertaking any genuine entrepreneurial restructuring with which to enhance economic efficiency; when they can rake in an even greater haul of loot by selling the firm smartly back to the next debt-swollen suckers in line (probably into the little man's sagging pension funds via the inevitable, well-hyped IPO[iii]); when they can scatter fees and commissions (and often political "contributions") liberally along the way – then we're clearly well past the point of reason or endorsement.[8]

Noting the "outrageously skewed" incomes made by bank traders at the top of the field (including Henry Paulson, who made over $30 million at Goldman Sachs the previous year), Corrigan asked rhetorically:

Why train to be a farmer or a pharmacologist, when you can join Merrill Lynch and become a millionaire in your mid-20s, using someone else's "capital" and benefiting from being an insider in the great Ponzi scheme in which we live?

All major markets are now thought to be subject to the behind-the-scenes maneuverings of big financial players, and these manipulations are being done largely with what Corrigan calls "phantom money." A June 2006 article in <u>Barron's</u> noted that the

---

[iii] Initial public offering.

bond market today is dominated by banks and government entities, and that they are not buying the bonds for their interest income. Rather, *"The reality is that [they] are only interested in currency manipulation and market contrivement."*[9]

To understand what is really going on behind the scenes, we need to understand the tools used by Big Money to manipulate markets. In the next chapter, we'll take a look at the investment vehicle known as the "short sale," which underlies many of those more arcane tools known as "derivatives." A massive wave of short selling was blamed for turning the Roaring Twenties into the Great Depression, and the same sort of manipulations are going on today under different names.

# Chapter 19
# BEAR RAIDS AND SHORT SALES: DEVOURING CAPITAL MARKETS

*"Lions, and tigers, and bears – oh my!  Lions, and tigers, and bears!"*

– Dorothy and her friends lost in the forest, <u>The Wizard of Oz</u>

The "Crash" that initiated the Great Depression wasn't a one-time occurrence.  It continued for nearly four years after 1929, stoked by speculators who made huge profits not only on the market's meteoric rise but as it was plummeting.  "Unrestrained financial exploitations have been one of the great causes of our present tragic condition," Roosevelt complained in 1933.  A four-year industry-wide "bear raid" reduced the Dow Jones Industrial Average (a leading stock index) to only 10 percent of its former value.  A *bear raid* is the practice of targeting stock for take-down, either for quick profits or for corporate takeover.  Whenever the market decline slowed after the 1929 crash, speculators would step in to sell millions of dollars worth of stock they did not own but had ostensibly borrowed just for purposes of sale, using the device known as the "short sale."  When done on a large enough scale, short selling can actually force prices down, allowing assets to be picked up very cheaply.

Here is how it works: stock prices are set on the trading floor by traders (those people you see wildly yelling, waving and signaling to each other on TV), whose job is to match buyers with sellers.  Short sellers willing to sell at any price are matched with the low-ball buy orders.  Since stock prices are set according to supply and demand, when sell orders overwhelm buy orders, the price drops.  The short sellers then buy the stocks back at the lower price and pocket the difference. Today, speculators have to drop the price only enough to trigger the automatic *stop loss orders* and *margin calls*[1] of the big *mutual funds* and *hedge funds*.[2] A cascade of sell orders follows, and the price plummets.

The short sale is explained by market analyst Richard Geist using a simple analogy:

> Pretend that you borrowed your neighbor's lawn mower, which your neighbor generously says you may keep for a couple of weeks while he's on vacation. You're thinking of buying a lawn mower anyway so you've been researching the latest sales and have seen your neighbor's lawn mower on sale for $300, marked down from $500. While you're mowing your lawn, a passerby stops and offers to buy the lawn mower you're using for $450. You sell him the lawn mower, then go out and buy the same one on sale for $300 and return it to your neighbor when he returns. Only now you've made a $150 on the deal.

Applying this analogy to a hypothetical stock trade, Geist writes:

> You believe Amazon is overvalued and its price is going to fall. So as a short seller, you borrow Amazon stock which, like the lawn mower, you don't own, from a broker and sell it into the market. . . .You borrow and sell 100 shares of Amazon at $50 per share, yielding a gain, exclusive of commissions, of $5,000. Your research proves correct and a few weeks later Amazon is selling for $35 per share. You then buy 100 shares of Amazon for $3500 and return the 100 shares to the broker. You then have closed your position, and in the meantime you've made $1500.[4]

---

[i]    A *stop loss order* is an order to sell when the price reaches a certain threshold. A *margin call* is a demand by a broker to a customer trading on *margin* (trading on credit or with borrowed funds) to add funds or securities to his margin account to bring it up to the percentage of the stock price required as a down payment by federal regulations. Most traders sell rather than pay the additional money.

[ii]    A *mutual fund* is a company that brings together money from many people and invests it. *Hedge funds* are investment companies that use high-risk techniques, such as borrowing money and selling short, in an effort to make extraordinary capital gains for their investors.

## The Hazards of Analogies

It sounds harmless enough when you are borrowing your neighbor's lawn mower with his "generous permission." But when short sellers sell stock they don't own, they don't actually get the permission of the real owners; and selling your neighbor's lawn mower won't affect lawn mower prices at Sears. In the stock market, by contrast, prices fluctuate from moment to moment according to the number of shares for sale. When millions of shares are "sold" without ever leaving the possession of their real owners, these "virtual" sales can force down the price, even when there has been no change in the underlying asset to justify the drop. Indeed, this can and often does happen when the news about the stock is *good*, because speculators want to take down the price so they can buy in cheaply. The price is not responding to "free market forces." It is responding to speculators with the collusive battering power to overwhelm the market with sell orders -- orders that are actually phony, because the "sellers" don't own the stock. Like fractional reserve lending, in which the same "reserves" are lent many times over, short selling has been called a fraud, one that damages the real shareholders and the company. Analyst David Knight explains it like this:

> *Short selling is a form of counterfeiting.*[i] When a company is founded, a certain number of shares are created. The entire value of that company is represented by that fixed number of shares. When an investor buys some of those shares and leaves them registered in his broker's street name, his broker makes those same shares available for someone else to sell short. *Once sold short, there are two investors owning the same shares of stock.*
>
> The price of stock shares are set by market forces, i.e., supply and demand. When there is a fixed supply of something, the price adjusts until demand is met. But when supply is not fixed, as when something is counterfeited, supply will exceed demand and the price will fall. Price will continue to fall as long as supply continues to expand beyond demand. Furthermore, price decline is not a linear function of supply expansion. At some point, if supply continues to expand beyond demand, the "bot-

---

[i] *Counterfeit*: to make a copy of, usually with the intent to defraud; to carry on a deception.

tom will fall out of the market," and prices will plunge.[6]

The lending of shares by a broker who holds them in trust for his customers is comparable to the goldsmiths' lending of gold held in trust for his depositors. The broker's customers may have agreed to lend out their shares in the fine print of their brokerage contracts, but they are probably not aware of it. They could avoid having their shares lent out by taking physical possession of the stock; but if they leave the stock with the broker (as nearly everyone does), it is in "street name" and can be lent out and "sold" without the real owners' knowledge, although they still believe in the company and have no intention of flooding the market with their shares.

An April 2006 article in <u>Bloomberg Markets</u> highlighted another serious problem with short selling. *The short seller is actually allowed to vote the shares at shareholder meetings.* To avoid having to reveal what is going on, stock brokers send proxies to the "real" owners as well; but that means there are duplicate proxies floating around. Just as bankers get away with lending the same money over and over because they know most people won't come to collect the cash, so brokers know that many shareholders won't go to the trouble of voting their shares. When too many proxies do come in for a particular vote, however, the totals are just reduced proportionately to "fit." But that means the real votes of real stock owners may be thrown out. Hedge funds are suspected of engaging in short selling *just* to vote on particular issues in which they are interested, such as hostile corporate takeovers. Since many shareholders don't send in their proxies, interested short sellers can swing the vote in a direction that is not in the best interests of those with a real stake in the corporation.[7]

Some of the damage caused by short selling was blunted by the Securities Act of 1933, which imposed an "uptick" rule and forbade "naked" short selling. The uptick rule requires a stock's price to be higher than its previous sale price before a short sale can be made, preventing a cascade of short sales when stocks are going down; but hedge funds have managed to avoid the rule by trading offshore, where they are unregulated. (See Chapter 20.) "Naked" short selling is the practice of selling stocks short without either owning *or* borrowing them. Like many of the regulations put in place during Roosevelt's New Deal, the rule against that practice, too, has been seriously eroded.

## The Nefarious, Ubiquitous Naked Short Sale

According to a November 2005 article in Time Magazine:

[N]aked short selling is illegal, *barring certain exceptions for brokers trying to maintain an orderly market.* In naked short selling, you execute the sale without borrowing the stock. The SEC noted in a report last year the "pervasiveness" of the practice. *When not caught, this kind of selling has no limits and allows a seller to drive down a stock.*[8]

A May 2004 Dow Jones report confirmed that naked short selling is "a manipulative practice that can drive a company's stock price sharply lower."[9] The exception that has turned the rule into a sham is a July 2005 SEC ruling allowing the practice by "market makers." Market makers are the brokers who actually do most of the buying and selling of stock today. Ninety-five percent of short sales are now done by broker-dealers and market makers.[10] Market making is one of the lucrative pursuits of those ten giant U.S. banks called "money center banks," which currently hold almost half the country's total banking assets. (More on this in Chapter 34.)

A story run on FinancialWire in March 2005 underscored the pervasiveness and perniciousness of naked short selling. A man named Robert Simpson purchased all of the outstanding stock of a small company called Global Links Corporation, totaling a little over one million shares. He put all of this stock in his sock drawer, then watched as *60 million* of the company's shares traded hands over the next two days. *Every outstanding share changed hands nearly 60 times in those two days, although they were safely tucked away in his sock drawer.* The incident substantiated allegations that a staggering number of "phantom" shares are being traded around by brokers in naked short sales. Short sellers are expected to "cover" by buying back the stock and returning it to the pool, but Simpson's 60 million shares were obviously never bought back, since they were not available for purchase; and the same thing is believed to be going on throughout the market.[11]

The role of market makers is supposedly to provide liquidity in the markets, match buyers with sellers, and ensure that there will always be someone to supply stock to buyers or to take stock off sellers' hands. The exception allowing them to engage in naked short selling is justified as being necessary to allow buyers and sellers to execute their orders without having to wait for real counterparties to show up. But if you want potatoes or shoes and your local store runs out, you have to wait for delivery. Why is stock investment different? It has been argued that a highly liquid stock market is essential to ensure corporate funding and growth. That might be a good argument if the money actually went to the company, but *that is not where it goes.* The issuing company gets the money *only* when the stock is sold at an initial public offering (IPO). The stock exchange is a *secondary market* – investors buying from other stockholders, hoping they can sell the stock for more than they paid for it. Basically, it is gambling. Corporations have an easier time raising money through new IPOs if the buyers know they can turn around and sell their stock quickly; but in today's computerized global markets, real buyers should show up quickly enough without letting brokers sell stock they don't actually have to sell.

Short selling is sometimes justified as being necessary to keep a brake on the "irrational exuberance" that might otherwise drive popular stocks into dangerous "bubbles;" but if that were a necessary feature of functioning markets, short selling would also be rampant in the markets for cars, television sets and computers, which it obviously isn't. The reason it isn't is that these goods can't be "hypothecated" or duplicated on a computer screen the way stock shares can. Like fractional reserve lending, short selling is made possible because the brokers are not dealing with physical things but are simply moving numbers around on a computer monitor. Any alleged advantages to a company from the liquidity afforded by short selling are offset by the serious harm this sleight of hand can do to companies targeted for take-down in bear raids.

## The Stockgate Scandal

The destruction that naked short selling can do was exposed in a July 2004 <u>Investors Business Daily</u> articled called "Stockgate," which detailed a growing scandal involving market makers and their clearing agency the Depository Trust Company (DTC). The DTC is responsible for holding securities and for arranging for the receipt, delivery, and monetary settlement of securities transactions. The DTC is an arm of the Depository Trust and Clearing Corporation (DTCC), a private conglomerate owned collectively by broker-dealers and banks. The lawsuits called "Stockgate" alleged a coordinated effort by hedge funds, broker-deals and market makers to strip small and medium-sized public companies of their value. In comments before the Securities and Exchange Commission, C. Austin Burrell, a litigation consultant for the plaintiffs, maintained that "illegal Naked Short Selling has stripped hundreds of billions, if not *trillions*, of dollars from American investors." Over the six-year period before 2004, he said, the practice resulted in over 7,000 public companies being "shorted out of existence." Burrell maintained that as much as $1 trillion to $3 trillion may have been lost to naked short selling, and that more than 1,200 hedge fund and offshore accounts have been involved in the scandal.

The DTC's role is supposed to be to bring efficiency to the securities industry by retaining custody of some 2 million securities issues, effectively "dematerializing" most of them so that they exist only as electronic files rather than as countless pieces of paper. Once "dematerialized," the shares can be "re-hypothecated," something the Stockgate plaintiffs say is just a fancy term for "counterfeiting." They allege that the DTCC has an enormous pecuniary interest in the short selling scheme, because it gets a fee each time a journal entry is made in the "Stock Borrow Program." According to the court filings, almost one billion dollars annually are received by the DTCC for its Stock Borrow Program, in which the DTCC lends out many multiples of the actual certificates outstanding in a stock. Worse, the SEC itself reportedly has a stake in the deal, since it receives a transaction fee for each transaction facilitated by these loans of non-existent certificates. The SEC was instituted during the Great Depression specifically to prevent this sort of corrupt practice. The <u>Investors Business Daily</u> article observed:

> The largely unregulated DTC has become something of a defacto Czar presiding over the entire U.S. markets system . . . . And, as the SEC's July 28 ruling indicates, its monopoly over the electronic trading system appears even to be protected. The Depository Trust and Clearing Corp.'s two preferred shareholders are the New York Stock Exchange and the NASD, a regulatory agency that also owns the NASDAQ (NDAQ) and the embattled American Stock Exchange! . . . In an era when corporate governance is the primary interest for the SEC and state regulators, the DTCC is hardly a role model. Its 21 directors represent a virtual litany of conflict . . . . *The scandal has embroiled hundreds of companies and dozens of brokers and marketmakers, in a web of international intrigue, manipulative short-selling and cross-border actions and denials.*

A web of international intrigue and coordinated manipulation -- the image recalls the "spider webbing" described by Hans Schicht. The Stockgate plaintiffs expect to show that the "hypothecation" or counterfeiting of unregistered shares is a specific violation of the Securities Act of 1933 barring the "Sale of Unregistered Securities." Restrictions on short selling were put into the Securities Acts of 1933 and 1934, according to Burrell, because of first-hand evidence that the "*sheer scale of the crashes [after 1929] was a direct result of intentional manipulation of U.S. markets through abusive short selling.*" He maintains:

> There are numerous cases of a single share being lent ten or many more times, giving rise to the complaint that the DTCC has been electronically counterfeiting just as was done via printed certificates before the Crash. . . . Shares could be electronically created/counterfeited/kited without a registration statement being filed, and without the underlying company having any knowledge such shares are being sold or even in existence.[12]

In a website devoted to the Stockgate scandal called "The Faulking Truth," Mark Faulk wrote in April 2006 that the lawsuits and repeated calls for investigation and reform have made little headway and have been denied media attention. The SEC has imposed only minor penalties for infractions, which are perceived by the defendants as being merely a cost of doing business.[13] Like with antitrust regulation in the Gilded Age, the fox has evidently gotten inside the SEC hen house. The big money cartels the agency was designed to control are now pulling its strings.

Patrick Byrne is president of a company called Overstock.com, which has been an apparent target of naked short selling. In a slide presentation called "The Darkside of the Looking Glass: The Corruption of Our Capital Markets," he says the SEC has the data on how much naked short selling is going on, but it refuses to reveal the numbers, the players or the plays. Why? The information can hardly be called a matter of national security. The SEC calls it "proprietary information" that would reveal the short sellers' trading strategies if exposed. Byrne translates this to mean that if the thieves were found out, they could not keep stealing. Why are the regulators protecting them? He offers two theories: either they are looking forward to being thieves themselves when they go back into private practice, or they are afraid that if they blow the whistle, the whole economy will come crashing down along with the banks arranging the deals.[14]

## Financial Weapons of Mass Destruction?

Short selling is the modern version of the counterfeiting scheme used to bring down the Continental in the 1770s. When a currency is sold short, its value is diluted just as it would be if the market were flooded with paper currency. The short sale is the basis of many of those sophisticated trades called "derivatives," which have become weapons for destroying competitor businesses by parasitic mergers and takeovers. Billionaire investor Warren Buffett calls derivatives "financial weapons of mass destruction."[15] The term fits not only because these speculative bets are very risky for investors but because big institutional investors can use them to manipulate markets, cause massive currency devaluations, and force small vulnerable countries to do their bidding. Derivatives have been used to destroy the value of the national currencies of competitor countries, allowing national assets to be picked up at fire sale prices, just as the assets of the American public were snatched up by wealthy insiders after the crash of 1929. Defenders of free markets blame the targeted Third World countries for being unable to manage their economies, but the fault actually lies in a monetary scheme that opens their currencies to manipulation by foreign speculators who have access to a flood of "phantom money" borrowed into existence from foreign banks.

To clarify all this, in the next chapter we'll take another short detour into the shady world of "finance capitalism" to explore the arcane subject of derivatives and the hedge funds that have perfected their use . . . .

---

[i] The term "Third World" is now an anachronism, since there is no longer a "Second World" (the Soviet bloc). But the term is used here because it has a popularly understood meaning and is still widely used, and because the alternatives – "developing world" and "underdeveloped world" – may be misleading. Citizens of ancient Third World civilizations tend to consider their cultures more "developed" than some in the First World.

# Chapter 20
# HEDGE FUNDS
# AND DERIVATIVES:
# A HORSE OF A
# DIFFERENT COLOR

*"What kind of a horse is that? I've never seen a horse like that before!"*
*"He's the Horse of a Different Color you've heard tell about."*

– The Guardian of the Gate to Dorothy,
The Wizard of Oz

Just as a painted horse is still a horse, so derivatives and the hedge funds that specialize in them have been called merely a disguise, something designed to look "different enough from the last time so no one realizes what is happening." John Train, writing in The Financial Times, used this colorful analogy:

> [I]t is like the floor show in a seedy nightclub. A sequence of girls trots on the scene, first a collection of Apaches, then some ballerinas, then cowgirls and so forth. Only after a while does the bemused spectator realize that, in all cases, they were the same girls in slightly different costumes. . . . [T]he so-called hedge fund actually was an excuse for a margin account.[1]

*Hedge funds* are private funds that pool the assets of wealthy investors with the aim of making "absolute returns" -- making a profit whether the market goes up or down. To maximize their profits, they typically use credit borrowed against the fund's assets to "leverage" their investments. *Leverage* is the use of borrowed funds to increase purchasing power. The greater the leverage, the greater the possible gain (or loss). In futures trading, this leverage is called the *margin*. Leveraging on margin, or by borrowing money, allows investors to place many more bets than if they had paid the full price.

In the 1920s, wealthy investors engaged in "pooling" – combining their assets to influence the markets for their collective benefit. Like trusts and monopolies, pooling was considered to be a form of collusive interference with the normal market forces of supply and demand. Hedge funds are the modern-day variants of this scheme. They are usually run in off-shore banking centers such as the Cayman Islands to avoid regulation. Off-shore funds are exempt from margin requirements that restrict trading on credit, and from uptick rules that limit short sales to assets that are rising in price.

Hedge funds were originally set up to "hedge the bets" of investors, insuring against currency or interest rate fluctuations; but they quickly became instruments for manipulation and control. Many of the largest hedge funds are run by former bank or investment bank dealers, who have left with the blessings of their former employers. The banks' investment money is then placed with the hedge funds, which can operate in a more unregulated environment than the banks can themselves. *Hedge funds are now often responsible for over half the daily trading in the equity markets*, due to their huge size and the huge amounts of capital funding them.[2] That gives them an enormous amount of control over what the markets will do. In the fall of 2006, 8,282 of the 9,800 hedge funds operating worldwide were registered in the Cayman Islands, a British Overseas Territory with a population of 57,000 people. The Cayman Islands Monetary Authority gives each hedge fund at registration a 100-year exemption from any taxes, shelters the fund's activity behind a wall of official secrecy, allows the fund to self-regulate, and prevents other nations from regulating the funds.[3]

*Derivatives* are key investment tools of hedge funds. Derivatives are basically side bets that some underlying investment (a stock, commodity, market, etc.) will go up or down. They are not really "investments," because they don't involve the purchase of an asset. They are outside bets on what the asset will do. All derivatives are variations on futures trading, and all futures trading is inherently speculation or gambling. The more familiar types of derivatives include "puts" (betting the asset will go down) and "calls" (betting the asset will go up). Over 90 percent of the derivatives held by banks today, however, are "over-the-counter" derivatives – investment devices specially tailored to financial institutions, often having exotic and complex features, not traded on standard exchanges. They are not regulated, are hard to trace, and are very hard to understand.[4] Some critics say they are impossible to understand, because they were designed to be so complex and obscure as to mislead investors.[5]

At one time, tough rules regulated speculation of this sort. The Glass-Steagall Act passed during the New Deal separated commercial banking from securities trading; and the Commodities Futures Trading Commission (CFTC) was created in 1974 to regulate commodity futures and option markets and to protect market participants from price manipulation, abusive sales practices, and fraud. But the speculators have managed to get around the rules. Derivative traders claim they are not dealing in "securities" or "futures" because nothing is traded; and just to make sure, they induced Congress to empower the head of the CFTC to grant waivers to that effect, and they set up offshore hedge funds that remained small, unregistered and unregulated. They also had the Glass-Steagall Act repealed.

## A Bubble on a Ponzi Scheme

Executive Intelligence Review (EIR), The New Federalist and The American Almanac are publications associated with Lyndon LaRouche, a controversial political figure who has inspired a devoted following and a large body of research. The derivatives crisis is a favorite topic of those publications. In a 1998 interview, John Hoefle, the banking columnist for EIR, clarified the derivatives phenomenon using another colorful analogy. He said:

> During the 1980s, you had the creation of a huge financial bubble. . . . [Y]ou could look at that as fleas who set up a trading empire on a dog. . . . They start pumping more and more blood out of the dog to support their trading, and then at a certain point, the amount of blood that they're trading exceeds what they can pump from the dog, without killing the dog. The dog begins to get very sick. So being clever little critters, what they do, is they switch to trading in blood futures. And since there's no connection – they break the connection between the blood available and the amount you can trade, then you can have a real explosion of trading, and that's what the derivatives market represents. And so now you've had this explosion of trading in blood futures which is going right up to the point that now the dog is on the verge of dying. And that's essentially what the derivatives market is. *It's the last gasp of a financial bubble.*[6]

What has broken the connection between "the blood available and the amount you can trade" is that derivatives are *not* assets. They are just bets on what the asset will do, and the bet can be placed with very little "real" money down. Most of the money is borrowed from banks that create it on a computer screen as it is lent. The connection with reality has been severed so completely that the market for over-the-counter derivatives has now reached many times the money supply of the world. Since these private bets are unreported and unregulated, nobody knows exactly how much money is riding on them; but the Bank for International Settlements reported that in the first half of 2006, their "notional value" had soared to a record $370 trillion. The *notional value* of a derivative is a hypothetical number described as "the number of units of an asset underlying the contract, multiplied by the spot price of the asset." Synonyms for "notional" include "fanciful, not based on fact, dubious, imaginary." Just how fanciful these values actually are is evident in the numbers: *$370 trillion is 28 times the $13 trillion annual output of the entire U.S. economy.* In 2005, the total annual productive output of the world was only $44.4 trillion.[7] The significance of these unfathomable numbers was pondered in a September 2006 article in <u>MarketWatch</u> by Thomas Kostigen, who wrote:

> ... Considering the total value of the stock and bond markets combined amounts to only $65 trillion, *it's worth wondering how so much extra value can be squeezed out of instruments that are essentially fake.*
>
> ... Wall Street manufactures these products and trades them in a rather shadowy way that keeps the average investor in the dark. You cannot exactly look up the price of an equity derivative in your daily newspaper's stock table.
>
> ... [I]t wouldn't take all that much to create a domino effect of market mishap. And there is no net. The Securities Investor Protection Corporation, which insures brokerage accounts in the event of a brokerage-firm failure, recently announced its reserves. It has about $1.38 billion. That may sound like a lot. Compared with half a quadrillion, it's a pittance. Scary but true.[8]

How are these astronomical derivative sums even possible? The answer, again, is that derivatives are just *bets*, and gamblers can bet any amount of money they want. Gary Novak is a scientist with a website devoted to simplifying complex issues. He writes, "It's like two persons flipping a coin for a trillion dollars, and afterwards some-one owes a trillion dollars which never existed."[9]  He calls it "funny money."  Like the Mississippi Bubble, the derivatives bubble is built on something that doesn't really exist; and when the losers cannot afford to pay up on their futures bets, the scheme must collapse.  Either that, or the taxpayers will be saddled with the bill for the largest bailout in history.

In a 1994 report presented at the request of the House Committee on Banking, Finance and Urban Affairs, Christopher White used some other vivid imagery.  He said:

> The derivatives market . . . is the greatest bubble in history.  It dwarfs the Mississippi Bubble in France and the South Sea Island bubble in England.  *This bubble, like a cancer, has penetrated and taken over the entirety of our banking and credit system;* there is no major commercial bank, investment bank, mutual fund, etc. that is not dependent on derivatives for its existence.  These derivatives suck the life's blood out of our economy.  *Our farms, our factories, our nation's infrastructure, our living standards are being sucked dry to pay off interest payments, dividend yields as well as other earnings on the bubble.*[10]

How speculation in derivatives draws much-needed capital away from domestic productivity was explained by White with another analogy:

> It would be like going to the horse races to bet, not on the race, but on the size of the pot. Who would care about what's involved with getting the runners to the starting gate?

Since the gamblers don't care who wins, they aren't interested in feeding the horses or hiring stable hands.  They are only interested in money making money.  Today more money can be had at less risk by speculation in derivatives than by investing in the growth of a business, and this is particularly true if you are a very big bank with the ability to influence the way the bet goes.  The Office of the Comptroller of the Currency reported that in mid-2006, there were close to 9,000 commercial and savings banks in the United States.  However, 97 percent of U.S. bank-held derivatives were concentrated in the hands of just five banks; and topping the list were JPMorgan Chase and Citibank, the citadels of the Morgan and Rockefeller empires.[11]

## Derivative Wars

The seismic power of the new derivative weapons was demonstrated in 1992, when George Soros and his giant hedge fund Quantum Group, backed by Citibank and other powerful institutional speculators, used derivatives to collapse the currencies of Great Britain and Italy in a single day. The European Monetary System was taken down with them. According to White:

> They showed that day that the speculative cancer that had been unleashed had grown beyond the point that monetary authorities could control. Farmers who have been ruined by short-sellers on commodities markets know what this is all about: *selling what you do not own in order to buy it back later for less. . . . These are instruments of financial warfare, deployed against nations and the populations in much the same way the commodity market short-seller has been deployed to bankrupt the farmer.*[12]

More than $60 billion were poured into the 1992 onslaught against European currencies, and this money was largely borrowed from giant international banks. A 1997 report by an IMF research team confirmed that to fuel a speculative attack, hedge funds needed the backing of the banks, since few private parties were willing or able to make those very large and very risky investments.[13] By 1997, hedge funds had an estimated $100 billion in assets, which could be leveraged five to ten times, giving them up to a trillion dollars in battering power. An article in The Economist observed:

> That may sound a lot, particularly if hedge funds leverage their capital. But consider that the assets of rich-country institutional investors exceed $20 trillion. *Hedge funds are bit players compared with banks, mutual or pension funds, many of which engage in exactly the same types of speculation.*[14]

George Soros raised this defense himself, when his giant hedge fund was blamed for the Asian currency crisis of 1997-98. In The Crisis of Global Capitalism, he wrote:

> There has . . . been much discussion of the role of hedge funds in destabilizing the financial system . . . I believe the discussion is misdirected. Hedge funds are not the only ones to use leverage; *the proprietary trading desks of commercial and investment banks are the main players in derivatives and swaps. . . . [H]edge funds as a group did not equal in size the proprietary trading desks of banks and brokers . . . .* [15]

Between 1996 and 2005, the number of hedge funds more than doubled, and their capital grew from $200 billion to over $1 trillion. Between 1987 and 2005, derivatives betting on international interest rate and currencies grew from $865 billion to $201.4 trillion. This explosion in derivative bets was matched on the downside by an explosion in risk. When a mega-corporation or a debtor nation goes bankrupt, the banks that are derivatively hedging its bets can go bankrupt too. When Russia defaulted on its debts, LTCM went bankrupt and threatened to take the banks with interlocking investments down with it. A November 2005 Bloomberg report warned:

> The $12.4 trillion market for credit derivatives is dominated by too few banks, making it vulnerable to a crisis if one of them fails to pay on contracts that insure creditors from companies defaulting . . . . JPMorgan Chase & Co., Deutsche Bank AG, Goldman Sachs Group Inc. and Morgan Stanley are the most frequent traders in a market where the top 10 firms account for more than two-thirds of the debt-insurance contracts bought and sold.[16]

John Hoefle warns that the dog has already run out of blood. He writes:

> We are on the verge of the biggest financial blowout in centuries, bigger than the Great Depression, bigger than the South Sea bubble, bigger than the Tulip bubble. The derivatives bubble, in which Citicorp, Morgan, and the other big New York banks are unsalvageably overexposed, is about to pop. The currency warfare operations of the Fed, George Soros, and Citicorp have generated billions of dollars in profits, but have destroyed the financial system in the process. *The fleas have killed the dog, and thus they have killed themselves.*[17]

## How Can a Bank Go Bankrupt?

But, you may ask, how *can* these banks go bankrupt? Don't they have the power to create money out of thin air? Why doesn't a bank with bad loans on its books just write them off and carry on?

British economist Michael Rowbotham explains that under the accountancy rules of commercial banks, all banks are obliged to balance their books, making their assets equal their liabilities. They can *create* all the money they can find borrowers for, but if the money isn't paid back, the banks have to record a loss; and when they cancel or write off debt, their total assets fall. To balance their books by making their assets equal their liabilities, they have to take the money either from profits or from funds invested by the bank's owners; and if the loss is more than the bank or its owners can profitably sustain, the bank will have to close its doors.[18] The bank's owners are not those multi-million dollar CEOs who control the company and pay themselves generous bonuses when they generate big new loans and fees, or the interlocking directorships that shower financial favors on their cronies. The owners are the shareholders. Like with the recent exploitation of the bankrupt energy giant Enron, the profiteers plunging ahead with reckless risk-taking are the management, who can take their winnings and walk away, leaving the shareholders and the employees holding the bag.

Individual profiteering aside, however, banks are clearly taking a risk when they extend credit. Bankers will therefore argue that they deserve the interest they get on these loans, even if they did conjure the money out of thin air. *Somebody* has to create the national money supply. Why not the bankers?

One problem with the current system is that the government itself has been seduced into borrowing money created out of nothing and paying interest on it, when the government could have created the funds itself, debt- and interest-free. In the case of government loans, the banks take virtually no risk, since the government is always good for the interest; and the taxpayers get saddled with a crippling debt that could have been avoided.

Another problem with the fractional reserve system is simply in the math. Since *all* money except coins comes into existence as a debt to private banks, and the banks create only the principal when they make loans, there is never enough money in the economy to repay principal plus interest on the nation's collective debt. When the money supply was tethered to gold, this problem was resolved through periodic waves of depression and default that wiped the slate clean and started the cycle all over again. It was a brutal system for the farmers and laborers who got wiped out, and it allowed a financier class to get progressively richer while the actual producers got progressively poorer; but it did serve to maintain a certain stability in the money supply. Today, however, the Fed has taken on the task of preventing depressions, something it does by pumping more and more credit-money into the economy by funding a massive federal debt that no one ever expects to have to repay; and all this credit-money is extended at interest. At some point, the interest bill alone must exceed the taxpayers' ability to pay it; and according to U.S. Comptroller General David Walker, that day of reckoning is only a few years away.[19] We have reached the end of the line on the debt-money train and will have to consider some sort of paradigm shift if the economy is to survive.

A third problem with the current system is that giant international banks are now major players in global markets, not just as lenders but as investors. Banks have a grossly unfair advantage in this game, because they have access to *so much* money that they can influence the outcome of their bets. If you the individual investor sell a stock short, your modest investment won't do much to influence the stock's price; but a mega-bank and its affiliates can short so much stock that the value plunges. If the bank is one of those lucky institutions considered "too big to fail," it can rest easy even if its bet does go wrong, since the FDIC and the taxpayers will bail it out from its folly. In the case of international loans, the International Monetary Fund will bail it out. In Sean Corrigan's descriptive prose:

> [W]hen financiers and traders get paid enough to make Croesus kvetch for taking wholly asymmetric risks with phantom capital – risks underwritten by government institutions like the Fed and the FDIC . . . . – this is not exactly a fair card game.[20]

For every winner in this game played with phantom capital there is a loser; and the biggest losers are those Third World countries that have been seduced into opening their financial markets to currency manipulation, allowing them to be targeted in powerful speculative raids that can and have destroyed their currencies and their economies. Lincoln's economist Henry Carey said that the twin weapons used by the British empire to colonize the world were the "gold standard" and "free trade." The gold standard has now become the petrodollar standard, as we'll see in the next chapter; but the game is basically the same: crack open foreign markets in the name of "free trade," take down the local currency, and put the nation's assets on the block at fire sale prices. The first step in this process is to induce the country to accept foreign loans and investment. The loan money gets dissipated but the loans must be repaid. In the poignant words of Brazilian politician Luis Ignacio Silva:

The Third World War has already started. . . . The war is tearing down Brazil, Latin America, and practically all the Third World. Instead of soldiers dying, there are children. It is a war over the Third World debt, one which has as its main weapon, interest, a weapon more deadly than the atom bomb, more shattering than a laser beam.[21]

The Third World is fighting back, in a war it thinks was started by the First World; but the governments of the First World are actually victims as well. As Dr. Quigley revealed, the secret of the international bankers' success is that they have managed to control national money systems while letting them *appear* to be controlled by governments.[22] The U.S. government itself is the puppet of invisible puppeteers.

# Section III

# ENSLAVED BY DEBT:
# THE BANKERS' NET SPREADS
# OVER THE GLOBE

*"If I cannot harness you," said the Witch to the Lion, speaking through the bars of the gate, "I can starve you. You shall have nothing to eat until you do as I wish."*

– <u>The Wonderful Wizard of Oz</u>,
*"The Search for the Wicked Witch"*

# Chapter 21
# GOODBYE YELLOW BRICK ROAD:
# FROM GOLD RESERVES
# TO PETRODOLLARS

*"Once," began the leader, "we were a free people, living happily in the great forest, flying from tree to tree, eating nuts and fruit, and doing just as we pleased without calling anybody master. . . . [Now] we are three times the slaves of the owner of the Golden Cap, whosoever he may be."*

– *The Wonderful Wizard of Oz,*
"The Winged Monkeys"

The Golden Cap suggested the gold that was used by international financiers to colonize indigenous populations in the nineteenth century. The gold standard was a necessary step in giving the bankers' "fractional reserve" lending scheme legitimacy, but the ruse could not be sustained indefinitely. Eleazar Lord put his finger on the problem in the 1860s. When gold left the country to pay foreign debts, the multiples of banknotes ostensibly "backed" by it had to be withdrawn from circulation as well. The result was money contraction and depression. "The currency for the time is annihilated," said Lord, "prices fall, business is suspended, debts remain unpaid, panic and distress ensue, men in active business fail, bankruptcy, ruin, and disgrace reign." Roosevelt was faced with this sort of implosion of the money supply in the Great Depression, forcing him to take the dollar off the gold standard to keep the economy from collapsing. In 1971, President Nixon had to do the same thing internationally, when foreign creditors threatened to exhaust U.S. gold reserves by cashing in their paper dollars for gold.

Between those two paradigm-changing events came John F. Kennedy, who evidently had his own ideas about free trade, the Third World, and the Wall Street debt game.

## Kennedy's Last Stand

In <u>Battling Wall Street: The Kennedy Presidency</u>, Donald Gibson contends that Kennedy was the last President to take a real stand against the entrenched Wall Street business interests. Kennedy was a Hamiltonian, who opposed the forces of "free trade" and felt that industry should be harnessed to serve the Commonwealth. He felt strongly that the country should maintain its independence by developing cheap sources of energy. The stand pitted him against the oil/banking cartel, which was bent on *raising* oil prices to prohibitive levels in order to entangle the world in debt.

Kennedy has been accused of "reckless militarism" and "obsessive anti-communism," but Gibson says his plan for neutralizing the appeal of Communism was more benign: he would have replaced colonialist and imperialist economic policies with a development program that included low-interest loans, foreign aid, nation-to-nation cooperation, and some measure of government planning. The Wall Street bankers evidently had other ideas. Gibson quotes George Moore, president of First National City Bank (now Citibank), who said:

> With the dollar leading international currency and the United States the world's largest exporter and importer of goods, services and capital, it is only natural that U.S. banks should gird themselves to play the same relative role in international finance that the great British financial institutions played in the nineteenth century.

The great British financial institutions played the role of subjugating underdeveloped countries to the position of backward exporters of raw materials. It was the sort of exploitation Kennedy's foreign policy aimed to eliminate. He crossed the banking community and the International Monetary Fund when he continued to give foreign aid to Latin American countries that had failed to adopt the bankers' policies. Gibson writes:

> Kennedy's support for economic development and Third World nationalism and his tolerance for government economic planning, even when it involved expropriation of property owned by interests in the U.S., all led to conflicts between Kennedy and

elites within both the U.S. and foreign nations.[1]

There is also evidence that Kennedy crossed the bankers by seeking to revive a silver-backed currency that would be independent of the banks and their privately-owned Federal Reserve. The matter remains in doubt, since his Presidency came to an untimely end before he could play his hand;[2] but he did authorize the Secretary of the Treasury to issue U.S. Treasury silver certificates, and he was the last President to issue freely-circulating United States Notes (Greenbacks). When Vice President Lyndon Johnson stepped into the Presidential shoes, his first official acts included replacing government-issued United States Notes with Federal Reserve Notes, and declaring that Federal Reserve Notes could no longer be redeemed in silver. New Federal Reserve Notes were released that omitted the former promise to pay in "lawful money." In 1968, Johnson issued a proclamation that even Federal Reserve Silver Certificates could not be redeemed in silver. The one dollar bill, which until then had been a silver certificate, was made a Federal Reserve note, not redeemable in any form of hard currency.[3] United States Notes in $100 denominations were printed in 1966 to satisfy the 1878 Greenback Law requiring their issuance, but most were kept in a separate room at the Treasury and were not circulated. In the 1990s, the Greenback Law was revoked altogether, eliminating even that token issuance.

## Barbarians Inside the Gates

Although the puppeteers behind Kennedy's assassination have never been officially exposed, some investigators have concluded that he was another victim of the invisible hand of the international corporate/banking/military cartel.[4] President Eisenhower warned in his 1961 Farewell Address of the encroaching powers of the military-industrial complex. To that mix Gibson would add the oil cartel and the Morgan-Rockefeller banking sector, which were closely aligned. Kennedy took a bold stand against them all.

How he stood up to the CIA and the military was revealed by James Bamford in a book called Body of Secrets, which was featured by ABC News in November 2001, two months after the World Trade Center disaster. The book discussed Kennedy's threat to abolish the CIA's right to conduct covert operations, after he was presented with secret military plans code-named "Operation Northwoods" in 1962. Drafted by America's top military leaders, these bizarre plans included proposals to kill innocent people and commit acts of terrorism in U.S. cities, in order to create public support for a war against Cuba. Actions contemplated included hijacking planes, assassinating Cuban émigrés, sinking boats of Cuban refugees on the high seas, blowing up a U.S. ship, orchestrating violent terrorism in U.S. cities, and causing U.S. military casualties, all for the purpose of tricking the American public and the international community into supporting a war to oust Cuba's then-new Communist leader Fidel Castro. The proposal stated, "We could blow up a U.S. ship in Guantanamo Bay and blame Cuba," and that "casualty lists in U.S. newspapers would cause a helpful wave of national indignation."[5]

Needless to say, Kennedy was shocked and flatly vetoed the plans. The head of the Joint Chiefs of Staff was promptly transferred to another job. The country's youngest President was assassinated the following year. Whether or not Operation Northwoods played a role, it was further evidence of an "invisible government" acting behind the scenes. His disturbing murder was a wake-up call for a whole generation of activists. Things in the Emerald City were not as green as they seemed. The Witch and her minions had gotten inside the gates.

## Bretton Woods: The Rise and Fall
## of an International Gold Standard

Lyndon Johnson was followed in the White House by Richard Nixon, the candidate Kennedy defeated in 1960. In 1971, President Nixon took the dollar off the gold standard internationally, leaving currencies to "float" in the market so that they had to compete with each other as if they were commodities. Currency markets were turned into giant casinos that could be manipulated by powerful hedge funds, multinational banks and other currency speculators. William Engdahl, author of A Century of War, writes:

> In this new phase, control over monetary policy was, in effect, privatized, with large international banks such as Citibank, Chase Manhattan or Barclays Bank assuming the role that central banks had in a gold system, but *entirely without gold.* "Market forces" now could determine the dollar. And they did with a vengeance.[6]

It was not the first time floating exchange rates had been tried. An earlier experiment had ended in disaster, when the British pound and the U.S. dollar had both been taken off the gold standard in the

1930s. The result was a series of competitive devaluations that only served to make the global depression worse. The Bretton Woods Accords were entered into at the end of World War II to correct this problem. Foreign exchange markets were stabilized with an international gold standard, in which each country fixed its currency's global price against the price of gold. Currencies were allowed to fluctuate from this "peg" only within a very narrow band of plus or minus one percent. The International Monetary Fund (IMF) was set up to establish exchange rates, and the International Bank for Reconstruction and Development (the World Bank) was founded to provide credit to war-ravaged and Third World countries.[7]

The principal architects of the Bretton Woods Accords were British economist John Maynard Keynes and Assistant U.S. Treasury Secretary Harry Dexter White. Keynes envisioned an international central bank that had the power to create its own reserves by issuing its own currency, which he called the "bancor." But the United States had just become the world's only financial superpower and was not ready for that step in 1944. The IMF system was formulated mainly by White, and it reflected the power of the American dollar. The gold standard had failed earlier because Great Britain and the United States, the global bankers, had run out of gold. Under the White Plan, gold would be backed by U.S. dollars, which were considered "as good as gold" because the United States had agreed to maintain their convertibility into gold at $35 per ounce. As long as people had faith in the dollar, there was little fear of running out of gold, because *gold would not actually be used.* Hans Schicht notes that the Bretton Woods Accords were convened by the "master spider" David Rockefeller.[8] They played right into the hands of the global bankers, who needed the ostensible backing of gold to justify a massive expansion of U.S. dollar debt around the world.

The Bretton Woods gold standard worked for a while, but it was mainly because few countries actually converted their dollars into gold. Trade balances were usually cleared in U.S. dollars, due to their unique strength after World War II. Things fell apart, however, when foreign investors began to doubt the solvency of the United States. By 1965, the Vietnam War had driven the country heavily into debt. French President Charles DeGaulle, seeing that the United States was spending far more than it had in gold reserves, demanded that it convert 300 million of France's U.S. dollar holdings into gold. That request was honored, but it was followed by one that would have "broken the bank." Great Britain, having incurred the largest monthly trade deficit in its history, had been turned down by the IMF for a $300 billion loan and had tried to cash in its gold-backed dollars for the gold they supposedly represented. The sum amounted to fully one-third the gold reserves of the United States. The problem might have been alleviated in the short term by raising the price of gold, but that was not the agenda that prevailed. The gold price was kept at $35 per ounce, forcing President Nixon to renege on the gold deal and close the "gold window" permanently. To his credit, Nixon did not take this step until he was forced into it, although it had been urged by economist Milton Friedman in 1968.[9]

The result of taking the dollar off the gold standard was to finally take the brakes off the printing presses. *Fiat* dollars could now be generated and circulated to whatever extent the world would take them. The Witches of Wall Street proceeded to build a worldwide financial empire based on a "fractional reserve" banking system that used bank-created paper dollars in place of the time-honored gold. Dollars became the reserve currency for a global net of debt to an international banking cartel. It all worked out so well for the bankers that skeptical commentators suspected it had been planned that way. Professor Antal Fekete wrote in an article in the May 2005 <u>Asia Times</u> that the removal of the dollar from the gold standard was "the biggest act of bad faith in history." He charged:

> It is disingenuous to say that in 1971 the US made the dollar "freely floating." What the US did was nothing less than *throwing away the yardstick measuring value*. It is truly unbelievable that in our scientific day and age when the material and therapeutic well-being of billions of people depends on the increasing accuracy of measurement in physics and chemistry, dismal monetary science has been allowed to push the world into the Dark Ages by abolishing the possibility of accurate measurement of value. We no longer have a reliable yardstick to measure value. There was no open debate of the wisdom, or the lack of it, to run the economy without such a yardstick.[10]

Whether unpegging the dollar from gold was a deliberate act of bad faith might be debated, but the fact remains that gold was inadequate as a global yardstick for measuring value. The price of gold fluctuated widely, and it was subject to manipulation by speculators. Gold also failed as a global reserve currency, because there was not enough gold available to do the job. If one country had an outstanding balance of payments because it had not exported enough goods to match its imports, that imbalance was corrected by transferring reserves of gold between countries; and to come up with the gold, the debtor country would cash in its U.S. dollars for the metal, draining U.S. gold reserves. It was inevitable that the U.S. government (the global banker) would eventually run out of gold. Some proposals for pegging currency exchange rates that would retain the benefits of the gold standard without its shortcomings are explored in Chapter 46.

## The International Currency Casino

If the gold standard was flawed, the system of "floating" exchange rates that replaced it was much worse, particularly for Third World countries. Currencies were now valued merely by their relative exchange rates in the "free" market. Foreign exchange markets became giant casinos, in which the investors were just betting on the relative positions of different currencies. Smaller countries were left at the mercy of the major players – whether other countries, multinational corporations or multinational banks – which could radically devalue national currencies just by selling them short on the international market in large quantities. These currency manipulations could be so devastating that they could be used to strong-arm concessions from target economies. That happened, for example, during the Asian Crisis of 1997-98, when they were used to "encourage" Thailand, Malaysia, Korea and Japan to come into conformance with World Trade Organization rules and regulations.[11] (More on this in Chapter 26.)

The foreign exchange market became so unstable that crises could result just from rumors of economic news and changes in perception. Commercial risks from sudden changes in the value of foreign currencies are now considered greater even than political or market risks for conducting foreign trade.[12] Huge derivative markets have developed to provide hedges to counter these risks. The hedgers typically place bets both ways, in order to be covered whichever way the market goes. But derivatives themselves can be very risky and expensive, and they can further compound market instability.

The system of floating exchange rates was the same system that had been tried briefly in the 1930s and had proven disastrous; but there seemed no viable alternative after the dollar went off the gold standard, so most countries agreed to it. Nations that resisted could usually be coerced into accepting the system as a condition of debt relief; and many nations needed debt relief, after the price of oil suddenly *quadrupled* in 1974. That highly suspicious rise occurred soon after an oil deal was engineered by U.S. interests with the royal family of Saudia Arabia, the largest oil producer in OPEC (the Organization of the Petroleum Exporting Countries). The deal was evidently brokered by U.S. Secretary of State Henry Kissinger. It involved an agreement by OPEC to sell oil only for dollars in return for a secret U.S. agreement to arm Saudi Arabia and keep the House of Saud in power. According to John Perkins in his eye-opening book <u>Confessions of an Economic Hit Man</u>, the arrangement basically amounted to protection money, insuring that the House of Saud would not go the way of Iran's Prime Minister Mossadegh, who was overthrown by a CIA-engineered coup in 1954.[13]

The U.S. dollar had formerly been backed by gold. It was now "backed" by oil. Every country had to acquire Federal Reserve Notes to purchase this essential commodity. Oil-importing countries around the world suddenly had to export goods to get the dollars to pay their expensive new oil import bills, diverting their productive capacity away from feeding and clothing their own people. Countries that had a "negative trade balance" because they failed to export more goods than they imported were advised by the World Bank and the IMF to unpeg their currencies from the dollar and let them "float" in the currency market. The theory was that an "overvalued" currency would then become devalued naturally until it found its "true" level. Devaluation would make exports cheaper and imports more expensive, allowing the country to build up a positive trade balance by selling more goods than it bought. That was the theory, but as Michael Rowbotham observes, it has not worked well in practice:

> There is the obvious, but frequently ignored point that, whilst lowering the value of a currency may promote exports, it will also raise the cost of imports. This of course is intended to deter imports. But if the demand for imports is "inelastic," reflecting essential goods and services, contracts and preferences, then the net cost of imports may not fall, and may actually rise. Also, whilst the volume of exports may rise, appearing to promise greater earnings, *the financial return per unit of exports will fall. . .* Time and time again, nations devaluing their currencies have seen volumes of exports and imports alter slightly, but with little overall impact on the financial balance of trade.[14]

If the benefits of letting the currency float were minor, the downsides were major: the currency was now subject to rampant manipulation by speculators. The result was a disastrous roller coaster ride, particularly for Third World economies. Today, most currency trades are done purely for speculative profit. Currencies rise or fall depending on quantities traded each day. Bernard Lietaer writes in The Future of Money:

> Your money's value is determined by a global casino of unprecedented proportions: $2 trillion are traded per day in foreign exchange markets, *100 times more than the trading volume of all the stock markets of the world combined.* Only 2% of these foreign exchange transactions relate to the "real" economy reflecting movements of real goods and services in the world, and 98% are purely speculative. This global casino is triggering the foreign exchange crises which shook Mexico in 1994-5, Asia in 1997 and Russia in 1998.[15]

The alternative to letting the currency float is for a national government to keep its currency tightly pegged to the U.S. dollar, but governments that have taken that course have faced other hazards. The currency becomes vulnerable to the monetary policies of the United States; and if the country does not set its peg right, it can still be the target of currency raids. In the interests of "free trade," the government usually agrees to keep its currency freely convertible into dollars. That means it has to stand ready to absorb any surpluses or fill any shortages in the exchange market; and to do this, it has to have enough dollars in reserve to buy back the local currency of anyone wanting to sell. If the government guesses wrong and sets the peg too high (so that its currency will not really buy as much as the equivalent in dollars), there will be "capital flight" out of the local currency into the more valuable dollars. (Indeed, speculators can induce capital flight even when the peg isn't set too high, as we'll see shortly.) Capital flight can force the government to spend its dollar reserves to "defend" its currency peg; and when the reserves are exhausted, the government will either have to default on its obligations or let its currency be devalued. When the value of the currency drops, so does everything valued in it. National assets can then be snatched up by circling "vulture capitalists" for pennies on the dollar.

Following all this can be a bit tricky, but the bottom line is that there is no really safe course at present for most small Third World nations. Whether their currencies are left to float or are kept tightly pegged to the dollar, they can still be attacked by speculators. There is a third alternative, but few countries have been in a position to take it: the government can peg its currency to the dollar and *not* support its free conversion into other currencies.[16] Professor Henry C. K. Liu, the

Chinese American economist quoted earlier, says that China escaped the 1998 "Asian crisis" in this way. He writes:

> China was saved from such a dilemma because the yuan was not freely convertible. In a fundamental way, the Chinese miracle of the past half a decade has been made possible by its fixed exchange rate and currency control . . . .

But China too has been under pressure to let its currency float. Liu warns the country of his ancestors:

> [T]he record of the past three decades shows that neo-liberal ideology brought devastation to every economy it invaded . . . . China will not be exempt from such a fate when it makes the yuan fully convertible at floating rates.[17]

There is no real solution to this problem short of global monetary reform. China's money system is explored in detail in Chapter 27, and proposals for reforming the international system are explored in Chapter 46.

## Setting the Debt Trap:
## "Emerging Markets" for Petrodollar Loans

When the price of oil quadrupled in the 1970s, OPEC countries were suddenly flooded with U.S. currency; and these "petrodollars" were usually deposited in London and New York banks. They were an enormous windfall for the banks, which recycled them as low-interest loans to Third World countries that were desperate to borrow dollars to finance their oil imports. Like other loans made by commercial banks, these loans did not actually consist of money deposited by their clients. The deposits merely served as "reserves" for loans created by the "multiplier effect" out of thin air.[18] Through the magic of fractional-reserve lending, dollars belonging to Arab sheiks were multiplied many times over as accounting-entry loans. The "emerging nations" were discovered as "emerging markets" for this new international financial capital. Hundreds of billions of dollars in loan money were generated in this way.

Before 1973, Third World debt was manageable and contained. It was financed mainly through public agencies including the World Bank, which invested in projects promising solid economic success.[19] But things changed when private commercial banks got into the game. The banks were not in the business of "development." They were in the business of loan brokering. Some called it "loan sharking." The banks preferred "stable" governments for clients. Generally, that meant governments controlled by dictators. How these dictators had come to power, and what they did with the money, were not of immediate concern to the banks. The Philippines, Chile, Brazil, Argentina, and Uruguay were all prime loan targets. In many cases, the dictators used the money for their own ends, without significantly bettering the condition of the people; but the people were saddled with the bill.

The screws were tightened in 1979, when the U.S. Federal Reserve under Chairman Paul Volcker unilaterally hiked interest rates to crippling levels. Engdahl notes that this was done after foreign dollar-holders began dumping their dollars in protest over the foreign policies of the Carter administration. Within weeks, Volcker allowed U.S. interest rates to *triple*. They rose to over 20 percent, forcing global interest rates through the roof, triggering a global recession and mass unemployment.[20] By 1982, the dollar's status as global reserve currency had been saved, but the entire Third World was on the brink of bankruptcy, choking from usurious interest charges on their petrodollar loans.

That was when the IMF got in the game, brought in by the London and New York banks to enforce debt repayment and act as "debt policeman." Public spending for health, education and welfare in debtor countries was slashed, following IMF orders to ensure that the banks got timely debt service on their petrodollars. The banks also brought pressure on the U.S. government to bail them out from the consequences of their imprudent loans, using taxpayer money and U.S. assets to do it. The results were austerity measures for Third World countries and taxation for American workers to provide welfare for the banks. The banks were emboldened to keep aggressively lending, confident that they would again be bailed out if the debtors' loans went into default.

Worse for American citizens, the United States itself ended up a major debtor nation. Because oil is an essential commodity for every country, the petrodollar system requires other countries to build up huge trade surpluses in order to accumulate the dollar surpluses they need to buy oil. These countries have to sell more goods in dollars than they buy, to give them a positive dollar balance. That is true for every country except the United States, which controls the dollar and issues it at will. More accurately, the Federal Reserve and the private commercial banking system it represents control the dollar and issue it at will. Since U.S. economic dominance depends on the dollar recycling process, the United States has acquiesced in becoming "importer of last resort." The result has been to saddle it with a growing negative trade balance or "current account deficit." By 2000, U.S. trade deficits and net liabilities to foreign accounts were well over 22 percent of gross domestic product. In 2001, the U.S. stock market collapsed; and tax cuts and increased federal spending turned the federal budget surplus into massive budget deficits. In the three years after 2000, the net U.S. debt position almost doubled. The United States had to bring in $1.4 billion in foreign capital *daily*, just to fund this debt and keep the dollar recycling game going. By 2006, the figure was up to $2.5 billion daily.[21] The people of the United States, like those of the Third World, have become hopelessly mired in debt to support the banking system of a private international cartel.

# Chapter 22
# THE TEQUILA TRAP:
# THE REAL STORY BEHIND
# THE ILLEGAL ALIEN INVASION

*The Witch bade her clean the pots and kettles and sweep the floor and keep the fire fed with wood.  Dorothy went to work meekly, with her mind made up to work as hard as she could; for she was glad the Wicked Witch had decided not to kill her.*

– <u>The Wonderful Wizard of Oz</u>,
*"The Search for the Wicked Witch"*

Waves of immigrants are now pouring over the Mexican border into the United States in search of work, precipitating an illegal alien crisis for Americans.  Vigilante border patrols view these immigrants as potential terrorists, but in fact they are refugees from an economic war that has deprived them of their own property and forced them into debt bondage to a private global banking cartel. When Mexico was conquered in 1520, the mighty Aztec empire was ruled by the unsuspecting, hospitable Montezuma.  The Spanish General Cortes, propelled by the lure of gold, conquered by warfare, violence and genocide.  When Mexico fell again in the twentieth century, it was to a more covert form of aggression, one involving a drastic devaluation of its national currency.

If Montezuma's curse was his copious store of gold, for Mexico in the twentieth century it was the country's copious store of oil. According to William Engdahl, who tells the story in <u>A Century of War</u>, the first Mexican national Constitution vested the government with "direct ownership of all minerals, petroleum and hydro-carbons" in 1917.  When British and American oil interests persisted in an intense behind-the-scenes battle for these oil reserves, the Mexican government finally nationalized all its foreign oil holdings.  The move led the British and American oil majors to boycott Mexico for the next forty years. When new oil reserves were discovered in Mexico in the 1970s, President Jose Lopez Portillo undertook an impressive modernization and industrialization program, and Mexico became the most rapidly growing economy in the developing world. But according to Engdahl, the prospect of a strong industrial Mexico on the southern border of the United States was intolerable to certain powerful Anglo-American interests, who determined to sabotage Mexico's industrialization by securing rigid repayment of its foreign debt. That was when interest rates were *tripled*. Third World loans were particularly vulnerable to this manipulation, because they were usually subject to floating or variable interest rates.

Why did Mexico *need* to go into debt to foreign lenders? It had its own oil in abundance. It had accepted development loans earlier, but it had largely paid them off. The problem for Mexico was that it was one of those intrepid countries that had declined to let its national currency float. Mexico's dollar reserves were exhausted by speculative raids in the 1980s, forcing it to borrow *just to defend the value of the peso*.[2] According to Henry Liu, writing in <u>The Asia Times</u>, Mexico's mistake was in keeping its currency freely convertible into dollars, requiring it to keep enough dollar reserves to buy back the pesos of anyone wanting to sell. When those reserves ran out, it had to borrow dollars on the international market just to maintain its currency peg.[3]

In 1982, President Portillo warned of "hidden foreign interests" that were trying to destabilize Mexico through panic rumors, causing capital flight out of the country. Speculators were cashing in their pesos for dollars and depleting the government's dollar reserves in anticipation that the peso would have to be devalued. In an attempt to stem the capital flight, the government cracked under the pressure and did devalue the peso; but while the currency immediately lost 30 percent of its value, the devastating wave of speculation continued. Mexico was characterized as a "high-risk country," leading international lenders to decline to roll over their loans. Caught by peso devaluation, capital flight, and lender refusal to roll over its debt, the country faced economic chaos. At the General Assembly of the United Nations, President Portillo called on the nations of the world to prevent a "regression into the Dark Ages" precipitated by the unbearably high interest rates of the global bankers.

In an attempt to stabilize the situation, the President took the bold move of taking charge of the banks. The Bank of Mexico and the country's private banks were taken over by the government, with compensation to their private owners. It was the sort of move calculated to set off alarm bells for the international banking cartel. A global movement to nationalize the banks could destroy their whole economic empire. They wanted the banks privatized and under their control. The U.S. Secretary of State was then George Shultz, a major player in the 1971 unpegging of the dollar from gold. He responded with a plan to save the Wall Street banking empire by having the IMF act as debt policeman. Henry Kissinger's consultancy firm was called in to design the program. The result, says Engdahl, was "the most concerted organized looting operation in modern history," carrying "the most onerous debt collection terms since the Versailles reparations process of the early 1920s," the debt repayment plan blamed for propelling Germany into World War II.[4]

Mexico's state-owned banks were returned to private ownership, but they were sold strictly to domestic Mexican purchasers. Not until the North American Free Trade Agreement (NAFTA) was foreign competition even partially allowed. Signed by Canada, Mexico and the United States, NAFTA established a "free-trade" zone in North America to take effect on January 1, 1994. In entering the agreement, Carlos Salinas, the outgoing Mexican President, broke with decades of Mexican policy of high tariffs to protect state-owned industry from competition by U.S. corporations.

By 1994, Mexico had restored its standing with investors. It had a balanced budget, a growth rate of over three percent, and a stock market that was up fivefold. In February 1995, Jane Ingraham wrote in The New American that Mexico's fiscal policy was in some respects "superior and saner than our own wildly spendthrift Washington circus." Mexico received enormous amounts of foreign investment, after being singled out as the most promising and safest of Latin American markets. Investors were therefore shocked and surprised when newly-elected President Ernesto Zedillo suddenly announced a 13 percent devaluation of the peso, since there seemed no valid reason for the move. The following day, Zedillo allowed the formerly managed peso to float freely against the dollar. The peso immediately plunged by 39 percent.[5]

What was going on? In 1994, the U.S. Congressional Budget Office Report on NAFTA had diagnosed the peso as "overvalued" by 20 percent. The Mexican government was advised to unpeg the currency and let it float, allowing it to fall naturally to its "true" level. The theory was that it would fall by *only* 20 percent; but that is not what happened. *The peso eventually dropped by 300 percent – 15 times the predicted fall.*[6]  Its collapse was blamed on the lack of "investor confidence" due to Mexico's negative trade balance; but as Ingraham observes, investor confidence was quite high immediately before the collapse.  If a negative trade balance is what sends a currency into massive devaluation and hyperinflation, the U.S. dollar itself should have been driven there long ago.  By 2001, U.S. public and private debt totaled ten times the debt of all Third World countries combined.[7]

Although the peso's collapse was supposedly unanticipated, over 4 billion U.S. dollars suddenly and mysteriously left Mexico in the 20 days before it occurred.  Six months later, this money had twice the Mexican purchasing power it had earlier.  Later commentators maintained that lead investors with inside information precipitated the stampede out of the peso.[8]  These investors were evidently the same parties who profited from the Mexican bailout that followed.  When Mexico's banks ran out of dollars to pay off its creditors (which were largely U.S. banks), the U.S. government stepped in with U.S. tax dollars.  The Mexican bailout was engineered by Robert Rubin, who headed the investment bank Goldman Sachs before he became U.S. Treasury Secretary.  Goldman Sachs was then heavily invested in short-term dollar-denominated Mexican bonds.  The bailout was arranged the very day of Rubin's appointment.  Needless to say, the money provided by U.S. taxpayers never made it to Mexico.  It went straight into the vaults of Goldman Sachs, Morgan Stanley, and other big American lenders whose risky loans were on the line.[9]

The late Jude Wanniski was a conservative economist who was at one time a Wall Street Journal editor and adviser to President Reagan.  He cynically observed of this banker coup:

> There was a big party at Morgan Stanley after the Mexican peso devaluation, people from all over Wall Street came, they drank champagne and smoked cigars and congratulated themselves on how they pulled it off and they made a fortune. *These people are pirates, international pirates.*[10]

The loot was more than just the profits of gamblers who had bet the right way.  The pirates actually got control of Mexico's banks.  NAFTA rules had already opened the nationalized Mexican banking system to a number of U.S. banks, with Mexican licenses being granted to 18 big foreign banks and 16 brokers including Goldman Sachs.  But these banks could bring in no more than 20 percent of the system's total capital, limiting their market share in loans and securities holdings.[11]  They wanted the whole enchilada.  By 2004, all but one of

Mexico's major banks had been sold to foreign banks, which gained total access to the formerly closed Mexican banking market.[12]

The value of Mexican pesos and Mexican stocks collapsed together, supposedly because there was a stampede to sell and no one around to buy; but buyers with ample funds were sitting on the sidelines, waiting to pick over the devalued stock at bargain basement prices. The result was a direct transfer of wealth from the local economy to international money manipulators. The devaluation also precipitated a wave of privatizations (sales of public assets to private corporations), as the Mexican government tried to meet its spiraling debt crisis. In a February 1996 article called "Militant Capitalism," David Peterson blamed the rout on an assault on the peso by short-sellers. He wrote:

> The austerity measures that the U.S. government and the IMF forced on Mexicans in the aftermath of last winter's assault on the peso by short-sellers in the foreign exchange markets have been something to behold. Almost overnight, the Mexican people have had to endure dramatic cuts in government spending; a sharp hike in regressive sales taxes; at least one million layoffs (a conservative estimate); a spike in interest rates so pronounced as to render their debts unserviceable (hence El Barzon, a nation-wide movement of small debtors to resist property seizures and to seek a rescheduling of their debts); a collapse in consumer spending on the order of 25 percent by mid-year; and, in brief, a 10.5 percent contraction in overall economic activity during the second quarter, with more of the same sure to follow.[13]

By 1995, Mexico's foreign debt was more than twice the country's total debt payment for the previous century and a half. Per-capita income had fallen by almost a third from a year earlier, and Mexican purchasing power had fallen by well over 50 percent.[14] Mexico was propelled into a crippling national depression that has lasted for over a decade. As in the U.S. depression of the 1930s, the actual value of Mexican businesses and assets did not change during this speculator-induced crisis. What changed was simply that currency had been sucked out of the economy by investors stampeding to get out of the Mexican stock market, leaving insufficient money in circulation to pay workers, buy raw materials, finance loans, and operate the country. It was further evidence that when short-selling is allowed, currencies are driven into hyperinflation not by the market mechanism of "supply and demand" but by the concerted action of currency speculators. The flipside of this also appears to be true: the U.S. dollar remains strong despite its plunging trade balance, because it has been artificially manipulated *up* by the Fed. (More on this in Chapter 33.) Market manipulators, not free market forces, are in control.

## International Pirates Prowling in a Sea of Floating Currencies

Countries around the world have been caught in the same trap that captured Mexico. Henry C K Liu calls it the "Tequila Trap." He also calls it "a suicidal policy masked by the giddy expansion typical of the early phase of a Ponzi scheme." The lure in the trap is the promise of massive dollar investment. At first, returns are spectacular. But as with every Ponzi scheme, the returns eventually collapse, leaving the people massively in debt to a foreign banking cartel that will become their new economic masters.[15] The former Soviet states, the Tiger economies of Southeast Asia, and the Latin American banana republics all succumbed to these rapacious tactics. Local ineptitude and corrupt politicians are blamed, when the real culprits are international banking speculators armed with tsunami-sized walls of "credit" created on computer screens. Targeted countries are advised that to attract foreign investment, they must make their currencies freely convertible into dollars at prevailing or "floating" exchange rates, and they must keep adequate dollars in reserve for anyone who wants to change from one currency to another. After the trap is set, the speculators move in. Speculation has been known to bring down currencies and national economics in a single day. Michel Chossudovsky, Professor of Economics at the University of Ottawa, writes:

> The media tends to identify these currency crises as being the product of some internal mechanism, internal political weaknesses or corruption. The linkages to international finance are downplayed. *The fact of the matter is that currency speculation, using speculative instruments, was ultimately the means whereby these central bank reserves were literally confiscated by private speculators.*[16]

While economists debate the fiscal pros and cons of "floating" exchange rates, from a legal standpoint they represent a blatant fraud on the people who depend on a stable medium of exchange. They are as much a fraud as a grocer's scales with a rock on it. If a farmer's peso was worth thirty cents yesterday and is worth only five cents today, his dozen eggs have suddenly shrunk to two eggs, his dozen apples to two apples. The very notion that a country has to "defend" its currency shows that there is something wrong with the system. Inches don't have to defend themselves against millimeters but peacefully co-exist side by side with them on the same yardstick. A sovereign government has both the right and the duty to calibrate its medium of exchange so that it is a stable measure of purchasing power for its people. How a stable international currency yardstick might be devised is explored in Section VI.

## The Tequila Trap and "Free Trade"

The "Tequila Trap" is the contemporary version of what Henry Carey and the American nationalists warned against in the nineteenth century when they spoke of the dangers of opening a country's borders to "free trade." Carey said sovereign nations should pay their debts in their own currencies, issued Greenback-style by their own governments. Professor Liu also advocates this approach, which he calls "sovereign credit." Carey called it "national credit," something he defined as "a national system based entirely on the credit of the government with the people, not liable to interference from abroad." Carey also called it the "American system" to distinguish it from the "British system" of free trade.

Abraham Lincoln was forging ahead with that revolutionary model when he was assassinated. Carey and his faction, realizing that the country was facing the very real threat that the banking interests that had captured England would also capture America, then moved to form a bulwark against this encroaching menace by planting the seeds of the American system abroad. In the twentieth century, the British system did prevail in America; but the American system was quietly taking root overseas . . . .

# Chapter 23
# FREEING THE YELLOW WINKIES:
# THE GREENBACK SYSTEM
# FLOURISHES ABROAD

*The Cowardly Lion was much pleased to hear that the Wicked Witch had been melted by a bucket of water, and Dorothy at once unlocked the gate of his prison and set him free. They went in together to the castle, where Dorothy's first act was to call all the Winkies together and tell them that they were no longer slaves. There was great rejoicing among the yellow Winkies, for they had been made to work hard during many years for the Wicked Witch, who had always treated them with great cruelty.*

> – *The Wonderful Wizard of Oz,*
> "The Rescue"

Accarding to later commentators, Frank Baum's yellow Winkies represented the world's exploited and oppressed. In the late nineteenth century, the United States was engaged in an imperial war with the Philippines, which was vigorously opposed by William Jennings Bryan, the Populist Lion. The Chinese had been exploited in the Opium Wars, and Chinese immigrants worked like slaves on the railroads of the American West. To Henry Carey, they were all victims of the "British system," a form of political economy based on "free trade" and the "gold standard." He wrote in The Harmony of Interests in 1851:

> Two systems are before the world. . . . One looks to underworking [underpaying or exploiting] the Hindoo, and sinking the rest of the world to his level; the other to raising the standard of man throughout the world to our level. One looks to pauperism, ignorance, depopulation, and barbarism; the other to increasing

wealth, comfort, intelligence, combination of action, and civilization. One looks towards universal war; the other towards universal peace. *One is the English system; the other we may be proud to call the American system,* for it is the only one ever devised the tendency of which was that of *elevating* while *equalizing* the condition of man throughout the world.

In <u>The Slave Trade, Domestic and Foreign</u>, published in 1853, Carey wrote:

> By adopting the "free trade," or British, system, we place ourselves side by side with the men who have ruined Ireland and India, and are now poisoning and enslaving the Chinese people. By adopting the other, we place ourselves by the side of those whose measures tend not only to the improvement of their own subjects, but to the emancipation of the slave everywhere, whether in the British Islands, India, Italy, or America.

America had narrowly escaped the fate of the Irish, Indians and Chinese only because President Lincoln had stood up to the bankers, rejecting their usurious loans in favor of government-issued Greenbacks. He had sponsored a government program in which the country would convert its own raw materials into manufactured goods, funding its own internal development by generating its own money, avoiding interest payments and subservience to middlemen, foreign or domestic. When Lincoln was assassinated and the British system got the upper hand, Carey and the American nationalists saw the need to develop a network of allies against this imminent threat. They encouraged political factions in Russia, Japan, Germany and France to bring their governments in accord with Lincoln's policies, forming a potential alliance that could destroy the British empire's financial hegemony. That alliance would later be disrupted by two world wars, but the foundations had been laid.[1]

The hundredth anniversary of the American Revolution was commemorated in 1876 with a Centennial in Philadelphia organized by Henry Carey and his circle. It was a World Fair that celebrated human freedom and potential through collective efforts to develop science, technology, transportation and communications. The Careyites funded Thomas Edison's "invention factory," which displayed its first telegraphic inventions at the Centennial exposition. Later, Edison was challenged by Carey's Philadelphia group to develop electricity; and Edison's partner introduced electric street cars and subway trains. Many other countries had their own displays at the

Philadelphia Centennial as well, including the French, who donated the Statue of Liberty; and millions of people attended from all over the world. Foreign delegates met with the Philadelphia group to discuss industrialization and the development of an economic system in their own countries along the lines envisioned by Franklin and Lincoln.[2]

Tom Paine had called debt-free government-issued money the cornerstone of the American Revolution. The cornerstone had been rejected in America; but it was being studied by innovative leaders abroad, and some of them wound up rejecting the privately-created money of foreign financiers in favor of this home-grown variety. As Wall Street came to dominate American politics and the American media, these "nationalized" banking systems would be branded un-American; but they were actually made in America, patterned after the prototypes of Franklin, Lincoln, Carey and the American Greenbackers. Russia and China developed national banking systems on the American model in the nineteenth century, well before the communist revolutions that overthrew their monarchies. Ironically, the Marxist political system they later adopted was devised in Great Britain and retained the class structure of the "British system," with a small financial elite ruling over masses of laborers.[3] The American system of Franklin, Hamilton and Lincoln was something quite different. It celebrated private enterprise and the entrepreneurial spirit, while providing a collective infrastructure under which competitive capitalism could flourish. This protective government umbrella furnished checks and balances that prevented exploitation by monopolies and marauding foreign interests, allowed science and technology to bloom, and provided funding for projects that "promoted the general welfare," improving the collective human condition by drawing on the credit of the nation.

## The Russian Experience

America's alliance with Russia dated back to the 1850s, when Henry Carey helped turn American opinion in Russia's favor with his newspaper writings. Carey argued that America should back Russia against England in the Crimean War. Russia, in turn, sent ships to back Lincoln against the British-backed Confederacy. The American system of economics was introduced to St. Petersburg by the U.S. ambassador. In 1861, Tsar Alexander II abolished serfdom and launched an economic plan for developing agricultural science, communications, railroads, and other infrastructure; and America provided scientific and technological know-how to help Russia industrialize. In 1862, Russia established a uniform national currency, a national tax levy system, and a state-owned central bank.[4] By the beginning of World War I, the Russian State Bank had become one of the most influential lending institutions in Europe. It had vast gold reserves, actively granted credit to aid industry and trade, and was the chief source of funds for Russia's war effort.[5]

A group of Russian entrepreneurs fought to copy the American system advanced by Carey and his faction, but they faced stiff opposition from the landed nobility, who were backed by international banking interests. Although the Tsar had liberated the peasants, the nobility forced such onerous conditions on their freedom that they remained exploited and oppressed. The peasants had to pay huge "redemption fees" to their former masters, and they were given insufficient land to support themselves. World War I imposed further burdens. Most of the working men were taken to fight the war, and those who remained had to work grueling hours in serf-like conditions. The people were forced off the land into overcrowded cities, where famine broke out. The peasants did not actually initiate the Russian Revolution, but when the match was lit, they provided the tinder to set it ablaze.

## Overthrowing the Revolution

There were actually two Russian revolutions. The first, called the February Revolution, was a largely bloodless transfer of power from the Tsar to a regime of liberals and socialists led by Alexander Kerensky, who intended to instigate political reform along democratic lines. The far bloodier October Revolution was essentially a coup, in which Kerensky was overthrown by Vladimir Lenin with the support of Leon Trotsky and some 300 supporters who came with him from New York. Born Lev Bronstein, Trotsky was a Bolshevik revolutionary who had gone to New York after being expelled from France in 1916. He and his band of supporters returned to Russia in 1917 with substantial funding from a mystery Wall Street donor, widely thought to be Jacob Schiff of Kuhn Loeb. Trotsky's New York recruits later adopted Russian names and made up the bulk of the Communist Party leadership.[6]

Why was a second Russian revolution necessary? In <u>The Creature from Jekyll Island</u>, Ed Griffin observes that Trotsky and the Bolsheviks received strong support from the highest financial and political power centers in the United States, men who were supposedly "capitalists" and should have strongly opposed socialism and communism. Griffin argues that Lenin, Trotsky and their supporters were not sent to Russia to overthrow the Tsar. Rather, he says, "Their assignment from Wall Street was to overthrow the *revolution*." He quotes Eugene Lyons, a correspondent for United Press who was in Russia during the Revolution. Lyons wrote:

> Lenin, Trotsky and their cohorts did not overthrow the monarchy. *They overthrew the first democratic society in Russian history, set up through a truly popular revolution in March, 1917. . . .*
> They represented the smallest of the Russian radical movements. . . . But theirs was a movement that scoffed at numbers and frankly mistrusted multitudes. . . . Lenin always sneered at the obsession of competing socialist groups with their "mass base." "Give us an organization of professional revolutionaries," he used to say, "and we will turn Russia upside down."
> . . . Within a few months after they attained power, most of the tsarist practices the Leninists had condemned were revived, usually in more ominous forms: political prisoners, convictions without trial and without the formality of charges, savage persecution of dissenting views, death penalties for more varieties of crime than any other modern nation.[7]

The February Revolution sought to establish a democratic Russian republic, one with a self-contained monetary system along the lines suggested by Abraham Lincoln. According to Griffin, the October Revolution was commissioned by Wall Street to make sure this did not happen. Lenin, Trotsky and their supporters kept Russia in the hands of a small group of elite called the Communist Party, who were largely foreign imports. The Party kept Russian commerce open to "free trade," and it kept the banking system open to private manipulation. The country's banking system was nationalized in 1917 as the People's Bank of the Russian Republic, but this system was dissolved in 1920 as contradicting the Communist idea of a "moneyless economy."[8] Griffin writes:

> In 1922, the Soviets formed their first international bank. *It was not owned and run by the state as would be dictated by Communist theory but was put together by a syndicate of private bankers.* These included not only former Tsarist bankers, but representatives of German, Swedish, and American banks. Most of the foreign

capital came from England, including the British government itself. The man appointed as Director of the Foreign Division of the new bank was Max May, Vice President of Morgan's Guaranty Trust Company in New York.

. . . In the years immediately following the October Revolution, there was a steady stream of large and lucrative (read non-competitive) contracts issued by the Soviets to British and American businesses . . . U.S., British, and German wolves soon found a bonanza of profit selling to the new Soviet regime.[9]

## The Cold War

If these arrangements were so lucrative for Anglo-American business interests, why did the United States target Soviet Russia as the enemy in the Cold War following World War II? The plans of the international bankers evidently went awry after Lenin died in 1924. Trotsky, who was in line to become the new Soviet leader, got sick at the wrong time, and Stalin grabbed the reins of power. For the Trotskyites and their Wall Street backers, Stalinist Communism then became the enemy. Trotsky was expelled from Soviet Russia in 1928 and returned for a time to New York, meeting his death in Mexico in 1940 at the hands of a Soviet agent.

Through most of the rest of the twentieth century, the banking cartel fought to regain its turf in Russia. The "Neocons" (or "New Conservatives"), the group most associated with the Cold War, have been traced to the Trotskyites of the 1930s.[10] Srdja Trifkovic is a journalist who calls himself a "paleoconservative" (the "Old Right" as opposed to the "New Right"). He writes that the Neocons moved "from the paranoid left to the paranoid right" after emerging from the anti-Stalinist far left in the late 1930s and early 1940s.[11] They had discovered that capitalism suited their aims better than socialism, but they remained consistent in those aims, which were to prevail over the Russian regime and dominate the world economically and militarily. They succeeded on the Russian front when the Soviet economy finally collapsed in 1989. The Central Bank of the Russian Federation was added to the league of central banks operating independently of federal and local governments in 1991.[12]

The economic destruction of Russia and its satellites followed. Jude Wanniski, the Reagan-era insider quoted earlier, said that "shock therapy" was imposed on the Soviet countries after 1989 as an intentional continuation of the Cold War by other means. In a February 2005 interview shortly before he died, Wanniski acknowledged that he was at one time a Neocon himself; but he said that he had had to break with Neocon policies after the Iron Curtain came down. He revealed:

> We were all Cold Warriors, united in a very hard line against Communism in Moscow and in Beijing. [We] fought the Cold War together and we were proud at being successful in that Cold War without having a nuclear exchange. But when the Cold War ended . . . the Russians invited me to Moscow to try and help them turn their communist system into a market economy; and I was glad to do that, for free . . . but I had to break with my old friends because they said we didn't beat these guys enough, *we have to smash them into the ground, we want to feed them bad economic advice, "shock therapy," so that they will fall apart.*[13]

"Shock therapy" consisted of "austerity measures" imposed in return for financial assistance from the International Monetary Fund and its sister agency the World Bank. Also called "structural readjustment," these belt-tightening measures included eliminating food program subsidies, reducing wages, increasing corporate profits, and privatizing public industry. According to Canadian writer Wayne Ellwood, structural adjustment is "a code word for economic globalization and privatization – a formula which aims both to shrink the role of the state and soften the market for private investors."[14]

Mark Weisbrot, co-director of the Center for Economic and Policy Research, testified before Congress in 1998 that Russia's steep decline after 1989 was a direct result of the harsh policies of the IMF, which were used as tools for "subordinating the domestic economies of 'emerging market' countries to the whims of international financial markets." He told Congress:

> The IMF has presided over one of the worst economic declines in modern history. Russian output has declined by more than 40% since 1992 -- a catastrophe worse than our own Great Depression. Millions of workers are denied wages owed to them, a total of more than $12 billion. . . . These are the results of "shock therapy," a program introduced by the International Monetary Fund in 1992. . . . First there was an immediate de-control of prices. . . . [I]nflation soared 520% in the first three

months. Millions of people saw their savings and pensions reduced to crumbs.[15]

The IMF blamed the Russian hyperinflation on deficit spending by the government, but Weisbrot said it wasn't true. Rather, the real culprit was the IMF's insistence on "tight money":

> [F]or the first four years of "shock therapy," the government mostly stayed within the Fund's target range. [But] as the economic collapse continued, tax collection became increasingly difficult. . . . In addition, the necessary capital was not made available for the potentially "efficient" firms to modernize. . . . Foreign direct investment was supposed to play a key role in providing capital, but this never materialized, given the instability of the economy. During the first two years of "shock therapy," the outflow of capital exceeded inflow by two to four times. . . . *[T]he whole idea that Russian industry had to be destroyed, so that they could start from scratch on the basis of foreign investment, was wrong from the beginning.*

Instead of providing capital to promote productivity, Weisbrot said, the IMF squandered $5 billion on trying to support the plunging ruble in a futile attempt to maintain the exchange rate at 6 rubles to the dollar. The result was to deliver $5 billion into the hands of speculators while setting off panic buying and a new round of inflation. What was the point of trying to maintain the convertibility of the domestic currency into dollars? "The IMF argues that it is essential to creating a climate in which foreign direct investment can be attracted," Weisbrot said, "but that is clearly not worth the price in Russia, where the capital flows that were attracted were overwhelmingly speculative. This is another example of the IMF's skewed priorities, which have now brought Russia to a state of economic and political chaos."

Russia had succumbed to the same sort of "free trade" policy that allowed British financial interests to invade America in the nineteenth century. It had opened itself to dependence on money created out of nothing lent by others, money it could have created itself. Indeed, Russia *had* been creating its own money, before the wolf got in the door in the form of IMF "shock therapy."

The Soviet economic scheme had failed, but it wasn't because of its banking system. Economists blamed the Marxist theory that prices and employment must be determined by the State rather than left to market forces. The result was to stifle individual initiative and eliminate the mechanisms for setting prices and allocating resources provided by the free market. This was very different from the "American system" prescribed by Henry Carey and the American nationalists, who encouraged free markets and individual initiative under a collective infrastructure that helped the people to all rise together. The seeds of the American system just had not had a chance to grow properly in Russia. In other fields abroad, they took better root . . . .

# Chapter 24

# SNEERING AT DOOM:
# GERMANY FINANCES A WAR
# WITHOUT MONEY

*"Frightened? You are talking to a man who has laughed in the face of death, sneered at doom, and chuckled at catastrophe. I was petrified. Then suddenly the wind changed, and the balloon floated down into this noble city, where I was instantly proclaimed the First Wizard Deluxe. Times being what they were, I accepted the job, retaining my balloon for a quick getaway."*

– *The Wizard of Oz* ( *MGM film*)

If anyone had sneered at doom, it was the Germans after World War I. The bold wizardry by which they pulled themselves out of bankruptcy to challenge the world in a second world war rivaled the audacity of the Kansas balloonist who mesmerized Oz. The Treaty of Versailles had imposed crushing reparations payments on Germany. The German people were expected to reimburse the costs of the war for all participants -- *costs totaling three times the value of all the property in the country.* Speculation in the German mark had caused it to plummet, precipitating one of the worst runaway inflations in modern times. At its peak, a wheelbarrow full of 100 billion-mark banknotes could not buy a loaf of bread. The national treasury was completely broke, and huge numbers of homes and farms had been lost to the banks and speculators. People were living in hovels and starving. Nothing like it had ever happened before – the total destruction of the national currency, wiping out people's savings, their businesses, and the economy generally.

What to do? The German government followed the lead of the American Greenbackers and issued its own fiat money. Hjalmar Schacht, then head of the German central bank, is quoted in a bit of wit that sums up the German version of the "Greenback" miracle. An American banker had commented, "Dr. Schacht, you should come to America. We've lots of money and that's real banking." Schacht replied, "You should come to Berlin. We don't have money. That's *real* banking."[1]

The German people were in such desperate straits that they relinquished control of the country to a dictator, and in this they obviously deviated from the "American system," which presupposed a democratically-governed Commonwealth. But autocratic authority did give Adolf Hitler something the American Greenbackers could only dream about – total control of the economy. He was able to test their theories, and he proved that they worked. Like for Lincoln, Hitler's choices were to either submit to total debt slavery or create his own fiat money; and like Lincoln, he chose the fiat solution. He implemented a plan of public works along the lines proposed by Jacob Coxey and the Greenbackers in the 1890s. Projects earmarked for funding included flood control, repair of public buildings and private residences, and construction of new buildings, roads, bridges, canals, and port facilities. The projected cost of the various programs was fixed at one billion units of the national currency. One billion non-inflationary bills of exchange, called Labor Treasury Certificates, were then issued against this cost. Millions of people were put to work on these projects, and the workers were paid with the Treasury Certificates. The workers then spent the certificates on goods and services, creating more jobs for more people.

Within two years, the unemployment problem had been solved and the country was back on its feet. It had a solid, stable currency, no debt, and no inflation, at a time when millions of people in the United States and other Western countries were still out of work and living on welfare. Germany even managed to restore foreign trade, although it was denied foreign credit and was faced with an economic boycott abroad. It did this by using a barter system: equipment and commodities were exchanged directly with other countries, circumventing the international banks. This system of direct exchange occurred without debt and without trade deficits. Germany's economic experiment, like Lincoln's, was short-lived; but it left some lasting monuments to its success, including the famous Autobahn, the world's first extensive superhighway.[2]

According to Stephen Zarlenga in The Lost Science of Money, Hitler was exposed to the fiat-money solution when he was assigned by German Army intelligence to watch the German Workers Party after

World War I. He attended a meeting that made a deep impression on him, at which the views of Gottfried Feder were propounded:

> The basis of Feder's ideas was that the state should create and control its money supply through a nationalized central bank rather than have it created by privately owned banks, to whom interest would have to be paid. From this view derived the conclusion that finance had enslaved the population by usurping the nation's control of money.[3]

Zarlenga traces the idea that the state should create its own money to German theorists who had apparently studied the earlier American Greenback movement. Where Feder and Hitler diverged from the American Greenbackers was in equating the financiers who had enslaved the population with the ethnic race of the prominent bankers of the day. The result was to encourage a wave of anti-semitism that darkened Germany and blackened its leader's name. The nineteenth century Greenbackers saw more clearly what the true enemy was – not an ethnic group but a financial scheme, one that transferred the power to create money from the collective body of the people to a private banking elite. The grave human rights violations Germany fell into under Hitler might have been avoided by a stricter adherence to the "American system," keeping the reins of power with the people themselves.

While Hitler clearly deserved the opprobrium heaped on him for his later military and racial aggressions, he was immensely popular with the German people, at least for a time. Zarlenga suggests that this was because he temporarily rescued Germany from English economic theory – the theory that money must be borrowed against the gold reserves of a private banking cartel rather than issued outright by the government. Zarlenga also suggests that retaliation by the international bankers may have been a key factor prompting World War II:

> Perhaps [Germany] was expected to borrow gold internationally, and that would have meant external control over her domestic policies. Her decision to use alternatives to gold, would mean that the international financiers would be unable to exercise this control through the international gold standard, . . . and this may have led to controlling Germany through warfare instead.[4]

Dr. Henry Makow, a Canadian researcher, concurs that this may have been a chief reason Hitler had to be stopped: he had sidestepped the international bankers and created his own money. Makow quotes from the 1938 interrogation of C. G. Rakowsky, a Trotsky intimate, who revealed:

> [Hitler] took over for himself the privilege of manufacturing money and not only physical moneys, but also financial ones; he took over the untouched machinery of falsification and put it to work for the benefit of the state . . . . Are you capable of imagining what would have come . . . if it had infected a number of other states and brought about the creation of a period of autarchy. If you can, then imagine its counterrevolutionary functions . . . .[5]

*Autarchy* is a national economic policy that aims at achieving self-sufficiency and eliminating the need for imports. Countries that take protectionist measures and try to prevent free trade are sometimes described as autarchical. Rakowsky's statement recalls the 1865 London Times editorial warning that if Lincoln's Greenback plan were not destroyed, "that government will furnish its own money without cost. It will pay off debts and be without a debt. It will have all the money necessary to carry on its commerce. It will become prosperous beyond precedent in the history of the civilized governments of the world." Germany was well on its way to achieving those goals. Henry C K Liu writes of the country's remarkable transformation:

> The Nazis came to power in Germany in 1933, at a time when its economy was in total collapse, with ruinous war-reparation obligations and zero prospects for foreign investment or credit. Yet through an independent monetary policy of sovereign credit and a full-employment public-works program, the Third Reich was able to turn a bankrupt Germany, stripped of overseas colonies it could exploit, into the strongest economy in Europe within four years, even before armament spending began.[6]

In Billions for the Bankers, Debts for the People (1984), Sheldon Emry also commented on this development, writing:

> Germany issued debt-free and interest-free money from 1935 and on, accounting for its startling rise from the depression to a world power in 5 years. Germany financed its entire government and war operation from 1935 to 1945 without gold and without debt, and it took the whole Capitalist and Communist world to destroy the German power over Europe and bring Europe back

under the heel of the Bankers. Such history of money does not even appear in the textbooks of public (government) schools today.

What *does* appear in modern textbooks is the disastrous runaway inflation suffered in 1923 by the Weimar Republic (the common name for the republic that governed Germany from 1919 to 1933). The radical devaluation of the German mark is cited as the textbook example of what can go wrong when governments are given the unfettered power to print money. That is what it is cited for; but in the complex world of economics, things are not always as they seem.

## Another Look at the Weimar Hyperinflation

The Weimar financial crisis began with the crushing reparations payments imposed at the Treaty of Versailles. Hjalmar Schacht, who was currency commissioner for the Republic, complained:

> The Treaty of Versailles is a model of ingenious measures for the economic destruction of Germany. . . . [T]he Reich could not find any way of holding its head above the water other than by the inflationary expedient of printing bank notes.

That is what he said at first; but Zarlenga writes that Schacht proceeded in his 1967 book The Magic of Money "to let the cat out of the bag, writing in German, with some truly remarkable admissions that shatter the 'accepted wisdom' the financial community has promulgated on the German hyperinflation."[7] *He revealed that it was the privately-owned Reichsbank, not the German government, that was pumping new currency into the economy.* Like the U.S. Federal Reserve, the Reichsbank was overseen by appointed government officials but was operated for private gain. *What drove the wartime inflation into hyperinflation was speculation by foreign investors, who would sell the mark short, betting on its decreasing value.* Recall that in the short sale, speculators borrow something they don't own, sell it, then "cover" by buying it back at the lower price. Speculation in the German mark was made possible because the Reichsbank made massive amounts of currency available for borrowing, marks that were created on demand and lent at a profitable interest to the bank. When the Reichsbank could not keep up with the voracious demand for marks, other private banks were allowed to create them out of nothing and lend them at interest as well.[8]

Far from causing the Weimar hyperinflation, according to Schacht, it was the government that got it under control. The Reichsbank was put under strict government regulation, and prompt corrective measures were taken to eliminate foreign speculation by eliminating easy access to loans of bank-created money. Hitler then got the country back on its feet with his "Feder money" issued Greenback-style by the government.

Schacht actually disapproved of the new Feder money. He wound up getting fired as head of the Reichsbank when he refused to issue it (something that may have saved him at the Nuremberg trials). But he acknowledged in his later memoirs that Feder's theories had worked. Allowing the government to issue the money it needed had not produced the price inflation predicted by classical economic theory. Schacht surmised that this was because factories were sitting idle and people were unemployed. In this he agreed with Keynes: when the resources were available to increase productivity, adding money to the economy did not increase prices; it increased goods and services. Supply and demand increased together, leaving prices unaffected.

These revelations put the notorious hyperinflations of modern history in a different light . . . .

# Chapter 25
# ANOTHER LOOK AT THE INFLATION HUMBUG: SOME "TEXTBOOK" HYPERINFLATIONS REVISITED

*There is no subtler, no surer means of overturning the existing basis of society than to debauch the currency. The process engages all the hidden forces of economic law on the side of destruction, and does it in a manner which not one man in a million is able to diagnose.*

*– John Maynard Keynes,*
*Economic Consequences of the Peace (1919)*

The rampant runaway inflations of Third World economies are widely blamed on desperate governments trying to solve their economic problems by running the currency printing presses. However, closer examination generally reveals other hands to be at work. What causes merchants to raise their prices is *not* a sudden flood of money from customers competing for their products because the money supply has been pumped up with new currency. Rather, it is a dramatic increase in *the merchants' own costs* as a result of a radical devaluation of the local currency; and this devaluation can usually be traced to manipulations in the currency's floating exchange rate. Here are some noteworthy examples . . . .

## The Ruble Collapse in Post-Soviet Russia

The usual explanation for the drastic runaway inflation that afflicted Russia and its former satellites following the fall of the Iron Curtain is that their governments resorted to printing their own money, diluting the money supply and driving up prices. But as William

Engdahl shows in <u>A Century of War</u>, this is not what was actually going on. Rather, hyperinflation was a direct and immediate result of letting their currencies float in foreign exchange markets. He writes:

> In 1992 the IMF demanded a free float of the Russian ruble as part of its "market-oriented" reform. *The ruble float led within a year to an increase in consumer prices of 9,900 per cent, and a collapse in real wages of 84 per cent.* For the first time since 1917, at least during peacetime, the majority of Russians were plunged into existential poverty. . . . Instead of the hoped-for American-style prosperity, two-cars-in-every-garage capitalism, ordinary Russians were driven into economic misery.[1]

After the Berlin Wall came down, the IMF was put in charge of the market reforms that were supposed to bring the former Soviet countries in line with the Western capitalist economies that were dominated by the dollars of the private Federal Reserve and private U.S. banks. The Soviet people acquiesced, lulled by dreams of the sort of prosperity they had seen in the American movies. But Engdahl says it was all a deception:

> The aim of Washington's IMF "market reforms" in the former Soviet Union was brutally simple: destroy the economic ties that bound Moscow to each part of the Soviet Union . . . . *IMF shock therapy was intended to create weak, unstable economies on the periphery of Russia, dependent on Western capital and on dollar inflows for their survival -- a form of neocolonialism.* . . . The Russians were to get the standard Third World treatment . . . IMF conditionalities and a plunge into poverty for the population. A tiny elite were allowed to become fabulously rich in dollar terms, and manipulable by Wall Street bankers and investors.

It was an intentional continuation of the Cold War by other means, entrapping the economic enemy with loans of accounting-entry money. Interest rates would then be raised to unpayable levels, and the IMF would be put in charge of "reforms" that would open the economy to foreign exploitation in exchange for debt relief. Engdahl writes:

> The West, above all the United States, clearly wanted a deindustrialized Russia, to permanently break up the economic structure of the old Soviet Union. A major area of the global economy, which had been largely closed to the dollar domain for more than seven decades, was to be brought under its control. . . . The new oligarchs were "dollar oligarchs."

## The Collapse of Yugoslavia and the Ukraine

Things were even worse in Yugoslavia, which suffered what has been called the worst hyperinflation in history in 1993-94. Again, the textbook explanation is that the government was madly printing money. As one college economics professor put it:

> After Tito [the Yugoslavian Communist leader until 1980], the Communist Party pursued progressively more irrational economic policies. These policies and the breakup of Yugoslavia . . . led to heavier reliance upon printing or otherwise creating money to finance the operation of the government and the socialist economy. This created the hyperinflation.[2]

That was the conventional view, but Engdahl maintains that the reverse was actually true: the Yugoslav collapse occurred because the IMF *prevented* the government from obtaining the credit it needed from its own central bank. Without the ability to create money and issue credit, the government was unable to finance social programs and hold its provinces together as one nation.

The country's real problem, says Engdahl, was not that its economy was too weak but that it was too strong. Its "mixed model" combining capitalism and socialism was so successful that it threatened the bankers' IMF/shock therapy model:

> For over 40 years, Washington had quietly supported Yugoslavia, and the Tito model of mixed socialism, as a buffer against the Soviet Union. As Moscow's empire began to fall apart, Washington had no more use for a buffer – especially a nationalist buffer which was economically successful, one that might convince neighboring states in eastern Europe that a middle way other than IMF shock therapy was possible. The Yugoslav model had to be dismantled, for this reason alone, in the eyes of top Washington strategists. The fact that Yugoslavia also lay on a critical path to the potential oil riches of central Asia merely added to the argument.[3]

Yugoslavia was another victim of the Tequila Trap – the lure of wealth and development if it would open its economy to foreign investment and foreign loans. According to a 1984 Radio Free Europe report, Tito had made the mistake of allowing the country the "luxury" of importing more goods than it exported, and of borrowing huge sums of money abroad to construct hundreds of factories that never made a profit. When the dollars were not available to pay back these loans, Yugoslavia had to turn to the IMF for debt relief. The jaws of the whale then opened, and Yugoslavia disappeared within.

As a condition of debt relief, the IMF demanded wholesale privatization of the country's state enterprises. The result was to bankrupt more than 1,100 companies and produce more than 20 percent unemployment. IMF policies caused inflation to rise dramatically, until by 1991 it was over 150 percent. When the government was not able to create the money it needed to hold its provinces together, economic chaos followed, causing each region to fight for its own survival. Engdahl states:

> Reacting to this combination of IMF shock therapy and direct Washington destabilization, the Yugoslav president, Serb nationalist Slobodan Milosevic, organized a new Communist Party in November 1990, dedicated to preventing the breakup of the federated Yugoslav Republic. The stage was set for a gruesome series of regional ethnic wars which would last a decade and result in the deaths of more than 200,000 people.
>
> . . . In 1992 Washington imposed a total economic embargo on Yugoslavia, freezing all trade and plunging the economy into chaos, with hyperinflation and 70 percent unemployment as the result. The Western public, above all in the United States, was told by establishment media that the problems were all the result of a corrupt Belgrade dictatorship.

Similar interventions precipitated runaway inflation in the Ukraine, when the IMF "reforms" began with an order to end state foreign exchange controls in 1994. The result was an immediate collapse of the currency. The price of bread shot up 300 percent; electricity shot up 600 percent; public transportation shot up 900 percent. State industries that were unable to get bank credit were forced into bankruptcy. As a result, says Engdahl:

> Foreign speculators were free to pick the jewels among the rubble at dirt-cheap prices. . . . The result was that Ukraine, once the breadbasket of Europe, was forced to beg food aid from the U.S., which dumped its grain surpluses on Ukraine, further destroying local food self-sufficiency. Russia and the states of the former Soviet Union were being treated like the Congo or Nigeria, as sources of cheap raw materials, perhaps the largest sources in the world. . . . [T]hose mineral riches were now within the reach of Western multinationals for the first time since 1917.[4]

## The Case of Argentina

The same debt monster that swallowed the former Soviet economies was busy devouring assets in Latin America. In Argentina in the
late 1980s, inflation shot up by as much as 5,000 percent. Again, this
massive hyperinflation has been widely blamed on the government
madly printing money; and again, the facts turn out to be quite different.

Argentina had been troubled by inflation ever since 1947, when
Juan Peron came to power. Peron was a populist who implemented
many new programs for workers and the poor, but he did it with
heavy deficit spending and taxation rather than by issuing money
Greenback-style.[5] What happened to the Argentine economy after
Peron is detailed in a 2006 Tufts University article by Carlos Escudé,
Director of the Center for International Studies at Universidad del
CEMA in Buenos Aires, who writes that inflation did not become a
national crisis until the eight-year period following Peron's death in
1974. Then the inflation rate increased seven-fold, to an "astonish-
ing" 206 percent. But this jump, says Professor Escudé, was *not* caused
by a sudden printing of pesos. Rather, it was the result of an intentional, radical devaluation of the currency by the new government,
along with a 175 percent increase in the price of oil.

The devaluation was effected by dropping the peso's dollar peg to
a fraction of its previous value; and this was done, according to insiders, with the *intent* of creating economic chaos. One source revealed,
"*The idea was to generate an inflationary stampede to depreciate the debts
of private firms, shatter the price controls in force since 1973, and especially benefit exporters through devaluation.*" Economic chaos was welcomed by pro-market capitalists, who pointed to it as proof that the
interventionist policies of the former government had been counter-
productive and that the economy should be left to the free market.
Economic chaos was also welcomed by speculators, who found that
"[p]rofiteering was a much safer way of making money than attempt-
ing to invest, increase productivity, and compete in an economy characterized by financial instability, distorted incentives, and obstacles to
efficient investment."

From that time onward, writes Professor Escudé, "astronomically
high inflation led to the proliferation of speculative financial schemes
that became a hallmark of Argentine financial life." One suicidal policy
adopted by the government was to provide "exchange insurance" to

private firms seeking foreign financing. The risk of exchange rate fluctuations was thus transferred from private businesses to the government, encouraging speculative schemes that forced further currency devaluation. Another disastrous government policy held that it was unfair for private firms contracting with the State to suffer losses from financial instability or other unforeseen difficulties while fulfilling their contracts. Again the risks got transferred to the State, encouraging predatory contractors to defraud and exploit the government. The private contractors' lobby became so powerful that the government wound up agreeing to "nationalize" (or assume responsibility for) private external debts. The result was to transfer the debts of powerful private business firms to the taxpayers. When interest rates shot up in the 1980s, the government dealt with these debts by "liquidification," evidently meaning that private liabilities were reduced by depreciating the currency. Again, however, this hyperinflation was not the result of the government printing money for its operational needs but was caused by an intentional devaluation of the currency to reduce the debts of private profiteers in control of the government.[6]

Making matters worse, Argentina was one of those countries targeted by international lenders for massive petrodollar loans. When the rocketing interest rates of the 1980s made the loans impossible to pay back, concessions were required of the country that put it at the mercy of the IMF. Under a new government in the 1990s, Argentina dutifully tightened its belt and tried to follow the IMF's dictates. To curb the crippling currency devaluations, a "currency board" was imposed in 1991 that maintained a strict one-to-one peg between the Argentine peso and the U.S. dollar. The Argentine government and its central bank were prohibited *by law* from printing their own pesos, unless the pesos were fully backed by dollars held as foreign reserves.[7] The maneuver worked to prevent currency devaluations, but the country lost the flexibility it needed to compete in international markets. The money supply was fixed, limited and inflexible. The disastrous result was national bankruptcy, in 1995 and again in 2001.

In the face of dire predictions that the economy would collapse without foreign credit, Argentina then defied its creditors and simply walked away from its debts. By the fall of 2004, three years after a record default on a debt of more than $100 billion, the country was well on the road to recovery; and it had achieved this feat without foreign help. The economy grew by 8 percent for 2 consecutive years. Exports increased, the currency was stable, investors were returning, and unemployment had eased. "This is a remarkable historical event, one that challenges 25 years of failed policies," said Mark Weisbrot in an interview quoted in The New York Times. "While other countries are just limping along, Argentina is experiencing very healthy growth with no sign that it is unsustainable, and they've done it without having to make any concessions to get foreign capital inflows."[8]

In January 2006, Argentina's President Nestor Kirchner paid off the country's entire debt to the IMF, totaling 9.81 billion U.S. dollars. Where did he get the dollars? The Argentine central bank had been routinely issuing pesos to buy dollars, in order to keep the dollar price of the peso from dropping. The Argentine central bank had accumulated over 27 billion U.S. dollars in this way before 2006. Kirchner negotiated with the bank to get a third of these dollar reserves, which were then used to pay the IMF debt.[9]

That the bank had been "issuing" pesos evidently meant that it was creating money out of nothing. The result, however, was not inflationary, at least at first. According to a December 2006 article in The Economist, the newly-issued pesos just stimulated the economy, providing the liquidity that was sorely needed by Argentina's money-starved businesses. But by 2004, spare production had been used up and inflation had again become a problem. President Kirchner then stepped in to control inflation by imposing price controls and export bans. Critics said that these measures would halt investment, but according to The Economist:

> So far they have been wrong. Argentina does lack foreign investment. But its own smaller companies have moved quickly to expand capacity in response to demand. . . . Overall, investment has almost doubled as a percentage of GDP since 2002, from 11% to 21.4%, enough to sustain growth of 4% a year.[10]

When President Kirchner paid off the IMF debt in 2006, he had hoped to get the central bank's dollar reserves debt-free; but he was foiled by certain "international funds." One disgruntled Argentine commentator wrote:

> Kirchner tried until the last moment to get hold of the [central bank's] funds as if they were surplus, without contracting any debt, but *the international funds warned him that if he did so he would provoke strong speculation against the Argentine peso.* Kirchner folded like a hand of poker and indebted the State at a higher rate.[11]

The "international funds" that threatened a speculative attack on the currency were the so-called "vulture funds" that had previously bought Argentina's public debt, in some cases for as little as 20 percent of its nominal value. *Vulture funds* are international financial organizations that specialize in buying securities in distressed conditions, then circle like vultures waiting to pick over the remains of the rapidly weakening debtor. To avoid a speculative attack on its currency from these funds, the Argentine government was forced to issue public debt of $11 billion to absorb the pesos that had been issued to buy the dollars to pay a debt to the IMF of under $10 billion. To Kirchner, however, it was evidently worth the price to get out from under the thumb of the IMF, which he said had been "a source of demands and more demands," forcing "policies which provoked poverty and pain among Argentine people."[12]

## The Case of Zimbabwe

The same foreign banking spider that was entrapping economies in the former Soviet Union and Latin America was also at work in Africa. A case recently in the news is that of Zimbabwe, which in August 2006 was reported to be suffering from a crushing hyperinflation of around 1,000 percent a year. As usual, the crisis is blamed on the government frantically issuing money; and in this case, the government's printing presses have indeed been running. But the currency's radical devaluation was still the fault of speculators, and it might have been avoided if the government had used its printing presses in a more prudent way.

The crisis dates back to 2001, when Zimbabwe defaulted on its loans and the IMF refused to make the usual accommodations, including refinancing and loan forgiveness. Apparently, the IMF intended to punish the country for political policies of which it disapproved, including land reform measures that involved reclaiming the lands of wealthy landowners. Zimbabwe's credit was ruined and it could not get loans elsewhere, so the government resorted to issuing its own national currency and using the money to buy U.S. dollars on the foreign-exchange market. These dollars were then used to pay the IMF and regain the country's credit rating.[13] Unlike in Argentina, however, the government had to show its hand before the dollars were in it, leaving the currency vulnerable to speculative manipulation. According to a statement by the Zimbabwe central bank, the hyperinflation was caused by speculators who charged exorbitant rates for U.S. dollars, causing a drastic devaluation of the Zimbabwe currency.

The government's real mistake, however, may have been in playing the IMF's game at all. Rather than using its national currency to buy foreign fiat money to pay foreign lenders, it could have followed the lead of Abraham Lincoln and the Guernsey islanders and issued its own currency to pay for the production of goods and services for its own people. Inflation would have been avoided, because the newly-created "supply" (goods and services) would have kept up with "demand" (the supply of money); and the currency would have served the local economy rather than being siphoned off by speculators. That solution worked in Guernsey, but Guernsey is an obscure island without the gold and other marketable resources that make Zimbabwe choice spider-bait. Once a country has been caught in the foreign debt trap, escape is no easy matter. Even the mighty Argentina, which at one time was the world's seventh-richest country, was unable to stand up to the IMF and the "vulture funds" for long.

All of these countries have been victims of the Tequila Trap – succumbing to the enticement of foreign loans and investment, opening their currencies to speculative manipulation. Henry C K Liu writes that the seduction of foreign capital is a "financial narcotic that would make the Opium War of 1840 look like a minor scrimmage."[14] In the 1990s, a number of Southeast Asian economies found this out to their peril . . . .

# Chapter 26
# POPPY FIELDS, OPIUM WARS, AND ASIAN TIGERS

> *Now it is well known that when there are many of these flowers together, their odor is so powerful that anyone who breathes it falls asleep. And if the sleeper is not carried away from the scent of the flowers, he sleeps on and on forever.*
>
> *– The Wonderful Wizard of Oz,*
> *"The Deadly Poppy Field"*

The deadly poppy fields that captured Dorothy and the Lion were an allusion to the nineteenth century Opium Wars, which allowed the British to impose economic imperialism on China. The Chinese government, alarmed at the growing number of addicts in the country, made opium illegal and tried to keep the British East India Company from selling it in the country. Britain then forced the issue militarily, acquiring Hong Kong in the process.

To the Japanese, it was an early lesson in the hazards of "free trade." To avoid suffering the same fate themselves, they tightly sealed their own borders. When they opened their borders later, it was to the United States rather than to Britain. The Japanese Meiji Revolution of 1868 was guided by Japanese students of Henry Carey and the American nationalists and has been called an "American System Renaissance." Yukichi Fukuzawa, its intellectual leader, has been called "the Benjamin Franklin of Japan." The feudal Japanese warlords were overthrown and a modern central government was formed. The new government abolished the ownership of Japan's land by the feudal samurai nobles and returned it to the nation, paying the nobles a sum of money in return.[1]

How was this massive buyout financed? President Ulysses S. Grant had warned against foreign borrowing when he visited Japan in 1879.

He said, "Some nations like to lend money to poor nations very much. By this means they flaunt their authority, and cajole the poor nation. The purpose of lending money is to get political power for themselves." Great Britain had a policy of owning the central banks of the nations it occupied, such as the Hongkong and Shanghai Bank in China. To avoid that trap, Japan became the first nation in Asia to found its own independent state bank. The bank issued new fiat money which was used to pay the samurai nobles. The nobles were then encouraged to deposit their money in the state bank and to put it to work creating new industries. Additional money was created by the government to aid the new industries. No expense was spared in the process of industrialization. Money was issued in amounts that far exceeded annual tax receipts. The funds were, after all, just government credits – money that was internally generated, based on the credit of the government rather than on debt to foreign lenders.[2]

The Japanese economic model that evolved in the twentieth century has been called a "state-guided market system." The state determines the priorities and commissions the work, then hires private enterprise to carry it out. The model overcame the defects of the communist system, which put ownership and control in the hands of the state. Chalmers Johnson, president of the Japan Policy Research Institute, wrote in 1989 that the closest thing to the Japanese model in the United States is the military/industrial complex. The government determines the programs and hires private companies to implement them. The U.S. military/industrial complex is a form of state-sponsored capitalism that has produced one of the most lucrative and successful industries in the country.[3] The Japanese model differs, however, in that it achieved this result without the pretext of war. The Japanese managed to transform their warrior class into the country's industrialists, successfully shifting their focus to the peaceful business of building the country and developing industry. The old feudal Japanese dynasties became the multinational Japanese corporations we know today – Mitsubishi, Mitsui, Sumitomo, and so forth.

## The Assault of the Wall Street Speculators

The Japanese state-guided market system was so effective and efficient that by the end of the 1980s, Japan was regarded as the leading economic and banking power in the world. Its Ministry of International Trade and Industry (MITI) played a heavy role in guiding national economic development. The model also proved highly successful in the "Tiger" economies -- South Korea, Malaysia and other East Asian countries. East Asia was built up in the 1970s and 1980s by Japanese state development aid, along with largely private investment and MITI support. When the Soviet Union collapsed, Japan proposed its model for the former communist economies, and many began looking to Japan and South Korea as viable alternatives to the U.S. free-market system. State-guided capitalism provided for the general welfare without destroying capitalist incentive. Engdahl writes:

> The Tiger economies were a major embarrassment to the IMF free-market model. Their very success in blending private enterprise with a strong state economic role was a threat to the IMF free-market agenda. So long as the Tigers appeared to succeed with a model based on a strong state role, the former communist states and others could argue against taking the extreme IMF course. In east Asia during the 1980s, economic growth rates of 7-8 per cent per year, rising social security, universal education and a high worker productivity were all backed by state guidance and planning, albeit in a market economy – an Asian form of benevolent paternalism.[4]

High economic growth, rising social security, and universal education in a market economy – it was the sort of "Common Wealth" America's Founding Fathers had endorsed. But the model represented a major threat to the international bankers' system of debt-based money and IMF loans. To diffuse the threat, the Bank of Japan was pressured by Washington to take measures that would increase the yen's value against the dollar. The stated rationale was that this revaluation was necessary to reduce Japan's huge capital surplus (excess of exports over imports). The Japanese Ministry of Finance countered that the surplus, far from being a problem, was urgently required by a world needing hundreds of billions of dollars in railroad and other economic infrastructure after the Cold War. But the Washington contingent prevailed, and Japan went along with the program. By 1987, the Bank of Japan had cut interest rates to a low of 2.5 per cent. The result was a flood of "cheap" money that was turned into quick gains on the rising Tokyo stock market, producing an enormous stock market bubble. When the Japanese government cautiously tried to deflate the bubble by raising interest rates, the Wall Street bankers went on the attack, using their new "derivative" tools to sell the market short and bring it crashing down. Engdahl writes:

No sooner did Tokyo act to cool down the speculative fever, than the major Wall Street investment banks, led by Morgan Stanley and Salomon Bros., began using exotic new derivatives and financial instruments. *Their intervention turned the orderly decline of the Tokyo market into a near panic sell-off, as the Wall Street bankers made a killing on shorting Tokyo stocks in the process.* Within months, Japanese stocks had lost nearly $5 trillion in paper value.[5]

Japan, the "lead goose," had been seriously wounded. Washington officials proclaimed the end of the "Japanese model" and turned their attention to the flock of Tiger economies flying in formation behind.

## Taking Down the Tiger Economies:
## The Asian Crisis of 1997

Until then, the East Asian countries had remained largely debt-free, avoiding reliance on IMF loans or foreign capital except for direct investment in manufacturing plants, usually as part of a long-term national goal.  But that was before Washington began demanding that the Tiger economies open their controlled financial markets to free capital flows, supposedly in the interest of "level playing fields."  Like Japan, the East Asian countries went along with the program.  The institutional speculators then went on the attack, armed with a secret credit line from a group of international banks including Citigroup.

They first targeted Thailand, gambling that it would be forced to devalue its currency and break from its peg to the dollar.  Thailand capitulated, its currency was floated, and it was forced to turn to the IMF for help.  The other geese then followed one by one.  Chalmers Johnson wrote in The Los Angeles Times in June 1999:

> The funds easily raped Thailand, Indonesia and South Korea, then turned the shivering survivors over to the IMF, not to help victims, but to insure that no Western bank was stuck with non-performing loans in the devastated countries.[6]

Mark Weisbrot testified before Congress, "In this case the IMF not only precipitated the financial crisis, it also prescribed policies that sent the regional economy into a tailspin."  The IMF had prescribed the removal of capital controls, opening Asian markets to speculation by foreign investors, when what these countries really needed was a supply of foreign exchange reserves to *defend* themselves against speculative currency raids. At a meeting of regional finance ministers in 1997, the government of Japan proposed an Asian Monetary Fund (AMF) that would provide the needed liquidity with fewer conditions than were imposed by the IMF. But the AMF, which would have directly competed with the IMF of the Western bankers, met with strenuous objection from the U.S. Treasury and failed to materialize. Meanwhile, the IMF failed to provide the necessary reserves, while insisting on very high interest rates and "fiscal austerity." The result was a liquidity crisis (a lack of available money) that became a major regional depression. Weisbrot testified:

> *The human cost of this depression has been staggering.* Years of economic and social progress are being negated, as the unemployed vie for jobs in sweatshops that they would have previously rejected, and the rural poor subsist on leaves, bark, and insects. In Indonesia, the majority of families now have a monthly income less than the amount that they would need to buy a subsistence quantity of rice, and nearly 100 million people – half the population – are being pushed below the poverty line.[7]

In 1997, more than 100 billion dollars of Asia's hard currency reserves were transferred in a matter of months into private financial hands. In the wake of the currency devaluations, real earnings and employment plummeted virtually overnight. The result was mass poverty in countries that had previously been experiencing real economic and social progress. Indonesia was ordered by the IMF to unpeg its currency from the dollar barely three months before the dramatic plunge of the *rupiah*, its national currency. In an article in <u>Monetary Reform</u> in the winter of 1998-99, Professor Michel Chossudovsky wrote:

> This manipulation of market forces by powerful actors constitutes *a form of financial and economic warfare*. No need to re-colonize lost territory or send in invading armies. In the late twentieth century, the outright "conquest of nations," meaning the control over productive assets, labor, natural resources and institutions, can be carried out in an impersonal fashion from the corporate boardroom: commands are dispatched from a computer terminal, or a cell phone. Relevant data are instantly relayed to major financial markets – often resulting in immediate disruptions in the functioning of national economies. "Financial warfare" also

applies complex speculative instruments including the gamut of derivative trade, forward foreign exchange transactions, currency options, hedge funds, index funds, etc. *Speculative instruments have been used with the ultimate purpose of capturing financial wealth and acquiring control over productive assets.*

Professor Chossudovsky quoted American billionaire Steve Forbes, who asked rhetorically:

Did the IMF help precipitate the crisis? This agency advocates openness and transparency for national economies, yet it rivals the CIA in cloaking its own operations. Did it, for instance, have secret conversations with Thailand, advocating the devaluation that instantly set off the catastrophic chain of events? . . . Did IMF prescriptions exacerbate the illness? These countries' monies were knocked down to absurdly low levels.[8]

Chossudovsky warned that the Asian crisis marked the elimination of national economic sovereignty and the dismantling of the Bretton Woods institutions safeguarding the stability of national economies. Nations no longer have the ability to control the creation of their own money, which has been usurped by marauding foreign banks.[9]

## Malaysia Fights Back

Most of the Asian geese succumbed to these tactics, but Malaysia stood its ground. Malaysian Prime Minister Mahathir Mohamad said the IMF was using the financial crisis to enable giant international corporations to take over Third World economies. He contended:

They see our troubles as a means to get us to accept certain regimes, to open our market to foreign companies to do business without any conditions. [The IMF] says it will give you money if you open up your economy, but doing so will cause all our banks, companies and industries to belong to foreigners. . . .

They call for reform but this may result in millions thrown out of work. I told the top official of IMF that if companies were to close, workers will be retrenched, but he said this didn't matter as bad companies must be closed. I told him the companies became bad because of external factors, so you can't bankrupt them as it was not their fault. But the IMF wants the companies to go bankrupt.[10]

Mahathir insisted that his government had not failed. Rather, it had been victimized along with the rest of the region by the international system. He blamed the collapse of Asia's currencies on an orchestrated attack by giant international hedge funds. Because they profited from relatively small differences in asset values, the speculators were prepared to create sudden, massive and uncontrollable outflows of capital that would wreck national economies by causing capital flight. He charged, "This deliberate devaluation of the currency of a country by currency traders purely for profit is a serious denial of the rights of independent nations." He said he had appealed to the international agencies to regulate currency trading to no avail, so he had been forced to take matters into his own hands. He had imposed capital and exchange controls, a policy aimed at shifting the focus from catering to foreign capital to encouraging national development. He fixed the exchange rate of the *ringgit* (the Malaysian national currency) and ordered that it be traded only in Malaysia. These measures did not affect genuine investors, he said, who could bring in foreign funds, convert them into ringgit for local investment, and apply to the Central Bank to convert their ringgit back into foreign currency as needed.

Western economists waited for the economic disaster they assumed would follow; but capital controls actually helped to stabilize the system. Before controls were imposed, Malaysia's economy had contracted by 7.5 percent. The year afterwards, growth projections went as high as 5 percent. Joseph Stiglitz, chief economist for the World Bank, acknowledged in 1999 that the Bank had been "humbled" by Malaysia's performance. It was a tacit admission that the World Bank's position had been wrong.[11]

David had stood up to Goliath, but the real threat to the international bankers was Malaysia's much more powerful neighbor to the north. The Chinese Dragon was not only still standing; it was breathing fire . . . .

# Chapter 27
# WAKING THE SLEEPING GIANT: LINCOLN'S GREENBACK SYSTEM COMES TO CHINA

*The flowers had been too strong for the huge beast and he had given up at last, falling only a short distance from the end of the poppy bed . . . . "We can do nothing for him," said the Tin Woodman sadly. "He is much too heavy to lift. We must leave him here to sleep . . . ."*

– The Wonderful Wizard of Oz,
*"The Deadly Poppy Field"*

Napoleon called China a sleeping giant. "Let him sleep," Napoleon said. "If he wakes, he will shake the world." China has now awakened and is indeed shaking the world. The Dragon has become so strong economically that it has been called the greatest threat to national security the United States faces, accounting for the greatest imbalance of any country in the U.S. trade budget deficit ($150 billion of $500 billion by 2004).[1]

This balance-of-trade problem is not new. The British were already complaining of it in the early nineteenth century. Then they discovered that exporting opium from India to China could offset their negative trade balance and give them control of China's financial system at the same time. The Chinese Emperor responded by banning the opium trade, after China started losing huge amounts of money to England. England then declared war, initiating the Opium War of 1840. The Chinese people wound up with two sets of imperial rulers, the British as well as their own.[2]

The leader of the revolution that finally overthrew 2,000 years of Chinese imperial rule was Dr. Sun Yat-sen, now revered as the father of modern China by Nationalists and Communists alike. Like the leaders of the Japanese Meiji revolution of the 1860s, he was a protegé of a group of American nationalists of the Lincoln/Carey faction. Sun's fundamental principles, known as the "Three Principles of the People," were based on the concept presented by Lincoln in the Gettysburg Address: "government of the people, by the people, and for the people." Sun was educated in Hawaii, where he built up his revolutionary organization at the house of Frank Damon, the son of Reverand Samuel Damon, who had run the Hawaii delegation to the American Centennial in Philadelphia in 1876. Frank Damon provided money, support and military training to Sun's organization; and Hawaii became its base for making a revolutionary movement in China.[3]

The Chinese Republic was proclaimed just before World War I. After Sun's death, the Nationalists lost control of mainland China to the Chinese Communists, who founded the People's Republic of China in 1949; but the Communists retained much of the "American system" in creating their monetary scheme, which was a Chinese variation of Lincoln's Greenback program. Before that, banknotes had been issued by a variety of private banks. After 1949, these banknotes were recalled and the *renminbi* (or "people's currency") became the sole legal currency, issued by the People's Bank of China, a wholly government-owned bank. The United States and other Western countries imposed an embargo against China in the 1950s, blocking trade between it and most of the rest of the world except the Soviet bloc. China then adopted a Soviet-style centrally-planned economy; but after 1978, it pursued an open-door policy and was transformed from a centrally-planned economy back into a market economy.[4] Private industry is now flourishing in China, and privatization has been creeping into its banking system as well; but it still has government-owned banks that can issue national credit for domestic development.[5]

By 2004, China was leading the world in economic productivity, growing at 9 percent annually. In the first quarter of 2007, its economic growth was up to a remarkable 11.1 percent, with retail sales climbing 15.3 percent. The commonly-held explanation for this impressive growth is that the Chinese are willing to work for what amounts to slave wages; but the starving poor of Africa, Indonesia, and Latin America are equally willing, yet their economies are languishing. Something else distinguishes China, and one key difference is its banking system. China has a government-issued currency and a system of national banks that are actually owned by the nation.[6] According to <u>Wikipedia</u>, the People's Bank of China is "unusual in

acting as a national bank, *focused on the country not on the currency.*"
The notion of "national banking," as opposed to private "central
banking," goes back to Lincoln, Carey and the American nationalists.
Henry C K Liu distinguishes the two systems like this: a national bank
serves the interests of the nation and its people. A central bank serves
the interests of private international finance. He writes:

> A national bank does not seek independence from the
> government. The independence of central banks is a euphemism
> for a shift from institutional loyalty to national economic well-
> being toward institutional loyalty to the smooth functioning of
> a global financial architecture . . . [Today that means] the sacrifice
> of local economies in a financial food chain that feeds the issuer
> of US dollars. It is the monetary aspect of the predatory effects
> of globalization.
>
> Historically, the term "central bank" has been interchange-
> able with the term "national bank." . . . However, with the
> globalization of financial markets in recent decades, a central
> bank has become fundamentally different from a national bank.
>
> *The mandate of a national bank is to finance the sustainable
> development of the national economy . . . . [T]he mandate of a modern-
> day central bank is to safeguard the value of a nation's currency in a
> globalized financial market . . . through economic recession and
> negative growth if necessary. . . .* [T]he best monetary policy in the
> context of central banking is . . . set by universal rules of price
> stability, unaffected by the economic needs or political
> considerations of individual nations.[7]

In 1995, a Central Bank Law was passed in China granting central bank status to the People's Bank of China (PBoC), shifting the
PBoC away from its previous role as a national bank. But Liu says the
shift was in name more than in form:

> It is safe to say that the PBoC still follows the policy directives of
> the Chinese government . . . . Unlike the Fed which has an arms-
> length relationship with the US Treasury, the PBoC manages
> the State treasury as its fiscal agent. . . . Recent Chinese policy
> has shifted back in populist directions to provide affirmative
> financial assistance to the poor and the undeveloped rural and
> interior regions and to reverse blatant income disparity and
> economic and regional imbalances. It can be anticipated that
> this policy shift will raise questions in the capitalist West of the
> political independence of the PBoC. Western neo-liberals will

be predictably critical of the PBoC for directing money to where the country needs it most, rather than to that part of the economy where bank profit would be highest.[8]

Besides its "populist" banking system, China is distinguished by keeping itself free of the debt web of the IMF and the international banking cartel; and by refusing to let its currency float, a policy that has fended off the currency manipulations of international speculators. The value of the renminbi is kept pegged to the dollar; and unlike Mexico in the 1990s, China has such a huge store of dollar reserves that it is impervious to the assaults of speculators. In 2005, China succumbed to Western pressure and raised its dollar peg slightly; but the renminbi continued to be pegged to its dollar counterpart, and the government retained control of its value.

As in Hitler's Germany, the repression of human rights in China deserves serious censure; but something in its economy is clearly working, and to the extent that this is its self-contained monetary policy, the Chinese may have the nineteenth century American Nationalists to thank, through their student Dr. Sun Yat-Sen.

## The Mystery of Chinese Productivity

In the eighteenth century, Benjamin Franklin surprised his British listeners with tales of the booming economy in the American colonies, something he credited to the new paper *fiat* money issued debt-free by the government. In a May 2005 article titled "The Mystery of Mr. Wu," Greg Grillot gave a modern-day variant of this story involving a recent visit to China. He said he and a companion named Karim had interviewed a retired architect named Mr. Wu on his standard of living. Mr. Wu was asked through an interpreter, "How has your standard of living changed in the last two decades?" The interpreter responded, "Thirteen years ago, his pension was 250 yuan a month. Now it is 2,500 yuan. He recently had a cash offer to buy his home for US$300,000, which he's lived in for 50 years." Karim remarked to his companion, "Greg, something doesn't add up here. His pension shot up 900% in 13 years while inflation snoozed at 2-5% per annum. How could the government pay him that much more in such a short period of time?" Grillot commented:

> [T]he more you look around, the more you notice that no one seems to know, or care, how so many people can produce so much so cheaply . . . and sell it below production cost. How

does the Chinese miracle work? Are the Chinese playing with economic fire? All over Beijing, you find people selling things for less than they must have cost to make.

. . . Karim and I looked over the books of a Chinese steel company. Its year-over-year gross sales increased at a fine, steady clip . . . but despite these increasing sales, its debt ascended a bit faster than its sales. So its net profits slowly dwindled over time. . . . But it also looked like the company never pays down its debt. . . . If the Chinese aren't paying their debts. . . is there any limit to the amount of money the banks can lend? Just who are these banks, anyway?

Could this be the key? . . . *In the land of the world's greatest capitalists [meaning China], there's one business that isn't even remotely governed by free markets: the banks. In the simplest terms, the banks and the government are one and the same.* Like modern American banks, the Chinese banks (read: the Chinese government) freely loan money to fledgling and huge established businesses alike. *But unlike modern American banks (most of them, anyway), the Chinese banks don't expect businesses to pay back the money lent to them.*

Evidently the secret of Chinese national banking is that the government banks are not balancing their books! Grillot concluded that it was a dangerous game:

[E]ven if it's a deliberate policy, an economy can't be deliberately inefficient in allocating capital. Things cost money. They cannot, typically, cost less than the value of the raw materials to make them. The whole cannot be worth less than the sum of the parts. . . Some laws of economics . . . can be bent, but not broken . . . at least not without consequences."[9]

Benjamin Franklin's English listeners would no doubt have said the same thing about the innovative monetary scheme of the American colonies. Or could Professor Liu be right? Our entire economic world view may need to be reordered, "just as physics was reordered when we realized that the earth is not stationary and is not the center of the universe."[10]

How the Chinese economy can function on credit that never gets repaid may actually be no more mysterious than the workings of the U.S. economy, which carries nearly $9 trillion in *federal* debt that nobody ever expects to see repaid. The Chinese government, which can print its own money and doesn't need to go into debt, can afford to let some struggling businesses carry perpetual debt on their books instead. In both China and the United States, the money supply is continually being inflated; but the Chinese mechanism may be more efficient, because it does a better job of recycling the money. The new money from Chinese loans that may or may not get repaid goes into the pockets of laborers, increasing their wages and their pensions, giving them more money for producing and purchasing goods. Like in the early American colonies, China's newly-created money is increasing the overall productivity of its economy and the standard of living of its people, promoting the general welfare by leavening the whole loaf at once. In twenty-first century America, by contrast, the economy keeps growing mainly from "money making money." The proceeds go into the pockets of investors who already have more than they can spend on consumer goods. American tax relief also tends to go to these non-producing investors, while American workers are heavily taxed. Meanwhile, the Chinese government is cutting taxes and raising salaries for consumers, in an effort to encourage more spending on cars and household appliances. The Chinese government recently eliminated rural taxes altogether.[11] How could it afford to do this? Evidently its secret is that it creates its own Greenback-style funding.

## Another Blow to the Quantity Theory of Money

In March 2006, the People's Bank of China reported that its M2 money supply had increased by a whopping 18.8 percent from a year earlier.[12] Under classical economic theory, this explosive growth should have crippled the economy with out-of-control price inflation; but it didn't. By early 2007, inflation in China was running at only 2 to 3 percent. In 2006, China pushed past France and Great Britain to become the world's fourth largest economy, with domestic retail sales boosted by 13 percent and industrial production by 16.6 percent.[13] As noted earlier, China has managed to keep the prices of its products low for thousands of years, although its money supply has continually been flooded with new currency that has poured in to pay for those cheap products.[14] The "economic mystery" of China may be explained by the Keynesian observation that when workers and raw materials are available to increase productivity, adding money ("demand") does not increase prices; it increases goods and services. Supply keeps up with demand, leaving prices unaffected.

We've seen that the usual trigger of hyperinflation is not a freely flowing money supply but the sudden devaluation of the currency induced by speculation in the currency market. China has so far managed to resist opening its currency to speculation; but Professor Liu warns that it has been engaged in a dangerous flirtation with foreign investors, who are continually leaning on it to bring its policies in line with the West's. China is "hoping to reap the euphoria of market fundamentalism without succumbing to this narcotic addiction," Liu writes, but "every addict begins with the confidence that he/she can handle the drug without falling into addiction."[15] He observes:

> After two and a half decades of economic reform toward neo-liberal market economy, China is still unable to accomplish in economic reconstruction what Nazi Germany managed in four years after coming to power, i.e., full employment with a vibrant economy financed with sovereign credit without the need to export, which would challenge that of Britain, the then superpower. *This is because China made the mistake of relying on foreign investment instead of using its own sovereign credit. The penalty for China is that it has to export the resultant wealth to pay for the foreign capital it did not need in the first place.* The result after more than two decades is that while China has become a creditor to the US to the tune of nearing China's own gross domestic product (GDP), it continues to have to beg the US for investment capital.[16]

Liu's proposed solution to the international debt crisis is what he calls "sovereign credit" and Henry Carey called "national credit": sovereign nations should pay their debts in their own currencies, issued by their own governments. Liu writes:

> Sovereign debts in local currency usually do not carry any default risk since the issuing government has the authority to issue money in domestic currency to repay its domestic debts. . . . [S]overeign debts' default risks are exclusively linked to foreign-currency debts and their impact on currency exchange rates. For this reason, *any government that takes on foreign debt is recklessly exposing its economy to unnecessary risk from external sources.*[17]

Although Liu says "the issuing government has the authority to issue money in domestic currency to repay its domestic debts," in the United States today, newly-created dollars are not issued by the U.S. Treasury. They originate with the privately-owned Federal Reserve or private commercial banks, which create the money in the form of loans. Like those governments that "take on foreign debt," the U.S. government will therefore never be able to cure its mounting debt crisis under the current system. The only way out may be the sort of Copernican revolution envisioned by this Chinese American economist with his feet in two worlds.

## The Dragon and the Eagle

Although China has been flirting with foreign capital investment, it has so far managed to retain the power to issue its own national currency. It has reportedly been using that sovereign power to print up renminbi and exchange them with Chinese companies for U.S. dollars, which are then used to buy U.S. securities, U.S. technology, and oil.[18] Washington can hardly complain, because the Chinese have been instrumental in helping the U.S. government bankroll its debt. The Japanese have also engaged in these maneuvers, evidently with U.S. encouragement. (See Chapter 40.) The problem with funding U.S. deficit spending with *fiat* money issued by foreign central banks is the leverage this affords America's competitors. According to a January 2005 Asia Times article, "All Beijing has to do is to mention the possibility of a sell order going down the wires. It would devastate the U.S. economy *more than a nuclear strike.*"[19]

Ironically, the Dragon has risen to challenge the Eagle's hegemony by adopting a monetary scheme that was made in America. For the United States to get back the chips it has lost in the global casino, it may need to return to its roots and adopt the financial cornerstone the builders rejected. It may need to do this for another reason: its debt-ridden economy could be on the brink of collapse. Like for Lincoln in the 1860s, the only way out may be the Greenback solution. We'll look at that challenge in Section IV, after considering one more interesting Asian phenomenon . . . .

# Chapter 28
# RECOVERING THE JEWEL
# OF THE BRITISH EMPIRE:
# A PEOPLE'S MOVEMENT
# TAKES BACK INDIA

*Of course the truck was a thousand times bigger than any of the mice who were to draw it. But when all the mice had been harnessed, they were able to pull it quite easily.*

– *The Wonderful Wizard of Oz,*
*"The Queen of the Field Mice"*

India is a second sleeping giant that is shaking off its ancient slumber. Once called the jewel in the crown of the British Empire, it was the very symbol of imperialism. Today India and China together are called the twin engines of economic growth for the twenty-first century. Combined, they represent two-fifths of the world's population. Mahatma Gandhi unleashed the collective power of the Indian people in the 1940s, when he helped bring about the country's independence by leading a mass non-violent resistance movement against the British. India celebrated its freedom in 1947. But in the next half century, the entrenched moneyed interests managed to regain their dominance by other means.

According to a PBS documentary called "Commanding Heights," in the 1950s India was a Mecca for economists, who poured in from all over the world to advise the Indian government on how to set up the model economy. Their advice was generally that it should have a state-led model of industrial growth, in which the public or government sector would occupy the "commanding heights" of the economy.

Gandhi's economic ideal was a simple India of self-sufficient villages; but Pandhit Nehru, the country's first prime minister, wanted to industrialize and combine British parliamentary democracy with Soviet-style central planning. In the prototype that resulted, all areas of heavy industry – steel, coal, machine tools, capital goods – were government-owned; but India added a democratically-elected government with a Parliament and a prime minister. The country became the model of economic development for newly independent nations everywhere, the leader for the Third World in planning, government ownership, and control.[1]

Helping to shape the economics of Nehru and his successor Indira Gandhi in the 1960s was celebrated American economist John Kenneth Galbraith, who was appointed ambassador to India by President John F. Kennedy. Galbraith believed that the government had an active role to play in stimulating the economy through public spending. He wrote and advised on public sector institutions and recommended the nationalization of banks, airlines and other industries. India's banks were nationalized in 1969.

Disillusionment with the promise of Indian independence set in, however, as the private interests that had controlled colonial India continued to pull the strings of the new Indian State. In 1973, the country had a positive trade balance; but that was before OPEC entered into an agreement to sell oil only in U.S. dollars. In 1974, the price of oil suddenly quadrupled. India had total foreign exchange reserves of only $629 million to pay an annual oil import bill of $1,241 million, almost double its available reserves. It therefore had to get U.S. dollars, and to do that it had to incur foreign debt and divert farming and other industry to products that would sell on foreign markets. In 1977, Indira Gandhi was forced into elections, in which key issues were the IMF and the domestic "austerity" measures the IMF invariably imposed in return for international loans. Indira was pushed out and was replaced with a regime friendlier to the globalist agenda. Engdahl writes, "the heavy hand of Henry Kissinger was present . . . in close coordination with the British."[2]

India's recent economic history was detailed in a 2005 article by a non-partisan research group in Mumbai, India, called the Research Unit for Political Economy (R.U.P.E.). It states that India's development was supposed to have been carried out free of powerful foreign and domestic private interests; but the economy wound up tailored to those very interests, which the authors describe darkly as "large domestic and foreign capitalists; landlords and other feudal sections; big traders and other parasitic forces." The government embarked on a policy of engaging in investment by expanding external and internal debt. Loan money was accepted from the IMF even when there was no immediate compulsion to do it. Annual economic growth increased, but it was largely growth in the "unproductive" industries of finance and defense. External debt ballooned from $19 billion in 1980, to $37 billion in 1985, to $84 billion in 1990, culminating in a balance of payments crisis in 1990-91 and a crippling IMF "structural adjustment" loan. After 1995, the policies advocated by the World Bank were reinforced by the stringent requirements of the newly-formed World Trade Organization. According to the R.U.P.E. group:

> For the people at large the development of events has been devastating. The relative stability of certain sections – middle peasants, organised sector workers, educated employees and teachers – evaporated; and those whose existence was already precarious plummeted. It took time for people to arrive at the perception that what was happening was not merely a series of individual tragedies, but a broader social calamity linked to official policy. As they did so, they expressed their anger in whatever way they could, generally by throwing out whichever party was in power . . . .

> Yet the [new government] follows, indeed must follow, broadly the same policies as its predecessor. Any attempt to slow the pace is met with rebukes and pressure from imperialist countries and the domestic corporate sector. Indeed, there is no longer any need for them to intervene explicitly. With the last 14 years of financial liberalisation, the country is now enormously vulnerable to volatile capital flows. This fact alone would rule out any serious populist exercise: for the resources required would have to be gathered either from increased taxation or from fiscal deficits, either of which would alienate foreign speculators and could precipitate a sudden outflow of capital.[3]

## Miracles for Investors, Poverty for Workers

Like other Third World countries, India has been caught in the trap of accepting foreign loans and investment, making it vulnerable to sudden capital flows, subjecting it to the whims and wishes of foreign financial powers. Countries that have been lured into this trap have wound up seeking financial assistance from the IMF, which has then imposed "austerity policies" as a condition of debt relief. These austerities include the elimination of food program subsidies, reduction of wages, increases in corporate profits, and privatization of public industry. All sorts of public assets go on the block – power companies, ports, airlines, railways, even social-welfare services. Canadian critic Wayne Ellwood writes of this "privatization trap":

> Dozens of countries and scores of public enterprises around the world have been caught up in this frenzy, many with little choice. . . . [C]ountries forced to the wall by debt have been pushed into the privatization trap by a combination of coercion and blackmail. . . . How much latitude do poor nations have to reject or shape adjustment policies? Virtually none. *The right of governments . . . to make sovereign decisions on behalf of their citizens – the bottom line of democracy – is simply jettisoned.*[4]

In theory, these structural adjustment programs also benefit local populations by enhancing the efficiency of local production, something that supposedly happens as a result of exposure to international competition in investment and trade. But their real effect has been simply to impose enormous hardships on the people. Food and transportation subsidies, public sector layoffs, curbs on government spending, and higher interest and tax rates all hit the poor disproportionately hard.[5] Helen Caldicott, M.D., co-founder of Physicians for Social Responsibility, writes:

> Women tend to bear the brunt of these IMF policies, for they spend more and more of their day digging in the fields by hand to increase the production of luxury crops, with no machinery or modern equipment. It becomes their lot to help reduce the foreign debt, even though they never benefited from the loans in the first place. . . . Most of the profits from commodity sales in the Third World go to retailers, middlemen, and shareholders in the First World. . . . UNICEF estimates that half a million children die each year because of the debt crisis.[6]

Countries have been declared "economic miracles" even when their poverty levels have increased. The "miracle" is achieved through a change in statistical measures. The old measure, called the gross national product or GNP, attributed profits to the country that received the money. The GNP included the gross domestic product or GDP (the total value of the output, income and expenditure produced within a country's physical borders) plus income earned from investment or work abroad. The new statistical measure looks simply at GDP. Profits are attributed to the country where the factories, mines, or financial institutions are located, even if the profits do not benefit the country but go to wealthy owners abroad.[7]

In 1980, median income in the richest 10 percent of countries was 77 times greater than in the poorest 10 percent. By 1999, that gap had grown to 122 times greater. In December 2006, the United Nations released a reported titled "World Distribution of Household Wealth," which concluded that *50 percent of the world's population now owns only 1 percent of its wealth.* The richest 1 percent own 40 percent of all global assets, with the 37 million people making up that 1 percent all having a net worth of $500,000 or more. The richest 10 percent of adults own 85 percent of global wealth. Under current conditions, the debts of the poorer nations can never be repaid but will just continue to grow. *Today more money is flowing back to the First World in the form of debt service than is flowing out in the form of loans.* By 2001, enough money had flowed back from the Third World to First World banks to pay the principal due on the original loans six times over. But interest consumed so much of those payments that the total debt actually quadrupled during the same period.[8]

## China and India: Ahead of the Pack

The statistics for most Third World countries are dismal, but India has done better than most. China, which is politically still Communist, is technically part of the "Second World," but it too has had serious struggles with poverty. Advocates of the free-market approach rely largely on data from China and India to show that the approach is working to reduce poverty, but as Christian Weller and Adam Hersh wryly observed in a 2002 editorial:

> [T]o use India and China as poster children for the IMF/World Bank brand of liberalization is laughable. *Both nations have sheltered their currencies from global speculative pressures (a serious*

*sin, according to the IMF).* Both have been highly protectionist (India has been a leader of the bloc of developing nations resisting WTO pressures for laissez-faire openness). And both have relied heavily on state-led development and have opened to foreign capital only with negotiated conditions.[9]

The declines in poverty in China and India occurred largely *before* the big strides in foreign trade and investment of the 1990s. Something else has contributed to their economic resilience, and one likely contributor is that both countries have succeeded in protecting their currencies from speculators. Both were largely insulated from the Asian crisis of the 1990s by their governments' refusal to open the national currency to foreign speculation. In India, as in in China, private banking has made some inroads; but in 2006, 80 percent of India's banks were still owned by the government.[10] Government ownership has not made these banks inefficient or uncompetitive. A 2001 study of consumer satisfaction found that the State Bank of India ranked highest in all areas scored, beating both domestic and foreign private banks and financing institutions.[11]

## A Country of Many States and Disparities

Differing assessments of how India is faring may be explained by the fact that it is a very large country divided into many states, with economic policies that differ. In a June 2005 article in the London Observer, Greg Palast noted that in those Indian states where globalist free trade policies have been imposed, workers have been reduced to sweatshop conditions due to murderous competition between workers without union protection. But these are not the states where Microsoft and Oracle are finding their highly-skilled computer talent. In those states, says Palast, the socialist welfare model is alive and thriving:

> The computer wizards of Bangalore (in Karnataka state) and Kerala are the products of fully funded state education systems where, unlike the USA, no child is left behind. A huge apparatus of state-owned or state-controlled industries, redistributionist tax systems, subsidies of necessities from electricity to food, tight government regulation and affirmative action programs for the lower castes are what has created these comfortable refuges for Oracle and Microsoft.

. . . What made this all possible was not capitalist competitive drive (there was no corporate "entrepreneur" in sight), but the state's investment in universal education and the village's commitment to development of opportunity, not for a lucky few, but for the entire community. The village was 100% literate, 100% unionized, and 100% committed to sharing resources through a sophisticated credit union finance system.[12]

Conditions are much different in the state of Andhra Pradesh, where farming has been the target of a "poverty eradication" program of the British government. Andhra Pradesh has the highest number of farmer suicides in India. These tragedies have generally followed the amassing of unrepayable debts for expensive seeds and chemicals for export crops that did not produce the promised returns. An April 2005 article in the British journal <u>Sustainable Economics</u> traced the problem to a project called "Vision 2020":

[T]he UK's Department for International Development (DFID) and World Bank were financing a project, Vision 2020 [which] aimed to transform the state to an export led, corporate controlled, industrial agriculture model that was thought likely to displace up to 20 million people from the land by 2020. There were no ideas or planning for what such displaced millions were to do and despite these fundamental and profound upheavals in the food system, there had been little or no involvement of small farmers and rural people in shaping this policy.

Vision 2020 was backed by a loan from the World Bank and was to receive £100 million of UK aid, 60% of all DFID's aid budget to India. . . . There were about 3000 farmer suicides in Andhra Pradesh in the 4 years prior to the May 2004 election and since the election there have been 1300 further suicides.[13]

Vendana Shiva, one of the article's co-authors, later put the number of farmer suicides at 150,000 in the decade before 2006.[14] Shiva and co-authors noted that India's farmers, who make up 70 percent of the population, voted out the existing coalition government in May 2004; but the new leaders too had to take their marching orders from the World Bank, the World Trade Organization (WTO) and multinational corporations. They observed that a growing number of laws and policies are being pushed through the legislature that threaten to rob the poor of their seeds, their food, their health and their livelihoods, including:

- A new patent ordinance that introduces product patents on seeds and medicines, putting them beyond people's reach. Prices increase 10- to 100-fold under patent monopolies. Since India is also the source of low-cost generic medicines for Africa, the introduction of patent monopolies in India is likely to increase debt and poverty globally.

- New policies for water privatization have been introduced, including privatization of Delhi's water supply, pushing water tariffs up by 10 to 15 times. The policies threaten to deprive the poor of their fundamental right to water, diverting scarce incomes to pay water bills that are 10 times higher than needed to cover the cost of operations and maintenance.

- The removal of regulations on prices and volumes, allowing giant corporations to set up private markets, destroying local markets and local production. India produces thousands of crops on millions of farms, while agribusiness trades in only a handful of commodities. Their new central role in much less regulated Indian markets is likely to result in destruction of diversity and displacement of small producers and traders.

India's poor, however, are not taking all this lying down. Following Gandhi's example of mass non-cooperation with oppressive British laws, they have organized a nation-wide movement against the patent ordinance. Communities are creating "freedom zones" to protect themselves from corporate invasion in areas such as genetically modified seeds, pesticides, unfair contracts, and monopolistic markets. The grassroots movement has called for a rethinking of GATT (the General Agreement on Tariffs and Trade), which led to the creation of the WTO in 1995. The WTO requires the laws of every member to conform to its own and has the power to enforce compliance by imposing sanctions.[15]

## The WTO and the NWO

The United States is also a member of the WTO. Critics warn that Americans could soon be seeing international troops in their own streets. The "New World Order" that was heralded at the end of the Cold War was supposed to be a harmonious global village without restrictions on trade and with cooperative policing of drug-trafficking, terrorism and arms controls. But to the wary, it is the road to a one-world government headed by transnational corporations, oppressing the public through military means and restricting individual freedoms. Bob Djurdjevic, writing in the paleoconservative journal Chronicles in 1998, compared the NWO to the old British empire:

> Parallels between the British Empire and the New World Order Empire are striking. It's just that the British crown relied on brute force to achieve its objectives, while the NWO elite mostly use financial terrorism . . . The British Empire was built by colonizing other countries, seizing their natural resources, and shipping them to England to feed the British industrialists' factories. In the wake of the "red coats" invasions, local cultures were often trampled and replaced by a "more progressive" British way of life.
>
> The Wall Street-dominated NWO Empire is being built by colonizing other countries with foreign loans or investments. When the fish is firmly on the hook, the NWO financial terrorists pull the plug, leaving the unsuspecting victim high and dry. And begging to be rescued. In comes the International Monetary Fund (IMF). Its bailout recipes – privatization, trade liberalization and other austerity reforms – amount to seizing the target countries' natural and other resources, and turning them over to the NWO elites – just as surely as the British Empire did by using cruder methods.[16]

Americans tend to identify with these Wall Street banks and transnational corporations because they have U.S. addresses, but Djurdjevic warns that the international cartels do not necessarily have our best interests in mind. To the contrary, Main Street America appears to be their next takeover target . . . .

# Section IV

# THE DEBT SPIDER
# CAPTURES AMERICA

*"We are all threatened," answered the tiger, "by a fierce enemy which has lately come into this forest. It is a most tremendous monster, like a great spider, with a body as big as an elephant and legs as long as a tree trunk. . . . [A]s the monster crawls through the forest he seizes an animal with a leg and drags it to his mouth, where he eats it as a spider does a fly. Not one of us is safe while this fierce creature is alive."*

– <u>The Wonderful Wizard of Oz</u>,
*"The Lion Becomes the King of Beasts"*

# Chapter 29

# BREAKING THE BACK OF
# THE TIN MAN:
# DEBT SERFDOM FOR
# AMERICAN WORKERS

*"I worked harder than ever; but I little knew how cruel my enemy could be. She made my axe slip again, so that it cut right through my body."*

– *The Wonderful Wizard of Oz,*
*"The Rescue of the Tin Woodman"*

The mighty United States has been in the banking spider's sights for more than two centuries. This ultimate prize too may finally have been captured in the spider's web, choked in debt spun out of thin air. The U.S. has now surpassed even Third World countries in its debt level. By 2004, the debt of the U.S. government had hit $7.6 trillion, more than three times that of all Third World countries combined. Like the bankrupt consumer who stays afloat by making the minimum payment on his credit card, the government has avoided bankruptcy by paying just the interest on its monster debt; but Comptroller General David M. Walker warns that by 2009 the country may not be able to afford even that mounting bill. When the government cannot service its debt, it will have to declare bankruptcy, and the economy will collapse.[1]

Al Martin is a retired naval intelligence officer, former contributor to the Presidential Council of Economic Advisors, and author of a weekly newsletter called "Behind the Scenes in the Beltway." He observed in an April 2005 newsletter that the ratio of total U.S. debt to gross domestic product (GDP) rose from 78 percent in 2000 to 308 percent in April 2005. The International Monetary Fund considers a nation-state with a total debt-to-GDP ratio of 200 percent or more to be a "de-constructed Third World nation-state." Martin wrote:

> What "de-constructed" actually means is that a political regime in that country, or series of political regimes, have, through a long period of fraud, abuse, graft, corruption and mismanagement, effectively collapsed the economy of that country.[2]

Other commentators warn that the "shock therapy" tested in Third World countries is the next step planned for the United States. Editorialist Mike Whitney wrote in <u>CounterPunch</u> in April 2005:

> [T]he towering national debt coupled with the staggering trade deficits have put the nation on a precipice and a seismic shift in the fortunes of middle-class Americans is looking more likely all the time. . . . The country has been intentionally plundered and will eventually wind up in the hands of its creditors . . . . This same Ponzi scheme has been carried out repeatedly by the IMF and World Bank throughout the world . . . . *Bankruptcy is a fairly straight forward way of delivering valuable public assets and resources to collaborative industries, and of annihilating national sovereignty. After a nation is successfully driven to destitution, public policy decisions are made by creditors and not by representatives of the people.* . . . The catastrophe that middle class Americans face is what these elites breezily refer to as "shock therapy"; a sudden jolt, followed by fundamental changes to the system. In the near future we can expect tax reform, fiscal discipline, deregulation, free capital flows, lowered tariffs, reduced public services, and privatization.[3]

Catherine Austin Fitts was formerly the managing director of a Wall Street investment bank and was Assistant Secretary of the Department of Housing and Urban Development (HUD) under President George Bush Sr. She calls what is happening to the economy "a criminal leveraged buyout of America." She defines that as "buying a country for cheap with its own money and then jacking up the rents and fees to steal the rest." She also calls it the "American Tapeworm" model:

> [T]he American Tapeworm model is to simply finance the federal deficit through warfare, currency exports, Treasury and federal credit borrowing and cutbacks in domestic "discretionary" spending. . . . This will then place local municipalities and local leadership in a highly vulnerable position – one that will allow

them to be persuaded with bogus but high-minded sounding arguments to further cut resources. Then, to "preserve bond ratings and the rights of creditors," our leaders can be persuaded to sell our water, natural resources and infrastructure assets at significant discounts of their true value to global investors. . . . This will all be described as a plan to "save America" by recapitalizing it on a sound financial footing. In fact, this process will simply shift more capital continuously from America to other continents and from the lower and middle classes to elites.[4]

## The Destruction of the Great American Middle Class

In 1894, Jacob Coxey warned of the destruction of the great American middle class. That prediction is rapidly materializing, as the gap between rich and poor grows ever wider. The Federal Reserve reported in 2004 that:

- The wealthiest 1 percent of Americans held 33.4 percent of the nation's wealth, up from 30.1 percent in 1989; while the top 5 percent held 55.5 percent of the wealth.

- The poorest 50 percent of the population held only 2.5 percent of the wealth, down from 3.0 percent in 1989.

- The very wealthiest 1 percent of Americans owned a bigger piece of the pie (33.4 percent) than the poorest 90 percent (30.4 percent of the pie). They also owned 62.3 percent of the nation's business assets.

- The wealthiest 5 percent owned 93.7 percent of the value of bonds, 71.7 percent of nonresidential real estate, and 79.1 percent of the nation's stocks.[5]

Forbes Magazine reported that from 1997 to 1999, the wealth of the 400 richest Americans grew by an average of $940 million *each*, for a *daily* increase of $1.3 million *per person*.[6] Note that lists of this sort do not include the world's truly richest families, including the Rothschilds, the Warburgs, and a long list of royal families. Whether they consider it to be in bad taste or because they fear retribution from the bottom of the wealth pyramid, the super-elite do not make their fortunes public.

## Debt Peonage: Eroding the Protection of the Bankruptcy Laws

While the super-rich are amassing fortunes rivaling the economies of small countries, Americans in the lower brackets are struggling with food and medical bills. Personal bankruptcy filings more than doubled from 1995 to 2005. In 2004, more than 1.1 million consumers filed for bankruptcy under Chapter 7. A Chapter 7 bankruptcy stays on the debtor's credit record for ten years from the date of filing, but at least it wipes the slate clean. In 2005, even that escape was taken away for many debtors. Under sweeping new provisions to the Bankruptcy Code, many more people are now required to file under Chapter 13, which does not eliminate debts but mandates that they be repaid under a court-ordered payment schedule over a three to five year period.

Homestead exemptions have traditionally protected homes from foreclosure in bankruptcy; but not all states have them, and the statutes usually preserve only a fraction of the home's worth. Worse, the new bankruptcy provisions require home ownership for a minimum of 40 months to qualify for the exemption. That means that if you file for bankruptcy within 3.3 years of purchase, your home is no longer off limits to creditors.[7] In the extreme case, the homeowner could not just lose his home but could owe a "deficiency," or balance due, for whatever the creditor bank failed to get from resale. This balance could be taken from the debtor's paychecks over a five-year period. State "anti-deficiency" laws may prevent this.[i] But again not all states have them, and they apply only to the original mortgage on the home. If the buyer takes out a second mortgage or takes equity out of the home, anti-deficiency laws may not apply. The push to persuade homeowners to take out home equity loans recalls the 1920s campaign to persuade people to borrow against their homes to invest in the stock

---

[i]   If a home buyer fails to make the mortgage payments, the property is foreclosed and legal proceedings are brought by the lender. The property is then typically sold to pay the mortgage, and a deficiency between the sale price and the outstanding balance of the mortgage usually exists. Anti-deficiency laws apply in some states if the mortgage is a purchase money mortgage for the purchase of a dwelling occupied by the purchaser. Under these laws, the purchaser can walk away from the property without owing a deficiency judgment, and the lender can recover only the property and the proceeds of a subsequent sale; but the laws typically provide no protection for second mortgages, home equity lines, or mortgages on property not used as the purchaser's primary residence.

market. When the stock market crashed, their homes became the property of the banks. Elderly people burdened with medical and drug bills are particularly susceptible to those tactics today.

Another insidious change that has been made in the bankruptcy laws pertains to insolvent corporations. The law originally provided for the appointment of an independent bankruptcy trustee, whose job was to try to keep the business running and preserve the jobs of the workers. In the 1970s, the law was changed so that the plan of bankruptcy reorganization would be designed by the *banks* that were financing the restructuring. The creditors now came first and the workers had to take what was left. The downsizing of the airline industry, the steel industry, and the auto industry followed, precipitating masses of worker layoffs.[8]

Normally, it would fall to the individual States to provide a safety net for their citizens from personal disasters of this sort, but the States have been driven to the brink of bankruptcy as well. Diversion of State funds to out-of-control federal spending has left States with budget crises that have forced them to take belt-tightening measures like those seen in Third World countries. Social services have been cut for those most in need during an economic downturn, including services for childcare, health insurance, income support, job training programs and education. Social services are "discretionary" budget items, which have been sacrificed to the fixed-interest income of the creditors who are first in line to get paid.[9]

Billionaire philanthropist Warren Buffett has warned that America, rather than being an "ownership society," is fast becoming a "sharecroppers' society." Paul Krugman suggested in a 2005 <u>New York Times</u> editorial that the correct term is "debt peonage" society, the system prevalent in the post-Civil War South, when debtors were forced to work for their creditors. American corporations are assured of cheap, non-mobile labor of the sort found in Third World countries by a medical insurance system and other benefits tied to employment. People dare not quit their jobs, however unsatisfactory, for fear of facing medical catastrophes without insurance, particularly now that the escape hatch of bankruptcy has narrowed substantially. Most personal bankruptcies are the result of medical emergencies and other severe misfortunes such as job loss or divorce. The Bankruptcy Reform Act of 2005 eroded the protection the government once provided against these unexpected catastrophes, ensuring that working people are kept on a treadmill of personal debt. Meanwhile, loopholes allowing very wealthy people and corporations to go bankrupt and to shield their assets from creditors remain intact.[10]

## Graft and Greed in the Credit Card Business

The 2005 bankruptcy bill was written by and for credit card companies. Credit card debt reached $735 billion by 2003, more than 11 times the tab in 1980. Approximately 60 percent of credit card users do not pay off their monthly balances; and among those users, the average debt carried on their cards is close to $12,000. *This "sub-prime" market is actually targeted by banks and credit card companies*, which count on the poor, the working poor and the financially strapped to *not* be able to make their payments. According to a 2003 book titled The Two-Income Trap by Warren and Tyagi:

> More than 75 percent of credit card profits come from people who make those low, minimum monthly payments. And who makes minimum monthly payments at 26 percent interest? Who pays late fees, over-balance charges, and cash advance premiums? Families that can barely make ends meet, households precariously balanced between financial survival and complete collapse. These are the families that are singled out by the lending industry, barraged with special offers, personalized advertisements, and home phone calls, all with one objective in mind: get them to borrow more money.

"Payday" lender operations offering small "paycheck advance" loans have mushroomed. Particularly popular in poor and minority communities, they can carry usurious interest rates as high as 500 percent. The debt crisis has been blamed on the imprudent spending habits of people buying frivolous things; but Warren and Tyagi observe that two-income families are actually spending 21 percent *less* on clothing, 22 percent less on food, and 44 percent less on appliances than one-income families spent a generation earlier. The reason is that they are spending substantially *more* on soaring housing prices and medical costs.[11]

In 2003, the average family was spending 69 percent more on home mortgage payments in inflation-adjusted dollars than their parents spent a generation earlier, and 61 percent more on health needs. At the same time, real wages had stagnated or declined. Most people were struggling to get by with less; and in order to get by, many turned to credit cards to pay for basic necessities. Credit card companies and their affiliated banks capitalize on the extremity of poor and working-class people by using high-pressure tactics to sign up borrowers they know can't afford their loans, then jacking up interest rates or forcing customers to buy "insurance" on the loans.[12] People who can make only minimal payments on their credit card bills wind up in "debt peonage" to the banks. The scenario recalls the sinister observation made in the Hazard Circular circulated during the American Civil War:

> [S]lavery is but the owning of labor and carries with it the care of the laborers, while the European plan, led by England, is that *capital shall control labor by controlling wages. This can be done by controlling the money.* The great debt that capitalists will see to it is made out of the war, must be used as a means to control the volume of money.

The slaves kept in the pre-Civil War South had to be fed and cared for. People enslaved by debt must feed and house themselves.

## Usurious Loans of Phantom Money

The ostensible justification for allowing lenders to charge whatever interest the market will bear is that it recognizes the time value of money. Lenders are said to be entitled to this fee in return for foregoing the use of their money for a period of time. That argument might have some merit if the lenders actually *were* lending their own money, but in the case of credit card and other commercial bank debt, they aren't. *They aren't even lending their depositors' money. They are lending nothing but the borrower's own credit.* We know this because of what the Chicago Fed said in "Modern Money Mechanics":

> Of course, [banks] do not really pay out loans from the money they receive as deposits. If they did this, no additional money would be created. *What they do when they make loans is to accept promissory notes in exchange for credits to the borrowers' transaction accounts.* Loans (assets) and deposits (liabilities) both rise [by the same amount].[13]

Here is how the credit card scheme works: when you sign a merchant's credit card charge slip, you are creating a "negotiable instrument." A negotiable instrument is anything that is signed and convertible into money or that can be used as money. The merchant takes this negotiable instrument and deposits it into his merchant's checking account, a special account required of all businesses that accept credit. The account goes up by the amount on the slip, indicating that the merchant has been paid. The charge slip is forwarded to the credit card company (Visa, MasterCard, etc.), which bundles your charges and sends them to a bank. The bank then sends you a statement, which you pay with a check, causing your transaction account to be debited at your bank. At no point has a bank lent you its money or its depositors' money. Rather, your charge slip (a negotiable instrument) has become an "asset" against which credit has been advanced. The bank has done nothing but *monetize* your own I.O.U. or promise to repay.[14]

When you lend someone your *own* money, your assets go down by the amount that the borrower's assets go up. But when a *bank* lends *you* money, its assets go *up*. Its liabilities also go up, since its deposits are counted as liabilities; but the money isn't really there. It is *simply* a liability – something that is owed back to the depositor. The bank turns your promise to pay into an asset and a liability at the same time, balancing its books without actually transferring any pre-existing money to you.

The spiraling debt trap that has subjected financially-strapped people to usurious interest charges for the use of something the lenders never had to lend is a fraud on the borrowers. In 2006, profits to lenders just from interest charges and late fees on U.S. credit card debt came to $90 billion. An alternative for retaining the benefits of the credit card system without feeding a parasitic class of unnecessary middlemen is suggested in Chapter 41.

# Chapter 30
# THE LURE IN THE
# CONSUMER DEBT TRAP:
# THE ILLUSION OF
# HOME OWNERSHIP

*"There's no place like home, there's no place like home, there's no place like home . . . ."*

If the bait that caught Third World countries in the bankers' debt trap was the promise of foreign loans and investment, for Americans in the twenty-first century it is the lure of home ownership and the promise of ready cash from home equity loans. Increased rates of home ownership are cited as a bright spot for labor in an economy in which workers continue to struggle. Home ownership is touted as being higher than ever before, hitting a high of nearly 69 percent in 2004.[1] That figure, however, is highly misleading. Sixty-nine percent of *individuals* obviously don't own their own homes. The figure applies only to "households." And while legal title may be in the name of the buyer, the home isn't really "owned" by the household until the mortgage is paid off. Only 40 percent of homes are now owned "free and clear," and that figure includes properties owned as second homes, as vacation homes, and by landlords who have rented the property out to non-homeowners. Even homes that were at one time owned free and clear may now have mortgages on them, after the owners have been lured by lenders into taking cash out through home equity loans. As a result of refinancing and residential mobility, most mortgages on single-family properties today are less than four years old, which means they have a long way to go before they are paid off.[2] And if the mortgages are less than 3.3 years old, the homes are not subject to the homestead exemption and can be taken by the banks even if the strapped debtors file for bankruptcy.

*The touted increase in "home ownership" actually means an increase in debt.* Households today owe more debt relative to their disposable income than ever before. In late 2004, mortgage debt amounted to 85 percent of disposable income, a record high. The fact that interest rates approached historic lows appeared to keep payments manageable, but the total amount of debt rose faster for the typical family than interest rates declined. As a result, households still ended up paying a greater share of their incomes for their mortgages. Total U.S. mortgage debt increased by over 80 percent between 1991 and 2001, and residential debt grew another 50 percent between 2001 and 2005. From 2001 through 2005, outstanding mortgage debt rose from $5.3 trillion to $8.9 trillion, the biggest debt expansion in history. In 2004, U.S. household debt increased more than twice as fast as disposable income; and most of this new debt-money came from the housing market. Homeowners took equity out of their homes through home sales, refinancings and home equity loans totaling about $700 billion in 2004, more than twice the $266 billion taken five years earlier. Debts due to residential mortgages exceeded *$8.1 trillion*, a sum larger even than the out-of-control federal debt, which hit $7.6 trillion the same year.[3]

## Baiting the Trap: Seductively Low Interest Rates and "Teaser Rates"

The housing bubble was another ploy of the Federal Reserve and the banking industry for pumping accounting-entry money into the economy. In the 1980s, the Fed reacted to a stock market crisis by lowering interest rates, making investment money readily available, inflating the stock market to unprecedented heights in the 1990s. When the stock market topped out in 2000 and started downward, the Fed could have allowed it to correct naturally; but that alternative was politically unpopular, and it would have meant serious losses to the banks that own the Fed. The decision was made instead to prop up the market with even *lower* interest rates. The federal funds rate was dropped to 1.0 percent, launching a credit expansion that was even greater than in the 1990s, encouraging further speculation in both stocks and real estate.[4]

After the Fed set the stage, banks and other commercial lenders fanned the housing boom into a blaze with a series of high-risk changes in mortgage instruments, including variable rate loans that allowed nearly anyone to qualify to buy a home who was willing to take the bait. By 2006, about half of all U.S. mortgages were at "adjustable" interest rates. Purchasers were lulled by "teaser" rates into believing they could afford mortgages that in fact were liable to propel them into inextricable debt if not into bankruptcy. Property values have gotten so high today that the only way many young couples can even hope to become homeowners is to agree to an adjustable rate mortgage or ARM, a very risky type of mortgage loan in which the interest rate and payments fluctuate with market conditions. The risks of ARMs were explained in a December 2005 press release by the Office of the Comptroller of the Currency:

> [T]he initial lower monthly payment means that less principal is being paid. As a result, *the loan balance grows*, or amortizes negatively until the sixth year when payments are adjusted to ensure the principal is paid off over the remaining 25 years of the loan. In the case of a typical $360,000 payment option mortgage that starts at 6 percent interest, *monthly payments could increase by 50 percent in the sixth year if interest rates do not change. If rates jump two percentage points, to 8 percent, monthly payments could double.*[5]

Homeowners agreeing to this arrangement are gambling that either their incomes will increase to meet the payment burden or that the housing market will continue to go up, allowing them to sell the home before the sixth year at a profit. But the housing bubble has now topped out; and like in every Ponzi scheme, the vulnerable buyers who got in last will be left holding the bag when the bubble collapses.

Even borrowers who have fixed rate mortgages can wind up paying quite a bit more than they anticipated for their homes. Loans are structured so that the borrower who agrees to a 30-year mortgage at a fixed rate of 7 percent will actually pay about 2-1/2 times the list price of the house over the course of the loan. A house priced at $330,000 at 7 percent interest would accrue *$460,379.36* in interest, for a total tab of $790,379.36.[6] The bank thus actually gets a bigger chunk of the pie than the seller, although it never owned *either* the property *or* the loan money, which was created as it was lent; and home loans are completely secured, so the risk to the bank is very low. The buyer will pay about 2-1/2 times the list price to borrow money the bank never had until the mortgage was signed; and if he fails to pay the full 250 percent, the bank may wind up with the house.

For the first five years of a thirty-year home mortgage, most of the buyer's monthly payments consist of interest. For ARMs, the loans may be structured so that the first five years' payments consist *only* of interest, with a variable-rate loan thereafter. Since most homes change hands within five years, the average buyer who thinks he owns his own home finds on resale that most if not all of the equity still belongs to the lender. If interest rates go up in the meantime, home values will drop, and the buyer will be locked into higher payments for a less valuable house.

The Homestead Laws that gave settlers their own plot of land have been largely eroded by 150 years of the "business cycle," in which bankers have periodically raised interest rates and called in loans, creating successive waves of defaults and foreclosures. For most families, the days of inheriting the family home free and clear are a thing of the past. Some individual homeowners have made out well from the housing boom, but the overall effect has been to put the average family on the hook for a substantially more expensive mortgage than it would have had a decade ago. Again the real winners have been the banks. As market commentator Craig Harris explained in a March 2004 article:

> Essentially what has happened is that there was a sort of stealth transfer of net worth from the public to the banks to help save the system. The public took on the risk, went further into debt, spent a lot of money . . . and the banks' new properties have appreciated substantially. . . . They created the money and lent it to you, you spent the money to prop up the economy, and now they own the real property and you're on the hook to pay them back an inflated price [for] that property . . . They gave you a better rate but you paid more for the property which they now own until you pay them back.[7]

## The Impending Tsunami of Sub-prime Morgage Defaults

The same "sub-prime" market that has been targeted by credit card companies has become a lucrative market for those lenders eager to qualify anyone for a home mortgage willing to commit to one. Sub-prime mortgage lending grew more than 500 percent from 1994 to 2002. In a November 2005 article called "Surreal Estate on the San Andreas Fault," Gary North estimated that loans related to the housing market had grown to 80 percent of bank lending, and that much of this growth was in the sub-prime market, which had been hooked with ARMs that were very risky not only for the borrowers but for the lenders. North warned:

> . . . Even without a recession, the [housing] boom will falter because of ARMs . . . . These time bombs are about to blow, contract by contract.
>
> *If nothing changes -- if short-term rates do not rise -- monthly mortgage payments are going to rise by 60% when the readjustment kicks in.* Yet buyers are marginal, people who could not qualify for a 30-year mortgage. This will force "For Sale" signs to flower like dandelions in spring. . . .
>
> If you remember the S&L [savings and loan association] crisis of the mid-1980s, you have some indication of what is coming. The S&L crisis in Texas put a squeeze on the economy in Texas. Banks got nasty. They stopped making new loans. Yet the S&Ls were legally not banks. They were a second capital market. *Today, the banks have become S&Ls. They have tied their loan portfolios to the housing market.*
>
> I think a squeeze is coming that will affect the entire banking system. The madness of bankers has become unprecedented. . . Banks will wind up sitting on top of bad loans of all kinds because the American economy is now housing-sale driven.[8]

The savings and loan industry collapsed when interest rates were raised to unprecedented levels in the 1980s. The commercial banks' prime rate (the rate at which they had to borrow) reached 20.5 percent at a time when the S&Ls were earning only about 5 percent on mortgage loans made previously. The negative spread caused them huge losses. Today, banks are liable to off-load mortgages by selling them to Fannie Mae (the Federal National Mortgage Association) or Freddie Mac (the Federal Home Mortgage Corporation), which now own or guarantee over 40 percent of the U.S. mortgage market.[9] Fannie and Freddie then bundle up these mortgages and sell them as mortgage-backed securities (MBS) to investors. But the risk to the banks is still there, because the terms of the MBS allow non-performing loans to be sold back to the lender or to Fannie and Freddie.[10] (More on this in Chapter 31.) And the banks themselves are investing in MBS.

By January 2007, the housing boom had substantially cooled after a series of interest rate hikes imposed by the Fed. An article in The New York Times warned, "1 in 5 sub-prime loans will end in foreclosure . . . . About 2.2 million borrowers who took out sub-prime loans from

1998 to 2006 are likely to lose their homes." In an editorial the same month, Mike Whitney noted that when family members and other occupants are included, that could mean 10 million people turned out into the streets; and some analysts thought even that estimate was low. Whitney quoted Peter Schiff, president of an investment strategies company, who warned, "The secondary effects of the '1 out of 5' sub-prime default rate will be a chain reaction of rising interest rates and falling home prices engendering still more defaults, with the added foreclosures causing the cycle to repeat. In my opinion, when the cycle is fully played out we are more likely to see an 80% default rate rather than 20%." Whitney commented:

> 40 million Americans headed towards foreclosure? Better pick out a comfy spot in the local park to set up the lean-to. Schiff's calculations may be overly pessimistic, but his reasoning is sound. Once mortgage-holders realize that their homes are worth tens of thousands less than the amount of their loan they are likely to "mail in their house keys rather than make the additional mortgage payments." As Schiff says, "Why would anyone stretch to spend 40% of his monthly income to service a $700,000 mortgage on a condo valued at $500,000, especially when there are plenty of comparable rentals that are far more affordable?"[11]

As with the Crash of 1929, responsibility for all this is being pinned on the Federal Reserve, which blew up the housing bubble with "easy" credit, then put a pin in it by making credit much harder to get. Whitney writes:

> [The Fed] kept the printing presses whirring along at full-tilt while the banks and mortgage lenders devised every scam imaginable to put greenbacks into the hands of unqualified borrowers. ARMs, "interest-only" or "no down payment" loans etc. were all part of the creative financing boondoggle which kept the economy sputtering along after the "dot.com" crackup in 2000.
>
> ... Now, many of those same buyers are stuck with enormous loans that are about to reset at drastically higher rates while their homes have already depreciated 10% to 20% in value. This phenomenon of being shackled to a "negative equity mortgage" is what economist Michael Hudson calls the "New Road to Serfdom"; paying off a mortgage that is significantly larger than the current value of the house. The sheer magnitude of the problem is staggering.

Although the ability to adjust interest rates is considered a necessary and proper tool of the Fed in managing the money supply, it is also a form of arbitrary manipulation that can be used to benefit one group over another. The very notion that we have a "free market" is belied by the fact that investors, advisers and market analysts wait with bated breath to hear what the Fed is going to do to interest rates from month to month. The market is responding not to supply and demand but to top-down dictatorial control.

Financial weather forecasters now see two economic storm fronts forming on the horizon, and both have been blamed on the market manipulations of the Fed . . . .

# Chapter 31
# THE PERFECT FINANCIAL STORM

*Uncle Henry sat upon the doorstep and looked anxiously at the sky, which was even grayer than usual. . . . "There's a cyclone coming, Em," he called to his wife. . . . Aunt Em dropped her work and came to the door. . . . "Quick, Dorothy!" she screamed. "Run for the cellar!"*

*– The Wonderful Wizard of Oz,*
*"The Cyclone"*

The rare weather phenomenon known as "the perfect storm" occurs when two storm fronts collide. What analysts are calling "the perfect financial storm" is the impending collision of the two economic storm fronts of inflation and deflation. The American money supply is being continually pumped up with new money created as loans, but borrowers are increasingly unable to repay their loans, which are going into default. When loans are extinguished by default, the money supply contracts and deflation and depression result. The collision of these two forces can result in "stagflation" – price inflation without economic growth. That is a "category 1" financial storm. A "category 5" storm might result from a derivatives crisis in which major traders defaulted on their bets, or from a serious decline in the housing market. In a June 2005 newsletter, Al Martin stated that the General Accounting Office, the Office of the Comptroller of the Currency, and the Federal Housing Administration had privately warned that a decline of as much as 40 percent could occur in the housing market between 2005 and 2010; and that a housing decline of that magnitude could collapse the economy of the United States.[1]

## The Debt Crisis and the Housing Bubble

After a series of changes beginning in 2001 dropping the federal funds rate to unprecedented lows, housing prices began their inexorable climb, aided by a loosening of lending standards. Adjustable-rate loans, interest only loans, and no down payment loans drew many new home buyers into the market, putting steady upward pressure on prices. Soaring housing prices, in turn, deepened the debt crisis. To keep all this new debt-money afloat required a steady stream of new borrowers, prompting lenders to offer loans to shaky borrowers on more and more lax conditions. In 2005, a Mortgage Bankers Association survey found that high-risk adjustable and interest-only loans had grown to account for nearly half of new loan applications. Federal Reserve Governor Susan Schmidt Bies, speaking in October 2005, said that average U.S. housing prices had appreciated by more than 80 percent since 1997.

Rock-bottom interest rates salvaged stock market speculators and big investment banks from the 2000 recession, and they allowed some politically-popular tax cuts that favored big investors; but they were disastrous for the bond market, where retired people have traditionally invested for a safe and predictable return on their savings. By 2004, real returns after inflation on short-term interest rates were negative.[2] (That is, if you lent $100 to the government by buying its bonds this year, your investment might grow to be worth $102 next year; but after inflation it would be worth only $98.) The result was to force retired people living on investment income from the reliable bond market into the much riskier stock market. Today, stocks are owned by over half of Americans, the highest number in history.

The Fed's low-interest policies also discouraged foreign investors from buying U.S. bonds, and that is what precipitated the second financial storm front. Foreign investment money is relied on by the government to roll over its ballooning debt. New bonds must continually be sold to investors to replace the old bonds as they come due. The Fed has therefore been under pressure to raise interest rates, both to attract foreign investors and to keep a lid on inflation. Higher interest rates, however, mean that increasing numbers of homes will go into foreclosure; and when mortgages are voided out, the supply of credit-money they created shrinks with them. Although the sellers have been paid and the old loan money is still in the system, the banks have to balance their books, which means they can create less money in the form of new loans; and borrowers are harder to find, because higher interest rates are less attractive to them. In the last "normal" correction of the housing market, between 1989 and 1991, median home prices dropped by 17 percent, and 3.6 million mortgages went into default. Analysts estimated, however, that the same decline in 2005 would have produced *20 million* defaults, because the average equity-to-debt ratio (the percentage of a home that is actually "owned" by the homeowner) had dropped dramatically. The ratio went from 37 percent in 1990 to a mere 14 percent in 2005, a record low, because $3 trillion had been taken out of property equities in the previous four years to sustain consumer spending.[3]

What would 20 million defaults do to the money supply? Al Martin cites a Federal Reserve study reported by Alan Greenspan before the Joint Economic Committee in June 2005, estimating that *two trillion dollars would simply evaporate along with these uncollectible loans*. That means two trillion dollars less to spend on government programs, wages and salaries. In 2005, two trillion dollars was about one-fifth the total M3 money supply. Accompanying that radical contraction, analysts predicted that stocks and home values would plummet, income taxes would triple, Social Security and Medicare benefits would be slashed in half, and pensions and comfortable retirements would become things of the past. And that was assuming housing prices dropped by *only* 17 percent. A substantially higher drop was feared, with even more dire consequences.[4]

## Fannie and Freddie: Compounding the Housing Crisis with Derivatives and Mortgage-Backed Securities

In a June 2002 article titled "Fannie and Freddie Were Lenders," Richard Freeman warned that the housing bubble is the largest bubble in history, dwarfing anything that has gone before; and that it has been pumped up to its gargantuan size by Fannie Mae and Freddie Mac, twin volcanoes that are about to blow. Fannie and Freddie have dramatically expanded the ways money can be created by mortgage lending, allowing the banks to issue many more loans than would otherwise have been possible; but it all adds up to another Ponzi scheme, and it is approaching its mathematical limits.

Freeman focuses on the larger of these two institutional cousins, Fannie Mae (the Federal National Mortgage Association). He notes that if it were a bank, Fannie would now be the third largest bank in the world; and it makes enormous amounts of money in the real estate market for its private owners. Contrary to popular belief, Fannie Mae is not actually a government agency. It began that way under Roosevelt's New Deal, but it was later transformed into a totally private corporation, which issued stock that was bought by private investors. Eventually, it was listed on the stock exchange. Like the Federal Reserve, it is now "federal" only in name.

Before the late 1970s, there were only two principal forms of mortgage lending. The lender could issue a mortgage loan and keep it; or the lender could sell the loan to Fannie Mae and use the cash to make a second loan, which could also be sold to Fannie Mae, allowing the bank to make a third loan, and so on. Freeman gives the example of a mortgage-lending financial institution that makes five successive loans in this way for $150,000 each, all from an initial investment of $150,000. It sells the first four loans to Fannie Mae, which buys them with money made from the issuance of its own bonds. The lender keeps the fifth loan. At the end of the process, the mortgage-lending institution still has only one loan for $150,000 on its books, and Fannie Mae has loans totaling $600,000 on its books.

Then in 1979-81, policy changes were made that would flood the housing market with even more new money. Fannie Mae gathered its purchased mortgages from different mortgage-lending institutions and pooled them together, producing a type of lending vehicle called a Mortgage-Backed Security (MBS). Fannie might, for example, bundle one thousand 30-year fixed-interest mortgages, each worth roughly $100,000, and pool them into a $100 million MBS. It would put a loan guarantee on the MBS, for which it would earn a fee, guaranteeing that in the event of default it would pay the interest and principal due on the loans "fully and in a timely fashion." The MBS would then be sold as securities in denominations of $1,000 or more to outside investors, including mutual funds, pension funds, and insurance companies. The investors would become the owners of the MBS and would have a claim on the underlying principal and interest stream of the mortgage; but if anything went wrong, Fannie Mae was still responsible. The MBS succeeded in extending the sources of funds that could be tapped into for mortgage lending far into U.S. and international financial markets. It also substantially increased Fannie Mae's risk.

Then Fannie devised a fourth way of extracting money from the markets. It took the securities and pooled them again, this time into an instrument called a Real Estate Mortgage Investment Conduit or REMIC (also known as a "restructured MBS" or collateralized mortgage obligation). REMICs are very complex derivatives. Freeman writes, "*They are pure bets*, sold to institutional investors, and individuals, to draw money into the housing bubble." Roughly half of all of Fannie Mae's Mortgage Backed Securities have been transformed into these highly speculative REMIC derivative instruments. "Thus," says Freeman, "what started out as a simple home mortgage has been transmogrified into something one would expect to find at a Las Vegas gambling casino. Yet the housing bubble now depends on precisely these instruments as sources of funds."

Only the first of these devices is an "asset," something on which Fannie Mae can collect a steady stream of principal and interest. The others represent very risky obligations. These investment vehicles have fed the housing bubble and have fed off it, but at some point a wave of mortgage defaults is inevitable; and when that happens, the riskier mortgage-related obligations will amplify the crisis. They are particularly risky because they involve leveraging (making multiple investments with borrowed money). That means that when the bet goes wrong, many losses must be paid instead of one.

In 2002, Fannie Mae's bonds made up over $700 billion of its outstanding debt total of $764 billion. Only one source of income was available to pay the interest and principal on these bonds, the money Fannie collected on the mortgages it owned. If a substantial number of mortgages were to go into default, Fannie would not have the cash to pay its bondholders. Freeman observes that *no company in America has ever defaulted on as much as $50 billion in bonds, and Fannie Mae has over $700 billion – at least ten times more than any other corporation in America*. A default on a bonded debt of that size, he says, could end the U.S. financial system virtually overnight. Like those banking institutions considered "too big to fail," Fannie Mae has tentacles reaching into so much of the financial system that if it goes, it could take the economy down with it. A wave of home mortgage defaults would not alone have been enough to bring down the whole housing market, but adding the possibility of default on Fannie's riskier obligations, totaling over $2 trillion in 2002, the possibility of a system-wide default has been raised to "radioactive" levels. If a crisis in the housing mortgage market were to produce a wave of loan defaults, Fannie would not be able to meet the terms of the guarantees it put on $859 billion in Mortgage-Backed Securities, and the pension funds and other investors buying the MBS would suffer tens of billions of dollars in losses. Fannie's derivative obligations, which totaled $533 billion in 2002, could also go into default. These hedges are supposed to protect investors from risks, but the hedges themselves are very risky ventures. Fannie Mae has taken extraordinary measures to roll over shaky mortgages in order to obscure the level of default currently threatening the system; but as households with declining real standards of living are increasingly unable to pay rising home prices and the demands of ever larger mortgages and higher interest payments, mortgage defaults will rise. The leverage that has been built into the housing market could then unwind like a rubber band, rapidly de-leveraging the entire market.[5]

In 2003, Freddie Mac was embroiled in a $5 billion accounting scandal in which it was caught "cooking" the books to make things look rosier than they were. In 2004, Fannie Mae was caught in a similar scandal. In 2006, Fannie agreed to pay $400 million for its misbehavior ($50 million to the U.S. government and $350 million to defrauded shareholders), and to try to straighten out its books. But investigators said the accounting could be beyond repair, since some $16 billion had simply disappeared from the books.

Meanwhile, after blowing the housing bubble to perilous heights with a 1 percent prime rate, the Fed proceeded to let the air back out with a succession of interest rate hikes. By 2006, the housing boom was losing steam. Nervous investors wondered who would be shouldering the risk when the mortgages bundled into MBS slid into default. As one colorful blogger put it:

> So let me get this straight . . . . Is the following scenario below actually playing out?
>
> For starters ma n' pa computer programmer buy a 500K house in Ballard using a neg-am/i-o [negative amortization interest-only mortgage] sold to them by a dodgy local fly-by night lender. That lender immediately sells it off to some middle-man for a period of time. The middlemen take their cut and then sell that loan upstream to Fannie Mae/Freddie Mac before it becomes totally toxic and reaches critical mass. At which point FM/FM bundle that loan into a mortgage backed security and sell it to pension funds, foreign banks, etc. etc.
>
> What happens when those loans go into their inevitable default? Who owns the property at that point and is left holding the bag?[6]

Nobody on the blog seemed to know; but according to Freeman, Fannie Mae will be holding the bag, since it guaranteed payment of interest and principal in the event of default. When Fannie Mae can't pay, the pension funds and other institutions investing in its MBS will be left holding the bag; and *it is these pension funds that manage the investments on which the retirements of American workers depend.* When that happens, comfortable retirements could indeed be things of the past.

All of which is ominous enough, but an even greater peril is now lurking in the economic shadows . . . .

# Chapter 32

# IN THE EYE OF THE CYCLONE:
# HOW THE DERIVATIVES CRISIS HAS
# GRIDLOCKED THE BANKING SYSTEM

*In the middle of a cyclone the air is generally still, but the great pressure of the wind on every side of the house raised it up higher and higher, until it was at the very top of the cyclone; and there it remained and was carried miles and miles away.*

– *The Wonderful Wizard of Oz,*
"The Cyclone"

The looming derivatives crisis is another phenomenon often described with weather imagery. "The grey clouds are getting darker," wrote financial consultant Colt Bagley in 2004; "the winds only need to kick up and we'll have one heck of a financial cyclone in the making."[1] A decade earlier, Christopher White told Congress:

> Taken as a whole, the financial derivatives market, orchestrated by financiers, operates with the vortical properties of a powerful hurricane. It is so huge and packs such a large momentum, that it sucks up the overwhelming majority of the capital and cash that enters or already exists in the economy. It makes a mockery of the idea that a nation exercises sovereign control over its credit policy.[2]

Martin Weiss, writing in a November 2006 investment newsletter, calls the derivatives crisis "a global Vesuvius that could erupt at almost any time, instantly throwing the world's financial markets into turmoil ... bankrupting major banks ... sinking big-name insurance companies ... scrambling the investments of hedge funds ... overturning the portfolios of millions of average investors."[3]

John Hoefle's arresting image was of fleas on a dog. "The fleas have killed the dog," he said, "and thus they have killed themselves."[4] Colt Bagley also sees in the derivatives crisis the seeds of the banks' own destruction. He wrote in 2004:

> Once upon a time, the American banking system extended loans to productive agriculture and industry. *Now, it is a vast betting machine, gaming on market distortions of interest rates, stocks, currencies, etc.* . . . JP Morgan Chase Bank (JPMC) dominates the U.S. derivatives market . . . JPMC Bank alone has derivatives approaching four times the U.S. Gross Domestic Product of $11.5 trillion. Next come Bank of America and Citibank, with $14.9 trillion and $14.4 trillion in derivatives, respectively. The OCC [Office of the Comptroller of the Currency] reports that the top seven American derivatives banks hold 96% of the U.S. banking system's notional derivatives holding. If these banks suffer serious impairment of their derivatives holdings, *kiss the banking system goodbye.*

Martin Weiss envisions how this collapse might occur:

> Portfolio managers at a major hedge fund bet too much on declining interest rates and they lose. They don't have enough capital to pay up on the bet, and the counterparties in the transaction – the winners of the bet – can't collect. Result: Many of these winners, also low on capital, can't pay up on their own bets and debts in a series of other derivatives transactions. Suddenly, in a chain reaction that no government or exchange authority can halt, dozens of major transactions slip into default, each setting off dozens of additional defaults.
>
> Major U.S. banks you've trusted with your hard-earned savings lose billions. Their shares plunge. Their uninsured CDs are jeopardized.
>
> Mortgage lenders dramatically tighten their lending standards. Mortgage money virtually disappears. The U.S. housing market, already sinking, busts wide open.[5]

## Derivatives 101

Gary Novak has a website simplifying complex issues, which was quoted earlier. He explains the derivatives crisis like this: the banking system has become gridlocked, because its pretended assets are fake; and the fake assets have swallowed up the real assets. It all began with deregulation in the 1980s, when government regulation was considered an irrational scheme from which business had to be freed. But regulations are criminal codes, and eliminating them meant turning business over to thieves. The Enron and Worldcom defendants were able to argue in court that their procedures were legal, because the laws making them illegal had been wiped off the books. Government regulation prevented the creation of "funny money" without real value. When the regulations were eliminated, funny money became the order of the day. It manifested in a variety of very complex vehicles lumped together under the label of derivatives, which were often made intentionally obscure and confusing.

"Physicists were hired to write equations for derivatives which business administrators could not understand," Novak says. Derivatives are just bets, but they have been sold as if they were something of value, until the sales have reached astronomical sums that are far beyond anything of real value in existence. Pension funds and trust funds have bought into the Ponzi scheme, only to see their money disappear down the derivatives hole. Universities have been forced to charge huge tuitions although they are financed with huge trust funds, because their money has been tied up in investments that are basically worthless. However, the administrators are holding onto their bets, which are "given a pretended value, because heads roll when the truth comes to light." Nobody dares to sell and nobody can collect. The result is a shortage of liquidity in global financial institutions. The very thing derivatives were designed to create – market liquidity – has been frozen to immobility in a gridlocked game.[6]

The author of a blog called "World Vision Portal" simplifies the derivatives problem in another way. He writes:

> Anyone who has been to Las Vegas or at the casino on a cruise ship can understand it perfectly. A bank gambles and bets on certain pre-determined odds, like playing the casino dealer in a game of poker (banks call this "hedging their risks with derivative contracts"). When they have to show their cards at the end of the play, they either win or loose their bet; either the bank wins or the house wins (this is the end of the derivative contract term).
>
> For us small-time players, we might lose $10 or $20, but the big-time banks are betting hundreds of $Millions on each card hand. The worst part is that they have a gambling addiction and can't stop betting money that isn't theirs to bet with. . . .

Winners always leave the gambling table with a big smile and you can see the chips in their hand to know they won more than they had bet. But losers always walk away quietly and don't talk about how much they lost. If a bank makes a good profit (won their bet), they would be telling everyone that their derivative contracts have paid off and they're sitting pretty. In reality, the big-time gambling banks are not talking and won't tell anyone how much they gambled or how much they lost.

We've been hoodwinked and the game is pretty much over.[7]

The irony is that derivative bets are sold as a form of insurance against something catastrophic going wrong. Yet if something catastrophic *does* go wrong, the counterparties (the parties on the other side of the bet, typically hedge funds) are liable to fold their cards and drop out of the game. The "insured" are left with losses both from the disaster itself and from the loss of the premium paid for the bet. To avoid that result, the Federal Reserve, along with other central banks, a fraternity of big private banks, and the U.S. Treasury itself, have gotten into the habit of covertly bailing out losing counterparties. This was done when the giant hedge fund Long Term Capital Management went bankrupt in 1998. It was also evidently done in 2005, very quietly . . . .

## A Derivatives Crisis Orders of Magnitude Beyond LTCM?

Rumors of a derivatives crisis dwarfing even the LTCM debacle surfaced in May 2005, following the downgrading of the debts of General Motors and Ford Motor Corporation to "junk" (bonds having a credit rating below investment grade). Severe problems had apparently occurred at several large hedge funds directly linked to these downgradings. In an article in Executive Intelligence Review in May 2005, Lothar Komp wrote:

The stocks of the same large banks that participated in the 1998 LTCM bailout, and which are known for their giant derivatives portfolios – including Citigroup, JP Morgan Chase, Goldman Sachs, and Deutsche Bank – were hit by panic selling on May 10. Behind this panic was the knowledge that not only have these banks engaged in dangerous derivatives speculation on their own accounts, but, ever desperate for cash to cover their own deteriorating positions, they also turned to the even more speculative hedge funds, placing money with existing funds, or even setting up their own, to engage in activities they didn't care to put on their own books. The combination of financial desperation, the Fed's liquidity binge, and the usury-limiting effects of low interest rates, triggered an explosion in the number of hedge funds in recent years, as everyone chased higher, and riskier, returns. There can be no doubt that some of these banks, not only their hedge fund offspring, are in trouble right now.[8]

Dire warnings ensued of a derivatives crisis "orders of magnitude beyond LTCM." But reports of a major derivative blow-out were being publicly denied, says Komp, since any bank or hedge fund that admitted such losses without first working a bail-out scheme would instantly collapse. An insider in the international banking community said that "there is no doubt that the Fed and other central banks are pouring liquidity into the system, covertly. *This would not become public until early April [2006], at which point the Fed and other central banks will have to report on the money supply.*"[9]

We've seen that when the Fed "pours liquidity into the system," it is by "open market operations" that create money with accounting entries. But if it became widely known that the Fed were printing dollars wholesale, alarm bells would sound. Investors would rush to cash in their dollar holdings, crashing the dollar and the stock market, following the familiar pattern seen in Third World countries.[10] What to do? The Fed apparently chose to muffle the alarm bells. It announced that in March 2006, it would no longer be reporting M3. M3 has been the main staple of money supply measurement and transparent disclosure for the last half-century, the figure on which the world has relied in determining the soundness of the dollar. In a December 2005 article called "The Grand Illusion," financial analyst Rob Kirby wrote:

> On March 23, 2006, the Board of Governors of the Federal Reserve System will cease publication of the M3 monetary aggregate. The Board will also cease publishing the following components: large-denomination time deposits, repurchase agreements (RPs), and Eurodollars. . . . [These securities] are exactly where one would expect to find the "capture" of any large scale monetization effort that the Fed would embark upon – should the need occur.

A commentator going by the name of Captain Hook observed:

> [T]his is as big a deal as Nixon closing the "gold window" back in '71, and we all know what happened after that. . . . [I]t almost looks like the boys are getting ready to unleash Weimar Republic II on the world. . . . Can you say welcome to the "People's Republic of the United States of What Used to Be America"?. . . *[W]e just got another very "big signal" from U.S. monetary authorities that the rules of the game are about to change fundamentally, once again.*[11]

When Nixon closed the gold window internationally in 1971 and when Roosevelt did it domestically before that, the rules were changed to keep a bankrupt private banking system afloat. The change in the Fed's reporting habits in 2006 appears to have been designed for the same purpose. The Fed was soon rumored to be madly printing up $2 trillion in new Federal Reserve Notes.[12] Why? Some analysts pointed to the festering derivatives crisis, while others pointed to the housing crisis; but there were also rumors of a third cyclone on the horizon. Iran announced that it would be opening an oil market (or "bourse") in Euros in March 2006, sidestepping the 1974 agreement with OPEC to trade oil only in U.S. dollars. An article in the Arab online magazine Al-Jazeerah warned that the Iranian bourse "could lead to a collapse in value for the American currency, potentially putting the U.S. economy in its greatest crisis since the depression era of the 1930s."[13] Rob Kirby wrote:

> [I]f countries like Japan and China (and other Asian countries) with their trillions of U.S. dollars no longer need them (or require a great deal less of them) to buy oil . . . [and] begin wholesale liquidation of U.S. debt obligations, there is no doubt in my mind that the Fed will print the dollars necessary to redeem them – this would necessarily imply an absolutely enormous (can you say hyperinflation) bloating of the money supply – which would undoubtedly be captured statistically in M3 or its related reporting. It would appear that we're all going to be "flying blind" as to how much money the Fed is truly going to pump into the system . . . .[14]

For the Federal Reserve to "monetize" the government's debt with newly-issued dollars is nothing new. When no one else buys U.S. securities, the Fed routinely steps in and buys them with money created for the occasion. What is new, and what has analysts alarmed, is that the whole process is now occurring behind a heavy curtain of secrecy. Richard Daughty, an entertaining commentator who writes in The Daily Reckoning as the Mogambu Guru, commented in April 2006:

> There was . . . a flurry of excitement last week when there was a rumor that the Federal Reserve had printed up, suddenly, $2 trillion in cash. My initial reaction was, of course, "Hahahaha!" and my reasoning is thus: why would they go through the hassle? They can make electronic money with the wave of a finger, so why go through the messy rigamarole of dealing with ink and paper and all the problems of transporting it and counting it and storing it and blah blah blah?
>
> But . . . this whole "two trillion in cash" scenario has some, um, merit, especially if you are thinking that foreigners dumping American securities . . . would instantly be reflected in instantaneous losses in bonds and meteoric rises in interest rates and the entire global economic machine would melt down. Bummer.
>
> So maybe this could explain the "two trill in cash" plan: With this amount of cash, see, *the American government can pretty much buy all the government securities that any foreigners want to sell,* but the inflationary effects of creating so much money won't be felt in prices for awhile! Hahaha! They think this is clever![15]

It might be clever, if it really *were* the American government buying back its own securities; *but it isn't. It is the private Federal Reserve and private banks.* If dollars are to be printed wholesale and federal securities are to be redeemed with them, why not let Congress do the job itself and avoid a massive unnecessary debt to financial middlemen? If the government were to buy back its own bonds and take them out of circulation, it could not only escape a massive federal debt but could do this *without* producing inflation. Government securities are already included in the money supply (M3). They would just be turned into cash, leaving the overall money supply unchanged. When the *Federal Reserve* buys up government bonds with newly-issued money, on the other hand, the bonds aren't taken out of circulation. Instead, they become the basis for generating many times their value in new loans; and that result is *highly* inflationary. But that is a subject for Section V.

## The Orwellian Solution

The Fed succeeded in hiding its sleight of hand by concealing the numbers for M3, but inflation was obviously occurring. By the spring of 2006, oil, gold, silver and other commodities were skyrocketing. Then, mysteriously, these inflation indicators too got suppressed. In the British journal <u>Financial News Online</u> in October 2006, Barry Riley wryly observed:

> Until the summer, the trends appeared ominous. The Fed was raising short rates and inflation was climbing. The price of crude oil stopped short of $80 a barrel. Sales of new homes were dropping off a cliff. Then, as if by magic, everything changed. The oil price went into reverse, tumbling to under $60 with favourable implications for the Consumer Price Index measure of inflation . . . . Similarly, the gold bullion price – an indicator of the potential fragility of the dollar exchange rate – has crashed from its early summer high. The Dow Jones Average two weeks ago advanced to a high, at last beating the bubble top in January 2000.
>
> . . . [T]he pattern is curious. . . . Perhaps bonds and commodities have been anticipating a recession. But then why has the equity market climbed?
>
> Conspiracy theories have abounded since Hank Paulson, boss of Goldman Sachs, was nominated in May to become treasury secretary. He had no political qualifications but a powerful reputation as a market fixer. Was he brought in to shore up the financial and commodities markets ahead of [the November 2006 elections]?

Were the Fed and the money cartel dealing with an impending economic crisis by hiding the bad news in another way -- by actually manipulating markets? Catherine Austin Fitts, former assistant secretary of HUD, called it "the Orwellian scenario." In a 2004 interview, she darkly observed:

> [W]e've reached a point . . . where rather than let financial assets adjust, the powers that be now have [such] control of the economy through the banking system and through the governmental apparatus [that] they can simply steal more money . . . , whether it's [by keeping] the stock market pumped up, the derivatives going, or the gold price manipulated down. . . . In other words, you can adjust to your economy not by letting the

value of the stock market or financial assets fall, but you can use warfare and organized crime to liquidate and steal whatever it is you need to keep the game going. And that's the kind of Orwellian scenario whereby you can basically keep this thing going, but *in a way that leads to a highly totalitarian government and economy – corporate feudalism.*[16]

In support of this Orwellian interpretation, latter-day Paul Reveres note that domestic security measures are being tightened and civil rights are being stripped, mirroring IMF policies in Third World countries, where the "IMF riot" is actually anticipated and factored in when "austerity measures" are imposed.[17] Conspiracy theorists warn that the industrial/banking cartel has been trying to get the Constitution suspended under the Emergency Powers Act, martial law imposed under the Patriot and Homeland Security Acts, and the American democratic form of government replaced with a police state manipulated by the banking/military/industrial cartel.[18] They point to the use of the military to quell rioting in New Orleans following Hurricane Katrina (in violation of *posse comitatus*, a statute forbidding U.S. active military participation in domestic law enforcement), as well as the use of fully-armed private mercenaries, some of them foreign.[19] The scene recalled a 1992 conference of the secretive group known as the Bilderbergers, covertly taped by a Swiss delegate, at which former U.S. Secretary of State Henry Kissinger reportedly said:

> Today, America would be outraged if U.N. troops entered Los Angeles to restore order. Tomorrow they will be grateful! . . . The one thing every man fears is the unknown. When presented with this scenario, individual rights will be willingly relinquished for the guarantee of their well-being granted to them by the World Government.[20]

Suspicions have been voiced concerning the Federal Emergency Management Agency (FEMA), which was put in charge of disaster relief. Al Martin notes that FEMA started out in 1952 as the Federal Emergency Military Agency. He wrote in a November 2005 newsletter:

> FEMA is being upgraded as a federal agency, and upon passage of PATRIOT Act III, which contains the amendment to overturn *posse comitatus*, FEMA will be re-militarized, which will give the agency military police powers. . . . Why is all of this being done? Why is the regime moving to a militarized police state and to a dictatorship? *It is because of what Comptroller General David Walker said, that after 2009, the ability of the United States to continue to*

*service its debt becomes questionable.* Although the average citizen may not understand what that means, when the United States can no longer service its debt it collapses as an economic entity. We would be an economically collapsed state. *The only way government can function and can maintain control in an economically collapsed state is through a military dictatorship.*[21]

## The Parasite's Challenge: How to Feed on the Host Without Destroying It

Critics charge that warfare, terrorism, and natural disasters on an unprecedented scale are being used to justify massive federal borrowing, while diverting attention from the fact that the economy is drowning in a sea of governmental and consumer debt.[22] But while that may be true, policymakers are only doing what they have to do under the current monetary scheme. In an upside-down world in which debt is money and money is debt, *somebody* has to go into debt just to keep money in the system so the economy won't collapse. The old productive virtues – hard work, productivity and creativity – have gone out the window. The new producers of economic "growth" are borrowers and speculators. Henry C K Liu draws an analogy from physics:

> [W]henever credit is issued, money is created. The issuing of credit creates debt on the part of the counterparty, but debt is not money; credit is. If anything, debt is negative money, a form of financial antimatter. Physicists understand the relationship between matter and antimatter. . . . The collision of matter and antimatter produces annihilation that returns matter and antimatter to pure energy. The same is true with credit and debt, which are related but opposite. . . . The collision of credit and debt will produce an annihilation and return the resultant union to pure financial energy unharnessed for human benefit.[23]

Credit and debt cancel each other out and merge back into the great zero-point field from whence they came. To avoid that result and keep "money" in the economy, new debt must continually be created. When commercial borrowers aren't creating enough money by borrowing it into existence, the government must take over that function by spending money it doesn't have, justifying its loans in any way it can. Keeping the economy alive means continually finding ways to pump newly-created loan money into the system, while concealing the fact that this "money" has been spun out of thin air. These new loans don't necessarily have to be paid back. New money just has to be circulated, providing a source of funds to pay the extra interest that wasn't lent into existence by the original loans. A variety of alternatives for pumping liquidity into the system have been resorted to by governments and central banks, including:

1. Drastically lowering interest rates, encouraging borrowers to expand the money supply by going further and further into debt.

2. Instituting tax cuts and rebates that put money into people's pockets. The resulting budget shortfall is made up later with new issues of U.S. bonds, which are "bought" by the Federal Reserve with dollars printed up for the occasion.

3. Authorizing public works, space exploration, military research, and other projects that will justify massive government borrowing that never gets paid back.

4. Engaging in war as a pretext for borrowing, preferably a war that will drag on. People are willing in times of emergency to allow the government to engage heavily in deficit spending to defend the homeland.

5. Lending to Third World countries. If necessary, some of these impossible-to-repay loans can be quietly forgiven later without repayment.

6. Periodic foreclosures on the loan collateral, transferring the collateral back to the banks, which can then be resold to new borrowers, creating new debt-money. The result is the "business cycle" – periodic waves of depression that flush away debt with massive defaults and foreclosures, causing the progressive transfer of wealth from debtors to the banks.

7. Manipulation, or rigging, of financial markets -- including the stock market -- in order to keep investor confidence high and encourage further borrowing, until savings are heavily invested and real estate is heavily mortgaged, when the default phase of the business cycle can begin again.[24]

*Rigging the stock market?* At one time, writes New York Post columnist John Crudele, just mentioning that possibility got a person branded as a "conspiracy nut":

This country, the critics would say, never interferes with its free capital markets. Sure, there's intervention in the currencies markets. And, yes, the Federal Reserve does manipulate the bond market and interest rates through word and deed. But never, ever would such action be taken at the core of capitalism – the equity markets, which for better or worse must operate without interference. That's the way the standoff stayed until 1997 when – at the height of the Last of the Great Bubbles – someone in government decided it wanted the world to know that there was someone actually paying attention in case Wall Street could not handle its own problems. The Working Group on Financial Markets – affectionately known as the Plunge Protection Team – suddenly came out of the closet.[25]

# Chapter 33
# MAINTAINING THE ILLUSION: RIGGING FINANCIAL MARKETS

*The Dow is a dead banana republic dictator in full military uniform propped up in the castle window with a mechanical lever moving the cadaver's arm, waving to the Wall Street crowd.*

– Michael Bolser, <u>Midas</u> (April 2004)[1]

While people, businesses and local and federal governments are barreling toward bankruptcy, market bulls continue to insist that all is well; and for evidence, they point to the robust stock market. It's uncanny really. Even when there is every reason to think the market is about to crash, somehow it doesn't. Bill Murphy, editor of an informative investment website called <u>Le Metropole Cafe</u>, described this phenomenon in an October 2005 newsletter using an analogy from <u>The Wizard of Oz</u>:

> Every time it looks like the stock market is on the verge of collapse, it comes back with a vengeance. In May for example, there were rumors of derivative problems and hedge fund problems, which set up the monster rally into the summer. The London bombings . . . same deal. Now we just saw Katrina and Rita precipitate rallies. *There must be some mechanism at work, like the Wizard of Oz behind a curtain, pulling on strings and pushing buttons.*[2]

What sort of mechanism? John Crudele writes that the cat was let out of the bag by George Stepanopoulos, President Clinton's senior adviser on policy and strategy, in the chaos following the World Trade Center attacks. Stepanopoulos blurted out on "Good Morning America" on September 17, 2001:

"[T]he Fed in 1989 created what is called the Plunge Protection Team, which is the Federal Reserve, big major banks, representatives of the New York Stock Exchange and the other exchanges, and there – they have been meeting informally so far, and *they have kind of an informal agreement among major banks to come in and start to buy stock if there appears to be a problem.*

"They have, in the past, acted more formally.

"I don't know if you remember, but in 1998, there was a crisis called the Long Term Capital crisis. It was a major currency trader and there was a global currency crisis. And they, at the guidance of the Fed, *all of the banks got together when that started to collapse and propped up the currency markets. And they have plans in place to consider that if the stock markets start to fall.*"[3]

The Plunge Protection Team (PPT) is formally called the Working Group on Financial Markets (WGFM). Created by President Reagan's Executive Order 12631 in 1988 in response to the October 1987 stock market crash, the WGFM includes the President, the Secretary of the Treasury, the Chairman of the Federal Reserve, the Chairman of the Securities and Exchange Commission, and the Chairman of the Commodity Futures Trading Commission. Its stated purpose is to enhance "the integrity, efficiency, orderliness, and competitiveness of our Nation's financial markets and [maintain] investor confidence." According to the Order:

> To the extent permitted by law and subject to the availability of funds therefore, the Department of the Treasury shall provide the Working Group with such administrative and support services as may be necessary for the performance of its functions.[4]

In plain English, taxpayer money is being used to make the markets look healthier than they are. Treasury funds are made available, but the WGFM is not accountable to Congress and can act from behind closed doors. It not only can but it must, since if investors were to realize what was going on, they would not fall for the bait. "Maintaining investor confidence" means keeping investors in the dark about how shaky the market really is.

Crudele tracked the shady history of the PPT in his June 2006 <u>New York Post</u> series:

> Back during a stock market crisis in 1989, a guy named Robert Heller – who had just left the Federal Reserve Board – suggested that the government rig the stock market in times of dire emergency. . . . He didn't use the word "rig" but that's what he meant.

Proposed as an op-ed in the Wall Street Journal, it's a seminal argument that says when a crisis occurs on Wall Street "instead of flooding the entire economy with liquidity, and thereby increasing the danger of inflation, the Fed could support the stock market directly by buying market averages in the futures market, thus stabilizing the market as a whole."

The PPT was to be the Roman circus of the twenty-first century, distracting the masses with pretensions of prosperity. Instead of fixing the problem in the economy, the PPT would just "fix" the investment casino. Crudele wrote:

Over the next few years . . . whenever the stock market was in trouble someone seemed to ride to the rescue. . . . Often it appeared to be Goldman Sachs, which just happens to be where [newly-appointed Treasury Secretary] Paulson and former Clinton Treasury Secretary Robert Rubin worked.

For obvious reasons, the mechanism by which the PPT has ridden to the rescue isn't detailed on the Fed's website; but some analysts think they know. Michael Bolser, who belongs to an antitrust group called GATA (the Gold Anti-Trust Action Committee), says that PPT money is funneled through the Fed's "primary dealers," a group of favored Wall Street brokerage firms and investment banks. The device used is a form of loan called a "repurchase agreement" or "repo," which is a contract for the sale and future repurchase of Treasury securities. Bolser explains:

It may sound odd, but the Fed occasionally gives money ["permanent" repos] to its primary dealers (a list of about thirty financial houses, Merrill Lynch, Morgan Stanley, etc). *They never have to pay this free money back*; thus the primary dealers will pretty much do whatever the Fed asks if they want to stay in the primary dealers "club."

The exact mechanism of repo use to support the DOW is simple. The primary dealers get repos in the morning issuance . . . and then buy DOW index futures (a market that is far smaller than the open DOW trading volume). These futures prices then drive the DOW itself because the larger population of investors think the "insider" futures buyers have access to special information and are "ahead" of the market. Of course they don't have special information . . . *only special money in the form of repos.*[5]

The money used to manipulate the market is "Monopoly" money, funds created from nothing and given for nothing, just to prop up the market. Not only is the Dow propped up but the gold market is held down, since gold is considered a key indicator of inflation. If the gold price were to soar, the Fed would have to increase interest rates to tighten the money supply, collapsing the housing bubble and forcing the government to raise inflation-adjusted payments for Social Security. Most traders who see this manipulation going on don't complain, because they think the Fed is rigging the market to their advantage. But gold investors are routinely being fleeced; and the PPT's secret manipulations are creating a stock market bubble that will take everyone's savings down when it bursts, as bubbles invariably do. Unwary investors are being induced to place risky bets on a nag on its last legs. The people become complacent and accept bad leadership, bad policies and bad laws, because they think it is all "working" economically.

GATA's findings were largely ignored until they were confirmed in a carefully researched report released by John Embry of Sprott Asset Management of Toronto in August 2004.[6] An update of the report published in The Asia Times in 2005 included an introductory comment that warned, "the secrecy and growing involvement of private-sector actors threatens to foster enormous moral hazards." *Moral hazard* is the risk that the existence of a contract will change the way the parties act in the future; for example, a firm insured for fire may take fewer fire precautions. In this case, the hazard is that banks are taking undue investment and lending risks, believing they will be bailed out from their folly because they always have been in the past. The comment continued:

> *Major financial institutions may be acting as de facto agencies of the state, and thus not competing on a level playing field. There are signs that repeated intervention in recent years has corrupted the system.[7]*

In a June 2006 article titled "Plunge Protection or Enormous Hidden Tax Revenues," Chuck Augustin was more blunt, writing:

> . . . Today the markets are, without doubt, manipulated on a daily basis by the PPT. Government controlled "front companies" such as Goldman-Sachs, JP Morgan and many others collect incredible revenues through market manipulation. Much of this money is probably returned to government coffers,

however, enormous sums of money are undoubtedly skimmed by participating companies and individuals.

The operation is similar to the Mafia-controlled gambling operations in Las Vegas during the 50's and 60's but much more effective and beneficial to all involved. Unlike the Mafia, the PPT has enormous advantages. The operation is immune to investigation or prosecution, there [are] unlimited funds available through the Treasury and Federal Reserve, it has the ultimate insider trading advantages, and it fully incorporates the spin and disinformation of government controlled media to sway markets in the desired direction. . . . Any investor can imagine the riches they could obtain if they *knew* what direction stocks, commodities and currencies would move in a single day, especially if they could obtain unlimited funds with which to invest! . . . [T]he PPT not only cheats investors out of trillions of dollars, *it also eliminates competition that refuses to be "bought" through mergers. Very soon now, only global companies and corporations owned and controlled by the NWO elite will exist.*[8]

## The Exchange Stabilization Fund

Another regulatory mechanism that is as important -- and as suspect -- as the PPT is the "Exchange Stabilization Fund" (ESF). The ESF was authorized by Congress to keep sharp swings in the dollar's exchange rate from "upsetting" financial markets. Market analyst Jim Sinclair writes:

Don't think of the ESF as an investment type, or even as a hedge fund. The ESF has no office, traders, or trading desk. It does not exist at all, aside from a fund of money and accounts to keep records. It seems that orders come from the US Secretary of the Treasury, or his designate (which could be a partner of one of the international investment banks he comes from), to intervene in markets . . . . Have you ever wondered how these firms seem to be trading for their own accounts on the side of the government's interest? Have you wondered how these firms always seem to be profitable in their trading accounts, and how they wield such enormous positions? . . . Not only [are they] executing ESF orders, but in all probability, [they are] coat-tailing trades while pretending there is a Chinese Wall between ESF orders and their own trading accounts.[9]

This is all highly annoying to investors trying to place their bets based on what the market "should" be doing, particularly when they are competing with a bottomless source of accounting-entry funds. A research firm reporting on the unexpectedly high quarterly profits of Goldman Sachs in March 2004 wrote cynically:

> [W]ho does Goldman have to thank for the latest outsized quarterly earnings? Its "partner" in charge of financing the proprietary trading operation -- Alan Greenspan.[10]

Henry Paulson headed Goldman Sachs before he succeeded to U.S. Treasury Secretary in June 2006, following in the steps of Robert Rubin, who headed that investment bank before he was appointed Treasury Secretary just in time for Goldman and other investment banks to capitalize on the drastic devaluation of the Mexican peso in 1995. An October 2006 article in the conservative <u>American Spectator</u> complained that the U.S. Treasury was being turned into "Goldman Sachs South."[11]

## Collusion Between Big Business and Big Government: The CRMPG

Another organization suspected of colluding to rig markets is a private fraternity of big New York banks and investment houses called the Counterparty Risk Management Policy Group (CRMPG). "Counterparties" are parties to a contract, normally having a conflict of interest. The CRMPG's dealings were exposed in an article reprinted on the GATA website in September 2006, which was supported by references to the websites of the Federal Reserve and the CRMPG.[12] The author, who went by the name of Joe Stocks, maintained that the CRMPG was set up to bail out its members from financial difficulty by combining forces to manipulate markets, and that it was all being done with the approval of the U.S. government. Bailouts, he notes, have been around for a long time. A series of them occurred in the 1990s, beginning with the Mexican bailout finalized on the evening Robert Rubin was sworn in as U.S. Treasury Secretary. This was followed by the 1998 "Asian crisis" and then by the 1999 bailout of Long Term Capital Management (LTCM), a giant hedge fund dealing in derivatives. The CRMPG was formed in 1999 to handle the LTCM crisis and to develop a policy that would protect the financial world from another such threat in the future.

In May 2002, the SEC expressed concern that a certain major bank could become insolvent due to derivative issues. The problem bank was JP Morgan Chase (JPM). By the end of the year, the CRMPG had recommended that a new bank be founded that would be a coordinated effort among the members of the CRMPG. The Federal Reserve and the SEC approved, and JPM's problems suddenly disappeared. A "stealth bailout" had been engineered.

The same year saw a big jump in the use of "program trades" – large-scale, computer-assisted trading of stocks and other securities, using systems in which decisions to buy and sell are triggered automatically by fluctuations in price. The major program traders were members of the CRMPG. Members that had not had large proprietary trading units started them, including Citigroup, which was quoted as saying something to the effect that there was now less risk in trading due to "new" innovations in the field. (New innovations in what – market rigging?) In early 2002, program trading was running at about 25 percent of all shares traded on the New York Stock Exchange. By 2006, it was closer to 60 percent. About a year later, concerns were expressed in The Wall Street Journal that JPM was making huge profits in the risky business of trading its own capital:

> Profits have been increasing recently due to a small and low profile group of traders making big bets with the firm's money. Apparently, an eight man New York team has pulled in more than $100M of trading profit with the company . . .

In 2004, Fed Chairman Alan Greenspan renewed concerns about the exploding derivatives market, which had roughly doubled in size since 2000. He called on the major players to meet with the Fed to discuss their derivative exposure, and to submit a report on the actions it felt were necessary to keep the markets stable. The report, filed in July 2005, was addressed not to the head of the Fed but to the chairman of Goldman Sachs. It was written in obscure banker jargon that is not easy to follow, but you don't need to understand the details to get the sense that the nation's largest banks are colluding with their clients and with each other to manipulate markets. The document is all about working together for the greater good, but Stocks notes that this is not how free markets work. The antitrust laws are all about preventing this sort of collusion.

The report says, "we must preserve and strengthen the institutional arrangements whereby, at the point of crisis, industry groups and industry leaders, as well as supervisors, are prepared to work together in order to serve the larger and shared goal of financial stability." It continues:

> It is acceptable market practice for a financial intermediary's sales and trading personnel to provide their sophisticated counterparties with general market levels or "indications," including inputs and variables that may be used by the counterparty to calculate a value for a complex transaction. Additionally, if a counterparty requests a price or level for purposes of unwinding a specific complex transaction, and the financial intermediary is willing to provide such price or level, it is appropriate for the financial intermediary's sales and trading personnel to furnish this information.[14]

Stocks writes, "the big banks are being encouraged to share information. We know there are two sides to each trade. . . . How would you like to be on the other side of [one of their] pre-arranged trades?" He warns:

> Their collusion at their highest ranks to secure the financial stability of the largest financial institutions could be at odds with the investments of smaller institutions and may be at odds with the small investor's long term investments and goals. When LTCM failed many of us could have not cared less . . . . The bailout was simply put in place to save their own skins and the investors they serve.
>
> . . . We require public corporations to provide open and full disclosure with the public, why should the CRMPG be allowed to collude to rig the market against free market principles? . . . The CRMPG report gives them the outline to execute their strategy in collusion at the expense ultimately of the small investor . . . . Moral hazard has led to moral decay at the highest ranks of our financial institutions. *Move over PPT – the CRMPG is at the wheel now.*

## Market Manipulation and Politics

At first blush, the notion that banks and the government are working together to prevent a national economic crisis by manipulating markets sounds benignly paternal and protective; but the wizard's magic that makes money appear where none existed before can also be used to divest small investors of their savings and for partisan political gain. When the economy looks good, incumbents get re-elected. Michael Bolser has carefully tracked the Dow against the "repo" pool (the "free money" made available to favored investment banks). His charts show that the Fed has routinely "engineered" the Dow and the dollar to make the economy appear sounder than it is. When Bolser tracked the rise in the stock market at the start of the 2003 Iraq War, for example, he found that "the 'Iraq War Rally' was nothing of the sort. *It was a wholly Fed-engineered exercise.*"[15] The Orwellian possibilities were suggested by Alex Wallenstein in an April 2004 article:

> People would never give up their property rights voluntarily, directly. But if we can be sucked by Fed interest rate policy into no longer saving money (because stock market gains are so much higher than returns on CDs and savings bonds), and instead into throwing all of our retirement hopes and dreams at the stock market (that can be engineered into a catastrophic collapse in the blink of an eye), then we can all become "good little sheep." Then we can be made to march right up to be fleeced and then slaughtered and meat-packed for later consumption by our handlers.[16]

Even if an economic collapse is not being engineered intentionally, many experts are convinced that one is coming, and soon. In a 2005 book titled <u>The Demise of the Dollar</u>, Addison Wiggin observes:

> How can the government promise to pay its debts when the total of that debt keeps getting higher and higher? It's already out of control. . . . In fact, a collapse is inevitable and it's only a question of how quickly it is going to occur. The consequences will be huge declines in the stock market, savings becoming worthless, and the bond market completely falling apart. . . . It will be a rude awakening for everyone who has become complacent about America's invulnerability.[17]

## Is the Spider Losing Its Grip?

Hans Schicht has another slant on the approaching day of financial reckoning. He noted in 2003 that David Rockefeller, the "master spider," was then 88 years old:

> [W]herever we look, his central command is seen to be fading. Neither is there a capable successor in sight to take over the

reigns. Hyenas have begun picking up the pieces. Corruption is rife. Rivalry is breaking up the Empire.

What has been good for Rockefeller, has been a curse for the United States. Its citizens, government and country indebted to the hilt, enslaved to his banks. . . . The country's industrial force lost to overseas in consequence of strong dollar policies. . . . A strong dollar pursued purely in the interest of the banking empire and not for the best of the country. The USA, now degraded to a service and consumer nation. . . .

With Rockefeller leaving the scene, sixty years of dollar imperialism are drawing to a close . . . . As one of the first signs of change, the mighty dollar has come under attack, directly on the currency markets and indirectly through the bond markets. The day of financial reckoning is not far off any longer. . . . With Rockefeller's strong hand losing its grip and the old established order fading, the world has entered a most dangerous transition period, where anything could happen.[18]

## Or Has the Spider Just Moved Its Nest?

With Rockefeller losing his grip and no replacement in sight, there is evidence that the master spider may have moved its nest back across the Atlantic to London, armed with a navy of pirate hedge funds that rule the world out of the Cayman Islands. In a March 2007 article, Richard Freeman observed that the Cayman Islands are a British Overseas Protectorate. The Caymans function as "an epicenter for globalization and financial warfare," with officials who have been hand-selected by what Freeman calls the "Anglo-Dutch oligarchy":

> For the Anglo-Dutch oligarchy, closely intertwined banks and hedge funds are its foremost instruments of power, to control the financial system, and loot and devastate companies and nations. . . . The three island specks in the Caribbean Sea, 480 miles south from Florida's southern tip — which came to be known as the Caymans, after the native word for crocodile (caymana) — had for centuries been a basing area for pirates who attacked trading vessels. . . .
>
> In 1993, the decision was made to turn this tourist trap into a major financial power, through the adoption of a Mutual Funds Law, to enable the easy incorporation and/or registration of hedge funds in a deregulated system. . . .The 1993 Mutual

Fund Law had its effect: with direction from the City of London, the number of hedge funds operating in the Cayman Islands exploded: from 1,685 hedge funds in 1997, to 8,282 at the end of the third quarter 2006, a fivefold increase. Cayman Island hedge funds are four-fifths of the world total. Globally, hedge funds command up to $30 trillion of deployable funds. . . . According to reports, during 2005, *the hedge funds were responsible for up to 50% of the transactions on the London and New York stock exchanges.* . . . The hedge funds are leading a frenzied wave of mergers and acquisitions, which reached nearly $4 trillion last year, and they are buying up and stripping down companies from auto parts producer Delphi and Texas power utility TXU, to Office Equities Properties, to hundreds of thousands of apartments in Berlin and Dresden, Germany. This has led to hundreds of thousands of workers being laid off.

They are assisted by their Wall Street allies. Taken altogether, the hedge funds, with money borrowed from the world's biggest commercial and investment banks, have pushed the world's derivatives bubble well past $600 trillion in nominal value, and put the world on the path of the biggest financial disintegration in modern history.[19]

## The Cracking Economic Egg

The magnitude of the crisis and the desperate attempts to cover it up were suggested in June 2007, when two hedge funds belonging to Bear Stearns Company went bankrupt over derivatives bets involving subprime mortgages gone wrong. The parties were being leaned on to settle quietly, to avoid revealing that their derivatives were worth far less than claimed. But as Adrian Douglas observed in a June 30 article called "Derivatives" in *LeMetropoleCafe.com*:

This is not just an ugly, non-malignant tumor that can be conveniently cut off. This massive financial activity that bets on the outcome of the pricing of the underlying assets has corrupted the system such that those who would be responsible for paying out orders of magnitude more money than they have if the bets go against them are sucked into a black hole of moral and ethical destitution as they have no other choice but to manipulate the price of the underlying assets to prevent financial ruin.

Douglas observes that while derivatives may appear to be complex instruments, the concept is simple. They are insurance contracts against something happening, such as interest rates going up or the stock market going down. Unlike with ordinary insurance policies, however, these are not catastrophic risks that happen infrequently. They *will* happen eventually. And if a payout event is triggered, "unlike when a house burns down, there will not be just a handful of claims on any one day, payouts will be due in the trillions of dollars on the same day. It is the financial equivalent of a hurricane Katrina hitting every US city on the same day!" Douglas writes:

> Instead of stopping this idiotic sham business from growing to galactic proportions, all the authorities, and all the banks, and all the major financial institutions around the world have heralded it as the best thing since sliced bread. But now all these players are complicit in the crime. They are all on the hook. The stakes are now too high. They must manipulate the underlying assets on a daily basis to prevent triggering the payout of a major derivative event.

> Derivatives are a bet against volatility. Guess what has happened? Surprise, surprise! Volatility has vanished. The VIX [the Chicago Board Options Exchange Volatility Index] looks like an ECG when the patient has died! Gold has an unofficial $6 rule. The DOW is not allowed to drop more than 200 points and it must rally the following day. Interest rates must not rise, if they do the FED must issue more of their now secret M3, ship it offshore to the Caribbean and pretend that an unknown foreign bank is buying US Treasuries like crazy.

> *But the sham is coming unglued because the huge excess liquidity that has been injected into the system to prevent it from imploding is showing up as asset bubbles all over the place and shortages of raw materials are everywhere. There is massive inflation going on.* There is *no* major economy in the world not inflating their money supply by less than 10% annually.

His concluding observation is that when the derivative buyers realize what is going on and quit paying premiums for insurance that doesn't exist, "there will be a whole new definition of volatility!" And that brings us back to the parasite's challenge. When the bubble collapses, the banking empire that has been built on it must collapse as well . . . .

# Chapter 34
# MELTDOWN:
# THE SECRET BANKRUPTCY
# OF THE BANKS

*"See what you have done!" the Witch screamed. "In a minute I shall melt away.". . . With these words the Witch fell down in a brown, melted, shapeless mass and began to spread over the clean boards of the kitchen floor.*

> – *The Wonderful Wizard of Oz,*
> *"The Search for the Wicked Witch"*

The debt bubble is showing clear signs of imploding, and when it does it is likely to liquidate the private banking empire that has been built on it. To prevent that financial meltdown, the Witches of Wall Street and their European affiliates have resorted to desperate measures, including a giant derivatives bubble that is jeopardizing the whole shaky system. In a February 2004 article called "The Coming Storm," the London <u>Economist</u> warned that top banks around the world are now massively exposed to high-risk derivatives, and that there is a very real risk of an industry-wide meltdown. The situation was compared to that before the 1998 collapse of Long Term Capital Management, when "[b]ets went spectacularly wrong after Russia defaulted; financial markets went berserk, and LTCM, a very large hedge fund, had to be rescued by its bankers at the behest of the Federal Reserve."[1]

John Hoefle maintains that the Fed has been quietly rescuing banks ever since. Writing in November 2002, he contended that the banking system actually went bankrupt in the late 1980s, with the collapse of the junk bond market and the real estate bubble of that decade. The savings and loan sector collapsed, along with nearly every large Texas bank; and that was just the tip of the iceberg:

Citicorp was secretly taken over by the Federal Reserve in 1989, shotgun mergers were arranged for other giant banks, backdoor bailouts were given through the Fed's lending mechanisms, and bank examiners were ordered to ignore bad loans. *These measures, coupled with a headlong rush into derivatives and other forms of speculation, gave the banks a veneer of solvency while actually destroying what was left of the U.S. banking system.*

The big banks were in trouble because of big gambles that had not paid off – Third World loans that had gone into default, giant corporations that had gone bankrupt, massive derivative bets gone wrong. Like with the bankrupt giant Enron, profound economic weakness was masked by phony accounting that created a "veneer of solvency." Hoefle wrote:

The U.S. banks – especially the derivatives giants – are masters at this game, counting trillions of dollars of worthless IOUs – derivatives, overblown assets, and unpayable debts – on their books at face value, in order to appear solvent. In the late 1980s, the term "zombie" was used to refer to banks which manifested some mechanical signs of life but were in fact dead.

Between 1984 and 2002, bank failures were accompanied by a wave of consolidations and takeovers that reduced the number of banks by 45 percent. The top seven banks were consolidated into three – Citigroup, JP Morgan Chase, and Bank of America. Hoefle wrote:

The result of all these mergers is a group of much larger, and far more bankrupt, giant banks. . . . [A] similar process has played out worldwide. . . . The global list also includes two institutions which specialize in pumping up the U.S. real estate bubble. Both Fannie Mae and Freddie Mac specialize in converting mortgages into mortgage-backed securities, and will vaporize when the U.S. housing bubble pops.

Hoefle said the zombies have now taken over the asylum. In 2002, Bank One was rumored to be a buyer for the zombie giant JP Morgan Chase. (This merger actually occurred in 2004.) "It was ludicrous," Hoefle wrote, since on paper JP Morgan Chase had twice the assets of Bank One. "Still, letting Morgan fail, which it seems determined to do, is clearly unacceptable from the standpoint of the White House/Federal Reserve Plunge Protection Team."[2]

In a February 2004 article titled "Cooking the Books: U.S. Banks Are Giant Casinos," Michael Edward concurred in this assessment. He wrote that U.S. banks are engaging in "smoke and mirror accounting," in which they are merging with each other in order to hide their derivative losses with "paper asset" bookkeeping:

> . . . [T]he public is being conned into thinking that U.S. banks are still solvent because they show "gains" in their stock "paper" value. *If the U.S. markets were not manipulated, U.S. banks would collapse overnight along with the entire U.S. economy.*
>
> . . . Astronomical losses for U.S. banks (as well as most world banks) have been concealed with mispriced derivatives. The problem with this is that these losses don't have to be reported to shareholders, so in all truth and reality, *many U.S. banks are already insolvent. What that means is that U.S. banks have become nothing less than a Ponzi Scheme paying account holders with other account holder assets or deposits.*
>
> . . . Robbing Peter to pay Paul has never worked, and every Ponzi Scheme (illegal pyramid scam) has always ended abruptly with great losses for every person who invested in them. U.S. bank account holders are about to find this out.[3]

## Has Private Commercial Banking Become Obsolete?

Is this secret epidemic of bank insolvencies just the result of individual mismanagement and overreaching? Or does it mark the inevitable end times of a Ponzi scheme that is inherently unsustainable? When the dollar was on the gold standard, banks had to deal with periodic bank "runs" because they did not have sufficient gold to cover their transactions. The Federal Reserve was instituted early in the twentieth century to provide backup money to prevent such runs. That effort was followed 20 years later by the worst depression in modern history. The gold standard was then abandoned, allowing larger and larger debt bubbles to flood the system, resulting in the derivative and housing crises looming today. When those bubbles pop, the only option may be another change in the rules of the game, a Copernican shift of the sort envisioned by Professor Liu.

Robert Guttman, Professor of Economics at Hofstra University in New York, is another academician who feels the current banking system may have outlived its usefulness. In a 1994 text called How Credit-Money Shapes the Economy, he states, "*It may well be that banks, as currently constituted, are in the process of becoming obsolete. Increasingly their traditional functions can be carried out more effectively by other institutions . . . ."* He goes on:

> American banks have been hit over the last two decades by a variety of adverse developments. Their traditional functions, taking deposits and making loans, have been subjected to increasing competition from less-regulated institutions. In the face of such market erosion on both sides of their balance-sheet ledger, the banks have had to find new profit opportunities. . . . Even though most commercial banks have managed to survive the surge in bad-debt losses . . . , they still face major competitive threats from less-regulated institutions. It is doubtful whether they can stop the market inroads made by pension funds, mutual funds, investment banks, and other institutions that benefit from the "marketization" of our financial system. . . . The revolution in computer and communications technologies has enabled others to access and process data at low cost. *Neither lenders nor borrowers need banks anymore. Both sides may find it increasingly more appealing to deal directly with each other.*[4]

At the time he was writing, hundreds of banks had failed after writing off large chunks of non-performing loans to developing countries, farmers, oil drillers, real estate developers, and takeover artists. Commercial banks and thrifts facing growing bad-debt losses were forced to liquidate assets and tighten credit terms, producing a credit crunch that choked off growth. The banks were also facing growing competition from investment pools such as pension funds and mutual funds. The banks responded with a dramatic shift away from loans, their core business, to liquid bundles of claims sold as securities. The commercial banking business was also eroding, as corporations switched from loans to securities for funding. FDIC insurance, which was originally intended to protect individual savers against loss, took on the quite different function of bailing out failing institutions. "Such a shift in focus led directly to adoption of the FDIC's 'too-big-to-fail' policy in 1984," Guttman wrote. *"The result has been increasingly costly government intervention which now has bankrupted the system."*

## The Shady World of Investment Banking

As banks have lost profits in the competitive commercial lending business, they have had to expand into investment banking just to remain profitable. That expansion was facilitated in 1999, when the Glass-Steagall Act, which forbade commercial and investment banking in the same institutions, was repealed. Investment banking includes corporate fund-raising, mergers and acquisitions, brokering trades, and trading for the bank's own account.[5] Despite this merger of banking functions, however, profits continued to falter. According to a 2002 publication called "Growing Profits Under Pressure" by the Boston Consulting Group:

> As the effects of the economic downturn continue to erode corporate profits, large commercial banks – both global and regional – face growing pressures on their corporate- and investment-banking businesses. . . . From the outside, commercial banks confront increasing competition – particularly from global investment banks . . . that are competing more vigorously for commercial banks' traditional corporate transactions. In addition, commercial banks are finding that their corporate clients are increasingly becoming their rivals. . . . [C]ompanies today...meet more of their own banking needs themselves . . . .
> In recent years, many commercial banks have acquired investment banks, hoping to gain access to new clients . . . . But . . . investment-banking revenues have suffered with the decline in mergers and acquisitions, equity capital markets, and trading activities. All too often, costs have continued to rise.[6]

An article in the June 2006 Economist reported that even with the success of bank trading departments, the overall share values of investment banks were falling. Evidently this was because investors suspected that the banks' returns had been souped up by trading with borrowed money, and they feared the risks involved.[7]

Meanwhile, banking as a public service has been lost to the all-consuming quest for profits. As noted in Chapter 18, investment banks make most of their profits from trading for their own accounts rather than from servicing customers. According to William Hummel in Money: What It Is, How It Works, the ten largest U.S. banks hold almost half the country's total banking assets. These banks, called "money market banks" or "money center banks," include Citibank, JPMorgan Chase, and Bank of America. They are large conglomerates that combine commercial banking with investment banking. However, *very little of their business is what we normally think of as banking* – taking deposits, providing checking services, and making consumer or small business loans. Rather, says Hummel, they mainly engage in four activities:

- *Portfolio business* – asset accumulation and funding for their own accounts, something they do by borrowing money cheaply and selling the acquired assets at a premium;

- *Corporate finance* – corporate lending and public offerings;

- *Distribution* – the sale of the banks' own securities, including treasuries, municipal securities, and Euro CDs; and

- *Trading* – largely market-making.[8]

Recall that market makers are the players chiefly engaged in naked short selling, an inherently fraudulent practice. (Chapter 19.) Patrick Byrne, who has been instrumental in exposing the naked shorting scandal, states that as much as 75 percent of the profits of big investment banks may come from their role as "prime brokers." He calls that a fancy word for the stock loan business -- renting the same stock several times over.[9] According to an article in Forbes, "prime brokerage" is "the business of catering to hedge funds; particularly, lending securities to funds so they can execute their trading strategies."[10] We've seen that hedge funds are groups of investors colluding to acquire companies and bleed them of their assets, speculate in derivatives, manipulate markets, and otherwise make profits for themselves at the expense of workers and smaller investors.

The big money center banks facilitating these dubious practices are also the banks that must periodically be bailed out by the Fed and the government because they are supposedly "too big to fail." Yet these banks are not even providing what we normally think of as banking services! They are "too big to fail" only because they are responsible for a giant Ponzi scheme that has the entire economy in its death grip. They have created a perilous derivatives bubble that has generated billions of dollars in short-term profits but has destroyed the financial system in the process. Collusion among mega-banks has made derivative trading less risky. However, this has not served the larger community but has hurt small investors and the budding corporations targeted by "vulture capitalism." The fleas' gain has been the dog's loss.

## The Secret Nationalization of the Banks

In a March 2007 article called "Too Big to Bail (Out)," Dave Lewis observes that the next major bank bailout may exceed the capacity of the taxpayers to keep the private banking boat afloat. Lewis is a veteran Wall Street trader who remembers the 1980s, when banks actually *could* fail. The "too big to fail" concept came in at the end of the 1980s, when the savings and loans collapsed and Citibank lost 50 percent of its share price. In 1989, Congress passed the Financial Institutions Reform, Recovery and Enforcement Act, which bailed out the S&Ls with taxpayer money. Citibank's share price also recouped its losses. In 1991, a Wall Street investment bank called Salomon Brothers threatened bankruptcy, after the New York Fed Chief announced that the bank would no longer be able to participate in auctions of U.S. Treasuries after being caught submitting false bids. Warren Buffett, whose company owned 12 percent of the stock of Salomon Brothers, negotiated heavily with Treasury Secretary Nicholas Brady; and Salomon Brothers was saved. After that, says Lewis, "too big to fail" became standard policy:

> It is now 16 years later, the thin edge of the wedge has done its thing and the circuit is now complete. *The financial industry has been, in a sense, nationalized.* Credit rating agencies . . . will now simply assume government support for large financial institutions. . . . [But] there are limits to the amount of support even the mighty US taxpayers can provide . . . . If the derivatives inspired collapse of LTCM was a problem how much more problematic would be a similarly inspired derivatives collapse at JPMorgan given their US$62.6T in exposure. According to the Office of the Comptroller of the Currency . . . , this US$62.6T in derivatives exposure is funded by assets of only US$1.2T. . . . And who will fill in the gap, US taxpayers? *Are we now willing to upend social harmony, or what little that remains, by breaking promises of social security and other "entitlements" in order to keep big banks that mismanaged their investment portfolios afloat?* And all this, by the way, while the upper class has been enjoying its biggest tax breaks in decades.
>
> . . . The $150B bail out of the S&Ls in the late 80s caused a recession and cost George Bush the Elder a second term. I wonder what effects a $1T or even $5T bail out would cause . . . . Short of a military dictatorship, I can't imagine a bail out of that size

for that reason passing through Congress. . . .

What if the problem arises due to a collapse of some intervention scheme? Will US taxpayers be expected to bail out a covert scheme to keep the price of gold down? or oil? More to the point, *could* US taxpayers bail out such schemes? . . . [I]n the event support was needed and could be obtained under these conditions, why would anyone want to buy US bonds?[11]

If the financial industry has indeed been nationalized, and if we the taxpayers are footing the bill, we can and should demand a banking system that serves the taxpayers' interests rather than working at cross-purposes with them.

## The Systemic Bankruptcy of the Banks

Only a few big banks are considered too big to fail, entitling them to taxpayer bailout; but in some sense, *all* banks operating on the fractional reserve system are teetering on bankruptcy. Recall the definition of the term: "being unable to pay one's debts; being insolvent; having liabilities in excess of a reasonable market value of assets held." In an article called "Fractional Reserve Banking," Murray Rothbard put it like this:

[Depositors] think of their checking account as equivalent to a warehouse receipt. If they put a chair in a warehouse before going on a trip, they expect to get the chair back whenever they present the receipt. Unfortunately, while banks depend on the warehouse analogy, the depositors are systematically deluded. *Their money ain't there.*

An honest warehouse makes sure that the goods entrusted to its care are there, in its storeroom or vault. But banks operate very differently . . . Banks make money by literally creating money out of thin air, nowadays exclusively deposits rather than bank notes. This sort of swindling or counterfeiting is dignified by the term "fractional-reserve banking," which means that bank deposits are backed by only a small fraction of the cash they promise to have at hand and redeem.[12]

Before 1913, if too many of a bank's depositors came for their money at one time, the bank would have come up short and would have had to close its doors. That was true until the Federal Reserve Act shored up the system by allowing troubled banks to "borrow" money from the Federal Reserve, which could create it on the spot by selling government securities to a select group of banks that created the money as bookkeeping entries on their books. By rights, Rothbard said, the banks should be put into bankruptcy and the bankers should be jailed as embezzlers, just as they would have been before they succeeded in getting laws passed that protected their swindling. Instead, big banks are assured of being bailed out from their folly, encouraging them to take huge risks because they are confident of being rescued if things go amiss. This "moral hazard" has now been built into the decision-making process. But small businesses don't get bailed out when they make risky decisions that put them under water. Why should big banks have that luxury? In a "free" market, big banks should be free to fail like any other business. It would be different if they actually *were* indispensable to the economy, as they claim; but these global mega-banks spend most of their time and resources making profits for themselves, at the *expense* of the small consumer, the small investor, and small countries.

There are more efficient ways to get the banking services we need than by continually feeding and maintaining the parasitic banking machine we have now. It may be time to cut the mega-banks loose from the Fed's apron strings and let them deal with the free market forces they purport to believe in. Without the collusion of the Plunge Protection Team, the CRMPG and the Federal Reserve, some major banks could soon wind up in bankruptcy. The Federal Deposit Insurance Corporation (FDIC) deals with bankrupt banks by putting them into receivership, a form of bankruptcy in which a company can avoid liquidation by reorganizing with the help of a court-appointed trustee. When a bank is put into receivership, the trustee is the FDIC, an agency of the federal government. In return for bailing the bank out, the FDIC has the option of retaining the bank as a public asset. Why this might not be the disaster for the larger community that has been predicted, and might even work out nicely to the public's benefit, is discussed in Section VI.

## Shelter from the Storm

Whiles we are waiting for these developments, what can we do to protect ourselves and our assets? Like Auntie Em, market "bears" warn to run for the cellar. They say to prepare for the coming storm by getting out of U.S. stocks, the U.S. dollar, and excess residential real estate, and investing instead in gold and silver, precious metal stocks, oil stocks, foreign stocks, and foreign currencies. Many good books and financial newsletters are available on this subject.[13]

People in serious Doomsday mode go further. They recommend storing canned and dry food, drinking water, and organic seeds for sprouting and planting; investing in a water purifier, light source, stove and heater that don't depend on functioning electrical outlets; keeping extra cash in the family safe for when the banks suddenly close their doors; and storing gold and silver coins for when paper money becomes worthlesss. They recommend starting a garden in the backyard, a hydroponic garden (plants grown in water), or a window-box garden; or joining a local communal farming project. People facing financial collapse in other countries are better prepared to deal with it than Americans are, because they have been farming their own small gardens and surviving in barter economies for centuries. Americans need to study, form groups, and practice in order to be prepared. Many good Internet websites are also available on this subject. Community currency options are discussed in Chapter 36.

While those are all prudent alternatives in the event of economic collapse, in the happier ending to our economic fairytale, the financial system would be salvaged *before* it collapses. We can stock the cellar just in case there is a cyclone, but to succumb to the fear of scarcity is to let the Wicked Witch prevail, to let the cartel once again wind up with all the houses and the stock bargains. What then of the American dream, the liberty and justice for all in a land of equal opportunity promised by the Declaration of Independence and the Constitution? The irony is that our economic nightmare is built on an illusion. We have been tricked into believing we are inextricably mired in debt, when the "debt" was for an advance of "credit" that was ours all along. While trouble boils and bubbles in the pots of the Witches of Wall Street, the Good Witch remains waiting in the wings, waiting for us to remember our magic slippers and come into our power . . . .

# Section V

# THE MAGIC SLIPPERS: TAKING BACK THE MONEY POWER

*"You had to find it out for yourself. Now those magic slippers will take you home in two seconds."*

– Glinda the Good Witch to Dorothy

# Chapter 35
# STEPPING FROM SCARCITY INTO TECHNICOLOR ABUNDANCE

*Somewhere over the rainbow*
*Skies are blue,*
*And the dreams that you dare to dream*
*Really do come true.*

*– Song immortalized by Judy Garland*
*in the 1939 musical* The Wizard of Oz

One of the most dramatic scenes in the MGM version of The Wizard of Oz comes when Dorothy's cyclone-tossed house falls from the sky. The world transforms, as she opens the door and steps from the black and white barrenness of a Kansas farmhouse into the technicolor wonderland of Oz. The world transforms again when Dorothy and her companions don green-colored glasses as they enter the Emerald City. In the Wizard's world, reality can be changed just by looking at things differently. Historian David Parker wrote of Baum's fairytale:

> [T]he book emphasized an aspect of theosophy that Norman Vincent Peale would later call "the power of positive thinking": theosophy led to "a new upbeat and positive psychology" that "opposed all kinds of negative thinking – especially fear, worry and anxiety." It was through this positive thinking, and not through any magic of the Wizard, that Dorothy and her companions (as well as everyone else in Oz) got what they wanted.[1]

It would become a popular Hollywood theme – Dumbo's magic feather, Pollyanna's irrepressible positive thinking, the Music Man's "think system" for making beautiful music, the "Unsinkable" Molly

Brown. Thinking positively is not just the stuff of children's fantasies but is deeply ingrained in the American psyche. "I have learned," said Henry David Thoreau, "that if one advances confidently in the direction of his dreams, and endeavors to live the life he has imagined, he will meet with a success unexpected in common hours." William James, another nineteenth century American philosopher, said, "The greatest discovery of my generation is that a human being can alter his life by altering his attitudes of mind." Franklin Roosevelt broadcast this upbeat message in his Depression-era "fireside chats," in which he entered people's homes through that exciting new medium the radio and galvanized the country with encouraging words. "The only thing we have to fear is fear itself," he said in 1933, when the "enemy" was poverty and unemployment. Andrew Carnegie, one of the multi-millionaire Robber Barons, was another firm believer in achievement through positive thinking. "It is the mind that makes the body rich," he maintained. Believing that financial success could be reduced to a simple formula, he commissioned a newspaper reporter named Napoleon Hill to interview over 500 millionaires to discover the common threads of their success. Hill then memorialized the results in his bestselling book <u>Think and Grow Rich</u>.

Thinking positively was a trait of the Robber Barons themselves, who for all their mischief were a characteristically American phenomenon. They thought big. If there was a criminal element to their thinking, it was a crime the law had not yet codified. The Wild West, the Gold Rush, the Gilded Age, the Roaring Twenties, bootlegging during Prohibition – all were part of the wild and reckless youth of the nation. The Robber Barons were a product of the American capitalist spirit, the spirit of believing in what you want and making it happen. An aspect of a "free" market is the freedom to steal, which is why economics must be tempered with the Constitution and the law. That was the fatal flaw in the laissez-faire free market economics of the nineteenth century: it allowed opportunists to infiltrate and monopolize industry. The Founding Fathers saw the necessity of designing a government that would protect the inalienable rights of the people from the power grabs of the unscrupulous. The capitalist spirit of achieving one's dreams needed to operate within an infrastructure that insured and supported a fair race. Naming the villains and locking them up could help temporarily; but to create a millennial utopia, the legal edifice itself had to be secured.

## Waking from the Spell

When Frank Baum wrote his famous fairytale at the turn of the twentieth century, the notion that a life of scarcity could be transformed in an instant into one of universal abundance did not seem entirely far-fetched. It was an era of miracles, when scientists were bringing electricity, mechanized transportation, and the promise of free energy to America. Explosive technological advances evoked visions of a utopian future filled with modern transportation and communication facilities, along with jobs, housing and food for all.[2]

Catapulting the country into universal abundance was possible, but it didn't happen. Instead, a darker form of witchcraft enthralled the country. By the time The Wizard of Oz was made into a musical in the 1930s, the economy had again fallen into a major depression. Yip Harburg, who wrote the lyrics to "Somewhere Over the Rainbow," had a long list of hit songs, including "Brother, Can You Spare a Dime?" Harburg was not actually a member of the Communist Party, but he was a staunch advocate of a variety of left-leaning causes. His Hollywood career came to a halt when he was blacklisted in the 1950s, another visionary fallen to an agenda of fear and control.

But by the end of the twentieth century, science had again reached a stage of development where abundance for all seemed within reach. Buckminster Fuller said in 1980:

> We are blessed with technology that would be indescribable to our forefathers. We have the wherewithal, the know-it-all to feed everybody, clothe everybody, and give every human on Earth a chance. We know now what we could never have known before – that *we now have the option for all humanity to make it successfully on this planet in this lifetime.* Whether it is to be Utopia or Oblivion will be a touch-and-go relay race right up to the final moment.

The race between Utopia and Oblivion reflects two different visions of reality. One sees a world capable of providing for all. The other sees a world that is too small for its inhabitants, requiring the annihilation of large segments of the population if the rest are to survive. The prevailing scarcity mentality focuses on shortages of oil, water and food. But the real shortage, as Benjamin Franklin explained to his English listeners in the eighteenth century, is in the medium of exchange. If sufficient money could be made available to develop alternative sources of energy, alternative means of extracting water from the environment, and more efficient ways of growing food, there *could* be abundance for all. The notion that the government could simply *print* the money it needs is considered unrealistically utopian and inflationary; yet banks create money all the time. The chief reason the U.S. government can't do it is that a private banking cartel already has a monopoly on the practice.

Growth in M3 is no longer officially being reported, but by 2007, reliable private sources put it at 11 percent per year.[3] That means over one trillion dollars are now being added to the economy annually. Where does this new money come from? Since the country went off the gold standard in 1933, it couldn't have come from new infusions of gold. *All* of this additional money must have been created by banks as loans. As soon as the loans are paid off, the money must be borrowed all over again, just to keep money in the system; and it is *here* that we find the real cause of global scarcity: *somebody is paying interest on most of the money in the world all of the time.* A dollar accruing interest at 5 percent, compounded annually, becomes two dollars in about 14 years. At that rate, *banks siphon off as much in interest every 14 years as there was money in the entire world 14 years earlier.* That explains why M3 has increased by 100 percent or more every 14 years since the Federal Reserve first started tracking it in 1959. According to a Fed chart titled "M3 Money Stock," M3 was about $300 billion in 1959. In 1973, 14 years later, it had grown to $900 billion. In 1987, 14 years after that, it was $3,500 billion; and in 2001, 14 years after that, it was $7,200 billion.[4] To meet the huge interest burden required to service all this money-built-on-debt, the money supply must continually expand; and for that to happen, borrowers must continually go deeper into debt, merchants must continually raise their prices, and the odd men out in the bankers' game of musical chairs must continue to lose their property to the banks. Wars, competition and strife are the inevitable results of this scarcity-driven system.

The obvious solution is to eliminate the parasitic banking scheme that is feeding on the world's prosperity. But how? The Witches of Wall Street are not likely to release their vice-like grip without some sort of revolution; and a violent revolution would probably fail, because the world's most feared military machine is already in the hands of the money cartel. Violent revolution would just furnish them with an excuse to test their equipment. The first American Revolution was fought before tasers, lasers, tear gas, armored tanks, and depleted uranium weapons. Fortunately or unfortunately, in the eye of today's economic cyclone, we may have to do no more than watch and wait, as the global pyramid scheme collapses of its own weight. In the end, what is likely to bring the house of cards down is that the Robber Barons have lost control of the propaganda machine. Their intellectual foe is the Internet, that last bastion of free speech, where even the common blogger can find a voice. As President John Adams is quoted as saying of the revolution of his day:

> The Revolution was effected before the war commenced. The Revolution was in the hearts and minds of the people. . . . *This radical change in the principles, opinions, sentiments, and affections of the people, was the real American Revolution.*

Today the corporate media are gradually losing control of public opinion; but the Money Machine is still shrouded in mystery, largely because the subject is so complex and forbidding. Richard Russell is a respected financial analyst who has been publishing The Dow Theory Letter for over half a century. He observes:

> The creation of money is a total mystery to probably 99 percent of the US population, and *that most definitely includes the Congress and the Senate. The takeover of US money creation by the Fed is one of the most mysterious and ominous acts in US history.* . . . The legality of the Federal Reserve has never been "tried" before the US Supreme Court.[5]

We the people could try bringing suit before the Supreme Court; but the courts, like the major media, are now largely under the spell of the financial/corporate cartel. There are honest and committed judges, congresspersons and reporters who could be approached; but to make a real impact will take a vigorous movement from an awakened and aroused populace ready to be heard and make a difference, a popular force too strong to be ignored. When a certain critical mass of people has awakened, the curtain can be thrown aside and the Wizard's hand can be exposed. But before we can build a movement, we need to be ready with an action plan, an ark that will keep us afloat when the flood hits. What sort of ark might that be? We'll begin by looking at a number of alternative models that have been developed around the world . . . .

## Perpetual Christmas in Guardiagrele, Italy

One interesting experiment in alternative financing was reported in the October 7, 2000 <u>Wall Street Journal</u>. It was the brainchild of Professor Giacinto Auriti, a wealthy local academic in Guardiagrele, Italy. According to the <u>Journal</u>:

> Prof. Auriti . . . hopes to convince the world that central bankers are the biggest con artists in modern history. His main thesis: For centuries, central banks have been robbing the common man by the way they put new money in circulation. Rather than divide the new cash among the people, they lend it through the banking system, at interest. This practice, he argues, makes the central banks the money's owners and makes everyone else their debtors. He goes on to conclude that this debt-based money has roughly half the purchasing power it would have if it were issued directly to the populace, free.

To prove his thesis, Professor Auriti printed up and issued his own debt-free bills, called *simec*. He agreed to trade simec for lire, and to redeem each simec for two lire from local merchants. The result:

> Armed with their *simec*, the townsfolk -- and later their neighbors elsewhere in central Italy's Abruzzo region -- stormed participating stores to snap up smoked prosciutto, designer shoes and other goods at just half the lire price.
>
> "At first, people thought this can't be true, there must be a rip-off hidden somewhere," says Antonella Di Cocco, a guide at a local museum. "But once people realized that the shopkeepers were the only ones taking the risk, they just ran to buy all these extravagant things they never really needed." Often, they raided their savings accounts in the process.
>
> The participating shopkeepers, some of whom barely eked out a living before the *simec* bonanza, couldn't have been happier. "Every day was Christmas," Pietro Ricci recalls from behind the counter of his cavernous haberdashery.
>
> Neither Mr. Ricci nor his fellow merchants were stuck with their *simec* for long. Once a week, they turned them in to Prof. Auriti, recouping the full price of their goods.
>
> "We doubled the money in people's pockets, injecting blood into a lifeless body," says Prof. Auriti. "People were so happy, they thought they were dreaming."

Non-participating stores, meanwhile, remained empty week after week. . . . By mid-August, says the professor, a total of about 2.5 billion *simec* had circulated.[6]

The professor had primed the pump by doubling the town's money supply. As a result, goods that had been sitting on the shelves for lack of purchasing power started to move. The professor himself lost money on the deal, since he was redeeming the *simec* at twice what he had charged for them; but the local merchants liked the result so much that they eventually took over the project. When there were enough *simec* in circulation for the system to work without new money, the professor was relieved of having to put his own money into the venture. The obvious limitation of his system is that it requires a wealthy local benefactor to get it going. Ideally, the benefactor would be the government itself, issuing permanent money in the form of the national currency.

## Private Silver and Gold Exchanges

People concerned about the soundness of the dollar may like the idea of trading in privately-issued precious metal coins. Private silver and gold exchanges go back for centuries. The U.S. dollar is defined in the Constitution in terms of silver, and at one time people could bring their own silver to the mint to be turned into coins. In 1998, a private non-profit organization call NORFED (the National Organization for the Repeal of the Federal Reserve Act and the Internal Revenue Code) began issuing a currency called the Liberty Dollar, which is backed by gold and silver. Liberty Dollars take the form of minted metal pieces, gold and silver certificates, and electronic currency. The coins come as $5, $10, and $20 Silver Liberties and a $1,000 Gold Liberty, while certificates come as $5, $10, and $20 silver certificates and a $1,000 gold certificate.

Legally, says NORFED, the Liberty Dollar certificates are receipts guaranteeing that the holder has ownership of a certain sum of silver or gold stored in a warehouse in Coeur d'Alene, Idaho. The silver is insured and audited monthly, and the Certificates are reported to be more difficult to counterfeit even than Federal Reserve Notes. Liberty Dollars are marketed at a discount and are exchanged at participating neighborhood stores dollar for dollar with U.S. dollars. NORFED has also "digitized" its gold and silver dollars, making them tradeable online or through electronic funds. By 2006, NORFED claimed a circulation of $20 million, making the Liberty Dollar the second most popular American currency after Federal Reserve Notes.[7]

That was true, at least, until September 2006, when a spokesman for the U.S. Mint declared the coins to be illegal because they could be confused with U.S. coins. "The United States Mint is the only entity that can produce coins," said the spokesman.[8] The pronouncement underscored one of the hazards of alternative currencies: their legal standing can be challenged. Privately-issued money may also be refused by merchants, and it is not accepted by banks.

Liberty Dollar certificates also involve a substantial markup, which makes them worth quite a bit less than their face value in precious metal. Even when precious metal coins are issued by governments, the value of the metal must be kept well below the face value of the coins, in order to keep them from being smelted for their metal content whenever the metal's market value goes up. The silver that backs the NORFED Certificates is only about half the face value of the Certificates (depending on the variable silver market). The difference goes to NORFED for its costs and to support its efforts to have the Federal Reserve and federal income tax abolished. However, the dilution in the value of the currency would seem to defeat the purpose of holding precious metals, which is to preserve value. Gold and silver are excellent ways to *store* value, but you don't need to use them as a medium of exchange. You can just buy bullion or coins and keep them in a safe place.

Even that alternative can be cumbersome. "GoldMoney" is an online precious metals exchange that overcomes the problems of storage and exchange by providing a convenient way to own and transfer gold without actually dealing with the physical metal. According to its website, when you buy "goldgrams," you own pure gold in a secure vault in London. GoldMoney can be used as currency by "clicking" goldgrams online from one account to another.[9] Online gold is a hassle-free way to invest in gold, but it too has drawbacks as a currency. It involves a certain markup, and its value fluctuates with the volatile gold market. People on fixed incomes with fixed rents generally prefer not to gamble. They like to know exactly what they have in the bank. The gold versus *fiat* question is explored further in Chapter 36.

## Community Banking:
## The Grameen Bank of Bangladesh

Another innovation in community financing is the community-owned bank. Desperately poor people have often been kept that way because they lacked the collateral necessary to qualify for loans from private corporate banks. The Grameen (or "Village") Bank of Bangladesh is designed so that ownership and control remains in the hands of the borrowers. As soon as a borrower accumulates sufficient savings, she buys one (and only one) share in the bank, for the very modest sum of three U.S. dollars. According to the Grameen Bank's website, 92 percent of the bank is now owned by its borrowers, with the Bangladesh government owning the remaining 8 percent. The interest rate for loans is set by the bank's board so that after paying all expenses, the bank makes a modest profit, which is returned to the shareholder-borrowers in the form of dividends. The rate of interest is 20 percent on a "working capital" loan and 8 percent on home loans. The Grameen Bank website reports that 54 percent of its borrowers have crossed the poverty line and another 27 percent are very close to it, beginning with loans of as little as $50.[10] By August 2006, the bank had served 5 million borrowers over a period of 25 years.[11]

The Grameen Bank has asserted its independence from the private corporate banking system by providing loans to people who would otherwise be considered bad credit risks, but the currency it lends is still the national currency, issued by the government and controlled by big corporate banks. Other community models operate independently of big banks, precious metals, *and* the government . . . .

# Chapter 36
# THE COMMUNITY CURRENCY MOVEMENT: SIDESTEPPING THE DEBT WEB WITH "PARALLEL" CURRENCIES

*It is as ridiculous for a nation to say to its citizens, "You must consume less because we are short of money," as it would be for an airline to say, "Our planes are flying, but we cannot take you because we are short of tickets."*

-- Sheldon Emry, <u>Billions for the Bankers, Debts for the People</u>

"Money" is a token representing value. A monetary system is a contractual agreement among a group of people to accept those tokens at an agreed-upon value in trade. The ideal group for this contractual agreement is the larger community called a nation, but if that larger group can't be brought to the task, any smaller group can enter into an agreement, get together and trade. Historically, community currencies have arisen spontaneously when national currencies were scarce or unobtainable. When the German mark became worthless during the Weimar hyperinflation of the 1920s, many German cities began issuing their own currencies. Hundreds of communities in the United States, Canada and Europe did the same thing during the Great Depression, when unemployment was so high that people had trouble acquiring dollars. People lacked money but had skills, and there was plenty of work to be done. Complementary local currencies quietly co-existed along with official government money, increasing liquidity and facilitating trade. Like the medieval tally, these currencies were simply credits attesting that goods or services had been received, entitling the bearer to trade the credit for an equivalent value in goods or services in the local market.

Community currencies now operate legally in more than 35 countries, and there are over 4,000 local exchange programs worldwide. Local or private exchange systems come in a variety of forms. Besides private gold and silver exchanges, they include local paper money, computerized systems of credits and debits, systems for bartering labor, and systems for trading local agricultural products. What distinguishes them from most national currencies is that they are not created as a debt to private banks, and they don't get siphoned off from the community to private banks in the form of interest. They stay in town, stimulating local productivity. Local currencies can "prime the pump" with new money, funding local projects without adding to the community debt. Many governments actively support them, and others give unofficial support. Experience shows that these additions to the money supply strengthen rather than threaten national financial stability. Besides their monetary functions, local exchange systems have served to bring communities together, funding cooperative businesses where members can sell goods, new skills can be learned, and public markets can be held.

## Creative Responses to Disaster:
## The Example of Argentina

In 1995, Argentina went bankrupt. The government had adopted all the policies mandated by the International Monetary Fund, including "privatization" (the sale of public assets to private corporations) and pegging the Argentine peso to the U.S. dollar. The result was an overvalued peso, massive economic contraction, and collapse of the financial system. People rushed to their banks to withdraw their life savings, only to be told that their banks had permanently closed.

Lawns soon turned into vegetable gardens, and local systems sprang up for bartering goods. One environmental group held a massive yard sale, where people brought what they had to sell and received tickets representing money in exchange. The tickets were then used to barter the purchase of other goods. This system of paper receipts for goods and services developed into the Global Exchange Network (*Red Global de Trueque* or RGT), which went on to become the largest national community currency network in the world. The model spread throughout Central and South America, growing to 7 million members and a circulation valued at millions of U.S. dollars per year.

Other financial innovations were devised in Argentina at the local provincial government level. Provinces short of the national currency resorted to issuing their own. They paid their employees with paper receipts called "Debt-Cancelling Bonds" that were in currency units equivalent to the Argentine Peso. These could be called "negotiable bonds" (bonds that are legally transferable and negotiable as currency), except that they did not pay interest. They were closer to the "non-interest-bearing bonds" proposed by Jacob Coxey in the 1890s for funding state and local projects. The bonds canceled the provinces' debts to their employees and could be spent in the community. The Argentine provinces had actually "monetized" their debts, turning their bonds or I.O.U.s into legal tender.[1]

Studies showed that in provinces in which the national money supply was supplemented with local currencies, prices not only did not rise but actually declined compared to other Argentine provinces. Local exchange systems allowed goods and services to be traded that would not otherwise have been on the market, causing supply and demand to increase together. The system had some flaws, including the lack of adequate controls against counterfeiting, which allowed large amounts of inventory to be stolen with counterfeit scrip. By the summer of 2002, the RGT had shrunk to 70,000 members; but it still remains a remarkable testament to what can be done at a grassroots level, when neighbors get together to trade with their own locally-grown currency.

## Alternative Paper Currencies in the United States

More than 30 local paper currencies are now available in North America. One that has been particularly successful is the Ithaca HOUR, originated by Paul Glover in Ithaca, New York. The HOUR is paper scrip that reads on the back:

> This is money. This note entitles the bearer to receive one hour of labor or its negotiated value in goods and services. Please accept it, then spend it. Ithaca HOURS stimulate local business by recycling our wealth locally, and they help fund new job creation. Ithaca HOURS are backed by real capital: our skills, our muscles, our tools, forests, fields and rivers.

One Ithaca HOUR is considered to be the equivalent of ten dollars, the average hourly wage in the area. More highly skilled services are negotiated in multiples of HOURS. A directory is published every couple of months that lists the goods and services people in the community are willing to trade for HOURS, and there is an HOUR bank. People can use HOURS to pay rent, shop at the farmers' market, or buy furniture. The local hospital accepts them for medical care. Several million Ithaca HOURS' worth of transactions have occurred since 1991. A Home Town Money Starter Kit is available for $25 or 2-1/2 HOURS from Ithaca MONEY, Box 6578, Ithaca, New York 14851.

Another successful credit program was originated by Edgar Cahn, a professor of law at the University of the District of Columbia, to help deal with inadequate government social programs. Like Glover, Cahn set out to create a new kind of money that was independent of both government and banks, one that could be created by people themselves. The unit of exchange in his system, called a "Time Dollar," parallels the Ithaca HOUR in being valued in man/hours. In a landmark ruling, the Internal Revenue Service held that Cahn's service plan was not "barter" in the commercial sense and was therefore tax-exempt. The ruling helped the program to spread quickly around the country. Cahn notes that social as well as economic benefits have resulted from this sort of program:

> [T]he very process of earning credits knits groups together . . . . They begin having pot-luck lunches; and they begin forming neighborhood crime watch things, and they begin looking after each other and checking in; and they begin to set up food bank coops. [The process] seems to act as a catalyst for the creation of group cohesion in a society where that kind of catalyst is difficult to find.[2]

Local scrip has also been used to tide farmers over until harvest. "Berkshire Farm Preserve Notes" were printed by a farmer when a bank in rural Massachusetts refused to lend him the money he needed to make it through the winter. Customers would buy the Notes for $9 in the winter and could redeem them for $10 worth of vegetables in the summer. With small family farms rapidly disappearing, local currencies of this type are a way for the community to help farm families that have been abandoned by the centralized monetary system. Private currencies provide the tools to bind communities together, support local food growers and maintain food supplies.[3]

Bernard Lietaer, author of The Future of Money, describes other private currency innovations, including a system devised in Japan for providing for elderly care that isn't covered by national health insurance. People help out the elderly in return for "caring relationship tickets" that are put into a savings account. They can then be used when the account holder becomes disabled, or can be sent electronically to elderly relatives living far away, where someone else will administer care in return for credits.

Another interesting model described by Lietaer is found in Bali, where communities have a dual money system. Besides the national currency, the Balinese use a local currency in which the unit of account is a block of time of about three hours. The local currency is used when the community launches a local project, such as putting on a festival or building a school. The villagers don't have to compete with the outside world to generate this currency, which can be used to accomplish things for which they would not otherwise have had the funds.[4]

## The Frequent Flyer Model:
## Supplemental Credit Systems

Another innovation that has served to expand the medium of exchange is the development of corporate credits such as airline frequent flyer miles, which can now be "earned" and "spent" in a variety of ways besides simply flying on the issuing airline. In some places, frequent flyer miles can be spent for groceries, telephone calls, taxis, restaurants and hotels. Bernard Lietaer proposes extending this model to local governments, to achieve community ends without the need to tax or vote special appropriations. For example, a system of "carbon credits" could reward consumers for taking measures that reduce carbon emissions. The credits would be accepted as partial payment for other purchases that serve to reduce carbon emissions, producing a snowball effect; and businesses accepting the credits could use them to pay local taxes.[5]

## Parallel Electronic Currencies:
## The LETS System

Alternative currency systems got a major boost with the advent of computers. No longer must private coins be minted or private bills be printed. Trades can now be done electronically. The first electronic currency system was devised after IBM released its XT computer to the public in 1981. Canadian computer expert Michael Linton built an accounting database, and in 1982 he introduced the Local Exchange Trading System (LETS), a computerized system for recording transactions and keeping accounts.

Like Cotton Mather more than two centuries earlier, Linton had redefined money. In his scheme, it was merely "an information system for recording human effort." A LETS credit comes into existence when a member borrows the community's credit to purchase goods or services. The credit is extinguished when the member gives goods or services back to the community in satisfaction of his obligation to repay the credits. The exchange operates without any form of "backing" or "reserves." Like the tally system of medieval England, it is just an accounting scheme tallying credits in and debits out. LETS credits cannot become scarce any more than inches can become scarce. They are tax-free and interest-free. They can be stored on a computer without even printing a paper copy. They are simply information. There are now at least 800 Local Exchange Trading Systems (LETS) in Europe, New Zealand, and Australia. They are less popular in the United States, but community currency enthusiast Tom Greco feels they will become more popular as conventional economies continue to decline and more people become "marginalized."

In a website called "Travelling the World Without Money," Australian enthusiast James Taris tells of his personal experiences with the LETS system. At a time when he had quit his job and was watching his money carefully, he attended a LETS group meeting in his local community, where he learned that he could obtain a variety of services just for contributing an equivalent amount of his time. The result was the first and best professional massage he had ever had, a luxury for which he could not justify paying $60 cash when he was gainfully employed. He "paid" for this and other services by learning various Internet and desktop publishing skills and contributing those skills to the group, something he quite enjoyed. He has been demonstrating the potential of the system by traveling around the world with very little conventional money.[6]

"Friendly Favors" is a LETS-type computerized exchange system that has grown beyond the local community into a worldwide database of over 12,000 members. The system tracks the exchange of "Thankyou's," a unit of measure considered to be the equivalent of one dollar saved due to a friendly discount or favor received. The database also stores the photos, resumes, talents, interests and community-building skills of participants. Developed by Sergio Lub and Victor Grey of Walnut Creek, California, *www.favors.org* is a non-commercial service "to interconnect those envisioning a world that works for all." Unlike most LETS systems, which have evolved among people short of money looking for alternative ways to trade, the Friendly Favors membership includes people who are financially well off and highly credentialed, who are particularly interested in the human resources potential of the system. As of May 2004, the Friendly Favors membership was spread over more than 100 countries and its database was shared by over 200 groups with a collective membership of over 42,000, making it potentially the largest source of human resources available on the Internet.

A number of good Internet sites are devoted to the community currency concept, including *ithacahours.com; madisonhours.org;* Carol Brouillet's site at *communitycurrency.org;* and The International Journal of Community Currency Research at *geog.le.ac.uk/ijccr.* For a good general discussion of alternative money proposals, see Tom Greco's Monetary Education Project at *reinvestingmoney.com.* The definitive source for LETS information is Landsman Community Services, Ltd., 1600 Embleton Crescent, Courtenay, British Columbia V9n 6N8, Canada; telephone (604) 338-0213.

## Limitations of Local Currency Systems

Local exchange systems demonstrate that "money" need not be something that is scarce or for which people have to compete. Money is simply credit. As Benjamin Franklin observed, credit turns prosperity tomorrow into ready money today. Credit can be had without gold, banks, governments or even printing presses. It can all be done on a computer.

The concept is good, but there are some practical limitations to the LETS model and other community currency systems as currently practiced. One is that the usual incentives for repayment are lacking. Interest is not charged, and there may be no time limit for repayment. If you have ever lent money to a relative, you know the problem. Debts can go unpaid indefinitely. You can lean on your relatives because you know where to find them; but in the anonymity of a city or a nation, borrowers on the honor system can just disappear into the night. Some alternatives for keeping community members honest have been suggested by Tom Greco, who writes:

[T]here is always the possibility that a participant may choose to not honor his/her commitment, opting out of the system and refusing to deliver value equivalent to that received. There are three possible ways, which occur to me, of handling that risk. The first possibility is to use a "funded" exchange in which each participant surrenders or pledges particular assets as security against his/her commitment. . . . A second possibility, is to maintain an "insurance" pool, funded by fees levied on all transactions, to cover any possible losses. A third possibility . . . is reliance upon group co-responsibility, i.e. having each participant within an affinity group bear responsibility for the debits of the others.[7]

Those are possibilities, but they are not so practical or so workable as the contractual agreements used today, with interest charges and late penalties enforceable in court. Of course, contractual agreements to repay could be made enforceable in court without including interest provisions. They could be enforced by foreclosing on collateral or garnishing wages. But eliminating interest from the money system would also eliminate the incentive for lenders to lend, and it would encourage speculation. If credit were made available without time limits or interest charges, people would simply borrow all the free money they could get, then compete to purchase bonds, stocks, and other income-producing assets with it, generating speculative asset bubbles. Imposing a significant cost on borrowing deters this sort of rampant speculation and ensures that borrowers borrow only so much as they need for only so long as they need it.

In Moslem communities, interest is avoided because usury is forbidden in the Koran. To avoid infringing religious law, Islamic lawyers have gone to great lengths to design contracts that avoid interest charges. The most common alternative is a contract in which the banker buys the property and sells it to the client at a higher price, to be paid in installments over time. But the effect is the same as charging interest: more money is owed back if the sum is paid over time than if it had been paid immediately. In large Western metropolises, where mobility is high and religion is not a pervasive factor, interest is considered a reasonable charge acknowledging the time value of money. The objection of Greco and others to charging interest turns on the "impossible contract" problem – the problem of finding principal and interest to pay back loans in a monetary scheme in which only the principal is put into the money supply. But that problem can be resolved in other ways. A proposal for retaining the benefits of the interest system while avoiding the "impossible contract" problem is explored in Chapter 42.

A more serious limitation of private "supplemental" currencies is that they fail to deal with the mammoth debt spider that is sucking the lifeblood from the national economy. "Supplemental" currencies all assume a national currency that is being supplemented. Taxes must still be paid in the national currency, and so must bills for telephone service, energy, gasoline, and anything else that isn't made by someone in the local currency group. That means community members must still belong to the national money system. As Stephen Zarlenga observes:

> [S]uch local currencies *do not stop the continued mismanagement of the money system at the national level* – they can't stop the continued dispensation of monetary injustice from above through the privately owned and controlled Federal Reserve money system. *Ending that injustice should be our monetary priority.*[8]

The *national* money problem can be solved only by reforming the *national* currency. And that brings us back to the "money question" of the 1890s – Greenbacks or gold?

# Chapter 37
# THE MONEY QUESTION:
# GOLDBUGS AND GREENBACKERS
# DEBATE

*You shall not crucify mankind upon a cross of gold.*
*-- William Jennings Bryan, 1896 Democratic Convention*

At opposite ends of the debate over the money question in the 1890s were the "Goldbugs," led by the bankers, and the "Greenbackers," who were chiefly farmers and laborers.[1] The use of the term "Goldbug" has been traced to the 1896 Presidential election, when supporters of gold money took to wearing lapel pins of small insects to show their position. The Greenbackers at the other extreme were suspicious of a money system dependent on the bankers' gold, having felt its crushing effects in their own lives. As Vernon Parrington summarized their position in the 1920s:

> To allow the bankers to erect a monetary system on gold is to subject the producer to the money-broker and measure deferred payments by a yardstick that lengthens or shortens from year to year. The only safe and rational currency is a national currency based on the national credit, sponsored by the state, flexible, and controlled in the interests of the people as a whole.[2]

The Goldbugs countered that currency backed only by the national credit was too easily inflated by unscrupulous politicians. Gold, they insisted, was the only stable medium of exchange. They called it "sound money" or "honest money." Gold had the weight of history to recommend it, having been used as money for 5,000 years. It had to be extracted from the earth under difficult and often dangerous circumstances, and the earth had only so much of it to relinquish. The supply of it was therefore relatively fixed. The virtue of gold was that it was a rare commodity that could not be inflated by irresponsible governments out of all proportion to the supply of goods and services.

The Greenbackers responded that gold's scarcity, far from being a virtue, was actually its major drawback as a medium of exchange. Gold coins might be "honest money," but their scarcity had led governments to condone *dishonest* money, the sleight of hand known as "fractional reserve" banking. Governments that were barred from creating their own paper money would just borrow it from banks that created it and then demanded it back with interest. As Stephen Zarlenga notes in <u>The Lost Science of Money</u>:

> [A]ll of the plausible sounding gold standard theory could not change or hide the fact that, in order to function, the system had to mix paper credits with gold in domestic economies. Even after this addition, the mixed gold and credit standard could not properly service the growing economies. They periodically broke down with dire domestic and international results. [In] the worst such breakdown, the Great Crash and Depression of 1929-33, . . . it was widely noted that those countries did best that left the gold standard soonest.[3]

The debate between these two camps still rages. However, today the Goldbugs are not the bankers but are in the money reform camp along with the Greenbackers. Both factions are opposed to the current banking system, but they disagree on how to fix it. That is one reason the modern money reform movement hasn't made much headway politically. As Machiavelli said in the sixteenth century, "He who introduces a new order of things has all those who profit from the old order as his enemies, and he has only lukewarm allies in all those who might profit from the new." Maverick reformers continue to argue among themselves, while the bankers and their hired economists march in lockstep, fortified by media they have purchased and laws they have gotten passed, using the powerful leverage of their bank-created fiat money.

Congressman Ron Paul of Texas is one of the few contemporary politicians to boldly challenge the monetary scheme in Congress. He is also a Goldbug, who argued in a February 2006 address to Congress:

> It has been said, rightly, that he who holds the gold makes the rules. In earlier times it was readily accepted that fair and honest trade required an exchange for something of real value . . . . [A]s governments grew in power they assumed monopoly control over money. . . . [I]n time governments learned to

outspend their revenues [and sought] more gold by conquering other nations. . . . When gold no longer could be obtained, their military might crumbled.

. . . Today the principles are the same, but the process is quite different. Gold no longer is the currency of the realm; paper is. The truth now is: "He who prints the money makes the rules". . . . Since printing paper money is nothing short of counterfeiting, the issuer of the international currency must always be the country with the military might to guarantee control over the system.

. . . The economic law that honest exchange demands only things of real value as currency cannot be repealed. The chaos that one day will ensue from our 35-year experiment with worldwide fiat money will require a return to money of real value.[4]

Modern-day Greenbackers, while having the highest regard for Congressman Paul's valiant one-man crusade, would no doubt debate the details; and one highly debatable detail is that it is the *government* that now has monopoly control over money, and it is the *government* that is counterfeiting the money supply. Wars are fought, the Greenbackers would say, not to preserve the dollars of the U.S. government but to preserve the Federal Reserve Notes of a private banking cartel. It is *this* private cartel that has monopoly control over money, and its monopoly grew out of a shell game called "fractional reserve banking," *which grew out of the very "gold standard" the Goldbugs seek to reinstate.* We have been deluded into thinking that what is wrong with the system is that the government has a monopoly over creating the money supply. The government lost its monopoly when King George forbade the colonies from printing their own money in the eighteenth century. Banks have created most of the national money supply for most of our national history. The government itself must beg from this private cartel to get the money it needs; and it is this mounting debt to an elite class of banker-financiers, not profligate government spending on social goods, that has brought the United States and most other countries to the brink of bankruptcy. If Congress had used its Constitutional power to create money to fund its own operations, it would not have needed to pursue imperialistic foreign wars to extort money from its neighbors.

## Is Gold a Stable Measure of Value?

Goldbugs maintain that the value of money needs to be pegged to something to keep it consistent and dependable. In a September 2002 statement urging Congress to abolish the Federal Reserve, Ron Paul argued:

> [A]bolishing the Federal Reserve and returning to a constitutional system will enable America to return to the type of monetary system envisioned by our nation's founders: one where the value of money is consistent because it is tied to a commodity such as gold. Such a monetary system is the basis of a true free-market economy.[5]

Again the Greenbacker camp might agree in part and disagree in part. They would agree that money needs to be pegged to something to keep it stable, but they would question whether the price of gold is stable enough to act as such a peg. The nineteenth century farmers knew the problem firsthand, having seen their profits shrink as the gold price went up. Real-world models are hard to come by today, but one is furnished by the real estate market in Vietnam, where sales are now undertaken in gold. When the price of gold soared to over $500 an ounce in the fall of 2005, buyers suddenly had to pay tens of millions more Vietnamese *dong* for a house valued at 1,000 *taels* of gold. As a result, the real estate market ground to a halt.[6]

The purpose of "money" is to tally the value of goods and services traded, facilitating commerce between buyers and sellers. If the yardstick by which value is tallied keeps stretching and shrinking itself, commerce is impaired. During the Gold Rush of the 1850s, the supply of gold shot up, and consumer prices shot up with it. From 1917 to 1920, the gold supply surged again, as gold came pouring into the country in exchange for war materials. The money supply became seriously inflated and consumer prices doubled, although the money supply was supposedly being strictly regulated by the Federal Reserve.[7] During the 1970s, the value of gold soared from $40 an ounce to $800 an ounce, dropping back to a low of $255 in February 2001. If you were on a fixed income and paying your rent in gold coins that you had stashed away earlier, you would have made out well in the 1970s; but you might be paying double or triple the effective rent thereafter. Again, people on fixed incomes generally prefer a currency that has a fixed and predictable value, even if it is made of paper. Some alternatives for pegging currencies that would be more stable than the price of gold alone are discussed in Chapter 46.

## Practical Limitations of Using Gold as Money

Beyond the question of price stability, there are major practical problems involved in using gold as a medium of exchange. If *only* gold is used, pennies, nickels and dimes will be so small that they will get lost in your wallet; while large purchases such as houses will have to be transacted in gold bars too heavy to carry in a suitcase. To be workable and efficient, the monetary system needs to be supplemented with checkbook money and electronic money; but that means exposing it to the same tampering and manipulation to which the current fiat system is subject.

There is also the problem, discussed earlier, of keeping gold coins in circulation. If the coins are stamped with a value that is the actual market value of the metal at the time the coins are produced, they are liable to get smelted for their metal as soon as its market value goes up. Coins are therefore usually issued with a face value (or nominal value) that is far in excess of their intrinsic worth.[8] But that destroys the very thing the coins are supposed to be good for – preserving value.

A more serious downside of using gold as a medium of exchange is that productivity becomes tied to the availability of the metal. When gold flooded the market after a major gold discovery in the nineteenth century, there was plenty of money to hire workers, so production and employment went up. When gold was scarce, as when the bankers raised interest rates and called in loans, there was insufficient money to hire workers, so production and employment went down. But what did the availability of gold have to do with the ability of farmers to farm, of miners to mine, of builders to build? Not much. The Greenbackers argued that the work should come *first*. Like in the medieval tally system, the "money" would follow, as a receipt acknowledging payment. The paper money issued by the government *did* represent something of real value, but it wasn't gold. The Greenback was a receipt for a quantity of goods or services delivered to the government, which the bearer could then trade in the community for other goods or services of equivalent value. The receipt was simply a tally, an accounting tool for measuring value.

Goldbugs argue that there will always be enough gold in a gold-based money system to go around, because prices will naturally adjust downward so that supply matches demand.[9] But we've seen that this fundamental premise of the classical "quantity theory of money" has not worked well in practice. The drawbacks of limiting the medium of exchange to precious metals were obvious as soon as the Founding Fathers decided on a precious metal standard at the Constitutional Convention, when the money supply contracted so sharply that farmers rioted in the streets in Shay's Rebellion. When gold left the country during the Great Depression, a vicious deflationary spiral was initiated in which insufficient money to pay workers led to demand falling off, which led to more goods remaining unsold, which caused even more workers to get laid off. Fruit was left to rot in the fields, because it wasn't economical to pick it and sell it.

To further clarify these points, here is a hypothetical. You are shipwrecked on a desert island . . . .

## Shipwrecked with a Chest of Gold Coins

You and nine of your mates wash ashore with a treasure chest containing 100 gold coins. You decide to divide the coins and the essential tasks equally among you. Your task is making the baskets used for collecting fruit. You are new to the task and manage to turn out only ten baskets the first month. You keep one and sell the others to your friends for one coin each, using your own coins to purchase the wares of the others.

So far so good. By the second month, your baskets have worn out but you have gotten much more proficient at making them. You manage to make twenty. Your mates admire your baskets and say they would like to have two each; but alas, they have only one coin to allot to basket purchase. You must either cut your sales price in half or cut back on production. The other islanders face the same problem with their production potential. The net result is price deflation and depression. You have no incentive to increase your production, and you have no way to earn extra coins so that you can better your standard of living.

The situation gets worse over the years, as the islanders multiply but the gold coins don't. You can't afford to feed your young children on the meager income you get from your baskets. If you make more baskets, their price just gets depressed and you are left with the number of coins you had to start with. You try borrowing from a friend, but he too needs his coins and will agree only if you will agree to pay him interest. Where is this interest to come from? There are not enough coins in the community to cover this new cost.

Then, miraculously, another ship washes ashore, containing a chest with 50 more gold coins. The lone survivor from this ship agrees to lend 40 of his coins at 20 percent interest. The islanders consider this a great blessing, until the time comes to pay the debt back, when they realize there are no extra coins on the island to cover the interest. The creditor demands lifetime servitude instead. The system degenerates into debt and bankruptcy, just as the gold-based system did historically in the outside world.

Now consider another scenario . . . .

## Shipwrecked with an Accountant

You and nine companions are shipwrecked on a desert island, but your ship is not blessed (or cursed) with a chest of gold coins. "No problem," says one of your mates, who happens to be an accountant. He will keep "count" of your productivity with notched wooden tallies. He assumes the general function of tally-maker and collector and distributor of wares. For this service he pays himself a fair starting wage of ten tallies a month.

Your task is again basket-weaving. The first month, you make ten baskets, keep one, and trade the rest with the accountant for nine tallies, which you use to purchase the work/product of your mates. The second month, you make twenty baskets, keep two, and request eighteen tallies from the accountant for the other baskets. This time you get your price, since the accountant has an unlimited supply of trees and can make as many tallies as needed. They have no real value in themselves and cannot become "scarce." They are just receipts, a measure of the goods and services on the market. By collecting eighteen tallies for eighteen baskets, you have kept your basket's price stable, and you now have some extra money to tuck under your straw mattress for a rainy day. You take a month off to explore the island, funding the vacation with your savings.

When you need extra tallies to build a larger house, you borrow them from the accountant, who tallies the debt with an accounting entry. You pay principal and interest on this loan by increasing your basket production and trading the additional baskets for additional tallies. Who pockets the interest? The community decides that it is not something the tally-maker is rightfully entitled to, since the credit he extended was not his own but was an asset of the community, and he is already getting paid for his labor. The interest, you decide as a group, will be used to pay for services needed by the community --

clearing roads, standing guard against wild animals, caring for those who can't work, and so forth. Rather than being siphoned off by a private lender, the interest goes back into the community, where it can be used to pay the interest on other loans.

When you and your chosen mate are fruitful and multiply, your children make additional baskets, and your family's wealth also multiplies. There is no shortage of tallies, since they are pegged to the available goods and services. They multiply along with this "real" wealth; but they don't inflate *beyond* real wealth, because tallies and "wealth" (goods and services) always come into existence at the same time. When you are comfortable with your level of production -- say, twenty baskets a month -- no new tallies are necessary to fund your business. The system already contains the twenty tallies needed to cover basket output. You receive them in payment for your baskets and spend them on the wares of the other islanders, keeping the tallies in circulation. The money supply is permanent but expandable, growing as needed to cover real growth in productivity and the interest due on loans. Excess growth is avoided by returning money to the community, either as interest due on loans or as a fee or tax for other services furnished to the community.

## The NESARA Bill: Restoring Constitutional Money

One other proposal should be explored before leaving this chapter. Harvey Barnard of the NESARA Institute in Louisiana has suggested a way to retain the silver and gold coinage prescribed in the Constitution while providing the flexibility needed for national growth and productivity. The Constitution gives Congress the exclusive power "to coin Money, regulate the Value thereof, and of foreign Coin, and fix the Standard of Weights and Measures." Under Barnard's bill, called the National Economic Stabilization and Recovery Act (NESARA), the national currency would be issued exclusively by the government and would be of three types: standard silver coins, standard gold coins, and Treasury credit-notes (Greenbacks). The Treasury notes would replace all debt-money (Federal Reserve Notes). The precious metal content of coins would be standardized as provided in the Constitution and in the Coinage Act of 1792, which make the silver dollar coin the standard unit of the domestic monetary system. To prevent coins from being smelted for their metal content, the coins would not be stamped with a face value but would just be named "silver dollars," "gold eagles," or fractions of those coins. Their values would then be left to float in relation to the Treasury credit-note and each other. Exchange rates would be published regularly and would follow global market values. Congress would not only mint coins from its own stores of gold and silver but would encourage people to bring their private stores to be minted and circulated. Other features of the bill include abolition of the Federal Reserve System, purchase by the U.S. Treasury of all outstanding capital stock of the Federal Reserve Banks, return of the national currency to the public through a newly-created U.S. Treasury Reserve System, and replacement of the federal income tax system with a 14 percent sales and use tax (exempting specified items including groceries and rents).[10]

The NESARA proposal might work, but the question remains, why use gold at all? If the government can issue *both* paper money *and* precious metal coins, the coins won't serve as much of a brake on inflation. So why go to the trouble of minting them, or to the inconvenience of carrying them around? The problem with the current financial scheme is not that the dollar is not redeemable in gold. It is that the whole monetary edifice is a pyramid scheme based on debt to a private banking cartel. Money created privately as multiple "loans" against a single "reserve" is fraudulent on its face, whether the "reserve" is a government bond or gold bullion.

Precious metals can preserve value in the event of economic collapse, and community currencies are viable alternative money sources when other money is not to be had. But in the happier ending to our economic fairytale, the national money supply would be salvaged *before* it collapses; and what is threatening to collapse the dollar today is not that it is not backed by gold. It is that 99 percent of the U.S. money supply is owed back to private lenders at interest. The result is a massive and growing federal debt, on which the interest burden alone will soon be more than the taxpayers can afford to pay. The debt is impossible to repay in the pre-Copernican world in which money is created as a debt to private banks, but the Wizard of Oz might have said we have just been looking at the matter wrong. We have allowed our money to rotate in the firmament around an elite class of financiers, when it should be rotating around the collective body of the people. When that Copernican shift is made, the water of a free-flowing money supply can transform the arid desert of debt into the green abundance envisioned by our forefathers. *We can have all the abundance we need without taxes or debt. We can have it just by eliminating the financial parasite that is draining our abundance away.*

# Chapter 38
# THE FEDERAL DEBT:
# A CASE OF
# DISORGANIZED THINKING

*"As for you my fine friend, you're a victim of disorganized thinking. You are under the unfortunate delusion that simply because you have run away from danger, you have no courage. You are confusing courage with wisdom."*

– *The Wizard of Oz to the Lion*

The Wizard of Oz solved impossible problems just by looking at them differently. The Wizard showed the Cowardly Lion that he had courage all along, showed the Scarecrow that he had a brain all along, showed the Tin Woodman that he had a heart all along. If the Kingdom of Oz had had a Congress, the Wizard might have shown it that it had the means to pay off its national debt all along. It could pay off the debt by turning its bonds into what they should have been all along – legal tender.

The day is fast approaching when the U.S. Congress may have no other alternative but to pay off its debt in this way. The federal debt has reached crisis proportions. U.S. Comptroller General David M. Walker warned in September 2003:

> We cannot simply grow our way out of [the national debt]. . . . The ultimate alternatives to definitive and timely action are not only unattractive, they are arguably infeasible. Specifically, raising taxes to levels far in excess of what the American people have ever supported before, cutting total spending by unthinkable amounts, or further mortgaging the future of our children and grandchildren to an extent that our economy, our competitive posture and the quality of life for Americans would be seriously threatened.[1]

In the 1930s, economist Alvin Hansen told President Roosevelt that plunging the country into debt did not matter, because the public debt was owed to the people themselves and never had to be paid back. But even if that were true in the 1930s (which is highly debatable), it is clearly not true today. Nearly half the public portion of the federal debt is now owed to foreign investors, who are not likely to be so sanguine about continually refinancing it, particularly when the dollar is rapidly shrinking in value. Al Martin cites a study authorized by the U.S. Treasury in 2001, finding that for the government to keep servicing its debt as it has been doing, by 2013 it will have to have raised the personal income tax rate to 65 percent. And that's just to pay the interest on the national debt. When the government can't pay the interest, it will be forced to declare bankruptcy and the economy will collapse. Martin writes:

> The economy of the rest of the planet would collapse five days later. . . . The only way the government can maintain control in a post-economically collapsed environment is through currency and through military might, or internal military power. . . . And that's what U.S. citizens are left with . . . supersized bubbles and really scary economic numbers.[2]

Compounding the problem, Iran and other oil producers are now moving from dollars to other currencies for their oil trades. If oil no longer has to be traded in dollars, a major incentive for foreign central banks to hold U.S. government bonds will disappear. British journalist John Pilger, writing in The New Statesman in February 2006, suggested that the real reason for the aggressive saber-rattling with Iran was not Iran's nuclear ambitions but was the effect of the world's fourth-biggest oil producer and trader breaking the dollar monopoly. He noted that Iraqi President Saddam Hussein had done the same thing before he was attacked.[3] In an April 2005 article in Counter Punch, Mike Whitney warned of the dire consequences to follow when the "petrodollar" standard is abandoned:

> This is much more serious than a simple decline in the value of the dollar. If the major oil producers convert from the dollar to the euro, the American economy will sink almost overnight. If oil is traded in euros then central banks around the world would be compelled to follow and *America will be required to pay off its enormous $8 trillion debt.* That, of course, would be doomsday for the American economy. . . . If there's a quick fix, I have no idea what it might be.[4]

The quick fix, however, was the Wizard's stock in trade. He might have suggested fixing the problem by changing the rules by which the game is played. In 1933, Franklin Roosevelt pronounced the country officially bankrupt, exercised his special emergency powers, waved the royal Presidential *fiat*, and ordered the promise to pay in gold removed from the dollar bill. The dollar was instantly transformed from a promise to pay in legal tender into legal tender itself. Seventy years later, Congress could again acknowledge that the country is officially bankrupt, propose a plan of reorganization, and turn its debts into "legal tender." Alexander Hamilton showed two centuries ago that Congress could dispose of the federal debt by "monetizing" it, but Congress made the mistake of delegating that function to a private banking system. Congress just needs to rectify its error and monetize the debt itself, by buying back its own bonds with newly-issued U.S. Notes.

If that sounds like a radical solution, consider that *it is actually what is being done right now -- not by the government but by the private Federal Reserve.* The problem is that when the *Fed* buys back the government's bonds with newly-issued Federal Reserve Notes, it doesn't take the bonds out of circulation. Two sets of securities (the bonds and the cash) are produced where before there was only one. This highly inflationary result could be avoided by allowing the government to buy back its *own* bonds and simply voiding them out.

## The Mysterious Pirates of the Caribbean

"Monetizing" the government's debt by buying federal securities with newly-issued cash has been engaged in by the Fed and its affiliated banks for the last century. But this scheme evidently went into high gear in 2005, when China and Japan, the two largest purchasers of U.S. federal debt, cut back on their purchases of U.S. securities. Market bears had long warned that when foreign creditors quit rolling over their U.S. bonds, the U.S. economy would collapse. They were therefore predicting the worst; but somehow, no disaster resulted. The bonds were still getting sold. The question was, to whom? The Fed identified the buyers as a mysterious new U.S. creditor group called "Caribbean banks." The financial press said they were offshore hedge funds. But Canadian analyst Rob Kirby, writing in March 2005, said that if they *were* hedge funds, they must have performed extremely poorly for their investors, raking in losses of 40 percent in January

2005 alone; and *no such losses were reported by the hedge fund community.*
He wrote:

> The foregoing suggests that *hedge funds categorically did not buy*
> *these securities.* The explanations being offered up as plausible
> by officialdom and fed to us by the main stream financial press
> are not consistent with empirical facts or market observations.
> There are no wide spread or significant losses being reported by
> the hedge fund community from ill gotten losses in the Treasury
> market. . . . [W]ho else in the world has pockets that deep, to
> buy 23 billion bucks worth of securities in a single month?  One
> might surmise that a printing press would be required to come
> up with that kind of cash on such short notice . . . . [M]y
> suggestion . . . is that history is indeed repeating itself and maybe
> Pirates still inhabit the Caribbean.  *Perhaps they are aided and*
> *abetted in their modern day financial piracy by Wizards and*
> *Snowmen[i] with printing presses, who reside in Washington.*[5]

In September 2005, this bit of wizardry happened again, after
Venezuela liquidated roughly $20 billion in U.S. Treasury securities
following U.S. threats to Venezuela.  Again the anticipated response
was a plunge in the dollar, and again no disaster ensued.  Other buyers
had stepped in to take up the slack, and chief among them were the
mysterious "Caribbean banking centers."  Rob Kirby wrote:

> I wonder who really bought Venezuela's 20 or so billion they
> "pitched."  Whoever it was, perhaps their last name ends with
> Snow or Greenspan. . . . [T]here are more ways than one might
> suspect to create the myth (or reality) of a strong currency – at
> least temporarily![6]

Those incidents may just have been dress rehearsals for bigger
things to come.  When the Fed announced that it would no longer be
publishing figures for M3 beginning in March 2006, analysts wondered
what it was we weren't supposed to know.  March 2006 was the
month Iran announced that it would begin selling oil in Euros.  Some
observers suspected that the Fed was gearing up to use newly-printed
dollars to buy back a flood of U.S. securities dumped by foreign central
banks.  Another possibility was that the Fed had already been engaging
in massive dollar printing to conceal a major derivatives default and
was hiding the evidence.[7]

---

[i]  An allusion to John Snow, then U.S. Treasury Secretary.

Whatever the answer, the question raised here is this: if the Fed can buy back the government's bonds with a flood of newly-printed dollars, leaving the government in debt to the Fed and the banks, why can't the government buy back the bonds with its *own* newly-printed dollars, debt-free? The inflation argument long used to block that solution simply won't hold up anymore. The inflation issue is addressed in the next chapter. First, we'll consider just how easily this reverse sleight of hand might be pulled off, without burying the government in paperwork or violating the Constitution.

## How to Extinguish the National Debt with the Click of a Mouse

In the 1980s, a chairman of the Coinage Subcommittee of the U.S. House of Representatives pointed out that the national debt could be paid with a single coin. The Constitution gives Congress the power to coin money and regulate its value, and no limitation is put on the value of the coins it creates.[8] *The entire national debt could be extinguished with a single coin minted by the U.S. Mint, stamped with the appropriate face value.* Today this official might have suggested nine coins, each with a face value of one trillion dollars.

One problem with this clever solution is making change for a trillion dollar coin. If the government can stamp a piece of metal and call it a trillion dollars, it should be able to stamp paper money and call it the same thing. The value of a trillion dollar coin would obviously derive not from their metal content but simply from the numerical value stamped on it. As Andrew Jackson observed, when the Founding Fathers gave Congress the power to "coin" money, they did not mean to *limit* Congress to metal money and let the banks create the rest. They meant to give the power to create the entire national money supply to Congress. Jefferson said that Constitutions needed to be amended to suit the times; and today the "coin" of the times is paper money, checkbook money, and electronic money. The Constitutional provision that gives Congress "the power to coin money" needs to be updated to read "the power to create the national money supply in all its forms."

If that modification were made, *most of the government's debt could be paid online.* The simplicity of the procedure was demonstrated by the U.S. Treasury itself in January 2004, when it "called" or paid off a 30-year bond issue before the bond was due. The Treasury announced on January 15, 2004:

TREASURY CALLS 9-1/8 PERCENT BONDS OF 2004-09

The Treasury today announced the call for redemption at par on May 15, 2004, of the 9-1/8% Treasury Bonds of 2004-09, originally issued May 15, 1979, due May 15, 2009 (CUSIP No. 9112810CG1). There are $4,606 million of these bonds outstanding, of which $3,109 million are held by private investors. Securities not redeemed on May 15, 2004 will stop earning interest.

These bonds are being called to reduce the cost of debt financing. The 9-1/8% interest rate is significantly above the current cost of securing financing for the five years remaining to their maturity. In current market conditions, Treasury estimates that interest savings from the call and refinancing will be about $544 million.

*Payment will be made automatically by the Treasury for bonds in book-entry form*, whether held on the books of the Federal Reserve Banks or in TreasuryDirect accounts.[9]

The provision for payment "in book entry form" meant that no dollar bills, checks or other paper currencies would be exchanged. Numbers would just be entered into the Treasury's direct online money market fund ("TreasuryDirect"). The securities would merely change character – from interest-bearing to non-interest-bearing, from a debt owed to a debt paid. Bondholders failing to redeem their securities by May 15, 2004 could still collect the face amount of the bonds in cash. They would just not receive interest on the bonds.

The Treasury's announcement generated some controversy, since government bonds are usually considered good until maturity; but early redemption was actually allowed in the fine print on the bonds.[10] Provisions for early redemption are routinely written into corporate and municipal bonds, so that when interest rates drop, the issuer can refinance the debt at a lower rate. How did the Treasury plan to refinance this $4 billion bond issue at a lower rate? Any bonds not bought by the public would no doubt be bought by the banks. Recall the testimony of Federal Reserve Board Chairman Marriner Eccles:

When the banks buy a billion dollars of Government bonds as they are offered . . . *they actually create, by a bookkeeping entry, a billion dollars*.[11]

If the Treasury can cancel its promise to pay interest on a bond issue simply by announcing its intention to do so, and if it can refinance the principal with bookkeeping entries, *it can pay off the entire federal debt in that way*. It just has to announce that it is calling its bonds and other securities, and that they will be paid "in book-entry form." No cash needs to change hands. The funds can remain in the accounts where the bonds were held, to be reinvested somewhere else.

Note that the federal debt needn't be paid off all at once. It can be paid gradually as the securities come due. That provision is part of a proposal called the American Monetary Act drafted by the American Monetary Institute, an organization founded by Stephen Zarlenga for furthering monetary reform. An explanatory comment notes that redeeming the debt would be a gradual process, since the government's debts extend several decades into the future.[12] The American Monetary Act is discussed along with several other proposals for returning the power to create money to the federal government in Chapter 41.

# Chapter 39
# LIQUIDATING THE FEDERAL DEBT WITHOUT CAUSING INFLATION

*The national debt . . . answers most of the purposes of money.*

-- *Alexander Hamilton, "Report on the Public Credit,"*
*January 14, 1790*


The idea that the federal debt could be liquidated by simply printing up money and buying back the government's bonds with it is dismissed out of hand by economists and politicians on the ground that it would produce Weimar-style runaway inflation. But would it? Inflation results when the money supply increases faster than goods and services, and *replacing government securities with cash would not change the size of the money supply.* Federal securities are *already* money. They have been money ever since Alexander Hamilton made them the basis of the national money supply in the late eighteenth century. Converting federal securities into U.S. Notes would not cause prices to shoot up because consumers would have no more money to spend than they had before.

To review: the federal debt is composed of securities (bills, bonds and notes). A "security" is a type of transferable interest representing financial value. Federal securities are treated by the Fed and by the market itself just as if they were money. They are traded daily in enormous volume among banks and other financial institutions around the world just as if they were money.[1] If the government were to buy back its own bonds with cash, these instruments representing financial value would merely be converted from interest-bearing notes into non-interest-bearing legal tender. The funds would move from M2 and M3 into M1 (cash and checks), but the total money supply would remain the same.

That would be true if the *government* were to buy back its securities with cash, but *that is very different from what happens today.* When the *Fed* uses newly-issued Federal Reserve Notes to buy back federal bonds, *it does not void out the bonds.* Rather, they become the "reserves" for issuing many times their value in new loans. The new cash created to buy them is added to the money supply as well. That highly inflationary result could be avoided by simply authorizing the government to buy back its own bonds and taking them out of circulation.

## Swapping Government Bonds for Cash
## Would Not Affect Consumer Prices

Policy-makers track inflation by looking at the widest measure of the money supply, called "broad liquidity." According to Investopedia:

> Broad Liquidity [is] a category of the money supply which includes: all funds in M3, individual holdings in accounts, savings bonds, T-bills with maturity of less than one year, commercial papers, and banker's acceptances.[2]

"Broad liquidity" thus includes most government securities. If the government were to swap these securities for cash and take them out of circulation, the money supply would not increase and prices would not rise, because the bondholders would have no more spending money than they had before. Longer-term securities are not technically included in the definition of "broad liquidity," but the principle still holds: cashing them out would not affect consumer prices, because the bearers would be no richer than they were before. Consider this hypothetical:

You have $20,000 that you want to save for a rainy day. You deposit the money in an account with your broker, who recommends putting $10,000 into the stock market and $10,000 into corporate bonds, and you agree. How much money do you have in the account? $20,000. A short time later, your broker notifies you that your bonds have been unexpectedly called or turned into cash. You check your account on the Internet and see that where before it contained $10,000 in corporate bonds, it now contains $10,000 in cash. How much money do you have in the account? $20,000 (plus or minus some growth in interest and fluctuations in stock values). Paying off the bonds did not give you an additional $10,000, making you feel richer than before, prompting you to rush out to buy shoes or real estate you did not think you could afford before, increasing demand and driving up prices.

This result is particularly obvious when we look at the largest holders of federal securities, including Social Security and other institutional investors.

## Solving the Social Security Crisis

In March 2005, the federal debt clocked in at $7.713 trillion. Of that sum, $3.169 trillion, or 41 percent, was in "intragovernmental holdings" – government trust funds, revolving funds, and special funds. Chief among them was the Social Security trust fund, which held $1.705 trillion of the government's debt. The 59 percent owned by the public was also held largely by institutional investors – U.S. and foreign banks, investment funds, and so forth.[3]

Dire warnings ensued that Social Security was going bankrupt, since its holdings were invested in federal securities that the government could not afford to redeem. Defenders of the system countered that Social Security cannot actually go bankrupt, because it is a pay-as-you-go system. Today's retirees are paid with withdrawals from the paychecks of today's working people. It is only the fund's *excess* holdings that are at risk; and it is the government, not Social Security, that is teetering on bankruptcy, because it is the government that lacks the money to pay off its bonds.[4]

The issue here, however, is something else: what would happen if the Social Security crisis were resolved by simply cashing out its federal bond holdings with newly-issued U.S. Notes? Would dangerous inflation result? The answer is that it would not, because the Social Security fund would have no more money than it had before. The government would just be returning to the fund what the taxpayers thought was in it all along. The bonds would be turned into cash, which would stay in the fund where the money belonged, to be used for future baby-boomer pay-outs as intended.

## Cashing Out the Federal Securities of the Federal Reserve

Another governmental agency holding a major chunk of the federal debt is the Federal Reserve itself. The Fed now owns about ten percent of the government's outstanding securities.[5] If the government were to buy back these securities with cash, that money too would no doubt stay where it is, where it would continue to serve as the reserves against which loans were made. The cash would just replace the bonds, which would be liquidated and taken out of circulation. Again, consumer prices would not go up because there would be no more money in circulation than there was before.

That is one way to deal with the Federal Reserve's Treasury securities, but an even neater solution has been proposed: the government could just void out the bonds. Recall that the Federal Reserve acquired its government securities without consideration, and that a contract without consideration is void. (See Chapter 2.) Article 30 of the Federal Reserve Act of 1913 gave Congress the right to rescind or alter the Act at any time. If the Act were modified to make the Federal Reserve a truly federal agency, it would not need to keep reserves. It could issue "the full faith and credit of the United States" directly, without having to back its dollars with government bonds. (More on this in Chapter 41.)

## Cashing Out the Holdings of Foreign Central Banks

Other major institutional holders of U.S. government debt are foreign central banks. At the end of 2004, foreign holdings of U.S. Treasury debt came to about $1.9 trillion, roughly comparable to the $1.7 trillion held in the Social Security trust fund. Of that sum, foreign central banks owned 64 percent, or $1.2 trillion.[6]

What would cashing out those securities do to the money supply? Again, probably not much. Foreign central banks have no use for consumer goods, and they do not invest in real estate. They keep U.S. dollars in reserve to support their own currencies in global markets and to have the dollars available to buy oil as required under a 1974 agreement with OPEC. They keep dollars in reserve *either* as cash *or* as U.S. securities. Holding U.S. securities is considered to be the equivalent of holding dollars that pay interest.[7] If these securities were turned into cash, the banks would probably just keep the cash in reserve in place of the bonds – and count themselves lucky to have their dollars back, on what is turning out to be a rather risky investment. Fears have been voiced that the U.S. government may soon be unable to pay even the interest on the federal debt. When that happens, the U.S. can either declare bankruptcy and walk away, or it can buy back the bonds with newly-issued fiat money. Given the choice, the investors will no doubt be happy to accept the fiat money, which they can spend on real goods and services in the economy.

Foreign central banks are already reducing their reserves of U.S. securities, since the dollar has been losing value in foreign exchange markets, making it an unprofitable investment. They have no more interest in seeing the global system collapse than the United States does, because their economies are now dependent on the U.S. economy and on U.S. dollars. They have therefore been moving discreetly; but the tide is rolling out, and U.S. bonds will be coming back to U.S. shores whether we like it or not. The question for the U.S. government is simply who will take up the slack when the creditors quit rolling over U.S. debt. Today, when no one else wants the bonds sold at auction, the Fed and its affiliated banks step in and buy them with dollars created for the occasion, creating two sets of securities (the bonds and the cash) where before there was only one. This inflationary duplication could be avoided if Congress were to buy back the bonds itself and just void them out. It could then avoid the debt problem in the future by following the lead of the Guernsey islanders and simply refusing to go into debt. Rather than issuing bonds to meet its costs, it could issue dollars directly.

What has analysts worried today is that as foreign central banks cash out their U.S. securities, U.S. dollars will come flooding back into U.S. markets, hyperinflating the money supply and driving up consumer prices. But we've seen that this predicted result has not materialized in China, although foreign money has been flooding the Chinese economy for thousands of years. In 2005, China's money supply increased by a whopping 18.8 percent without creating runaway inflation, apparently because the influx of new money stimulated productivity, driving up supply along with demand. American factories and industries are now laying off workers because they lack customers. A return of U.S. dollars to U.S. shores could prime the pump, giving lagging American industries the boost they need to again become competitive with the rest of the world. We are continually being urged to "shop" for the good of the economy. What would be so bad about having our dollars returned to us by some foreigners who wanted to do a little shopping? The American economy may particularly need a boost after the housing bubble collapses. In the boom years, home refinancings have been a major source of consumer spending dollars. If the money supply shrinks by $2 trillion in the next housing correction, as some analysts have predicted, a supply of spending dollars from abroad could be just the quick fix the economy needs to ward off a deflationary crisis. There is the concern that U.S. assets could wind up in the hands of foreign owners, but there is not much we can do about that short of imposing high tariffs or making foreign ownership illegal. We owe them the money and they have the bonds to prove it. We can't stop them from spending it. But that is a completely different issue from the effects of cashing out their bonds with fiat dollars, which would give them no more claim to our assets than they have with the bonds. In the long run, they would have less claim to U.S. assets, since their dollar investments would no longer be accruing additional dollars in interest.

## Prelude to a Dangerous Stock Market Bubble?

Even if cashing out the government's bonds did not inflate consumer prices, would it not trigger dangerous inflation in the stock market, the bond market and the real estate market, the likely targets of the freed-up money? If the government's securities were paid off gradually as they came due, new money would enter those markets only gradually, moderating any inflationary effects. But even if the debt were paid off all at once, it is submitted that investors would not be hurt. Indeed, they could be quite pleased with the result.

In December 2005, the market value of all publicly traded companies in the United States was reported at $15.8 trillion.[8] Assume that fully half the $8 trillion then invested in government securities got reinvested in the stock market. The level of stock market investment would have increased by 25 percent -- a dramatic rise, but not an unprecedented one. The S&P 500 (a stock index tracking 500 companies in leading industries) actually *tripled* from 1995 to 2000, and no great disaster resulted.[9] Much of that rise was due to the technology bubble, which later broke; but by 2006, the S&P had gained back most of its losses. High stock prices are actually good for investors, who make money across the board. Stocks are not household necessities that shoot out of reach for ordinary consumers when prices go up. The stock market is the casino of people with money to invest. Anyone with any amount of money can jump in at any time, at any level. If the market continues to go up, investors will make money on resale. Although this may *look* like a Ponzi scheme, it really isn't as long as the stocks are bought with cash rather than debt. Like with the inflated values of prized works of art, stock prices would go up due to increased demand; and as long as the demand remained strong, the stocks would maintain their value.

Stock market bubbles are bad only when they burst, and they burst because they have been artificially pumped up in a way that cannot be sustained. The market crash of 1929 resulted because investors were buying stock largely on credit, thinking the market would continue to go up and they could pay off the balance from profits. The stock market became a speculative pyramid scheme, in which most of the money invested in it did not really exist.[10] The bubble burst when reserve requirements were raised, making money much harder to borrow. In the scenario considered here, the market would not be pumped up with borrowed money but would be infused with cold hard cash, the permanent money received by bondholders for their government bonds. The market would go up and stay up. At some point, investors would realize that their shares were overpriced relative to the company's assets and would find something else to invest in; but that correction would be a normal one, not the sudden collapse of a bubble built on credit with no "real" money in it. There would still be the problem of speculative manipulation by big banks and hedge funds, but that problem too can be addressed -- and it will be, in Chapter 43.

As for the real estate market, cashing out the federal debt would probably have little effect on it. Foreign central banks don't buy real estate, and neither do Social Security and other trust funds; and individual investors would not be likely to make the leap into real estate either, since cashing out their bonds would give them no more money than they had before. Their ability to buy a house would therefore not have changed. People generally hold short-term T-bills as a convenient way to "bank" money at a modest interest while keeping it liquid. They hold longer-term Treasury notes and bonds, on the other hand, for a safe and reliable income stream. Neither purpose would be served by jumping into real estate, which is a very illiquid investment that does not return profits until the property is sold. People wanting to keep their funds liquid would probably just move the cash into bank savings or checking accounts; while people wanting an income stream would move it into corporate bonds, certificates of deposit and the like. Another potential interest-generating option for these funds is explored in Chapter 41.

That just leaves the corporate bond market, which would hardly be hurt by an influx of new money either. Fresh young companies would have easier access to startup capital; promising inventions could be developed; new products would burst onto the market; jobs would be created; markets would be stimulated. New capital could only be good for productivity.

A final objection that has been raised to paying off the federal debt with newly-issued fiat money is that foreign lenders would be discouraged from purchasing U.S. government bonds in the future. But the Wizard's response to that argument would no doubt be, "So what?" Once the government reclaims the power to create money from the banks, it will no longer need to sell its bonds to investors. It will not even need to levy income taxes. It will be able to exercise its sovereign right to issue its own money, debt-free. That is what British monarchs did until the end of the seventeenth century, what the American colonists did in the eighteenth century, and what Abraham Lincoln did in the nineteenth century. It has also been proposed in the twenty-first century, not just by "cranks and crackpots" in the money reform camp but by none other than Federal Reserve Chairman Ben Bernanke himself. At least, that is what he appears to have proposed. The suggestion was made several years before he became Chairman of the Federal Reserve, in a speech that earned him the nickname "Helicopter Ben" . . . .

# Chapter 40
# "HELICOPTER" MONEY:
# THE FED'S NEW
# HOT AIR BALLOON

*"[I]t will be no trouble to make the balloon. But in all this country there is no gas to fill the balloon with, to make it float."*
*"If it won't float," remarked Dorothy, "it will be of no use to us."*
*"True," answered Oz. "But there is another way to make it float, which is to fill it with hot air."*

– The Wonderful Wizard of Oz,
*"How the Balloon Was Launched"*

Balloon imagery is popular today for describing the perilous state of the economy. Richard Russell wrote in The Dow Theory Letter in August 2006, "The US has become a giant credit, debt and deficit balloon. Can the giant debt-balloon be kept afloat? That's what we're going to find out in the coming months." Russell warned that we have reached the point where pumping more debt into the balloon is unsustainable, and that the solution of outgoing Fed Chairman Alan Greenspan was no solution at all. He merely concealed the M-3 statistics. "If you can't kill the messenger, at least hide him."[1]

The solution of Greenspan's successor Ben Bernanke is not entirely clear, since like his predecessors he has been playing his cards close to the chest. (Being tight-lipped actually appears to be part of the job description. When he tried to be transparent, he was roundly criticized for spooking the market.) In a speech he delivered when he had to be less cautious about his utterances, however, Dr. Bernanke advocated what appeared to be a modern-day version of Lincoln's Greenback solution: instead of filling the balloon with more debt, it could be filled with money issued debt-free by the government.

The speech was made in Washington in 2002 and was titled "Deflation: Making Sure 'It' Doesn't Happen Here." Dr. Bernanke stated that the Fed would not be "out of ammunition" to counteract deflation just because the federal funds rate had fallen to 0 percent. Lowering interest rates was not the only way to get new money into the economy. He said, "*the U.S. government has a technology, called a printing press (or, today, its electronic equivalent), that allows it to produce as many U.S. dollars as it wishes at essentially no cost.*"

He added, "One important concern in practice is that calibrating the economic effects of nonstandard means of injecting money may be difficult, *given our relative lack of experience with such policies.*"[2] If the government was inexperienced with the policies, they were not the usual "open market operations," in which the government prints bonds, the Fed prints dollars, and they swap stacks, leaving the government in debt for money created by the Fed. He said that the *government* could print money, and that it could do this *at essentially no cost*. The implication was that the government could create money *without* paying interest and *without* having to pay it back to the Fed or the banks.

Later in the speech Dr. Bernanke said, "A money-financed tax cut is essentially equivalent to Milton Friedman's famous 'helicopter drop' of money." Dropping money from helicopters was Professor Friedman's hypothetical cure for deflation. The "money-financed tax cut" recommended by Dr. Bernanke was evidently one in which *taxes would be replaced with money that was simply printed up by the government and spent into the economy.*

He added, "[I]n lieu of tax cuts, the government could increase spending on current goods and services *or even acquire existing real or financial assets.*" The government could reflate the economy by printing money and buying hard assets with it – assets such as real estate and corporate stock! That is what the earlier Populists had proposed: the government could buy whole industries and operate them at a profit. The Populists proposed nationalizing essential industries that had been monopolized by giant private cartels, including the railroads, steel -- and the banks. The profits generated by these industries would return to the government to be used in place of taxes.

## The Japanese Experiment

Dr. Bernanke went further than merely suggesting the "helicopter-money" solution.  He evidently carried it out, and on a massive scale.  More accurately, the Japanese carried it out at his behest.  During a visit to Japan in May 2003, he said in a speech to the Japanese:

> My thesis here is that cooperation between the monetary and fiscal authorities in Japan [the central bank and the government] could help solve the problems that each policymaker faces on its own.  Consider for example a tax cut for households and businesses that is explicitly coupled with incremental BOJ [Bank of Japan] purchases of government debt – *so that the tax cut is in effect financed by money creation.*[3]

Dr. Bernanke was advising the Japanese government that it could finance a tax cut by creating money!  (Note that this is easier to do in Japan than in the United States, since the Japanese government actually owns its central bank, the Bank of Japan.[4])  The same month, the Japanese embarked on what British economist Richard Duncan called "the most aggressive experiment in monetary policy ever conducted."[5]  In a May 2005 article titled "How Japan Financed Global Reflation," Duncan wrote:

> In 2003 and the first quarter of 2004, Japan carried out a remarkable experiment in monetary policy – remarkable in the impact it had on the global economy and equally remarkable in that *it went almost entirely unnoticed in the financial press.*  Over those 15 months, monetary authorities in Japan created ¥35 trillion . . . approximately 1% of the world's annual economic output.  ¥35 trillion . . . would amount to $50 per person if distributed equally among the entire population of the planet.  In short, *it was money creation on a scale never before attempted during peacetime.*
>
> Why did this occur?  *There is no shortage of yen in Japan* . . . . Japanese banks have far more deposits than there is demand for loans . . . . So, what motivated the Bank of Japan to print so much more money when the country is already flooded with excess liquidity?[6]

Duncan explained that the shortage of money was not actually in Japan.  *It was in the United States, where the threat of deflation had appeared for the first time since the Great Depression.*  The technology bubble of the late 1990s had popped in 2000, leading to a serious global economic slowdown in 2001. Before that, the Fed had been bent on curbing *inflation*; but now it had suddenly switched gears and was focusing on *reflation* – the intentional reversal of deflation through government intervention. Duncan wrote:

> *Deflation is a central bank's worst nightmare.* When prices begin to fall, interest rates follow them down. Once interest rates fall to zero, as is the case in Japan at present, central banks become powerless to provide any further stimulus to the economy through conventional means and monetary policy becomes powerless. The extent of the US Federal Reserve's concern over the threat of deflation is demonstrated in Fed staff research papers and the speeches delivered by Fed governors at that time. For example, in June 2002, the Board of Governors of the Federal Reserve System published a Discussion Paper entitled, "Preventing Deflation: Lessons from Japan's Experience in the 1990s." The abstract of that paper concluded ". . . we draw the general lesson from Japan's experience that when inflation and interest rates have fallen close to zero, and the risk of deflation is high, stimulus – both monetary and fiscal – should go beyond the levels conventionally implied by baseline forecasts of future inflation and economic activity."

Just how far beyond the conventional the Federal Reserve was prepared to go was demonstrated in the Japanese experiment, in which the Bank of Japan created 35 trillion yen over the course of the following year. The yen were then traded with the government's Ministry of Finance (MOF) for Japanese government securities, which paid virtually no interest. The MOF used the yen to buy approximately $320 billion in U.S. dollars from private parties, which were then used to buy U.S. government bonds.

Duncan wrote, "It is not certain how much of the $320 billion the MOF did invest into US Treasury bonds, but judging by their past behavior it is fair to assume that it was the vast majority of that amount." Assuming all the dollars were so used, the funds were sufficient to float 77 percent of the U.S. budget deficit in the fiscal year ending September 30, 2004. The effect of this unprecedented experiment, said Duncan, was *to finance a broad-based tax cut in the United States with newly-created money.* The tax cuts were made in America, but the money was made in Japan. Three large tax cuts took the U.S. budget from a surplus of $127 billion in 2001 to a deficit of $413 billion in 2004. The difference was a deficit of $540 billion, and it was largely "monetized" by the Japanese.

Duncan asked rhetorically, "Was the BOJ/MOF conducting Governor Bernanke's Unorthodox Monetary Policy on behalf of the Fed? . . . Was the BOJ simply serving as a branch of the Fed, as the Federal Reserve Bank of Tokyo, if you will?" If so, Duncan said, "*it worked beautifully*":

> The Bush tax cuts and the BOJ money creation that helped finance them at very low interest rates were the two most important elements driving the strong global economic expansion during 2003 and 2004. Combined, they produced a very global reflation. . . . US tax cuts and low interest rates fuelled consumption in the United States. In turn, growing US consumption shifted Asia's export-oriented economies into overdrive. China played a very important part in that process. . . . China used its large trade surpluses with the US to pay for its large trade deficits with most of its Asian neighbors, including Japan. The recycling of China's US Dollar export earnings explains the incredibly rapid "reflation" that began across Asia in 2003 and that was still underway at the end of 2004. Even Japan's moribund economy began to reflate.
>
> . . . *In 2004, the global economy grew at the fastest rate in 30 years. Money creation by the Bank of Japan on an unprecedented scale was perhaps the most important factor responsible for that growth.* In fact, ¥35 trillion could have made the difference between global reflation and global deflation. *How odd that it went unnoticed.*[7]

The Japanese experiment ended in March 2004, apparently because no more intervention was required. The Fed had agreed to begin raising interest rates, putting a stop to the flight from the dollar; and strong economic growth in the United States had created higher than anticipated tax revenues, reducing the need for supplemental budget funding. The experiment had "worked beautifully" to reduce deflation and provide the money for more U.S. government deficits, except for one thing: the U.S. government was now in debt to a foreign power for money the Japanese had created with an accounting entry -- money the U.S. government could have created itself.

## Can You Trust a Pirate?

After the Japanese experiment came the Caribbean experiment, which was discussed in Chapter 38. Joseph Stroupe, editor of <u>Global Events Magazine</u>, warned in 2004:

> [I]nternational support for the dollar and for related US economic and foreign policies is noticeably weakening, at a time when it is most needed to support an unprecedented and mushrooming mountain load of debt. . . . The appetite of the big Asian economies to continue buying dollar assets is waning . . . . Hence the possibility of a Twin Towers-like vertical collapse of the US economy is becoming greater, not lesser.[8]

That was the fear, but collapse was averted when "the Pirates of the Carribean" stepped in to pick up the unsold bonds, evidently at a substantial loss to themselves. As noted earlier, these traders must have been fronts for the Federal Reserve itself, which alone has pockets deep enough to pull off such a maneuver and absorb the loss. (See Chapter 38.) The Fed manipulates markets with accounting-entry money funneled through its "primary dealers" – a list of about 30 investment houses authorized to trade government securities, including Goldman Sachs, Morgan Stanley, and Merrill Lynch.[9] These banks then use the funds to buy government bonds, in the sort of maneuver that might be called "money laundering" if it were done privately. (See Chapter 33.)

In December 2005, M3 increased in a single week by $58.7 billion – *a 30 percent annualized rate of growth.* Financial adviser Robert McHugh compared this increase to the hyperinflation seen in banana republics. "This is nuts folks," he wrote, "unless there is an incredible risk out there we are not being told about. That is a lot of money for the Plunge Protection Team's arsenal to buy markets – stocks, bonds, currencies, whatever."[10]

The question is, can this secretive private cartel be *trusted* with so much unregulated power? Wouldn't it be cheaper and safer to give the power to create dollars to Congress itself, with full accountability and full disclosure to the public? Congress would not have to conceal the fact that it was financing its own debt. It would not even have to go into debt. It could just create the money in full view in an accountable way. The power to create money is given to Congress in the Constitution. Debt-free government-created money was the financial system that got the country through the American Revolution and the Civil War; the system endorsed by Franklin, Jefferson, and Lincoln; the system that Henry Clay, Henry Carey and the American Nationalists called the "American system." The government could simply acknowledge that it was pumping money into the economy. It could explain that the economy *needs* the government's money to prevent a dollar collapse, and that the cheapest and most honest way to do it is by creating the money directly and then spending it on projects that "promote the general welfare." Laundering the money through non-producing middlemen is giving the people's Constitutionally-ordained money-creating power away.

The usual objections to this solution are that it would be dangerously inflationary and that government is inherently "corrupt" and will be given too much power. But as will be detailed in Chapter 44, government-issued money would actually be *less* inflationary than the system we have now. And it is precisely *because* power and money corrupt that money creation needs to be done by a public body, exercised in full view and with full accountability. We can watch our congresspersons deliberating every day on C-SPAN. If the people's money isn't being spent for the benefit of the people, we can vote our representatives out. The bottom line is that *somebody* has to have the power to create money. We've seen that gold is too scarce and too inelastic to be the national money supply, at least without an expandable fiat-money system to back it up; and somebody has to create that fiat system. There are only three choices for the job: a private banking cartel, local communities acting separately, or the collective body of the people acting through their representative government.

Today we are operating with option #1, a private banking cartel, and it has brought the system to the brink of collapse. The privately-controlled Federal Reserve, which was chartered specifically to "maintain a stable currency," has allowed the money supply to balloon out of control. The Fed manipulates the money supply and regulates its value behind closed doors, in blatant violation of the Constitution and the antitrust laws. Yet it not only can't be held to account; it doesn't even have to explain its rationale or reveal what is going on.

Option #2, the local community fiat alternative, is basically the national fiat currency alternative on a smaller scale. As one commentator put it, what would you have more confidence in – the full faith and credit of Ithaca, New York (population 30,000), or the full faith and credit of the United States? The fiat currency of the *national* community has the full force of the nation behind it. And *even if* the politicians in charge of managing it turn out to be no less corrupt than private bankers, the money created by the government will be debt-free. Shifting the power to create money to Congress can relieve future generations of the burden of perpetual interest payments to an elite class of financial oligarchs who have advanced nothing of their own to earn it. The banking spider that has the country trapped in its debt web could be decapitated, returning national sovereignty to the people themselves.

# Section VI

# VANQUISHING THE DEBT SPIDER: A BANKING SYSTEM THAT SERVES THE PEOPLE

*The great spider was lying asleep when the Lion found him . . . .*
*It had a great mouth, with a row of sharp teeth a foot long; but its*
*head was joined to the pudgy body by a neck as slender as a wasp's*
*waist. This gave the Lion a hint of the best way to attack the creature.*
*. . . [W]ith one blow of his heavy paw, all armed with sharp claws, he*
*knocked the spider's head from its body.*

— *The Wonderful Wizard of Oz*,
"The Lion Becomes the King of Beasts"

# Chapter 41

# RESTORING NATIONAL SOVEREIGNTY WITH A TRULY NATIONAL BANKING SYSTEM

*"If I put an end to your enemy, will you bow down to me and obey me as the King of the Forest?" inquired the Lion.*
*"We will do that gladly," replied the tiger. . . .*
*"Take good care of these friends of mine," said the Lion, "and I will go at once to fight the monster."*

-- *The Wonderful Wizard of Oz,*
*"The Lion Becomes the King of Beasts"*

William Jennings Bryan, the Cowardly Lion of <u>The Wizard of Oz</u>, proved his courage by challenging the banking cartel's right to create the national money supply. He said in the speech that won him the Democratic nomination in 1896:

> *[W]e believe that the right to coin money and issue money is a function of government.* . . . Those who are opposed to this proposition tell us that the issue of paper money is a function of the bank and that the government ought to go out of the banking business. I stand with Jefferson . . . and tell them, as he did, that *the issue of money is a function of the government and that the banks should go out of the governing business.* . . . [W]hen we have restored the money of the Constitution, all other necessary reforms will be possible, and . . . until that is done there is no reform that can be accomplished.

The "money of the Constitution" was money created by the people themselves. Technically, the Constitution gave Congress the exclusive power only to "coin" money; but the Constitution was drafted in the eighteenth century, when most forms of money in use today either did not exist or were not recognized as money. Thomas Jefferson said that Constitutions needed to be updated to suit the times. A contemporary version of the Constitutional provision that "Congress shall have the power to coin money" would give Congress the exclusive power to create the national currency in all its forms.[i]

That would mean either abolishing the Federal Reserve or making it what most people think it now is – a truly *federal* agency. If the Federal Reserve were an arm of the U.S. government, the dollars it generated could go directly into the U.S. Treasury, without the need to add to a crippling federal debt by "funding" them with bonds. That would take care of 3 percent of the U.S. money supply, but what about the other 97 percent that is now created as commercial loans? Would giving Congress the exclusive power to create money mean the government would have to go into the commercial lending business?

Perhaps, but why not? As Bryan said, banking *is* the government's business, by Constitutional mandate. At least, that part of banking is the government's business that involves creating new money. The rest of the lending business could continue to be conducted privately, just as it is now. Recall that banks today account for only about 20 percent of total credit market debt. The rest is done by non-bank financial institutions, including finance companies, pension funds, mutual funds, insurance companies, and securities dealers. These institutions do not create the money they lend but merely recycle pre-existing funds.[1] If the power to create the national money supply were returned to the government, private banks would just join these non-bank lenders as recyclers of existing money. They would begin doing what most people think they do now: borrowing money at a low interest rate and lending it at a higher rate.

That sort of system would be more equitable and more Constitutional than what we have now, but it would also have some downsides that would have to be worked out. According to government officials who reviewed such a proposal recently in England, the chief downside would be that it would be likely to bankrupt the banks . . . .

---

[i] As an aside to community currency advocates: this would not prevent local organizations from issuing private currencies, which are not the national medium of exchange but are contractual agreements between private parties.

## The Fate of a British Proposal for Monetary Reform

The Bank of England was actually nationalized in 1946, but the monetary scheme did not change much as a result. The government took over the function of *printing* paper money; but in England, as in the United States, printed paper money makes up only a very small percentage of the money supply. The bankers still have the power to create money as loans, leaving them in control of the money spigots.[3] In <u>Monetary Reform: Making It Happen</u> (2003), James Robertson observed that 97 percent of Britain's money supply is now created by banks when they advance credit. The result is a grossly unfair windfall to the banks, which get the use of money that is properly an asset of the people. He proposed reforming the system so that it would be illegal for banks to create money as loans, just as it is illegal to forge coins or counterfeit banknotes. Only the central bank could create new money. Commercial banks would have to borrow existing money and relend it, just as non-bank financial institutions do now. In Robertson's proposed system, new money created by the central bank would not go directly to the commercial banks but would be given to the government to spend into circulation, where it would eventually find its way back to the banks and could be recycled by them as loans.[4]

It sounded good in theory, but when he ran the plan past several government officials, they objected that the banks would go broke under such a scheme. Depriving banks of the right to advance credit on the "credit multiplier" system (the British version of fractional reserve lending) would increase the costs of borrowing; would raise the costs of payment services; would force banks to cut costs, close branches and reduce jobs; and would damage the international competitiveness of British banks and therefore of the British economy as a whole.

An official with the title of Shadow Chancellor of the Exchequer warned, "Legislating against the credit multiplier would lead to the migration from the City of London of the largest collection of banks in the world. It would be a disaster for the British economy."

Another official bearing the title of Treasury Minister argued that "if banks were obliged to bid for funds from lenders in order to make loans to their customers, the costs to banks of extending credit would be significant, adversely affecting business investment, especially of small and medium-sized firms." This official wrote in an August 2001 letter:

It is evident that this proposal would cause a dramatic loss in profits to the banks – all else [being] equal they would still face the costs of running the payments system but would not be able to make profitable loans using the deposits held in current accounts. In this case, it is highly likely that banks will attempt to maintain their profitability by re-locating to avoid the restriction on their operations that the proposed reform involves.[5]

And there was the rub: in London, banking is very big business. If the banks were to move *en masse* to the Continent, the British economy could collapse like a house of cards.

## The 100 Percent Reserve Solution

A proposal similar to the Robertson plan was presented to the U.S. Congress by Representative Jerry Voorhis in the 1940s. Called "the 100 Percent Reserve Solution," it was first devised in 1926 by Professor Frederick Soddy of Oxford and was revived in 1933 by Professor Henry Simons of the University of Chicago. The plan was to require banks to establish 100 percent reserve backing for their deposits, something they could do by borrowing enough newly-created money from the U.S. Treasury to make up the shortfall.

"With this elegant plan," wrote Stephen Zarlenga in The Lost Science of Money, "all the bank credit money the banks have created out of thin air, through fractional reserve banking, would be transformed into U.S. government legal tender – real, honest money." The plan was elegant, but like the later Robertson proposal, it would have been quite costly for the banks. It died when Representative Voorhis lost his seat to Richard Nixon in a vicious campaign funded by the bankers.[6]

The 100 Percent Reserve Solution was revived by Robert de Fremery in a series of articles published in the 1960s.[7] Under his proposal, banks would have two sections, a deposit or checking-account section and a savings-and-loan section:

> The deposit section would merely be a warehouse for money. All demand deposits would be backed dollar for dollar by actual currency in the vaults of the bank. The savings-and-loan section would sell Certificates of Deposit (CDs)[ii] of varying maturities –

---

[ii] *Certificate of deposit (CD)*: a time deposit with a bank which bears a specific maturity date (from three months to five years) and a specified interest rate, much like bonds.

from 30 days to 20 years – to obtain funds that could be safely loaned for comparable periods of time. Thus money obtained by the sale of 30-day, one-year and five-year CDs, etc., could be loaned for 30 days, one year and five years respectively – not longer. Banks would then be fully liquid at all times and never again need fear a liquidity crisis.

The liquidity problem de Fremery was concerned with came from "borrowing short and lending long" – borrowing short-term deposits and committing them to long-term loans – a common practice that exposed banks to the risk that their depositors would withdraw their money before the loans came due, leaving the banks short of lendable funds. Banks today deal with a shortage of funds by borrowing them in the money market from other banks or the Fed, which can create new money out of thin air through "open market operations" to meet the demand. But the 100 percent reserve plan is an equitable solution that continues to have advocates.

One is the American Monetary Institute founded by Stephen Zarlenga, discussed earlier, which has drafted an American Monetary Act that would eliminate fractional reserve banking. It would impose a 100 percent reserve requirement on all checking-type bank accounts. As in de Fremery's proposal, these accounts could not be the basis for loans but would simply be "a warehousing and transferring service for which fees are charged." The Federal Reserve System would be incorporated into the U.S. Treasury, and all new money would be created by these government agencies. It would be spent into circulation to promote the general welfare, monitored in a way so that the amount would be neither inflationary nor deflationary. New money would be spent on infrastructure, including education and health care, creating jobs, re-invigorating local economies, and re-funding government at all levels. Banks would lend in the way most people think they do now: by acting as intermediaries that accepted savings deposits and lent them out to borrowers.[8]

A model Monetary Reform Act on the website of the documentary video <u>The Money Masters</u> would go even further: it would impose a 100 percent reserve requirement on *all* bank deposits, including savings deposits. Banks that serviced depositors could not lend at all, unless they were using their own money. If banks wanted to make loans of other people's money, they would have to set up separate institutions for the purpose, not called "banks," which could lend only pre-existing funds. The proposed Monetary Reform Act provides:

> By the end of the transition period, for every dollar deposited, banks must have a dollar of United States Notes on hand or invested in a Treasury Department Deposit account. All bank deposits shall be in demand accounts. . . . Banks or any other persons may establish separate associations, . . . not to be titled *banks*, such as investment trusts, mutual funds, brokerage or lending houses, to sell stock, to receive, borrow, lend or invest money at interest, but by the end of the transition period only from existing funds (*i.e.* United States Notes and Treasury Deposits).[9]

Banks making loans would join the other 80 percent of lending institutions that could lend only when they first had the money in hand. "Deposits" would not be counted as "reserves" against which loans could be made but would be held in trust for the sole and exclusive use of the depositors.

## How to Eliminate Fractional Reserve Banking Without Eliminating the Banks

Like the Robertson plan proposed in England, these proposals have been criticized on the ground that they would be likely to bankrupt the banks. But if the power to create the national money supply is going to be the exclusive domain of Congress, 100 percent backing will *have* to be required for any private bank deposits that can be withdrawn on demand, to avoid the electronic duplication that is the source of growth in the money supply today. And that means the banks will have to come up with enough money to "fund" all their outstanding loans. Recall what the Chicago Federal Reserve said in "Modern Money Mechanics":

> Of course, [banks] do not really pay out loans from the money they receive as deposits. . . . What they do when they make loans is to accept promissory notes in exchange for credits to the borrowers' transaction accounts. Loans (assets) and deposits (liabilities) both rise [by the same amount].

The "credits" (or loans) become "deposits" that represent "liabilities" of the banks, money the banks *owe* to the depositors. Federal Reserve Statistical Release H.8 puts the total "loans and leases in bank credit" of all U.S. banks as of April 2007 at $6 trillion.[10] Since banks today operate with minimal reserves (10 percent or even less), the banks might have to come up with 90 percent of $6 trillion in "real" money to meet a 100 percent reserve requirement. They could borrow the money from the government, but to service the loans they would have to raise interest rates and reduce the interest they paid to depositors, shrinking their profit margins, squeezing their customers and driving them into the arms of those non-bank competitors that have already cornered 80 percent of the loan market. Just the rumor that the banks were going to have to incur substantial new debt could make bank share values plummet.

In a December 2006 article called "A Plan for Monetary Reform," William Hummel suggests another alternative: the banks could sell their existing loans to investors.[11] Where could enough investors be found to fund close to $6 trillion in outstanding bank loans? Recall the nearly $9 trillion in bond money that would be freed up if the federal debt were paid off by "monetizing" it with new Greenback dollars. People who had previously stored their savings in government bonds would be looking for a steady source of income to replace the interest stream they had just lost. Investment fund managers, quick to see an opportunity, would no doubt form funds just for this purpose. They could buy up the banks' existing loans with money from their investors and bundle them as securities, the way Fannie Mae and Freddie Mac sell mortgage-backed securities now. The investors would be paid interest on these securities as it accrued on the loans. In that way the same Greenback dollars that "monetized" the federal debt could be used to monetize the $6 trillion in bank loans created with accounting entries by the banks.

Since the banks created the loans with accounting entries, the money they received for the sale of the loans would represent a windfall that should properly be turned over to the government; but even if the government got the proceeds, selling the loans would allow the banks to avoid incurring substantial new debt to meet the 100 percent reserve requirement. The banks' balance sheets would be wiped clean and they could start fresh with new loans, doing what most people think they do now: borrowing at a low interest rate and relending at a higher rate. However, the new limitations on bank lending could still make bank shares plummet, imposing an unfair burden on the unsuspecting shareholders, warranting some equitable division of the sale proceeds in compensation. Another possibility for relieving the shareholders of an unfair penalty would be for the government to simply buy out their shares at some equitable price. That option is explored in Chapter 43.

# A System of National Bank Branches to Service Basic Public Banking Needs

Hummel points out that if private banks could no longer lend their deposits many times over on a fractional reserve system, they would have little incentive to service the depository needs of the public. He writes:

> Depository functions are basically clerical and offer little opportunity for income other than fees for service. Banks have less incentive to seek customer deposits when they cannot be used to back the creation of new deposits, as in a fractional reserve system.

It would therefore make sense to simplify the banking business by transferring the depository role to a system of bank branches acting as one entity under the Federal Reserve. Such a system would have a number of advantages:

> Since all deposits would be entries in a common computer network, determining balances and clearing checks could be done instantly, thereby eliminating checking system float[iii] and its logistic complexities. . . .
>
> With the Fed operating as the sole depository, payments would only involve the transfer of deposits between accounts within a single bank. This would allow for instant clearing, eliminate the nuisance of checking system float, and significantly reduce associated costs. Additional advantages include the elimination of any need for deposit insurance, and ending overnight sweeps[iv] and other sterile games that banks play to get around the fractional reserve requirement.[12]

---

[iii] *Float*: the time that elapses between when a check is deposited into a bank account and the funds are available to the depositor, during which the bank is collecting payment from the payer's bank.

[iv] The *overnight sweep* is a tactic for maximizing the interest earned by a customer who has both a high-interest rate account and a low- or no-interest account at the same financial institution. Funds not being immediately used in the low-interest account are automatically transferred (swept) to the high-interest account, where they remain until the balance in the low-interest account drops below a certain minimum, when the funds are transferred back to the first account. The funds may be "swept" to the high-interest account either overnight or for longer periods.

In Hummel's model, the Fed would be the sole depository and only its branches would be called "banks." Institutions formerly called banks would have to close down their depository operations and would become "private financial institutions" (PFIs), along with finance companies, pension funds, mutual funds, insurance companies and the like. Some banks would probably sell out to existing PFIs. PFIs could borrow from the Fed just as banks do now, but the interest rate would be set high enough to discourage them from using the money just for investment. "When banks cannot create money for borrowers as they do now," Hummel writes, "there should be less temptation to advance loans for purely speculative games in the financial markets." He adds:

> Without the depository role, banks would no longer need the same number of branch offices. The Fed would probably offer to buy them in setting up its own depository branch offices. A logical way to proceed would be to gradually increase the reserve ratio requirement on existing depositories until it reached 100 percent.

In How Credit-Money Shapes the Economy, Robert Guttman makes a similar proposal. He notes that the public's basic banking needs are fairly simple. We need a safe place to keep our money and a practical way to transfer it to others. Those needs could be served by a government agency on the model of the now-defunct U.S. Postal Savings System, which operated successfully from 1911 to 1967, providing a safe and efficient place for customers to save and transfer funds. It issued U.S. Postal Savings Bonds in various denominations that paid annual interest, as well as Postal Savings Certificates and domestic money orders.[13]

The U.S. Postal Savings System was set up to get money out of hiding, attract the savings of immigrants accustomed to saving at post offices in their native countries, provide safe depositories for people who had lost confidence in private banks, and furnish more convenient depositories for working people than were provided by private banks. (At that time post offices had longer hours than banks, being open from 8 a.m. to 6 p.m. six days a week.) The postal system paid two percent interest on deposits per year. The minimum deposit was $1 and the maximum was $2,500. Savings in the system spurted to $1.2 billion during the 1930s and jumped again during World War II, peaking in 1947 at almost $3.4 billion. The U.S. Postal Savings System was shut down in 1967, not because it was inefficient but because it became unnecessary after private banks raised their interest rates and offered the same governmental guarantees as the postal savings system.[14] The services offered by a modern system of federally-operated bank branches would have to be modified to reflect today's conditions, but the point is that the government has done this before and could do it again.

## Solving the Credit Card Problem

Another thing that would need to be worked out if banks could only recycle existing funds is the servicing of credit cards. Hummel notes that private banks would be barred from engaging in that business in a 100 percent reserve system.[15] We've seen that when a bank issues credit against a customer's charge slip, the charge slip is considered a "negotiable instrument" that becomes an "asset" against which the bank creates a "liability" in the form of a deposit. The bank balances its books without debiting its own assets or anyone else's account. The bank is thus creating new money, something that private banks could no longer do under a 100 percent reserve system. But the ability to get ready credit simply against the borrower's promise to pay is an important service that would be sorely missed if banks could no longer engage in it. If your ability to use your credit card were contingent on your bank's ability to obtain scarce funds in a competitive market, you might find, when you went to pay your restaurant bill, that credit had been denied because your bank was out of lendable funds.

The notion that money has to "be there" before it can be borrowed is based on the old commodity theory of money. Theorists from Cotton Mather to Benjamin Franklin to Michael Linton (who designed the LETS system) have all defined "money" as something else. It is simply "credit" – an advance against the borrower's promise to repay. Credit originates with that promise, not with someone else's deposit of something valuable in the bank. Credit is not dependent on someone else having given up his rights to an asset for a period of time, and "reserves" are not necessary for advancing it. *What is wrong with the current system is not that money is advanced as a credit against the borrower's promise to repay but that the interest on this advance accrues to private banks that gave up nothing of their own to earn it.* This problem could be rectified by turning the business of extending credit over to a system of truly *national* banks, which would be authorized to advance the "full faith and credit of the United States" as agents of

Congress, which is authorized to create the national money supply under the Constitution.

Credit card services are actually an extension of the depository functions of banks. The link with bank deposits is particularly obvious in the case of those debit cards that can be used to trigger ATM machines to spit out twenty dollar bills. When you make a transfer or withdrawal on your debit card, the money is immediately transferred out of your account, just as if you had written a check. When you use your credit card, the link is not quite so obvious, since the money doesn't come out of your account until later; but it is still *your* money that is being advanced, not someone else's. Again, your promise to pay becomes an asset and a liability of the bank at the same time, without bringing any of the bank's or any other depositor's money into the deal. The natural agency for handling this sort of transaction would be an institution that was authorized *both* to deal with deposits *and* to create credit-money with accounting entries. A truly "national" bank would be authorized to create credit-money as an agency of Congress. A government banking agency would not be driven by the profit motive to gouge desperate people with exorbitant interest rates. Credit could be extended on credit cards at interest rates that were reasonable, predictable and fixed.

## Old Banks Under New Management

The branch offices set up by the Federal Reserve to handle the depository and credit card needs of the public would not need to be new entities, and they would not need to take over the whole banking business. They could be existing banks that had been bought by the government or picked up in bankruptcy. As we'll see in Chapter 43, the same mega-banks that handle a major portion of the nation's credit card business today may already be insolvent, making them prime candidates for FDIC receivership and government takeover. If just those banking giants were made government agencies, they might provide enough branches to service the depository and credit card needs of the citizenry, leaving the lending of pre-existing funds to private financial institutions, just as is done now.

Note too that the government would not actually have to *run* these new bank branches. The FDIC could just hire new management or give the old management new guidelines, redirecting them to operate the business for the benefit of the public. As in any corporate acquisition, not much would need to change beyond the names on the stock certificates. Business could carry on as before. The employees would just be under new management. The banks could advance loans as accounting entries, just as they do now. The difference would be that interest on advances of credit, rather than going into private vaults for private profit, would go into the coffers of the government. *The "full faith and credit of the United States" would become an asset of the United States.*

## A Money Supply That Regulates Itself?

Hummel points to another limitation of a 100 percent reserve system. The extension of credit by private banks plays an important role in regulating the national money supply. Public borrowing is the natural determinant of monetary growth. When banks extend credit, the money supply expands naturally to meet the needs of growth and productivity. If a 100 percent reserve requirement were imposed, the money supply could not grow in this organic way, so monetary growth would have to be brought about by some more artificial means.

One alternative that has been proposed is for the government to expand the money supply according to a set formula. Milton Friedman suggested a fixed 4 percent per year. But such a system would not allow for modifying the money supply to respond to external shocks or varying internal needs. Another alternative that has been proposed is to delegate monetary expansion to a monetary board of some sort, which would be authorized to determine how much new money the government could issue in any given period. But that alternative too would be subject to the vagaries of human error and manipulation for private gain. We've seen the roller-coaster results when the Fed has been allowed to manipulate the money supply by arbitrarily changing interest rates and reserve requirements. Fed tinkering in 1929 is blamed for bringing on the Great Depression.

Why does the money supply *need* to be manipulated by the Fed? Consumer loans are self-liquidating: the new money created when a loan is advanced eventually gets paid back and zeroes out automatically. But that result is skewed by the charging of interest and by the fact that the burgeoning *federal* debt never gets paid back but just keeps growing. The money supply expands because government securities (or debt) are sold to the Federal Reserve and commercial banks, which buy them with money created out of thin air; and it is *this* unchecked source of expansion that has to be regulated by artificial means. In a system without a federal debt and without interest, consumer debt could regulate itself. That sort of model is found, for example, in the LETS system, in which "money" is created whenever someone pays someone else with "credits," and it is liquidated when the outstanding credits are used up. Thus:

Jane bakes cookies for Sam. Sam pays Jane one LETS credit by crediting her account and debiting his. "Money" has just been created. Sam washes Sue's car, for which Sue gives Sam one LETS credit, extinguishing the debit in his account and creating one in hers. Sue babysits for Jane, who pays with the LETS credit Sam gave her. The books are now balanced. There is no longer any "money" in the system, but there is still plenty of "credit," which can be created by anyone just by doing work for someone else.

The LETS system is a community currency system in which no gold or other commodity is needed to make it work. "Money" (or "credit") is generated by the participants themselves. Projecting this account-tallying model onto the larger community known as a nation, money would come into existence when it was borrowed from the community-owned bank, and it would be extinguished as the loans were repaid. That is actually how money is generated now; but the creators of this public credit are not the community at large but are private bankers who distort the circular flow of the medium of exchange by siphoning off a windfall profit in the form of interest. The charging of interest, in turn, creates the "impossible contract" problem – the spiral of inflation and unrepayable debt resulting when only the principal is lent into the money supply without creating the interest necessary to pay back the loans. In community LETS systems, this problem is avoided because interest is not charged; but we've seen that interest serves some useful purposes. It encourages borrowers to repay their debts quickly, discourages speculation, and compensates lenders for foregoing the use of their money for a period of time. Eliminating interest would eliminate the bond market on which prudent savers and retired people rely to supplement their incomes. How can the benefits of the interest system be retained without triggering the impossible contract problem? As Benjamin Franklin might have said, "That is simple" . . . .

# Chapter 42
# THE QUESTION OF INTEREST:
# BEN FRANKLIN SOLVES THE
# IMPOSSIBLE CONTRACT PROBLEM

*"Back where I come from, we have universities, seats of great learning, where men go to become great thinkers, and when they come out, they think deep thoughts, and with no more brains than you have. But they have one thing that you haven't got, a diploma."*

– The Wizard of Oz to the Scarecrow

Like Andrew Jackson and Abraham Lincoln, Benjamin Franklin was a self-taught genius. He invented bifocals, the Franklin stove, the odometer, and the lightning rod. He was also called "the father of paper money." He did not actually devise the banking system used in colonial Pennsylvania, but he wrote about it, promoted it, and understood its superiority over the private British gold-based system. When the directors of the Bank of England asked what was responsible for the booming economy of the young colonies, Franklin explained that the colonial governments issued their own money, which they both *lent* and *spent* into the economy. He is reported to have said:

> [A] legitimate government can both spend and lend money into circulation, while banks can only lend significant amounts of their promissory bank notes . . . . Thus, when your bankers here in England place money in circulation, there is always a debt principal to be returned and usury to be paid. The result is that you have always too little credit in circulation . . . and that which circulates, all bears the endless burden of unpayable debt and usury.

A money supply created by *banks* was never sufficient, because the bankers created only the principal and not the interest to pay back their loans. A *government*, on the other hand, could not only *lend* but *spend* money into the economy, covering the interest shortfall and keeping the money supply in balance. In an article titled "A Monetary System for the New Millennium," Canadian money reform advocate Roger Langrick explains this in contemporary terms. He begins by illustrating the mathematical problem arising from a money supply created as a debt lent at interest:

> [I]magine the first bank which prints and lends out $100. For its efforts it asks for the borrower to return $110 in one year; that is it asks for 10% interest. Unwittingly, or maybe wittingly, the bank has created a mathematically impossible situation. The only way in which the borrower can return 110 of the bank's notes is if the bank prints, and lends, $10 more at 10% interest. . . .
>
> The result of creating 100 and demanding 110 in return, is that the collective borrowers of a nation are forever chasing a phantom which can never be caught; the mythical $10 that were never created. The debt in fact is unrepayable. Each time $100 is created for the nation, the nation's overall indebtedness to the system is increased by $110. The only solution at present is increased borrowing to cover the principal plus the interest of what has been borrowed.[1]

The better solution, says Langrick, is to allow the government to issue enough new debt-free Greenbacks to cover the interest charges not created by the banks as loans:

> Instead of taxes, government would be empowered to create money for its own expenses *up to the balance of the debt shortfall*. Thus, if the banking industry created $100 in a year, the government would create $10 which it would use for its own expenses. Abraham Lincoln used this successfully when he created $500 million of "greenbacks" to fight the Civil War.

In Langrick's example, a private banking industry pockets the interest, which must be replaced every year by a 10 percent issue of new Greenbacks; but there is another possibility. The loans could be advanced by the government itself. The interest would then return to the government and could be spent back into the economy in a circular flow, without the need to continually issue more money to cover the interest shortfall. Government as the only interest-charging lender might not be a practical solution today, but it is a theoretical extreme that can be contrasted with the existing system to clarify the issues. Compare these two hypothetical models:

## Bad Witch/Good Witch Scenarios

The Wicked Witch of the West rules over a dark fiefdom with a single private bank owned by the Witch. The bank issues and lends all the money in the realm, charging an interest rate of 10 percent. The Witch prints 100 witch-dollars, lends them to her constituents, and demands 110 back. The people don't have the extra 10, so the Witch creates 10 more on her books and lends them as well. The money supply must continually increase to cover the interest, which winds up in the Witch's private coffers. She gets progressively richer, as the people slip further into debt. She uses her accumulated profits to buy things she wants. She is particularly fond of little thatched houses and shops, of which she has an increasingly large collection. To fund the operations of her fiefdom, she taxes the people heavily, adding to their financial burdens.

Glinda the Good Witch of the South runs her realm in a more people-friendly way. All of the money in the land is issued and lent by a "people's bank" operated for their benefit. She begins by creating 110 people's-dollars. She lends 100 of these dollars at 10 percent interest and spends the extra 10 dollars into the community on programs designed to improve the general welfare – things such as pensions for retirees, social services, infrastructure, education, research and development. The $110 circulates in the community and comes back to the people's bank as principal and interest on its loans. Glinda again lends $100 of this money into the community and spends the other $10 on public programs, supplying the interest for the next round of loans while providing the people with jobs and benefits.

For many years, she just recycles the same $110, without creating new money. Then one year, a cyclone comes up that destroys many of the charming little thatched houses. The people ask for extra money to rebuild. No problem, says Glinda; she will just print more people's-dollars and use them to pay for the necessary labor and materials. Inflation is avoided, because supply increases along with demand. Best of all, *taxes are unknown in the realm.*

## A Practical Real-world Model

It sounds good in a fairytale, in a land with a benevolent queen and only one bank; but things are a bit different in the real world. For one thing, enlightened benevolent queens are hard to come by. For another thing, returning all the interest collected on loans to the government would require nationalizing not only the whole banking system but every other form of private lending at interest, an alternative that is clearly too radical for current Western thinking. A more realistic model would be a dual lending system, semi-private and semi-public. The government would be the initial issuer and lender of funds, and private financial institutions would recycle this money as loans. Private lenders would still be siphoning interest into their own coffers -- just not as much. The money supply would therefore still need to expand to cover interest charges -- just not by as much. The actual amount by which it would need to expand, and how this expansion could be achieved without creating dangerous price inflation, are addressed in Chapter 44.

## Interest and Islam

Instituting a system of government-owned banks may sound radical in the United States, but some countries have already done it; and some other countries are ripe for radical reform. Rodney Shakespeare, co-author of Seven Steps to Justice (2002) and author of The Modern Universal Paradigm (2007), suggests that significant monetary reform may come first in the Islamic community. Islamic scholars and economists are keenly aware of the limitations of the current Western system and are actively seeking change, and oil-rich Islamic countries may have the clout to pull it off. In a series of international conferences held in Malaysia, Indonesia and Bangladesh, Islamic thinkers have been working to come up with a viable alternative to the Western banking system.

The interest question is a major issue for these reformers, because usury is forbidden in the Koran. Western economists got around the religious proscription against usury by redefining the term to mean "excessive" interest, but Islamic purists still hold to the older interpretation. As noted earlier, Islamic lawyers have gone to great lengths to design contracts that avoid interest charges, in order to avoid infringing religious law. The most common alternative is a contract in which the banker buys the property and sells it to the client at a higher price, to be paid in installments over time. But skeptical Islamic scholars maintain that these arrangements merely amount to interest-bearing loans by other names. They use descriptive terms such as "the usury of deception" and "the jurisprudence of legal tricks."[2]

Unlike the "impossible contract" problem, which is a simple mathematical issue, the religious objection to charging interest is a moral one. People who have not labored for the money take it from those who have earned it by the sweat of their brows. But the morality objection too might be overcome by a model in which interest is returned to the community and spent on the public good. Like in the Sumerian temple societies of 3,000 B.C., interest income could be used to support widows, orphans, and other underprivileged people who have traditionally been victimized by the private commercial banking system. The Sumerian system worked until private money lenders got into the game and started skimming a perpetual tribute off the top. Then the holdings of the creditors got bloated at the expense of the debtors, distorting the natural flow of the medium of exchange and producing inexorable price inflation and inextricable debt. If the interest had been returned to the community, it could have been used to pay community expenses in place of taxes, keeping the currency circulating from the government to the people and back again. That was the system employed successfully not only by the ancient Sumerians but in some of the early American colonies.

## As American as Apple Pie

Today, government-owned banks are associated with socialism; but they would not have raised the eyebrows of our forefathers. We've seen that the American colonies had very successful publicly-owned banks that made commercial loans of newly-issued paper scrip. In the province of Pennsylvania, a public land bank generated enough money to eliminate the need for taxes. Some theorists have argued that governments *must* tax in order to draw excess money out of the system and prevent inflation. But the Pennsylvania experience showed that inflation would not result if the government *lent* new money into the economy, because the money would be drawn back out when the debt was repaid; and new money *spent* into the economy could be recycled back to the government in the form of interest due on loans and fees for other public services.

The national banking system envisioned by Franklin, Jefferson and Lincoln was something quite different from the modern socialist scheme. The Pennsylvania land banks allowed the government to pay its own way, making taxes unnecessary. Even the most successful modern Western democratic socialist countries, including Sweden and Australia, *do not* eliminate taxes. Rather than funding their governments with profits from national banking and other publicly-owned industries, they rely on heavy taxes imposed on the private sector. Sweden developed one of the largest welfare states in Europe after 1945, but it had few government-run industries.[3] India was off to a good start, but it got sucked into massive foreign debts by the engineered oil crisis of 1974 and a banker-manipulated Congress that took on unnecessary IMF debt.[4] The Australian Labor Party, while holding public ownership of infrastructure out as an ideal, has not had enough political power to put that ideal into practice -- at least not lately. At the turn of the twentieth century, Australia did have a very successful publicly-owned bank, one of which Ben Franklin would have approved.

Australia's Commonwealth Bank was a "people's bank" that not only issued paper money but made loans and collected interest on them. When private banks were demanding 6 percent interest, Commonwealth Bank financed the Australian government's First World War effort at an interest rate of a fraction of 1 percent. The result was to save Australians some $12 million in bank charges. After the First World War, the bank's governor used the bank's credit power to save Australians from the depression conditions in other countries. It financed production and home-building, and lent funds to local governments for the construction of roads, tramways, harbors, gasworks, and electric power plants. The bank's profits were paid to the national government and were available for the redemption of debt. This prosperity lasted until the bank fell to the twentieth century global drive for privatization. At the beginning of the twentieth century, Australia had a standard of living that was among the highest in the world; but after its bank was privatized, the country fell heavily into debt. By the end of the century, its standard of living had dropped to twenty-third.[5]

In the United States in the 1930s, Franklin Roosevelt developed a public banking institution that was similar to Australia's Commonwealth Bank: he reshaped the Reconstruction Finance Corporation into a source of cheap and abundant credit for developing the national infrastructure and putting the country back to work.[6] Besides the colonial land banks, Lincoln's Greenback system, and the

U.S. Postal Savings System, other U.S. experiments in government banking have included the Small Business Administration (SBA) and Fannie Mae and Freddie Mac. The SBA oversees loans to small businesses in an economic climate in which credit may be denied by private banks because there is not enough profit in the loans to warrant the risks. Fannie Mae and Freddie Mac were also developed as government agencies. They did not become embroiled in the corruption they are dealing with now until they became private corporations. (See Chapter 31.)

## The Myth of Government Inefficiency

A common objection to getting the government involved in business is that it is notoriously inefficient at those pursuits; but Betty Reid Mandell, author of Selling Uncle Sam, maintains that this reputation is undeserved. It has resulted largely because the only enterprises left to government are those from which private enterprise can't make a profit. She cites surveys showing that in-house operation of publicly-provided services is generally *more* efficient than contracting them out, while privatizing public infrastructure for private profit has typically led to *increased* costs, inefficiency, and corruption.[7] A case in point is the deregulation and privatization of electricity in California, which met with heavy criticism as an economic disaster for the state.[8] Complex publicly-provided services tend to break down with privatization, just from the complexity of contracting and supervising the contract. Privatization of the British rail system caused rate increases, rail accidents, and system breakdown, to the point that a majority of the British public now favors returning to government ownership and operation.

Catherine Austin Fitts concurs, drawing on her experience as Assistant Secretary of HUD. She writes:

> The public policy "solution" has been to outsource government functions to make them more productive. In fact, this jump in overhead is simply a subsidy provided to private companies and organisations that receive thereby a guaranteed return regardless of performance. We have subsidies and financing to support housing programs that make no economic sense except for the property managers and owners who build and manage it for layers of fees.[9]

Government services may *appear* to be inefficient because the local government doesn't have enough funding to do the job properly, but this inefficiency is not the result of a lack of motivation among government workers caused by inadequate "competition." Clerks working for the government have to compete and perform to hold onto their jobs just as clerks working for private industry do. To the clerk, there is not much difference whether she is working for the government or for a big multinational corporation. It is not "her" business. Either way, she is just getting paid to take orders and carry them out. Beating out the competition by cutthroat practices is not the only way to motivate workers. Pride of performance, a desire for promotion and higher salaries, and a belief in the team project are also effective prods. Recall the Indian study comparing service and customer satisfaction from private-sector and public-sector banks, in which the government-owned Bank of India came out on top in all areas surveyed.[10]

Banks that are government agencies would have a number of practical advantages that could actually make them *more* efficient in the marketplace than their private counterparts. A government banking agency could advance loans without keeping "reserves." Like in the tally system or the LETS system, it would just be advancing "credit." A truly national bank would not need to worry about going bankrupt, and it would not need an FDIC to insure its deposits. It could issue loans impartially to anyone who satisfied its requirements, in the same way that the government issues driver's licenses to anyone who qualifies. Loans could be issued at an interest rate that was modest and fixed, returning reliability and predictability to borrowing. The Federal Reserve would no longer have to tamper with interest rates to control the money supply indirectly, because it would have direct control of the national currency at its source.

## The Fear of Giving Big Government Even More Power

Another common objection to returning the power to create money to Congress is that a corrupt government would be given even more power. We generally think we want *less* government, not more. But America's Founding Fathers had a different view of the function of government. They thought it was to *protect* their liberties from the power grabs of the unscrupulous. The Declaration of Independence declared:

> [W]e hold these Truths to be self evident, that all men are created equal, that they are endowed by their Creator with certain

unalienable Rights, that among these are Life, Liberty, and the Pursuit of Happiness – *That to secure these Rights, Governments are instituted among Men, deriving their just Powers from the Consent of the Governed.*

Today the government is actually *run* by the money cartel. Big business holds all the cards, because its affiliated banks have appropriated the power to create money for themselves. These giant cartels can be brought to heel only by cutting off their source of power and returning it to its rightful sovereign owners, the people and their representative government. The problem with the current monetary scheme is not that the *government* is irresponsibly running the printing presses but that *private bankers* are covertly engaged in that practice. Bankers have monopolized the business of issuing and lending the national money supply, a function the Constitution delegates solely to Congress. What hides behind the banner of "free enterprise" today is a system in which giant corporate monopolies have used their affiliated banking trusts to generate unlimited funds to buy up competitors, the media, and the government itself, forcing truly independent private enterprise out. Big private banks are allowed to create money out of nothing, lend it at interest, foreclose on the collateral, and determine who gets credit and who doesn't. They can advance massive loans to their affiliated cartels and hedge funds, which use the money to raid competitors and manipulate markets. If some players have the power to create money and others don't, the playing field is not "level" but allows some favored players to dominate and coerce others.

Private enterprise needs publicly-operated police, courts and laws to keep corporate predators at bay. It also needs a system of truly national banks, in which the power to create the money and advance the credit of the people is retained by the people. We trust government with sweeping powers to declare and conduct wars, provide for the general welfare, and establish and enforce laws. Why not trust it to create the national money supply in all its forms? A system of truly "national" banks would return to the people their most valuable asset, the right to create their own money. Like the monarchs of medieval England, we the people of a sovereign nation would not be dependent on loans from a cartel of private financiers. We would have the power to issue our own money and fund our own government, and *we would no longer have to pay income taxes* . . . .

# Chapter 43
# BAILOUT, BUYOUT, OR
# CORPORATE TAKEOVER?
# BEATING THE ROBBER BARONS AT
# THEIR OWN GAME

*"Didn't you know water would be the end of me?" asked the Witch, in a wailing, despairing voice. . . . "In a few minutes I shall be all melted, and you will have the castle to yourself. . . . Look out – here I go!"*
– *The Wonderful Wizard of Oz,*
"The Search for the Wicked Witch"

In the happy ending to our economic fairytale, the drought of debt to a private banking monopoly is destroyed with the water of a freely-flowing public money supply. Among other salubrious results, *we the people never have to pay income taxes again.* That possibility is not just the fantasy of utopian dreamers but is the conclusion of some respected modern financial analysts. One is Richard Russell, the investment adviser quoted earlier, whose <u>Dow Theory Letter</u> has been in publication for nearly fifty years. In his April 2005 newsletter, Russell observed that the creation of money is a total mystery to probably 99 percent of the U.S. population. Then he proceeded to unravel the mystery in a few sentences:

> To simplify, when the US government needs money, it either collects it in taxes or it issues bonds. These bonds are sold to the Fed, and the Fed, in turn, makes book entry deposits. This "debt money" created out of thin air is then made available to the US government. But if the US government can issue Treasury bills, notes and bonds, it can also issue currency, as it did prior to the formation of the Federal Reserve. *If the US issued its own money,*

*that money could cover all its expenses, and the income tax wouldn't be needed.* So what's the objection to getting rid of the Fed and letting the US government issue its own currency? *Easy, it cuts out the bankers and it eliminates the income tax.*[1]

In a February 2005 article titled "The Death of Banking and Macro Politics," Hans Schicht reached similar conclusions. He wrote:

> If prime ministers and presidents would only be blessed with the most basic knowledge of the perversity of banking, they would not go onto their knees to the Central Banker and ask His Highness for loans . . . . *With a little bit of brains they would expropriate all banking institutions* . . . . *Expropriation would bring enough money into the national treasuries for the people not to have to pay taxes for years to come.*[2]

"Expropriation," however, means "to deprive of property," and that is not the American way. At least, it isn't in principle. The Robber Barons routinely deprived their competitors of property, but they did it by following accepted business practices: they purchased the property on the open market in a takeover bid. Their sleight of hand was in the funding used for the purchases. They had their own affiliated banks, which could "lend" money into existence with an accounting entry.

If the banking cartels can do it, so can the federal government. Commercial bank ownership is held as stock shares, and the shares are listed on public stock exchanges. The government could regain control of the national money supply by simply buying up some prime bank stock at its fair market price.

Buying out the entire banking industry would not be necessary, since the depository and credit needs of consumers could be served by a much smaller banking force than is prowling the capital markets right now. The recycling of funds as loans could be left to private banks and those non-bank financial institutions that are already serving 80 percent of that market. Buying out the whole industry would not be necessary, but it might be the equitable thing to do, since if the government were to take back the power to create money from the banks, bank stock could plummet. If commercial banks could no longer make loans with accounting entries, the banks' shareholders would probably *vote* to be bought out if given the choice.

Assume for purposes of argument, then, that Congress had decided to reclaim the whole commercial banking industry, as an assortment of populist writers have suggested. What would that cost on the open market? At the end of 2004, the total book value (assets minus liabilities) of all U.S. commercial banks was reported at $850 billion.[3] "Book value" is what the shareholders would receive if the banks were liquidated and the shareholders were cashed out for exactly what the banks were worth. Shares trade on the stock market at substantially more than this figure, but the price is usually no more than a generous two times "book." Assuming that formula, around $1.7 trillion might be enough to purchase the whole U.S. commercial banking industry.

Too much for the government to pay?

Not if it were to create the money with accounting entries the way banks do now.

But wouldn't that be dangerously inflationary?

Not if Congress were to wait for a *deflationary* crisis; and we've seen that such a crisis is now looming on the horizon. The next correction in housing prices is expected to shrink the money supply by about $2 trillion. Fed Chairman Ben Bernanke suggested in 2002 that the government could counteract a major deflationary crisis by simply printing money and buying real assets with it. (See Chapter 40.) Buying the banking industry for $1.7 trillion in new Greenbacks could be just what the good doctor ordered.

## Bailout, Buyout, or FDIC Receivership?

The government *could* buy out the banks' shareholders, but it wouldn't necessarily have to. Enough bank branches to serve the public's needs might be picked up by the FDIC for free, just by conducting an independent audit of the big derivative banks and putting any found to be insolvent into receivership.

Recall Murray Rothbard's contention that the whole commercial banking system is bankrupt and belongs in receivership. (Chapter 34.) Banks owe depositors many times the amount of money they have on "reserve." They have managed to avoid a massive run on the banks by lulling their depositors into a false sense that all is well, using devices such as FDIC deposit insurance and a "reserve system" that allows banks to borrow money created out of nothing from the Federal Reserve. But that bailout system is provided at taxpayer expense. By rights, said Rothbard, the whole banking system should be put into receivership and the bankers should be jailed as embezzlers.

If the taxpayers were to withdraw the taxpayer-funded props holding up a bankrupt banking system, the banks, or at least some of them, could soon collapse of their own weight; and the first to go would probably be the big derivative banks that have been called "zombie banks" – banks that are already bankrupt and are painted with a veneer of solvency by a team of accountants adept at "creative accounting." Insolvent banks are dealt with by the FDIC, which can proceed in one of three ways. It can order a *payout*, in which the bank is liquidated and ceases to exist. It can arrange for a *purchase and assumption*, in which another bank buys the failed bank and assumes its liabilities. Or it can take the *bridge bank* option, in which the FDIC replaces the board of directors and provides the capital to get it running in exchange for an equity stake in the bank.[4] An "equity stake" means an ownership interest: the bank's stock becomes the property of the government.

The bridge bank option was taken in 1984, when Chicago's Continental Illinois became insolvent. Continental Illinois was the nation's seventh largest bank, and its insolvency was the largest bank failure that had ever occurred in the United States. Ed Griffin writes:

> Federal Reserve Chairman Volcker told the FDIC that it would be unthinkable to allow the world economy to be ruined by a bank failure of this magnitude. So, the FDIC assumed $4.5 billion in bad loans and, *in return for the bailout, took 80% ownership of the bank in the form of stock. In effect, the bank was nationalized . . . . The United States government was now in the banking business.*
>
> . . . Four years after the bailout of Continental Illinois, the same play was used in the rescue of BankOklahoma, which was a bank holding company. The FDIC pumped $130 million into its main banking unit and took warrants for 55% ownership. . . *By accepting stock in a failing bank in return for bailing it out, the government had devised an ingenious way to nationalize banks without calling it that.*[5]

The FDIC sold its equity interest in Continental Illinois after the bank got back on its feet in 1991, but the bank was effectively nationalized from 1984 to 1991. Griffin decries this result as being antithetical to capitalist notions; but as William Jennings Bryan observed, banking *is* the government's business, by constitutional mandate. The right and the duty to create the national money supply were entrusted to Congress by the Founding Fathers. If Congress is going to take back the power to create money, it will *have* to take control of the lending business, since over 97 percent of the money supply is now created as commercial loans.

As Dave Lewis observed, in some sense the big banks considered "too big to fail" are *already* nationalized, since their survival depends on a system of taxpayer-funded bailouts. (See Chapter 34.) If taxpayer money is keeping the ship from sinking, the taxpayers are entitled to step in and take the helm. Banking institutions supported by taxpayer money can and should be made public institutions operated for the benefit of the taxpayers.

### Some Choice Bank Stock Ripe for FDIC Plucking?

Continental Illinois may not be the largest U.S. bank to have been bailed out from bankruptcy. We've seen evidence that Citibank became insolvent in 1989 and was quietly bailed out with the help of the Federal Reserve, and that JPMorgan Chase (JPM) followed suit in 2002. (Chapters 33 and 34.) These are the country's two largest banks, and they are the banks that are the most perilously over-exposed in the massive derivatives bubble. Recall the 2006 report by the Office of the Comptroller of the Currency, finding that 97 percent of U.S. bank-held derivatives are in the hands of just five banks; and that the first two banks on the list are JPM and Citibank. According to Martin Weiss in a November 2006 newsletter:

> The biggest [derivatives] player, JPMorgan Chase, is a party to $57 trillion in notional value of derivatives. Its total credit exposure adds up to $660 billion, a stunning 748% of the bank's risk-based capital. In other words, for every dollar of its net worth, JPMorgan Chase is *risking* $7.48 in derivatives. All it would take is for 13.3% of its derivatives to go bad . . . and JPMorgan's capital would be wiped out, gone. . . . Citibank isn't far behind – with $4.24 at risk for every dollar of capital, more than double what it was just a few years ago.[6]

These two banks are prime candidates for receivership, and the FDIC might not even have to wait for a massive derivatives crisis in order to proceed. It might just need to take a close look at the banks' books. JPM and Citibank were both defendants in the Enron scandal, in which they were charged with fraudulently cooking their books to make things look rosier than they were. To avoid judgment, they wound up paying $300 million to settle the suits; but while a settlement avoids having to admit liability, evidence in the case clearly showed fraudulent activities.[7] Banks with a record of engaging in such tactics could still be engaging in them. A penetrating look at their books might confirm that their complex derivatives schemes were illegal pyramid schemes concealing insolvency, as critics have charged. (See Chapter 34.) If the banks are insolvent, they belong in receivership.

JPM and Citibank have many branches and an extensive credit card system. Recall that JPM now issues the most Visas and MasterCards of any bank nationwide, and that it holds the largest share of U.S. credit card balances. If just these two banks were acquired by the government in receivership, they might be sufficient to service the depository, check clearing, and credit card needs of the citizenry. That result would also make a very satisfying ending to our story. JPM and Citibank are the money machines of the empires of Morgan and Rockefeller, the Robber Barons whose henchmen plotted at Jekyll Island to impose their Federal Reserve scheme on the American people. They induced William Jennings Bryan to endorse the Federal Reserve Act by leading him to believe that it provided for a national money supply issued by the government rather than by private banks. It would only be poetic justice for these massive banking conglomerates to become truly "national" banking institutions, serving the public interest at last.

### Time for an Audit of the Banks and a Tax on Derivatives?

Even if the mega-banks (or some of them) are already bankrupt, we might not hear about it without an independent Congressional audit. John Hoefle writes, "Major financial crises are never announced in the newspapers but are instead treated as a form of national security secret, so that various bailouts and market-manipulation activities can be performed behind the scenes." The bailouts are primarily conducted by the Federal Reserve, a private corporation answerable to the private banks that are its real owners. Hoefle argues that Congress delegated the money-creating power to the Federal Reserve in violation of its Constitutional mandate, making the Fed's activities illegal. He maintains:

> This is not an academic question, as the Fed is actively involved in looting the American population for the benefit of giant U.S. and global financial institutions, and the global casino. *Few Americans have any idea the extent to which the Fed and its system reach into their pockets on a daily basis, and the extent to which their standard of living has been eroded by the financier-led deindustrialization of the United States. . . .* [N]ot only do we suffer from an inadequate infrastructure, but we have lost the benefits

of those breakthroughs which would have occurred, the technologies which would have been developed, had the parasites not taken over the economy. It is the failure to push back the boundaries of science that is responsible for most of our problems today.[8]

In order to bring the largely-unreported derivatives scheme into public view and under public control, Hoefle favors a tax on all derivative trades. This form of tax is called a "Tobin tax," after economist James Tobin, who received a Bank of Sweden Prize in Economics in 1981. Hoefle notes that even a very modest tax of one-tenth of one percent would bring derivative trades out into the open, allowing them to be traced and regulated; and because derivative trading is in such high volume, the tax would have the further benefit of generating significant revenue for the government.

Dean Baker, of the Center for Economic and Policy Research in Washington, is another advocate of a tax on derivatives. He points out that financial transactions taxes have been successfully implemented in the past and have often raised substantial revenue. Until recently, every industrialized nation imposed taxes on trades in its stock markets; and several still do. Until 1966, the United States placed a tax of 0.1 percent on shares of stock when they were first issued, and a tax of 0.04 percent when they were traded. A tax of 0.003 percent is still imposed on stock trades to finance SEC operations.[9]

Baker notes that the vast majority of stock trades and other financial transactions are done by short term traders who hold assets for less than a year and often for less than a day. Unlike long-term stock investment, these trades are essentially a form of gambling. He writes, "When an investor buys a share of stock in a company that she has researched and holds it for ten years, this is not gambling. But when a day trader buys a stock at 2:00 P.M. and sells it at 3:00 P.M., this is gambling. Similarly, the huge bets made by hedge funds on small changes in interest rates or currency prices is a form of gambling." When poor and middle income people gamble, they usually engage in one of the heavily taxed forms such as buying lottery tickets or going to the race track; but wealthier people who gamble in the stock market escape taxation. Baker argues that a tax on derivative trades would only be fair, equalizing the rules of the game:

> Insofar as possible, taxes should be shifted away from productive activity and onto unproductive activity. In recognition of this basic economic principle, the government . . .

already taxes most forms of gambling quite heavily. For example, gambling on horse races is taxed at between 3.0 and 10.0 percent. Casino gambling in the states where it is allowed is taxed at rates between 6.25 and 20.0 percent. State lotteries are taxed at a rate of close to 40 percent. Stock market trading is the only form of gambling that largely escapes taxation. This is doubly inefficient. The government has no reason to favor one form of gambling over others, and it is far better economically to tax unproductive activities than productive ones.

. . . From an economic standpoint, the nation is certainly no better off if people do their gambling on Wall Street rather than in Atlantic City or Las Vegas. In fact, there are reasons to believe that the nation is better off if people gamble in Las Vegas, since gambling on Wall Street can destabilize the functioning of financial markets. Many economists have argued that speculators cause the price of stocks and other assets to diverge from their fundamental values.[10]

A tax on short-term trades would impose a significant tax on speculators while leaving long-term investors largely unaffected. It could also make a substantial contribution toward the government's budget needs. According to Baker, a tax of 0.25 percent imposed on each purchase or sale of a share of stock, along with a comparable tax on the transfer of other assets such as bonds, options, futures, and foreign currency, could easily have raised $120 billion in 2000; and that figure would be substantially higher today.

## Solving the Derivatives Crisis

A derivatives tax might do more than just raise money for the government. Hoefle maintains that it could actually kill the derivatives business, since even a very small tax leveraged over many trades would make them unprofitable. Killing the derivatives business, in turn, could propel some very big banks into bankruptcy; but the fleas' loss could be the dog's gain. The handful of banks in which 97 percent of U.S. bank-held derivatives are concentrated are the same banks that are engaging in vulture capitalism, bear raids through collusive short selling, and a massive derivatives scheme that allows them to manipulate markets and destroy businesses. A tax on derivatives could expose these corrupt practices and bring both the schemes and the culpable banks under public control.

# Chapter 44
# THE QUICK FIX:
# GOVERNMENT THAT PAYS
# FOR ITSELF

*The strange creatures set the travelers down carefully before the*
*gate of the City . . . and then flew swiftly away . . . .*
*"That was a good ride," said the little girl.*
*"Yes, and a quick way out of our troubles," replied the Lion.*

> – *The Wonderful Wizard of Oz,*
> *"The Winged Monkeys"*

A tax on derivatives could be a useful tool, but the ideal government would be one that was self-sustaining, without imposing
*either* taxes *or* a mounting debt on its citizens. As Richard Russell
observed, if the U.S. issued its own money, that money could cover all
its expenses, and taxes would not be necessary. If the Federal Reserve
were made what most people think it now is – an arm of the *federal
government* – and if it had been vested with the exclusive authority to
create the national money supply in all its forms, the government would
have access to enough money to spend on anything it needed or
wanted. The obvious problem with that "quick fix" is that it would
eventually produce serious inflation, unless the money were siphoned
back out of the economy in some way. The questions considered in
this chapter are:

- *How much* new money could the government put into the economy
  annually without creating dangerous price inflation?

- Would that be enough to replace income taxes? How about other
  taxes?

- Would it be enough to avoid the "impossible contract" problem by
  furnishing the money necessary to cover the interest that isn't
  advanced in commercial loans?

## No More Income Taxes!

Assume that the Federal Reserve had used its new Greenback-issuing power to buy back the entire outstanding federal debt, and that it had acquired enough bank branches (either by purchase or by FDIC takeover in receivership) to service the depository and credit needs of the public. What impact would those alterations have on the federal income tax burden? To explore the possibilities, we'll use U.S. data for FY 2005 (the fiscal year ending September 2005), the last year for which M3 was reported:

- Total individual income taxes in FY 2005 came to $927 billion.

- Taxpayers paid $352 billion in interest that year on the federal debt. If the debt had been paid off, this interest could have been cut from the national budget, reducing the tax burden by that sum.[1]

- Total assets in the form of bank credit for all U.S. commercial banks in FY 2005 were reported at $7.4 trillion.[2] Assuming an average collective interest rate on bank loans of about 5 percent, approximately 370 billion dollars were thus paid in interest that year. If roughly half this sum had gone to a newly-formed *national* banking system -- for loans made at the federal funds rate to private lending institutions, interest on credit card debt, loans to small businesses, and so forth -- the government could have earned around $185 billion in interest in FY 2005.

Adding these two adjustments together, the public tax bill might have been reduced by around $537 billion in FY 2005. Deducting this sum from $927 billion leaves $390 billion. This is the approximate sum the government would have had to generate in new Greenbacks to eliminate federal income taxes altogether in FY 2005.

What would adding $390 billion do to the money supply and to consumer prices? In 2005, M3 was $9.7 trillion. Adding $390 billion would have expanded M3 by only 4 percent -- Milton Friedman's modest target rate, and *far less* than the money supply *actually* grew in 2006. That was the year the Fed quit reporting M3, but the figures have been calculated privately by other sources. Economist John Williams has a website called "Shadow Government Statistics," which exposes and analyzes the flaws in current U.S. government data and reporting. He states that in July 2006, the annual growth in M3 was *over 9 percent*.[3] We've seen that this growth must have come from fiat money created as loans by the Federal Reserve and the banks.[4] Thus if new debt-free Greenbacks had been issued by the Treasury instead, inflation of the money supply could actually have been *reduced* – from 9 percent to a modest 4 percent – *without* cutting government programs or adding to a burgeoning federal debt.

## Horn of Plenty: Avoiding Inflation by Increasing Supply and Demand Together

New Greenbacks in the sum of $390 billion dollars would have been enough to eliminate income taxes, but according to Keynes, the government could have issued quite a bit more than that without significantly inflating prices. He said that if the funds were used to put the unemployed to work making new goods and services, new currency could safely be added up to the point of full employment without creating price inflation. The gross domestic product (GDP) would just increase by the value of the newly-made goods and services, keeping supply and demand in balance. We've seen that the Chinese money supply increased by *18.8 percent* in 2005 without creating runaway inflation. Rather, the country pushed ahead to become the world's fourth-largest economy. (Chapter 27.)

How much is the U.S. work force under-employed today? In the first half of 2006, the official unemployment rate was 4.6 percent; but critics said the figure was low, because it included only people applying for unemployment benefits. It did not include those who were no longer eligible for benefits, those who had given up, or those whose skills and education were under-utilized – people working part-time who wanted to work full-time, engineers working as taxi drivers, computer programmers working as store clerks, and so forth. According to Williams' "Shadow Government Statistics" website, *the real U.S. unemployment figure in early 2006 was a full 12 percent.*[5]

The reported GDP in 2005 was $12.5 trillion. If Williams' unemployment figure is correct, $12.5 trillion represented only 88 percent of the country's productive capacity in 2005. Extrapolating upwards, 100 percent productive capacity would have generated a GDP of $14.2 trillion, or $1.7 trillion more than was actually produced in 2005. *That means another $1.7 trillion in new Greenbacks could have been spent into the economy for productive purposes in 2005 without creating significant price inflation.*

What could you do with $1.7 trillion ($1,700 billion)? According to a United Nations report, in 1995 a mere *$80 billion* added to existing resources would have been enough to cut world poverty and hunger in half, achieve universal primary education and gender equality, reduce under-five mortality by two-thirds and maternal mortality by three-quarters, reverse the spread of HIV/AIDS, and halve the proportion of people without access to safe water world-wide.[6]

For comparative purposes, here are some typical U.S. government outlays: $76 billion went for education in FY 2005, $26.6 billion went for natural resources and the environment, and $69.1 billion went for veteran's benefits. Under our projected scenario, these and other necessary services could have been expanded and many others could have been added, while at the same time *eliminating* federal income taxes *and* the federal debt, *without* creating dangerous inflation. The government would have money for programs that have always been needed but today appear to be beyond its budget, including improved education, environmental cleanup and preservation, basic universal health coverage, restoration of infrastructure, independent medical research, and development of alternative energy sources.

## Keeping the Economic Bathtub from Overflowing

One glitch in this model is that the $1.7 trillion added to the economy would not be a one-time payment. Even when full employment had been reached, the newly employed would need to be paid and the new programs would need to be funded. Wouldn't adding that much new money *every* year throw the economy into hyperinflation?

It probably would, if liquidity were not drained back out of the economic bathtub in other ways. The government could pump in all the new money it wanted, if it had ways to recycle the funds back to itself. The next time around, the government could spend this recycled money instead of issuing new money, keeping the money supply stable.

Recycling money back to the Treasury is usually done through taxes, but a more equitable and satisfying solution would be for the government to invest in productive industries that would return income to the public purse. If the government were to venture into the business of banking, for example, income would return to it as interest on loans. Another money-producing option would be for the government to invest in infrastructure that could generate income. Wind and ocean wave energies are obvious examples. Unlike scarce oil resources that are non-renewable and come from a plot of ground someone owns, the wind and the waves are inexhaustible and belong to everyone;

and once the necessary infrastructure is set up, no further investment is necessary beyond maintenance to keep these energy generators going. They are natural perpetual motion machines, powered by the moon, the tides and the weather. Wind farms could be set up on publicly-owned lands across the country. Denmark, the leading wind power nation in the world, today satisfies 20 percent of its electricity needs with clean energy produced at Danish wind farms. Wave energy can average 65 megawatts per mile of coastline in favorable locations, and the West Coast of the United States is more than 1,000 miles long. The government could charge a reasonable fee to users for this harnessed energy.

Besides what the government could do to recycle excess liquidity out of the economy, there are major deflationary forces now on the horizon that are threatening to shrink the money supply into a major depression, *unless* the federal government steps in to refill the economic tub with liquidity. We've seen that the money supply could contract by $1.7 trillion or more just from the next correction in the housing market; and when the derivatives bubble collapses, substantially more debt-money will disappear. The Federal Reserve reports that the fastest-growing portion of the U.S. debt burden is in the "financial sector" (meaning mainly the banking sector), which was responsible for $12.5 trillion in debt in 2005. This explosive growth is attributed largely to speculation in derivatives, which are highly leveraged. The buyer of a derivative might, for example, put up 5 percent while a bank loan provides the rest.[7] The debt ratio of the financial sector zoomed from a mere 5 percent of the economy's national income in 1957 to *126 percent* in 2005, a growth rate 23 times greater than general economic growth.[8] Recall that in 2006, only 5 major U.S. banks held 97 percent of derivatives, including the "zombie" banks that were already bankrupt and were being propped up by manipulative market intervention. The whole edifice is built on sand; and when it collapses, the masses of debt-money it created will vanish with it in the waves, massively deflating the money supply, leaving plenty of room for the government to add money back in.

A more positive factor serving to make room for new Greenback dollars is that debt will disappear as this new money replaces it. As unemployed and under-employed people acquire incomes they can live on, they will no longer need to take out loans at exorbitant interest rates to pay their bills. Home buyers with money to spare will pay down their mortgages, and fewer "sub-prime" borrowers will be induced to acquire new mortgages, since aggressive lending tactics will have disappeared along with the fractional reserve banking system that made them profitable. A tax imposed on derivatives could put a brake on the exploding derivatives bubble and its accompanying debt burden; and if the big derivative banks were put into receivership before the bubble popped, the derivative Ponzi scheme might be carefully unwound by the FDIC, liquidating large amounts of "virtual" debt with it. As these sources of debt-money were reduced, there would be increasing room for growth through government programs funded with new Greenbacks.

## Solving the Impossible Contract Problem

That just leaves the "impossible contract" problem. We've seen that over 99 percent of the money supply is now borrowed into existence from the banking system, and that these loans are all at interest to the banks. That means more money is always owed back in principal and interest than was advanced in the form of loans. A dollar borrowed at 5 percent interest becomes a debt of two dollars in 14 years. That means the money supply has to double every 14 years just to produce the interest to service the debt to keep the money supply in existence; and as the money supply inflates, so do prices. An inflating money supply isn't necessarily bad so long as the new money is used to produce new goods and services; but in this case it is being drained off for the non-productive purpose of paying a service charge to private banks for lending money they never had to lend.

Roger Langrick's solution to the impossible contract problem is to authorize the government to issue enough new money to match the outstanding collective interest bill of the nation. (Chapter 42.) But that bill could be a prohibitive sum today. The provincial government of Pennsylvania succeeded in spending enough new money into the economy to cover its collective interest tab without producing Weimar-style inflation, but the Colony of Pennsylvania wasn't drowning in debt. "Neither a borrower nor a lender be," said Benjamin Franklin in a bygone era before betting with borrowed money became the favorite game of speculators. By 2006, outstanding public and private debt in the United States came to a staggering $44 *trillion*. Assuming an average interest rate of 5 percent, interest on the collective debt came to about $2.2 trillion. This sum would have to be matched with new Greenbacks to avoid the impossible contract problem under Roger Langrick's proposal. Adding $2.2 trillion to an M3 of $9.7 trillion would expand the money supply by 23 percent, too much for comfort even under Keynes' expansive formula.

The collective interest tab could, however, be trimmed by reducing the total debt in various ways. Paying off the federal debt would have shaved $8 trillion from the overall debt in 2005. Another $1.9 trillion could have been trimmed from the total interest-bearing debt by refinancing state and local government debt with interest-free loans from the federal government (an option discussed below). In 2005, those two adjustments would have reduced the total outstanding debt burden to about $34 trillion. At 5 percent, the interest bill would have been $1.7 trillion, the very sum by which the money supply could have been expanded without producing inflation under Keynes' formula. With these adjustments in the debt burden, then, the syndrome of unrepayable debt and ever-inflating prices created by the "impossible contract" problem could indeed have been eliminated, just as it was in colonial Pennsylvania.

## A Helping Hand to the States

The federal government's largesse could also spill over into state and local budgets. In the interest of preserving a single national currency, state and local governments would not be able to issue new Greenbacks to fund their programs (although they could issue other forms of credit, such as tax credits for fuel efficiency; see Chapter 36). However, the federal government could offer loans to state and local governments interest-free. That is what Jacob Coxey proposed in the 1890s – "non-interest-bearing bonds" to fund local public projects, to be issued by the local government and pledged to the federal government in exchange for federally-issued Greenback dollars.

Relieving state and local governments of the burden of paying interest would give a major boost to local economies. Today, local governments often pay more in interest on loans for local projects than they pay for labor and materials.[9] State and local governments are good credit risks and do not need the prod of interest charges to encourage them to make timely payments on their loans. To discourage local officials from borrowing "free" money just to speculate with it, the funds could be earmarked for specific approved purposes, and a strict repayment schedule could be imposed.

How would the loans be repaid? The money *could* come from taxes; but again, a more satisfying solution would be for state and local governments to raise revenue through fee-generating enterprises of various sorts, turning local economies into the sort of cooperative profit-generating endeavors implied in the term "Common Wealth."

## A Government That Pays Dividends to Its Citizens?

There may be a way that not only federal income taxes but *all* taxes -- state, local and federal -- could be eliminated. In fact, *the government could be paying dividends to us.* So writes Walter Burien, an investment adviser and accountant who has spent many years peering into government books. He notes that the government is composed of 54,000 different state, county, and local government entities, including school districts, public authorities, and the like; and that all of them keep their financial assets in liquid investment funds, bond financing accounts and corporate stock portfolios. The only income that must be reported in government budgets is that from taxes, fines and fees; but the stock holdings of government entities can be found in official annual reports known as CAFRs (Comprehensive Annual Financial Reports), which must be filed with the federal government by local, county and state governments. According to Burien, these annual reports show that virtually every U.S. city, county, and state has vast amounts of money stashed away in surplus funds, with domestic and international stock holdings collectively totaling trillions of dollars.[10]

Some of these stock holdings are pure surplus held as "slush funds" (funds raised for undesignated purposes). Others belong to city and county employees as their pension funds. Unlike the federal Social Security fund, which must be invested in U.S. government securities, the funds in state and local government pension investment programs can be invested in anything – common stock, bonds, real estate, derivatives, commodities. Where Social Security depends on taxing future generations, state and local retirement systems can invest in assets that are income-producing, making them self-sufficient. The slush funds that represent "pure surplus," says Burien, have been kept concealed from taxpayers, even as taxes are being raised and citizens are being told to expect fewer services from the government. He maintains that with prudent government management, not only could taxes be abolished, but citizens could start receiving dividend checks. This is already happening in Alaska, where oil investments have allowed the state to give rebates to taxpayers (around $2,000 per person in 2000).[11]

Burien's thesis is controversial and would take some serious investigation to be substantiated, but combined with allegations by Catherine Austin Fitts and others that trillions of dollars have simply been "lost" to "black ops" programs, it raises intriguing possibilities. The government may be far richer than we know. An honest government truly intent on providing for the general welfare could find the funds for all sorts of programs that are sorely needed but today are considered too expensive to be within reach. Roger Langrick concludes:

> With computerization, robotics, advances in genetics and food growing, we have the potential to turn the planet into a sustainable ecosystem capable of supporting all. . . . This is not a time to be saddled with an 18th century money system designed around the endless rape of the planet, [one] based on the robber baron mentality and flawed with Unrepayable Debt. . . . *A new monetary system with enough government control to ensure funding of vital issues could unlock the creative potential of the entire nation.*[12]

# Chapter 45

# GOVERNMENT WITH HEART: SOLVING THE PROBLEM OF THIRD WORLD DEBT

*"Remember, my fine friend, a heart is not judged by how much you love, but by how much you are loved by others."*

– The Wizard of Oz to the Tin Woodman, MGM film

In the nineteenth century, the corporation was given the legal status of a "person" although it was a person without heart, incapable of love and charity. Its sole legal motive was to make money for its stockholders, ignoring such "external" costs as environmental destruction and human oppression. The U.S. government, by contrast, was designed to be a social organism *with* heart. The Founding Fathers stated as their guiding principles that all men are created equal; that they are endowed with certain inalienable rights, including life, liberty and the pursuit of happiness; and that the function of government is to "provide for the general welfare."

If the major corporate banking entities that are now in control of the nation's money supply were made agencies of the U.S. government, they could incorporate some of these humanitarian standards into their business models; and one important humanitarian step these public banks would be empowered to take would be to forgive unfair and extortionate Third World debt. Most Third World debt today is held by U.S.-based international banks.[1] If those banks were made federal agencies (either by purchasing their stock or by acquiring them in receivership), the U.S. government could declare a "Day of Jubilee" -- a day when oppressive Third World debts were forgiven across the board. The term comes from the Biblical Book of Leviticus, in which Jehovah Himself, evidently recognizing the mathematical impossibility of continually collecting debts at interest compounded annually, declared a day to be held every 49 years, when debts would be forgiven and the dispossessed could return to their homes.

Unlike when Jehovah did it, however, a Day of Jubilee declared by the U.S. government would not be an entirely selfless act. If the United States is going to pay off its international debts with new Greenbacks, it is going to need the goodwill of the world. Forgiving the debts of our neighbors could encourage them to forgive ours. Other countries have no more interest in seeing the international economy collapse than we do; but if they are "spooked" by the market, they could rush to dump their dollars along with everyone else, bringing the whole shaky debt edifice down. Forgiving Third World debt could show our good intentions, quell market jitters, and get everyone on the same page. Our shiny new monetary scheme, rather than appearing to be more sleight of hand, could unveil itself as a millennial model for showering abundance everywhere.

Forgiving Third World debt could have a number of other important benefits, including a reduction in terrorism. In a 2004 book called The Debt Threat: How Debt Is Destroying the Developing World and Threatening Us All, Noreena Hertz notes that "career terrorists" are signing up for that radical employment because it pays a salary when no other jobs are available. Relieving Third World debt would also help protect the global environment, which is being destroyed piece by piece to pay off international lenders; and it could help prevent the spread of diseases that are being bred in impoverished conditions abroad.

The United States has actually been looking for a way to cancel Third World debt. It just hasn't been able to reach agreement with its fellow IMF members on how to do it. When the IMF talks of "forgiving" debt, it isn't talking about any acts of magnanimous generosity on the part of the banks. It is talking about shifting the burden of payment from the debtor countries to the wealthier donor countries, or drawing on the IMF's gold reserves to insure that the banks get their money. In the fall of 2004, the United States decided that Iraq's $120 billion debt should be canceled; but if oil-rich Iraq merited debt cancellation, much poorer countries would too. Under the Heavily Indebted Poor Country (HIPC) Initiative of 1996, rich nations agreed to cancel $110 billion in debt to poor nations; but by the fall of 2004, only about $31 billion had actually been canceled. The thirty or so poorest nations, most of them in Africa, still had a collective outstanding debt of about $200 billion.

At a meeting of finance ministers, the United States took the position that the debts of all the poorest nations should be canceled outright. The sticking point was where to get the funds. One suggestion was to revalue and sell the IMF's gold; but objection was raised that this would simply be another form of welfare to banks that had made risky loans, encouraging them to continue in their profligate loan-sharking.[2]

The Wizard of Oz might have said this was another instance of disorganized thinking. The problem could be solved in the same way that it was created: by sleight of hand. The debts could be canceled simply by voiding them out on the banks' books. No depositors or creditors would lose any money, because no depositors or creditors advanced their own money in the original loans. According to British economist Michael Rowbotham, writing in 1998:

> [O]f the $2,200 billion currently outstanding as Third World, or developing country debt, the vast majority represents money created by commercial banks in parallel with debt. In no sense do the loans advanced by the World Bank and IMF constitute monies owed to the "creditor nations" of the World Bank and IMF. The World Bank co-operates directly with commercial banks in the creation and supply of money in parallel with debt. The IMF also negotiates directly with commercial banks to arrange combined IMF/commercial "loan packages."
>
> As for those sums loaned by the IMF from the total quotas supplied by member nations, these sums also do not constitute monies owed to "creditor" nations. The monies subscribed as quotas were initially created by commercial banks. *Both quotas and loans are owed, ultimately, to commercial banks.*

If the money is owed to commercial banks, it was created with accounting entries. Rowbotham observes that Third World debt represents a liability on the banks' books only because the rules of banking say their books must be balanced. He suggests two ways the rules of banking might be changed to liquidate unfair and oppressive debts:

> The first option is to remove the obligation on banks to maintain parity between assets and liabilities, or, to be more precise, to allow banks to hold reduced levels of assets equivalent to the Third World debt bonds they cancel. Thus, if a commercial bank held $10 billion worth of developing country debt bonds, after cancellation it would be permitted in perpetuity to have a

$10 billion dollar deficit in its assets. This is a simple matter of record-keeping.

The second option, and in accountancy terms probably the more satisfactory (although it amounts to the same policy), is to cancel the debt bonds, yet permit banks to retain them for purposes of accountancy. The debts would be cancelled so far as the developing nations were concerned, but still valid for the purposes of a bank's accounts. The bonds would then be held as permanent, non-negotiable assets, at face value.[3]

Third World debt could be eliminated with the click of a mouse!

## Stabilizing Exchange Rates in a Floating Sea of Trade

Old debts could be wiped off the books, but the same debt syndrome will strike again unless something is done to stabilize national currencies. As long as currencies can be devalued by speculators, Third World countries will be exporting goods for a fraction of their value and over-paying for imports, keeping the national balance sheet in the red. The U.S. dollar itself could soon be at risk. If global bondholders start dumping their bond holdings in large quantities, short sellers could fan the flames, collapsing the value of the dollar just as speculators collapsed the German mark in 1923.

To counteract commercial risks from sudden changes in the value of foreign currencies, corporations today feel compelled to invest heavily in derivatives, "hedging" their bets by buying puts and calls so they can win either way. But derivatives themselves are quite risky and expensive, and they can serve to compound the risk. Some other solution is needed that can return predictability, certainty and fairness to international contracts. The Bretton Woods gold standard worked to prevent devaluations and huge trade deficits like the United States now has with China, but gold ultimately failed as a currency peg. The U.S. government (the global banker) had insufficient gold reserves for clearing international trade balances, and it eventually ran out of gold. Gold alone has also proved to be an unstable measure of value, since its own value fluctuates widely. Some new system is needed that retains the virtues of the gold standard while overcoming its limitations.

## From the Dollar Peg to "Full Dollarization"?

One solution that has been tried is for countries to stabilize their currencies by pegging them directly to the U.S. dollar. The maneuver has worked to prevent currency devaluations, but the countries have lost the flexibility they need to compete in international markets. In Argentina between 1991 and 2001, a "currency board" maintained a strict one-to-one peg between the Argentine peso and the U.S. dollar. The money supply was fixed, limited and inflexible. The dire result was national bankruptcy, in 1995 and again in 2001.[4]

The extreme form of dollar pegging is called "full dollarization." The fully dollarized country simply abandons its local currency and uses *only* U.S. dollars. Ecuador converted to full dollarization in 2000, and El Salvador did it in 2002.[5] Certain benefits were realized, including reduced interest rates, reduced inflation, a stable currency, and a measure of economic growth. But when neighboring countries devalued their own currencies, the "dollarized" countries' products became more expensive and less competitive in global markets. Dollarized countries also lost the ability to control their own money supplies. When the El Salvador government incurred unexpected expenses, it could not finance them either by issuing its own currency or by issuing bonds that would be funded by its own banks, since neither the government nor the bankers had the ability to create dollars. The country's money supply was fixed and limited, forcing the government to cut budgeted programs to make up the difference; and that seriously hurt the poor, since welfare programs got slashed first.

## The Single Currency Solution

Another proposed solution to the floating currency conundrum is for the world to convert *en masse* to a single currency. Proponents say this would do on a global level what the standardized dollar bill did on a national level for the United States, and what the Euro did on a regional level for the European Union. But critics point out that the world is *not* one nation or one region, and they question who would be authorized to issue this single currency. Letting all governments issue it would leave the global money supply vulnerable to irresponsible governments that issued too much. Limiting its issue to a few individuals, on the other hand, would eliminate national sovereignty. If those individuals were the same financial elite who now control the dollar, the result would essentially be "full dollarization" for the world. Countries would not be able to issue their own currencies or draw on their own credit when they needed it for internal purposes. Like in El Salvador, their supply of currency would be limited and fixed. Whenever they had crises that put unusual demands on the national budget, they would not have the option of generating new money to meet those demands. They would be forced to tighten their belts and pursue "austerity measures," cutting out social goods essential to the poor; or to borrow from some global central bank such as the IMF, with all the globalization hazards that alternative has been shown to entail. Scarcity rather than abundance would be the order of the day.

A sovereign nation needs to be able to regulate its own money supply according to its own monetary policies; issue its own national currency; and contract debts and pay for them in that currency, without having to resort to a "reserve currency" over which it has no control. Rather than a single global currency, what is needed is a single stable *yardstick* against which governments can value their currencies, some independent measure in which merchants can negotiate their contracts and be sure of getting what they bargained for. But how is such a yardstick to be calibrated? Feet and meters can be calibrated and their relationship can be fixed because the yardstick against which they are measured is solid; but in the world of fluctuating supply and demand, the ground itself is moving. Some unit of value is needed that can withstand currency movements because it is independent of them. But what sort of unit might that be?

# Chapter 46
# BUILDING A BRIDGE:
# TOWARD A NEW BRETTON WOODS

*[S]uddenly they came to another gulf across the road. . . . [T]hey sat down to consider what they should do, and after serious thought the Scarecrow said, "Here is a great tree, standing close to the ditch. If the Tin Woodman can chop it down, so that it will fall to the other side, we can walk across it easily."*

*"That is a first-rate idea," said the Lion. "One would almost suspect you had brains in your head, instead of straw."*

– *The Wonderful Wizard of Oz,*
"The Journey to the Great Oz"

John Maynard Keynes had an idea. Instead of pegging currencies to the price of a single commodity -- gold -- they could be pegged to a "basket" of commodities: wheat, oil, copper, and so forth. He did not elaborate much on this idea, perhaps because the world economy was not then troubled by wild devaluations from speculative currency trading, and the statistical calculations for such a standard would have been hard to make on a daily basis in the 1940s. But Michael Rowbotham has elaborated on the proposal, calling it "a profound and democratic idea" that is "vital to any future sustainable and just world economy." He writes:

> Today, wheat grown in one country may, due to a devalued currency, cost a fraction of wheat grown in another. This leads to the country in which wheat is cheaper becoming a heavy exporter – regardless of need, or the capacity to produce better quality wheat in other locations. In addition, currency values can change dramatically and the situation can reverse. Critically, such wheat "prices" bear no relation to genuine comparative

advantage of climate, soil type, geography and even less to indigenous/local/regional needs. Neither does it have any stabilising element that would promote a long-term stability of production with relation to need. . . . [B]y imputing value to a nation's produce, and allowing this to determine the value of a nation's currency, one is imputing value to its resources, its labourers and acknowledging its own needs.[1]

An international trade unit could be established that consisted of the value of a basket of commodities broad enough to be representative of national products and prices and to withstand the manipulations of speculators. "With today's sophisticated trading data," says Rowbotham, "we could, literally, have a register of all globally traded commodities used to determine currency values." Although this unit for measuring value would include the *price* of gold and other commodities, it would not actually *be* gold or any other commodity, and it would not be a currency. It would just be a yardstick for pegging currencies and negotiating contracts. A global unit for pegging value would allow currencies to be exchanged across national borders at exact conversion rates, just as miles can be exactly converted into kilometers, and watches can be precisely set when crossing international date lines. Exchange rates would not be fixed forever, but they would be fixed everywhere. Changes in exchange rates would reflect the national market for real goods and services, not the international market for currencies. *Like in the Bretton Woods system, in which currencies were pegged to gold, there would be no room for speculation or hedging.* But the peg would be more stable than in the Bretton Woods system; and because it would not trade as a currency itself, it would not be in danger of becoming scarce.

## Private Basket-of-Commodities Models

To implement such a standard globally would take another round of Bretton Woods negotiations, which might not happen any time soon. In the meantime, private exchange systems have been devised on the same model, which are instructive in the meantime for understanding how such a system might work.

Community currency advocate Tom Greco has designed a "credit clearing exchange" that expands on the LETS system. It involves an exchange of credits tallied on a computer, without resorting to physical money at all. Values are computed using a market basket standard. The system is designed to provide merchants with a means of negotiating contracts privately in international trade units, which are measured against a basket of commodities rather than in particular currencies. Greco writes:

> The use of a market basket standard rather than a single commodity standard has two major advantages. First, it provides a more stable measure of value since fluctuation in the market price of any single commodity is likely to be greater than the fluctuation in the average price of a group of commodities. The transitory effects of weather and other factors affecting production and prices of individual commodities tend to average out. Secondly, the use of many commodities makes it more difficult for any trader or political entity to manipulate the value standard for his or her own advantage.[2]

In determining what commodities should be included in the basket, Greco suggests the following criteria. They should be (1) traded in several relatively free markets, (2) traded in relatively high volume, (3) important in satisfying basic human needs, (4) relatively stable in price over time, and (5) uniform in quality or subject to quality standards. Merchants using the credit clearing exchange could agree to accept payment in a national currency, but the amount due would depend on the currency's value in relation to this commodity-based unit of account. Once the unit had been established, the value of any circulating currency could be determined in relation to it, and exchange rates could be regularly computed and published for the benefit of traders.

Bernard Lietaer has proposed a commodity-based currency that he calls "New Currency," which could be initiated unilaterally by a private central bank without the need for new international agreements. The currency would be issued by the bank and backed by a basket of from three to a dozen different commodities for which there are existing international commodity markets. For example, 100 New Currency could be worth 0.05 ounces of gold, plus 3 ounces of silver, plus 15 pounds of copper, plus 1 barrel of oil, plus 5 pounds of wool. Since international commodity exchanges already exist for those resources, the New Currency would be automatically convertible to other national currencies.[3] Lietaer has also proposed an exchange system based on a basket-of-commodities standard that could be used privately by merchants without resorting to banks. Called the Trade Reference Currency (TRC), it involves the actual acquisition of commodities by an intermediary organization. The details are found on the TRC website at *www.terratrc.org*.

## Valuing Currencies Against the Consumer Price Index

Money reform advocate Frederick Mann, author of <u>The Economic Rape of America</u>, had another novel idea. Writing in 1998, he suggested that a private unit of exchange could be valued against *either* a designated basket of commodities, *or* the Commodity Research Bureau Index (CRB), *or* the Consumer Price Index (CPI). Using standardized price indices would make the unit particularly easy to calculate, since the figures for those indices are regularly reported around the world.

Mann called his currency unit the "Riegel," after E. C. Riegel, who wrote on the subject in the first half of the twentieth century. For the "basket" option, Mann proposed using cattle, cocoa, coffee, copper, corn, cotton, heating oil, hogs, lumber, natural gas, crude oil, orange juice, palladium, rough rice, silver, soybeans, soybean meal, soybean oil, sugar, unleaded gas, and wheat, in proportions that worked out to about $1 million in American money. This figure would be divided by 1 million to get 1 Riegel, making the Riegel worth about $1 in American money.

Another option would be to use the Commodity Research Bureau Index, which includes gold along with other commodities. But Mann noted that the CRB would give an unrealistic picture of typical prices, because individuals don't buy those commodities on a daily basis. A better alternative, he said, was the Consumer Price Index, which tallies the prices of things routinely bought by a typical family. In the United States, CPI figures are prepared monthly by the U.S. Bureau of Labor Statistics. Prices used to calculate the index are collected in 87 urban areas throughout the country and include price data from approximately 23,000 retail and service establishments, and data on rents from about 50,000 landlords and tenants.

When Mann was writing in 1998, the CPI was about $160. He suggested designating 1 Riegel as the CPI divided by 160, which would have again made it about $1 in 1998 prices.[4] Converting the cost of one Riegel's worth of goods in American dollars to the cost of those goods in other currencies would then be a simple mathematical proposition. The CPI's "core rate," which is used to track inflation, currently excludes goods with high price volatility, including food, energy, and the costs of owning rather than renting a home.[5] But to be a fair representation of the consumer value of a currency at any particular time, those essential costs would probably need to be factored in as well.

## A New Bretton Woods?

These proposals involve private international currency exchanges, but the same sort of reference unit could be used to stabilize exchange rates among official national currencies. Several innovators have proposed solutions to the exchange rate problem along these lines. Besides Michael Rowbotham in England, they include Lyndon LaRouche in the United States and Dr. Mahathir Mohamad in Malaysia, two political figures who are controversial in the West but have large followings and substantial influence internationally.

LaRouche shares the label "perennial candidate" with Jacob Coxey, having run for U.S. President eight times. He also shares a number of ideas with Coxey, including the proposal to make cheap national credit available for putting the unemployed to work developing national infrastructure. LaRouche has launched an appeal for a new Bretton Woods Conference to reorganize the world's financial system, a plan he says is endorsed by many international leaders. It would call for:

1. A new system of fixed exchange rates,

2. A treaty between governments to ban speculation in derivatives,

3. The cancellation or reorganization of international debt, and

4. The issuance of "credit" by national governments in sufficient quantity to bring their economies up to full employment, to be used for technical innovation and to develop critical infrastructure.[6]

La Rouche's proposed system of exchange rates would be based on an international unit of account pegged against the price of an agreed-upon basket of hard commodities. With such a system, he says, it would be "the currencies, not the commodities, [which are] given implicitly adjusted values, as based upon the basket of commodities used to define the unit."[7]

Dr. Mahathir is the outspoken Malaysian prime minister credited with sidestepping the "Asian crisis" that brought down the economies of his country's neighbors. (See Chapter 26.) The Middle Eastern news outlet <u>Al Jazeera</u> describes him as a visionary in the Islamic world, who has proven to be ahead of his time.[8] As noted earlier,

Islamic movements for monetary reform are of particular interest today because oil-rich Islamic countries are actively seeking alternatives for maintaining their currency reserves, and they may be the first to break away from the global bankers' private money scheme. In international conferences and forums, Islamic scholars have been vigorously debating monetary alternatives.

In 2002, Dr. Mahathir hosted a two-day seminar called "The Gold Dinar in Multilateral Trade," in which he expounded on the Gold Dinar as an alternative to the U.S. dollar for clearing trade balances. Islamic proposals for monetary reform have generally involved a return to gold as the only "sound" currency, but Dr. Mahathir stressed that he was not advocating a return to the "gold standard," in which paper money could be exchanged for its equivalent in gold on demand. Rather, he was proposing a system in which only trade *deficits* would be settled in gold. A British website called "Tax Free Gold" explains the proposed Gold Dinar system like this:

> It is not intended that there should be an actual gold dinar coin, or that it should be used in everyday transactions; *the gold dinar would be an international unit of account for international settlements between national banks.* If for example the balance of trade between Malaysia and Iran during one settlement period, probably three months, was such that Iran had made purchases of 100 million Malaysian Ringgits, and sales of 90 million Ryals, the difference in the value of these two amounts would be paid in gold dinars. . . . From the reports of the Malaysian conferences, we deduce that the gold dinar would be one ounce of gold or its equivalent value.[9]

At the 2002 seminar, Dr. Mahathir conceded that gold's market value is an unsound basis for valuing the national currency or the prices of national goods, because the value of gold is quite volatile and is subject to manipulation by speculators just as the U.S. dollar is. He said he was thinking instead along the lines of a basket-of-commodities standard for fixing the Gold Dinar's value. Pegging the Dinar to the value of an entire basket of commodities would make it more stable than if it were just tied to the whims of the gold market. The Gold Dinar has been called a direct challenge to the IMF, which forbids gold-based currencies; but that charge might be circumvented if the Dinar were actually valued against a basket of commodities, as Dr. Mahathir has proposed. It would then not be a gold "currency" but would be merely an international unit of account.

## The Urgent Need for Change

Other Islamic scholars have been debating how to escape the debt trap of the global bankers. Tarek El Diwany is a British expert in Islamic finance and the author of The Problem with Interest (2003). In a presentation at Cambridge University in 2002, he quoted a 1997 United Nations Human Develop Report underscoring the massive death tolls from the debt burden to the international bankers. The report stated:

> Relieved of their annual debt repayments, the severely indebted countries could use the funds for investments that in Africa alone would save the lives of about 21 million children by 2000 and provide 90 million girls and women with access to basic education.[10]

El Diwany commented, "The UNDP does not say that the bankers are killing the children, it says that the debt is. But who is creating the debt? The bankers are of course. *And they are creating the debt by lending money that they have manufactured out of nothing.* In return the developing world pays the developed world USD 700 million per day net in debt repayments."[11] He concluded his Cambridge presentation:

> But there is hope. The developing nations should not think that they are powerless in the face of their oppressors. Their best weapon now is the very scale of the debt crisis itself. A coordinated and simultaneous large scale default on international debt obligations could quite easily damage the Western monetary system, and the West knows it. There might be a war of course, or the threat of it, accompanied perhaps by lectures on financial morality from Washington, but would it matter when there is so little left to lose? In due course, every oppressed people comes to know that it is better to die with dignity than to live in slavery. Lenders everywhere should remember that lesson well.

We the people of the West can sit back and wait for the revolt, or we can be proactive and work to solve the problem at its source. We can start by designing legislation that would disempower the private international banking spider and empower the people worldwide. To be effective, this legislation would need to be negotiated internationally, and it would need to include an agreement for pegging or stabilizing national currencies on global markets.

## A Proposal for an International Currency Yardstick
## That Is Not a Currency

That brings us back to the question of how best to stabilize national currencies. The simplest and most comprehensive measure for calibrating an international currency yardstick seems to be the Consumer Price Index proposed by Mann, modified to reflect the real daily expenditures of consumers. To show how such a system might work, here is a hypothetical example. Assume that one International Currency Unit (ICU) equals the Consumer Price Index or some modified version of it, multiplied by some agreed-upon fraction:

On January 1 of our hypothetical year, a computer sampling of all national markets indicates that the value of one ICU in the United States is one dollar. The same goods that one dollar would purchase in the United States can be purchased in Mexico for 20 Mexican pesos and in England for half a British pound. These are the actual prices of the selected goods in each country's currency within its own borders, as determined by supply and demand. When you cross the Mexican border, you can trade a dollar bill for 10 pesos or a British pound for 20 pesos. On either side of the border, one ICU worth of goods can be bought with those sums of money in their respective denominations.

Carlos, who has a business in Mexico, buys 10,000 ICUs worth of goods from Sam, who has a business in the United States. Carlos pays for the goods with 2,000,000 Mexican pesos. Sam takes the pesos to his local branch of the now-federalized Federal Reserve and exchanges them at the prevailing exchange rate for 10,000 U.S. dollars. The Fed sells the pesos at the prevailing rate to other people interested in conducting trade with Mexico. When the Fed accumulates excess pesos (or a positive trade balance), they are sold to the Mexican government for U.S. dollars at the prevailing exchange rate. If the Mexican government runs out of U.S. dollars, the U.S. government can either keep the excess pesos in reserve or it can buy anything it wants that Mexico has for sale, including but not limited to gold and other commodities.

The following year, Mexico has an election and a change of governments. The new government decides to fund many new social programs with newly-printed currency, expanding the supply of Mexican pesos by 10 percent. Under the classical quantity theory of money, this increase in demand (money) will inflate prices, pushing the price of one ICU in Mexico to around 22 Mexican pesos. That is the conventional theory, but Keynes maintained that if the new pesos were used to produce new goods and services, supply would increase along with demand, leaving prices unaffected. (See Chapter 16.) Whichever theory proves to be correct, the point here is that the value of the peso would be determined by the actual price on the Mexican market of the goods in the modified Consumer Price Index, not by the quantity of Mexican currency traded on international currency markets by speculators.

Currencies would no longer be traded as commodities fetching what the market would bear, and they would no longer be vulnerable to speculative attack. They would just be coupons for units of value recognized globally, units stable enough that commercial traders could "bank" on them. If labor and materials were cheaper in one country than another, it would be because they were more plentiful or accessible there, not because the country's currency had been devalued by speculators. *The national currency would become what it should have been all along – a contract or promise to return value in goods or services of a certain worth, as measured against a universally recognized yardstick for determining value.*

# Chapter 47

# OVER THE RAINBOW: GOVERNMENT WITHOUT TAXES OR DEBT

*"Toto, I have a feeling we're not in Kansas anymore. We must be over the rainbow!"*

Going over the rainbow suggested a radical visionary shift, a breakthrough into a new way of seeing the world. We have come to the end of the Yellow Brick Road, and only a radical shift in our concepts of money and banking will save us from the cement wall looming ahead. We the people got lost in a labyrinth of debt when we allowed paper money to represent an illusory sum of gold held by private bankers, who multiplied it many times over in the guise of "fractional reserve" lending. The result was a Ponzi scheme that has pumped the global money supply into a gigantic credit bubble. As bond investor Bill Gross said in a February 2004 newsletter, we have been "skipping down this yellow brick road of capitalism, paved not with gold, but with thick coats of debt/leverage that requires constant maintenance."

The levees that have kept a flood of debt-leverage from collapsing the economy showed signs of cracking on February 27, 2007, when the Dow Jones Industrial Average suddenly dropped by more than 500 points. The drop was triggered by a series of events like those initiating the Great Crash of 1929. A nearly 9 percent decline in China's stock market set off a wave of selling in U.S. markets to satisfy "margin calls" (requiring investors using credit to add cash to their accounts to bring them to a certain minimum balance). The Chinese drop, in turn, was triggered by an intentional credit squeeze by Chinese officials, who were concerned that Chinese homeowners were mortgaging their homes and businessmen were pledging their businesses as collateral to play the over-leveraged Chinese stock market, just as American investors did in the 1920s.[1] Commentators suggested that the Dow fell by *only* 500 points because of the behind-the-scenes maneuverings of the Plunge Protection Team, the Counterparty Risk Management Policy Group and the Federal Reserve.[2] But it was all just window-dressing, a dog and pony show to keep investors lulled into complacency, inducing them to keep betting on a stock market nag on its last legs. A bigger crisis next time might not be so easy to conceal behind a facade of prosperity.

Like at the end of the Roaring Twenties, we are again looking down the trough of the "business cycle," mortgaged up to the gills and at risk of losing it all. We own nothing that can't be taken away. The housing market could go into a tailspin and so could the stock market. The dollar could collapse and so could our savings. Even social security and pensions could soon be things of the past. Before the economy collapses and our savings and security go with it, we need to reverse the sleight of hand that created the bankers' Ponzi scheme. The Constitutional provision that "Congress shall have the power to coin money" needs to be updated so that it covers the national currency in all its forms, including the 97 percent now created with accounting entries by private commercial banks. That modest change could transform the dollar from a vice for wringing the lifeblood out of a nation of sharecroppers into a bell for ringing in the millennial abundance envisioned by our forefathers. The government could actually *eliminate* taxes and the federal debt while *expanding* the services it provides.

## The Puzzle Assembled

The pieces to the monetary puzzle have been concealed by layers of deception built up over 400 years, and it has taken some time to unravel them; but the picture has now come clear, and we are ready to recap what we have found. The global debt web has been spun from a string of frauds, deceits and sleights of hand, including:

• *"Fractional reserve" banking.* Formalized in 1694 with the charter for the Bank of England, the modern banking system involves credit issued by private bankers that is ostensibly backed by "reserves." At one time, these reserves consisted of gold; but today they are merely government securities (promises to pay). The banking system lends these securities many times over, essentially counterfeiting them.

- *The "gold standard."* In the nineteenth century, the government was admonished not to issue paper *fiat* money on the ground that it would produce dangerous inflation. The bankers insisted that paper money had to be backed by gold. What they failed to disclose was that there was not nearly enough gold in their own vaults to back the privately-issued paper notes laying claim to it. The bankers themselves were dangerously inflating the money supply based on a fictitious "gold standard" that allowed them to issue loans many times over on the same gold reserves, collecting interest each time.

- *The "Federal" Reserve.* Established in 1913 to create a national money supply, the Federal Reserve is not federal, and today it keeps nothing in "reserve" except government bonds or I.O.U.s. It is a private banking corporation authorized to print and sell its own Federal Reserve Notes to the government in return for government bonds, putting the taxpayers in perpetual debt for money created privately with accounting entries. Except for coins, which make up only about one one-thousandth of the money supply, the *entire* U.S. money supply is now created by the private Federal Reserve and private banks, by extending loans to the government and to individuals and businesses.

- *The federal debt and the money supply.* The United States went off the gold standard in the 1930s, but the "fractional reserve" system continued, backed by "reserves" of government bonds. The federal debt these securities represent is never paid off but is continually rolled over, forming the basis of the national money supply. As a result of this highly inflationary scheme, by January 2007 the federal debt had mushroomed to $8.679 trillion and was approaching the point at which the interest alone would be more than the public could afford to pay.

- *The federal income tax.* Considered unconstitutional for over a century, the federal income tax was legalized in 1913 by the Sixteenth Amendment to the Constitution. It was instituted primarily to secure a reliable source of money to pay the interest due to the bankers on the government's securities, and that continues to be its principal use today.

- *The Federal Deposit Insurance Corporation and the International Monetary Fund.* A principal function of the Federal Reserve was to bail out banks that got over-extended in the fractional-reserve shell game, using money created in "open market" operations by the Fed. When the Federal Reserve failed in that backup function, the FDIC and then the IMF were instituted, ensuring that mega-banks considered "too big to fail" would get bailed out no matter what unwarranted risks they took.

• *The "free market."* The theory that businesses in America prosper or fail due to "free market forces" is a myth. While smaller corporations and individuals who miscalculate their risks may be left to their fate in the market, mega-banks and corporations considered too big to fail are protected by a form of federal welfare available only to the rich and powerful. Other distortions in free market forces result from the covert manipulations of a variety of powerful entities. Virtually every market is now manipulated, whether by federal mandate or by institutional speculators, hedge funds, and large multinational banks colluding on trades.

• *The Plunge Protection Team and the Counterparty Risk Management Policy Group (CRMPG).* Federal manipulation is done by the Working Group on Financial Markets, also known as the Plunge Protection Team (PPT). The PPT is authorized to use U.S. Treasury funds to rig markets in order to "maintain investor confidence," keeping up the appearance that all is well. Manipulation is also effected by a private fraternity of big New York banks and investment houses known as the CRMPG, which was set up to bail its members out of financial difficulty by colluding to influence markets, again with the blessings of the government and to the detriment of the small investors on the other side of these orchestrated trades.

• *The "floating" exchange rate.* Manipulation and collusion also occur in international currency markets. Rampant currency speculation was unleashed in 1971, when the United States defaulted on its promise to redeem its dollars in gold internationally. National currencies were left to "float" against each other, trading as if they were commodities rather than receipts for fixed units of value. The result was to remove the yardstick for measuring value, leaving currencies vulnerable to attack by international speculators prowling in these dangerous commercial waters.

• *The short sale.* To bring down competitor currencies, speculators use a device called the "short sale" – the sale of currency the speculator does not own but has theoretically "borrowed" just for purposes of sale. Like "fractional reserve" lending, the short sale is actually a form of counterfeiting. When speculators sell a currency short in massive quantities, its value is artificially forced down, forcing down the value of goods traded in it.

- *"Globalization" and "free trade."* Before a currency can be brought down by speculative assault, the country must be induced to open its economy to "free trade" and to make its currency freely convertible into other currencies. The currency can then be attacked and devalued, allowing national assets to be picked up at fire sale prices and forcing the country into bankruptcy. The bankrupt country must then borrow from international banks and the IMF, which impose as a condition of debt relief that the national government may not issue its own money. If the government tries to protect its resources or its banks by nationalizing them for the benefit of its own citizens, it is branded "communist," "socialist" or "terrorist" and is replaced by one that is friendlier to "free enterprise." Locals who fight back are termed "terrorists" or "insurgents."

- *Inflation myths.* The runaway inflation suffered by Third World countries has been blamed on irresponsible governments running the money printing presses, when in fact these disasters have usually been caused by speculative attacks on the national currency. Devaluing the currency forces prices to shoot up overnight. "Creeping inflation" like that seen in the United States today is also blamed on governments irresponsibly printing money, when it is actually caused by *private banks* inflating the money supply with *debt*. Banks advance new money as loans that must be repaid with interest, but the banks don't create the interest necessary to service the loans. New loans must continually be taken out to obtain the money to pay the interest, forcing prices up in an attempt to cover this new cost, spiraling the economy into perpetual price inflation.

- *The "business cycle."* As long as banks keep making low-interest loans, the money supply expands and business booms; but when the credit bubble gets too large, the central bank goes into action to deflate it. Interest rates are raised, loans are "called," and the money supply shrinks, forcing debtors into foreclosure, delivering their homes and farms to the banks. This is called the "business cycle," as if it were a natural condition like the weather. In fact, it is a natural characteristic only of a monetary scheme in which money comes into existence as a debt to private banks for "reserves" of something lent many times over.

- *The home mortgage boondoggle.* Most of the money created by banks today originates with the "monetization" of home mortgages. The borrower thinks he is borrowing pre-existing funds, when the bank is just turning his promise to repay into an "asset" secured by real property. By the time the mortgage is paid off, the borrower has usually paid the bank more in interest than was owed on the original loan; and if he defaults, the bank winds up with the house, although the money advanced to purchase it was created out of thin air.

• *The housing bubble.* The dollar and the economy are currently being supported by a housing boom that was initiated when the Fed pushed interest rates to very low levels after the stock market collapsed in 2000, significantly shrinking the money supply. "Easy" credit pumped the money supply back up and saved the market investments of the Fed's member banks, but it also led to a housing bubble that must eventually burst, sending the economy to the trough of the "business cycle" once again.

• *The Adjustable Rate Mortgage or ARM.* After interest rates were dropped to very low levels, the housing bubble was fanned into a blaze through a series of high-risk changes in mortgage instruments, including variable rate loans that have allowed nearly anyone to qualify to buy a home who will take the bait. About half of all U.S. mortgages today are at "adjustable" interest rates. Purchasers are lulled by "teaser" rates into believing they can afford mortgages that are liable to propel them into inextricable debt if not into bankruptcy. Payments can increase by 50 percent after 6 years just by their terms, and can increase by 100 percent if interest rates go up by a mere 2 percent in 6 years.

• *The secret bankruptcy of the banks.* The banks themselves are taking enormous risks with these housing loans, as well as with very risky investments known as "derivatives," which are basically side bets that a company's stock or some other asset will go up or down. Banks have been led into these dangerous waters because traditional commercial banking has proven to be an unprofitable venture. While banks have the power to create money as loans, they also have the obligation to balance their books; and when borrowers default, the losses must be made up from the banks' profits. Faced with a wave of bad debts and lost business, banks have kept afloat by branching out into the economically destructive derivatives business, and by colluding with each other and the government to arrange periodic stealth bailouts when banks considered "too big to fail" become insolvent.

• *"Vulture capitalism" and the derivatives cancer.* At one time, banks served the community by providing loans to developing businesses; but today this essential credit function is being replaced by a form of "vulture capitalism," in which bank investment departments and affiliated hedge funds are buying out shareholders and bleeding businesses of their profits, using loans of "phantom money" created on a computer screen. Banks are also funding speculative derivative bets, in which money that should be going into economic productivity is merely gambled on money making money in the casino of the markets. Outstanding derivatives are now counted in the hundreds of trillions of dollars, many times the money supply of the world.

• *Moral hazard.* The derivatives bubble is showing clear signs of imploding; and when it does, those banks considered too big to fail will expect to be bailed out from the consequences of their risky loans just as they have been in the past . . . .

## Waking Up in Kansas

It is at this point in our story, if it is to have a happy ending, that we the people must snap ourselves awake, stand up, and say "Enough!" The bankers' extremity is our opportunity. We can be kept indebted and enslaved only if we continue to underwrite bank profligacy. As Mike Whitney wrote in March 2007, "The Federal Reserve will keep greasing the printing presses and diddling the interest rates until someone takes away the punch bowl and the party comes to an end."[3] It is up to us, an awakened and informed populace, to take away the punch bowl. Private commercial banking as we know it is obsolete, and the vulture capitalist investment banking that has come to dominate the banking business is a parasite on productivity, serving its own interests at the expense of the public's. Rather than propping up a bankrupt banking system, Congress could and should put insolvent banks into receivership, claim them as public assets, and operate them as agencies serving the depository and credit needs of the people.

Besides the imploding banking system, a second tower is now poised to fall. The U.S. federal debt is close to the point at which just the interest on it will be more than the taxpayers can afford to pay; and just when foreign investors are most needed to support this debt, China and other creditors are threatening to demand not only the interest but the principal back on their hefty loans. The debt has reached its mathematical limits, forcing another paradigm shift if the economy is to survive. Will the collapse of the debt-based house of cards be the end of the world as we know it? Or will it be the way through the looking glass, a clarion call for change? We can step out of the tornado into debtors' prison, or we can step into the technicolor cornucopia of a money system based on the ingenuity and productivity that are the true wealth of a nation and its people.

## Home at Last

In the happy ending to our modern monetary fairytale, Congress takes back the power to create money in all its forms, including the money created with accounting entries by private banks. Highlights of this satisfying ending include:

• Elimination of personal income taxes, allowing workers to keep their wages, putting spending money in people's pockets, stimulating economic growth.

• Elimination of a mounting federal debt that must otherwise burden and bind future generations.

• The availability of funds for a whole range of government services that have always been needed but could not be afforded under the "fractional reserve" system, including improved education, environmental cleanup and preservation, universal health care, restoration of infrastructure, independent medical research, and development of alternative energy sources.

• A social security system that is sufficiently funded to support retirees, replacing private pensions that keep workers chained to unfulfilling jobs and keep employers unable to compete in international markets.

• Elimination of the depressions of the "business cycle" that have resulted when interest rates and reserve requirements have been manipulated by the Fed to rein in out-of-control debt bubbles.

• The availability of loans at interest rates that are not subject to unpredictable manipulation by a private central bank but remain modest and fixed, something borrowers can rely on in making their business decisions and in calculating their risks.

• Elimination of the aggressive currency devaluations and economic warfare necessary to sustain a money supply built on debt. Exchange rates become stable, the U.S. dollar becomes self-sustaining, and the United States and other countries become self-reliant, trading freely with their neighbors without being dependent on foreign creditors or having to dominate and control other countries and markets.

This happy ending is well within the realm of possibility, but it won't happen unless we the people get our boots on and start marching. We have become conditioned by our television sets to expect some hero politician to save the day, but the hero never appears, because both sides dominating the debate are controlled by the banking/industrial cartel. Nothing will happen until we wake up, get organized, and form a plan. What sort of plan? The platform of a revamped Populist/Greenback/American Nationalist/Whig Party might include:

1. A bill to update the Constitutional provision that "Congress shall have the power to coin money" so that it reads, "Congress shall have the power to create the national currency in all its forms, including not only coins and paper dollars but the nation's credit issued as commercial loans."

2. A call for an independent audit of the Federal Reserve and the giant banks that own it, including an investigation of:

    • The creation of money through "open market operations,"

    • The market manipulations of the Plunge Protection Team and the CRMPG,

    • The massive derivatives positions of a small handful of mega-banks and their use to rig markets, and

    • The use of "creative accounting" to mask bank insolvency. Any banks found to be insolvent would be delivered into FDIC receivership and to the disposal of Congress.

3. Repeal of the Sixteenth Amendment to the Constitution, construed as authorizing a federal income tax.

4. Either repeal of the Federal Reserve Act as in violation of the Constitution, or amendment of the Act to make the Federal Reserve a truly federal agency, administered by the U.S. Treasury.

5. Public acquisition of a network of banks to serve as local bank branches of the newly-federalized banking system, either by FDIC takeover of insolvent banks or by the purchase of viable banks with newly-issued U.S. currency. Besides serving depository banking functions, these national banks would be authorized to service the credit needs of the public by advancing the "full faith and

credit of the United States" as loans. Interest on advances of the national credit would be returned to the Treasury to be used in place of taxes.

6. Elimination of money creation by private "fractional reserve" lending. Private lending would be limited to the recycling of existing money or to the lending of new funds borrowed from the newly-federalized Federal Reserve.

7. Authorization for the Treasury to buy back and retire all of its outstanding federal debt, using newly-issued U.S. Notes or Federal Reserve Notes. In most cases this could be done online, without physical paper transfers.

8. Authorization for Congress, acting through the Treasury, to issue new currency annually to be spent on programs that promote the general welfare. To keep supply in balance with demand and prevent inflation, the new currency would be spent on programs that contributed new goods and services to the economy, and it would be limited to a sum equal to the unused productive capacity of the national work force.

9. Authorization for Congress to fund programs that would return money to the Treasury in place of taxes, including the development of cheap effective energy alternatives (wind, solar, ocean wave, etc.), which could be sold to the public for a fee.

10. Regulation and control of the exploding derivatives crisis, either by imposing a modest .25 percent tax on all derivative trades in order to track and regulate them, or by imposing an outright ban on derivatives trading. If the handful of banks responsible for 97 percent of all derivative trades were found after audit to be insolvent, they could be put into receivership and their derivative trades could be unwound by the FDIC as receiver.

11. Initiation of a new round of international agreements modeled on the Bretton Woods Accords, addressing the following monetary issues, among others:

    • The pegging of national currency exchange rates to the value either of an agreed-upon standardized price index or an agreed-upon "basket" of commodities;

    • The international regulation of or elimination of speculation in derivatives, short sales, and other forms of trading used to manipulate markets; and

- The elimination of burdensome and unfair international debts. This could be done by simply writing the debts off the books of the issuing banks, reversing the sleight of hand by which the loan money was created in the first place.

12. Other domestic reforms that might be addressed include election reform, campaign finance reform, lobby reform, media reform, the development of sustainable energy, widespread affordable housing, and basic universal health coverage.

Like the earlier Greenback and Populist Parties, this grassroots political party might not win any major elections; but it could raise awareness, and when the deluge hit, it could provide an ark. We need to spark a revolution in the popular understanding of money and banking while free speech is still available on the Internet, in independent media and in books. New ideas and alternatives need to be communicated and put into action before the door to our debtors' prison slams shut. The place to begin is in the neighborhood, with brainstorming sessions in living rooms in the Populist tradition. The Populists were the people, and what they sought was a people's currency. Reviving the "American system" of government-issued money would not represent a radical departure from the American tradition. It would represent a radical return. Like Dorothy, we the people would finally have come home.

# GLOSSARY

*Adjustable Rate Mortgage (ARM)*: a type of mortgage loan program in which the interest rate and payments are adjusted as frequently as every month. The purpose of the program is to allow mortgage interest rates to fluctuate with market conditions.

*Bankrupt*: unable to pay one's debts, insolvent, having liabilities in excess of a reasonable market value of assets held.

*Bear raid*: the practice of targeting the stock of a particular company for take-down by massive short selling, either for quick profits or for corporate takeover.

*Bears versus bulls*: Bears think the market will go down; bulls think it will go up.

*Book value*: the total assets of a company minus its liabilities such as debt.

*Bubble*: an illusory inflation in price that is grossly out of proportion to underlying values.

*Business cycle*: a predictable long-term pattern of alternating periods of economic growth (recovery) and decline (recession).

*Capitalization*: market value of a company's stock.

*Cartel*: a combination of producers of any product joined together to control its production, sale and price, so as to obtain a monopoly and restrict competition in that industry or commodity.

*Central bank*: a non-commercial bank, which may or may not be independent of government, which has some or all of the following functions: conduct monetary policy; oversee the stability of the financial system; issue currency notes; act as banker to the government; supervise financial institutions and regulate payments systems.

*Chinese walls*: information barriers implemented in firms to separate and isolate persons within a firm who make investment decisions from persons within a firm who are privy to undisclosed material information which may influence those decisions, in order to safeguard inside information and ensure there is no improper trading.

*Compound interest*: interest calculated not only on the initial principal but on the accumulated interest of prior payment periods.

*Conspiracy*: an agreement between two or more persons to commit a crime or accomplish a legal purpose through illegal action.

*Counterfeit*: to make a copy of, usually with the intent to defraud.

*Counterparties*: parties to a contract, usually having a potential conflict of interest. Within the financial services sector, the term market counterparty is used to refer to national banks, governments, national monetary authorities and multinational monetary organizations such as the World Bank Group, which act as the ultimate guarantor for loans and indemnities. The term may also be applied to companies acting in that role.

*Currency*: Money in any form when in actual use as a medium of exchange, facilitating the transfer of goods and services.

*Customs*: duties on imported goods.

*Deficit spending*: government spending in excess of what the government takes in as tax revenue.

*Deflation*: A contraction in the supply of money or credit that results in declining prices; the opposite of inflation.

*Demand deposits*: bank deposits that can be withdrawn on demand at any time without notice. Most checking and savings accounts are demand deposits.

*Depository*: a bank that holds funds deposited by others and facilitates exchanges of those funds.

*Derivative*: A financial instrument whose characteristics and value depend upon the characteristics and value of an "underlier," typically a commodity, bond, equity or currency. Familiar examples of derivatives include "futures" and "options."

*Discount*: The difference between the face amount of a note or mortgage and the price at which the instrument is sold on the market.

*Equity*: ownership interest in a corporation.

*Equity market*: the stock market – a system through which company shares are traded, offering investors an opportunity to participate in a company's success through an increase in its stock price.

*Excise taxes*: internal taxes imposed on certain non-essential consumer goods.

*Federal funds rate*: the rate that banks charge each other on overnight loans made between them.

*Federal Reserve*: the central bank of the United States; a system of banks charged with regulating the U.S. money supply, mainly by buying and selling U.S. securities and setting the discount interest rate (the interest rate at which the Federal Reserve lends money to commercial banks). Although designated "federal," the Federal Reserve is actually a private banking corporation.

*Federal Reserve banks*: The banks that carry out Federal Reserve operations, including controlling the money supply and regulating member banks. There are 12 District Feds, headquartered in Boston, New York, Philadelphia, Cleveland, St. Louis, San Francisco, Richmond, Atlanta, Chicago, Minneapolis, Kansas City, and Dallas.

*Floating exchange rate*: a foreign exchange rate that is not fixed by national authorities but varies according to supply and demand.

*Fiat*: Latin for "let it be done;" an arbitrary order or decree.

*Fiat money*: Legal tender, especially paper currency, authorized by a government but not based on or convertible into gold or silver.

*Fiscal year*: The U.S. government's fiscal year begins on October 1 of the previous calendar year and ends on September 30.

*Float*: The number of shares of a security that are outstanding and available for trading by the public.

*Fraud*: a false representation of a matter of fact, whether by words or by conduct, by false or misleading allegations, or by concealment of that which should have been disclosed, which deceives and is intended to deceive another so that he shall act upon it to his legal injury.

*Free trade*: trade between nations unrestricted by import duties, export bounties, domestic production subsidies, trade quotas, or import licenses. Critics say that in more developed nations, free trade results in jobs being "exported" abroad, where labor costs are lower; while in less developed nations, workers and the environment are exploited by foreign financiers, who take labor and raw materials in exchange for paper money the national government could have created itself.

*Globalization*: the tendency of businesses, technologies, or philosophies to spread throughout the world, or the process of making them spread throughout the world.

*Gold standard*: a monetary system in which currency is convertible into fixed amounts of gold.

*Gross domestic product*: the value of all final goods and services produced in a country in a year.

*Hedge funds*: investment companies that use high-risk techniques, such as borrowing money and selling short, in an effort to make extraordinary capital gains for their investors.

*Hyperinflation*: a period of rapid inflation that leaves a country's currency virtually worthless.

*Inflation*: a persistent increase in the level of consumer prices or a persistent decline in the purchasing power of money, caused by an increase in available currency and credit beyond the proportion of available goods and services.

*Infrastructure*: the set of interconnected structural elements that provide the framework for supporting the entire structure. In a country, it consists of the basic facilities needed for the country's functioning, providing a public framework under which private enterprise can operate safely and efficiently.

*Investment banks* help companies and governments issue securities, help investors purchase securities, manage financial assets, trade securities and provide financial advice. Unlike commercial banks, they do not take deposits or make commercial loans; but the lines have blurred with the 1999 repeal of the Glass Steagall Act, which prohibited the same bank from taking deposits and underwriting securities. Leading investment banks include Merrill Lynch, Salomon Smith Barney, Morgan Stanley Dean Witter and Goldman Sachs.

*Legal tender*: money that must legally be accepted in the payment of debts.

*Leveraging*: buying with borrowed money. *Leverage* is the degree to which an investor or business is using borrowed money.

*Liquidity*: the ability of an asset to be converted into cash quickly and without discount.

*Margin*: an investor who buys on margin buys with money he doesn't have, borrowing a percentage of the purchase price from the broker, to be repaid when the stock or other investment goes up. People usually open margin accounts, not because they're short of cash, but because they can "leverage" their investment by buying many times the amount of stock they could have bought if they had paid the full price.

*Margin call*: a broker's demand on an investor using borrowed money to deposit additional money or securities to bring the margin account up to a certain minimum balance. If one or more of the investor's securities have decreased in value past a certain point, the broker will call and require the investor either to deposit more money in the account or to sell off some of the stock.

*Monetize*: to convert government debt from securities into currency that can be used to purchase goods and services.

*Money center bank*: a large bank in a major financial center which borrows from and lends to governments, corporations and other banks rather than to consumers.

*Money market*: the trade in short-term, low-risk securities, such as certificates of deposit and U.S. Treasury notes.

*Money supply*: the entire quantity of bills, coins, loans, credit, and other liquid instruments in a country's economy. "Liquid" instruments are those easily convertible to cash. The money supply has traditionally been reported by the Federal Reserve in three categories – M1, M2, and M3, although it quit reporting M3 after March 2006. M1 is what we usually think of as money – coins, dollar bills, and the money in our checking accounts. M2 is M1 plus savings accounts, money market funds, and other individual or "small" time deposits. M3 is M1 and M2 plus institutional and other larger time deposits (including institutional money market funds) and eurodollars (American dollars circulating abroad).

*Moral hazard*: the risk that the existence of a contract will change the behavior of the parties to it; for example, a firm insured for fire may take fewer fire precautions. In the case of banks, it is the hazard that they will expect to be bailed out from their profligate ways because they have been bailed out in the past.

*Mortgage*: A loan to finance the purchase of real estate, usually with specified payment periods and interest rates.

*Multiplier effect*: according to Investopedia, "the expansion of a country's money supply that results from banks being able to lend."

*Oligarchy*: government by a few, usually the rich, for their own advantage.

*Open market operations*: the buying and selling of government securities in the open market in order to expand or contract the amount of money in the banking system.

*Ponzi scheme*: a form of pyramid scheme in which investors are paid with the money of later investors. Charles Ponzi was an engaging Boston ex-convict who defrauded investors out of $6 million in the

1920s, in a scheme in which he promised them a 400 percent return on redeemed postal reply coupons. For a while, he paid earlier investors with the money of later investors; but eventually he just collected without repaying. The scheme earned him ten years in jail.

*Posse comitatus*: a statute preventing the U.S. active military from participating in American law enforcement.

*Plutocracy*: a form of government in which the supreme power is lodged in the hands of the wealthy classes; government by the rich.

*Privatization*: the sale of public assets to private corporations.

*Proprietary trading:* a term used in investment banking to describe when a bank trades stocks, bonds, options, commodities, or other items with its own money as opposed to its customers' money, so as to make a profit for itself. Although investment banks are usually defined as businesses which assist other business in raising money in the capital markets (by selling stocks or bonds), in fact most of the largest investment banks make the majority of their profit from trading activities.

*Receivership*: a form of bankruptcy in which a company can avoid liquidation by reorganizing with the help of a court-appointed trustee.

*Reflation*: the intentional reversal of deflation through monetary action by a government.

*Republic*: A political order in which the supreme power lies in a body of citizens who are entitled to vote for officers and representatives responsible to them.

*Repurchase agreement ("repo")*: The sale or purchase of securities with an agreement to reverse the transaction at an agreed future date and price. Repos allow the Federal Reserve to inject liquidity on one day and withdraw it on another with a single transaction.

*Reserve requirement*: The percentage of funds the Federal Reserve Board requires that member banks maintain on deposit at all times.

*Security*: A type of transferable interest representing financial value; an investment instrument issued by a corporation, government, or other organization that offers evidence of debt or equity.

*Short sale*: Borrowing a security and selling it in the hope of being able to repurchase it more cheaply before repaying the lender. A *naked short sale* is a short sale in which the seller does not buy shares to replace those he borrowed.

*Specie*: precious metal (usually gold or silver) used to back money.

*Structural adjustment*: a term used by the International Monetary Fund (IMF) for the changes it recommends for developing countries that want new loans, including internal changes (notably privatization and deregulation) as well as external ones (especially the reduction of barriers to trade); a package of "free market" reforms designed to create economic growth to generate income to pay off accumulated debt.

*Tariff*: a tax placed on imported or exported goods (sometimes called a customs duty).

*Tight money*: insufficient money to go around, generally because the money supply has been intentionally contracted by the financial establishment.

*Time deposits*: deposits that the depositor knows are being lent out and that he can't have back for a certain period of time.

*Transaction deposit*: a term used by the Federal Reserve for checkable deposits (deposits on which checks can be drawn) and other accounts that can be used directly as cash without withdrawal limits or restrictions. They are also called *demand deposits*, since they can be withdrawn on demand at any time without notice. Most checking and savings accounts are demand deposits.

*Trust*: a combination of firms or corporations for the purpose of reducing competition and controlling prices throughout a business or an industry.

*Usury*: the practice of lending money and charging the borrower interest, especially at an exorbitant or illegally high rate.

*Uptick rule*: the SEC rule requiring that a stock's price be higher than its previous sale price before the stock may be sold short.

# SELECTED BIBLIOGRAPHY OF BOOKS
# AND SUGGESTED READING

Barber, Lucy, <u>Marching on Washington: The Forging of an American Political Tradition</u> (University of California Press, 2004).

Chicago Federal Reserve, <u>Modern Money Mechanics</u>, originally produced and distributed free by the Public Information Center of the Federal Reserve Bank of Chicago, Chicago, Illinois, now available on the Internet at http://landru.i-link-2.net/monques/mmm2.html.

De Fremery, Robert, <u>Rights Vs. Privileges</u> (San Anselmo, California: Provocative Press, undated).

Emry, Sheldon, <u>Billions for the Bankers, Debts for the People</u> (Phoenix, Arizona: America's Promise Broadcast, 1984), reproduced at www.libertydollar.org.

Engdahl, William, <u>A Century of War</u> (New York: Paul & Co., 1993).

Franklin, Benjamin, <u>The Autobiography of Benjamin Franklin</u> (Dover Thrift Edition, 1996).

Gatto, John Taylor, <u>The Underground History of American Education</u> (Oxford, New York: Oxford Village Press, 2000-2001).

Gibson, Donald, <u>Battling Wall Street: The Kennedy Presidency</u> (New York: Sheridan Square Press, 1994).

Goodwin, Jason, <u>Greenback</u> (New York: Henry Holt & Co., LLC, 2003).

Greco, Thomas, <u>Money and Debt: A Solution to the Global Debt Crisis</u> (Tucson, Arizona, 1990).

Greco, Thomas, <u>New Money for Healthy Communities</u> (Tucson, Arizona, 1994).

Griffin, G. Edward, <u>The Creature from Jekyll Island</u> (Westlake Village, California: American Media, 1998).

Guttman, Robert, How Credit-Money Shapes the Economy (Armonk, New York: M. E. Sharpe, 1994).

Hoskins, Richard, War Cycles, Peace Cycles (Lynchburg, Virginia: Virginia Publishing Company, 1985).

Lietaer, Bernard, The Future of Money: Creating New Wealth, Work and a Wiser World (Century, 2001).

Patman, Wright, A Primer on Money (Government Printing Office, prepared for the Sub-committee on Domestic Finance, House of Representatives, Committee on Banking and Currency, Eighty-Eighth Congress, 2nd session, 1964).

Perkins, John, Confessions of an Economic Hit Man (San Francisco: Berrett-Koehler Publishers, Inc., 2004).

Rothbard, Murray, Wall Street, Banks, and American Foreign Policy (Center for Libertarian Studies, 1995).

Rowbothan, Michael, Goodbye America! Globalisation, Debt and the Dollar Empire (Charlbury, England: Jon Carpenter Publishing, 2000).

Rowbotham, Michael, The Grip of Death: A Study of Modern Money, Debt Slavery and Destructive Economics (Charlbury, Oxfordshire: Jon Carpenter Publishing, 1998).

Schwantes, Carlos, Coxey's Army: An American Odyssey (Moscow, Idaho: University of Idaho Press, 1994).

Weatherford, Jack, The History of Money (New York: Crown Publishers, Inc., 1997).

Wiggin, Addison, The Demise of the Dollar ( Hoboken, New Jersey: John Wiley & Sons, 2005).

Zarlenga, Stephen, The Lost Science of Money (Valatie, New York: American Monetary Institute, 2002).

# Endnotes

## Introduction

1. Hans Schicht, "The Death of Banking and Macro Politics," 321gold.com/ editorials (February 9, 2005).

2. Carroll Quigley, <u>Tragedy and Hope: A History of the World in our Time</u> (New York: Macmillan Company, 1966), page 324.

3. Quoted in U. Ibrahim-Morrison, et al., "Building Sound Economic Foundations," <u>Alarm Magazine</u> (May 1995).

4. Henry C K Liu, "The Global Economy in Transition," <u>Asia Times</u> (September 16, 2003). For Liu's bio, see "The Complete Henry C K Liu," <u>Asia Times</u> (May 11, 2007).

5. In the Foreword to Irving Fisher, <u>100% Money</u> (1935), reprinted by Pickering and Chatto Ltd. (1996).

6. Quoted in "Someone Has to Print the Nation's Money . . . So Why Not Our Government?", <u>Monetary Reform Online</u>, reprinted from <u>Victoria Times Colonist</u> (October 16, 1996).

7. Michel Chossudovsky, University of Ottawa, "Financial Warfare," hartford-hwp.com (September 23, 1998).

8. Michael Hodges, "America's Total Debt Report," <u>Grandfather Economic Report</u>, http://whodges.home.att.net (2006).

9. "Crumbling Nation? U.S. Infrastructure Gets a 'D'", MSNBC.com (March 9, 2005).

10. Victor Thorn, "Who Controls the Federal Reserve System?", rense.com (May 9, 2002).

11. Christopher Mark, "The Grand Deception: The Theft of America and the World, Part III," prisonplanet.com (March 15, 2003).

12. Murray Rothbard, "The Solution," <u>The Freeman</u> (November 1995).

13. James Galbraith, "Self-fulfilling Prophets: Inflated Zeal at the Federal Reserve," <u>The American Prospect</u> (June 23, 1994).

14. Anton Chaitkin, "How Henry Carey and the American Nationalists Build the Modern World," <u>American Almanac</u> (May 1977).

## Chapter 1

1. Henry Littlefield, "The Wizard of Oz: Parable on Populism," American Quarterly 16 (Spring, 1964), page 50, reprinted at amphigory.com/oz.htm.

2. H. Rockoff, "'The Wizard of Oz' as a Monetary Allegory," <u>Journal of Political Economy</u> 98:739-60 (1990). See also Mark Lovewell, "Yellow Brick Road: The Economics Behind the Wizard of Oz," www.ryerson.ca/ ~lovewell/oz.html (2000); Bill O'Rahilly, "Goodbye, Yellow Brick Road," <u>Financial Times</u> (August 5, 2003).

3. Tim Ziaukas, "100 Years of Oz: Baum's 'Wizard of Oz' as Gilded Age Public Relations," <u>Public Relations Quarterly</u> (Fall 1998).

4. "Populism," <u>Wikipedia</u> (April 2006).

5. David Parker, "The Rise and Fall of The Wonderful Wizard of Oz as a 'Parable on Populism,'" <u>Journal of the Georgia Association of Historians</u> 15:49-63 (1995).

6. Lawrence Goodwin, paraphrased by Patricia Limerick in "The Future of Populist Politics" (speech at Colorado College, February 6, 1999).

7. Gretchen Ritter, Goldbugs and Greenbacks: The Antimonopoly Tradition and the Politics of Finance in America, 1865-1896 (Cambridge: Cambridge University Press, 1997), pages 8-9; Carlos Schwantes, Coxey's Army (Moscow, Idaho: University of Idaho Press, 1994); Neander97's Historical Trivia, "Militia Threatens March on Washington!", geocities.com/Athens/Forum/3807/features/hogan.html.

8. Texas State Historical Association, "Greenback Party," The Handbook of Texas Online (December 4, 2002).

9. Official Proceedings of the Democratic National Convention Held in Chicago, Illinois, July 7, 8, 9, 10, and 11, 1896 (Logansport, Indiana, 1896), pages 226–234, reprinted in The Annals of America, Vol. 12, 1895–1904: Populism, Imperialism, and Reform (Chicago: Encyclopedia Britannica, Inc., 1968), pages 100–105.

10. Jack Weatherford, The History of Money: From Sandstone to Cyberspace (New York: Three Rivers Press, 1998), page 176; John Corbally, "The Cross of Gold and the Wizard of Oz," The History of Money, http://home.earthlink.net/~jcorbally/eng218/rcross.html; Hugh Downs, "Odder than Oz," monetary.org (1998).

11. Wayne Slater interviewed in "Karl Rove – the Architect," Frontline, www.pbs.org (April 12, 2005).

12. D. Parker, op. cit.

13. John Algeo, "A Notable Theosophist: L. Frank Baum," Journal of the Theosophical Society in America (September 4, 1892).

14. T. Ziaukas, op. cit.

15. J. Corbally, op. cit.; D. Parker, op. cit.

16. Murray Rothbard, Wall Street, Banks, and American Foreign Policy (Center for Libertarian Studies, 1995).

17. Robert Blumen, "The Organization of Debt into Currency: On the Monetary Thought of Charles Holt Carroll," mises.org (April 27, 2006).

18. John Ascher, "Remembering President William McKinley," schillerinstitute.org (September 2001); Marcia Merry-Baker, et al., "Henry Carey and William McKinley," American Almanac (1995), Sherman Skolnick, "What Happened to America's Goldenboy?", skolnickreport.com.

19. Michael Rowbothan, Goodbye America! Globalisation, Debt and the Dollar Empire (Charlbury, England: Jon Carpenter Publishing, 2000), page 104.

## Chapter 2

1. Paul Sperry, "Greenspan: Financial Wizard of Oz," WorldNetDaily (2001).

2. Ibid.

3. Federal Reserve Bank of New York, "I Bet You Thought," page 186, quoted in G. Edward Griffin, The Creature from Jekyll Island (Westlake Village, California: American Media, 1998), page 19.

4. See Lewis v. United States, 680 F.2d 1239 (1982), in which a federal circuit court so held.

5. Wright Patman, A Primer on Money (Government Printing Office, prepared for the Sub-committee on Domestic Finance, House of Representatives, Committee on Banking and Currency, Eighty-Eighth Congress, 2nd session, 1964).

6. Quoted in Archibald Roberts, The Most Secret Science (Fort Collins, Colorado: Betsy Ross Press, 1984).

7. Benjamin Gisin, "The Mechanics of Money: A Danger to Civilization," American Monetary Institute Presentation (Chicago, September 2006).

8. "United States Mint 2004 Annual Report," usmint.gov.

9. "Money Supply," Wikipedia (October 2006).

10. Chicago Federal Reserve, Modern Money Mechanics (1963), originally produced and distributed free by the Public Information Center of the Federal Reserve Bank of Chicago, Chicago, Illinois, now available on the Internet at http://landru.i-link-2.net/monques/mmm2.html.

11. Chicago Federal Reserve, op. cit.; Patrick Carmack, Bill Still, The Money Masters: How International Bankers Gained Control of America (video, 1998), text at http://users.cyberone.com.au/myers/money-masters.html; William Bramley, The Gods of Eden (New York: Avon Books, 1989), pages 214-29.

12. Robert de Fremery, "Arguments Are Fallacious for World Central Bank," The Commercial and Financial Chronicle (September 26, 1963), citing E. Groseclose, Money: The Human Conflict, pages 178-79.

13. "A Landmark Decision," The Daily Eagle (Montgomery, Minnesota: February 7, 1969), reprinted in part in P. Cook, "What Banks Don't Want You to Know," www9.pair.com/xpoez/money/cook (June 3, 1993).

14. See Bill Drexler, "The Mahoney Credit River Decision," worldnewsstand.net/money/mahoney-introduction.html.

15. G. Edward Griffin, "Debt-cancellation Programs," freedomforceinternational.org (December 18, 2003).

16. William Hummel, "Non-banks Versus Banks," in Money: What It Is, How It Works, http://wfhummel.net (May 17, 2002).

17. See, e.g., California Civil Code Section 1598: "Where a contract . . . [is] wholly impossible of performance, . . . the entire contract is void."

18. Quoted in Stephen Zarlenga, The Lost Science of Money (Valatie, New York: American Monetary Institute, 2002), pages 345-46.

19. Bernard Lietaer, interviewed by Sarah van Gelder in "Beyond Greed and Scarcity," Yes! Magazine (Spring 1997).

20. Quoted in G. E. Griffin, The Creature from Jekyll Island (Westlake Village, California: American Media, 1998), pages 187-88.

21. Mark Stencel, "Budget Background: A Decade of Black Ink?", washingtonpost.com (February 2, 2000); "The Presidential Facts Page," The History Ring, scican.net/~dkochan; Robert Samuelson, "Rising Federal Debt Not Necessarily Negative," Washington Post Writers Group, in the Baton Rouge Advocate (October 9, 2003).

22. John K. Galbraith, Money: Whence It Came, Where It Went (Boston: Houghton Mifflin, 1975), page 90.

23. Erik Sorensen, "Economic Never-never Land," republicons.org (January 17, 2003). (Assume 3 feet per step. One mile = 5,280 feet, multiplied by 4 billion miles = 21,120 billion feet, divided by 3 feet per step = 7,040 billion, or 7.04 trillion, steps.)

24. George Humphrey, Common Sense (Austin, Texas: George Humphrey, 1998), page 5.

25. "Today's Boxscore," nationaldebt.org ($25,725 debt per capita as of January 7, 2005).

26. See "Confessions of a White House Insider", Time Magazine, time.com (January 19, 2004) (Vice President Dick Cheney citing President Ronald Reagan for the proposition that "deficits don't matter").

27. See Chapter 29.

## Chapter 3

1. Jason Goodwin, Greenback (New York: Henry Holt & Co., LLC, 2003), page 40.
2. H. A. Scott Trask, "Did the Framers Favor Hard Money?", lcwatch.com/special69.shtml (2002).
3. J. Goodwin, op. cit., page 43.
4. Ibid.; Jack Weatherford, The History of Money (New York: Crown Publishers, Inc., 1997), pages 132-35.
5. Alvin Rabushka, "Representation Without Taxation," Policy Review (Hoover Institution, Stanford University, August/September 2002).
6. Quoted by Congressman Charles Binderup in a 1941 speech, "How America Created Its Own Money in 1750: How Benjamin Franklin Made New England Prosperous," reprinted in Unrobing the Ghosts of Wall Street, http://reactor core.org/america created money.html.
7. Ibid.; Carmack & Still, op. cit.; expanded quote in "Contango: Dollar Future?", http://thefountainhead.typepad.com (March 16, 2006).
8. J. Goodwin, op. cit., pages 56-57.
9. Quoted in C. Binderup, op. cit.
10. Alexander Del Mar, History of Monetary Systems (1895), quoted in S. Zarlenga, op. cit., page 378.
11. S. Zarlenga, op. cit., pages 377-78.
12. Ibid., pages 385-86.
13. J. W. Schuckers, Finances and Paper Money of the Revolutionary War (Philadephia: J. Campbell & Son, 1874), quoted in S. Zarlenga, op. cit., pages 380-81.
14. S. Zarlenga, op. cit., pages 377-87; Carmack and Still, The Money Masters, op. cit.

## Chapter 4

1. Sheldon Emry, Billions for the Bankers, Debts for the People (Phoenix, Arizona: America's Promise Broadcast, 1984), reproduced at libertydollar.org.
2. James Newell, "Currency and Finance in the 18th Century," The Continental Line (Fall 1997).
3. Alexander Hamilton, Works, Part II, page 271, quoted in G. Edward Griffin, The Creature from Jekyll Island (Westlake Village, California: American Media, 1998), page 316.
4. Jason Goodwin, Greenback (New York: Henry Holt & Co., LLC, 2003), pages 95-115.
5. Vernon Parrington, Main Currents in American Thought, Volume 1, Book 3, Part 1, Chapter 3, "Alexander Hamilton" (1927); reprinted at http://xroads.virginia.edu/~HYPER/Parrington/vol1/bk03_01_ch03.html.
6. Lyndon LaRouche, "Alexander Hamilton," in Economics: The End of a Delusion (Leesburg, Virginia, 2002), pages 82-83.
7. "American Vs. British System," ibid., page 42.
8. J. Goodwin, op. cit., page 109.
9. Stephen Zarlenga, The Lost Science of Money (Valatie, New York: American Monetary Institute, 2002), pages 405-08.
10. J. Goodwin, op. cit.
11. Quoted in S. Zarlenga, op. cit., page 408.
12. Steven O'Brien, Hamilton (NewYork: Chelsea House Publishers, 1989), page 66.
13. Anton Chaitkin, "The Lincoln Revolution," Fidelio Magazine

(spring 1998); David Rivera, Final Warning (1997), republished at silverbearcafe.com.

## Chapter 5

1. Bernard Lietaer, The Mystery of Money (Munich, Germany: Riemann Verlag, 2000), pages 33-44.

2. Michael Hudson, "Reconstructing the Origins of Interest-bearing Debt," in Debt and Economic Renewal in the Ancient Near East (CDL Press, 2002).

3. B. Lietaer, op. cit., pages 48-49.

4. Richard Hoskins, War Cycles, Peace Cycles (Lynchburg, Virginia: Virginia Publishing Company, 1985), page 2.

5. Peter Vogelsang, et al., "Anti-semitism," Holocaust Education, www.holocaust-education.dk (2002).

6. Patrick Carmack, Bill Still, The Money Masters: How International Bankers Gained Control of America (video, 1998), text at http://users.cyberone.com.au/myers/money-masters.html.

7. Aristotle, Ethics 1133.

8. M. T. Clanchy, From Memory to Written Record, England 1066-1307 (Cambridge, Mass., 1979), page 96; see also page 95, n. 28, pl. VIII.

9. Dave Birch, "Tallies & Technologies," Journal of Internet Banking and Commerce, arraydev.com; "Tally Sticks," http://yamaguchy.netfirms.com/astle_d/tally_3.html; Carmack & Still, op. cit.; "Tally Sticks," National Archives, nationalarchives.gov.uk (November 7, 2005).

10. R. Hoskins, op. cit., page 39.

11. S. Zarlenga, op. cit., page 253, citing Peter Spufford, Money and Its Use in Medieval Europe (Cambridge University Press, 1988, 1993), pages 83-93.

12. R. Hoskins, op. cit., pages 37-45, 59-61.

13. James Walsh, The Thirteenth: Greatest of Centuries (New York: Catholic Summer School Press, 1907), chapter 1.

14. Poverty and Pauperism," Catholic Encyclopedia, online edition, newadvent.org. (2003).

15. R. Hoskins, op. cit., pages 37-45, 59-61.

## Chapter 6

1. Patrick Carmack, Bill Still, The Money Masters: How International Bankers Gained Control of America (video, 1998), text at http://users.cyberone.com.au/myers/money-masters.html.

2. Ibid.; Richard Hoskins, War Cycles, Peace Cycles (Lynchburg, Virginia: Virginia Publishing Company, 1985).

3. Stephen Zarlenga, The Lost Science of Money (Valatie, New York: American Monetary Institute, 2002), pages 266-69.

4. Carmack & Still, op. cit.

5. Ibid.

6. J. Lawrence Broz, et al., Paying for Privilege: The Political Economy of Bank of England Charters, 1694-1844 (January 2002), page 11, econ.barnard.columbia.edu.

7. Herbert Dorsey, "The Historical Influence of International Banking," http://usa-the-republic.com; Ed Griffin, The Creature from Jekyll Island (American Media: Westlake Village, California, 2002), pages 175-77.

8. S. Zarlenga, op. cit., page 228.

9. E. Griffin, op. cit.

10. J. Lawrence Broz, Richard Grossman, "Paying for Privilege: The Political Economy of Bank of England Charters, 1694-1844," econ.barnard.columbia.edu

(Weatherhead Center for International Affairs, Harvard University, January 2002).

11. Thomas Rue, "Nine Million Witches?", Harvest 11(3):19-20 (February 1991).

12. "Tally Sticks," op. cit.; R. Hoskins, op. cit.

13. Jack Weatherford, The History of Money (New York: Three Rivers Press, 1998), pages 130-32.

14. See Chapter 17.

**Chapter 7**

1. Charles Conant, A History of Modern Banks of Issue (New York: Putnam, 1909), quoted in Stephen Zarlenga, The Lost Science of Money (Valatie, New York: American Monetary Institute, 2002), page 413.

2. Gustavus Myers, History of the Great American Fortunes (New York: Random House, 1936), page 556, quoted in G. Edward Griffin, The Creature from Jekyll Island (Westlake Village, California: American Media, 1998), page 331.

3. G. E. Griffin, op. cit., pages 226-27; Patrick Carmack, Bill Still, The Money Masters: How International Bankers Gained Control of America (video, 1998), text at http://users.cyberone.com.au/myers/money-masters.html.

4. Carmack & Still, ibid.

5. Quoted in S. Zarlenga, op. cit., page 411.

6. Ibid., pages 410-13.

7. Thomas Jefferson, The Writings of Thomas Jefferson, Memorial Edition (Lipscomb and Bergh, editors, Washington, D.C., 1903-04), volume 15, pages 40-41.

8. S. Zarlenga, op. cit., page 416.

9. G. E. Griffin, op. cit., page 352.

10. Carmack & Still, op. cit.

11. Ibid.; David Rivera, Final Warning (1997), republished at silverbearcafe.com.

**Chapter 8**

1. Anton Chaitkin, "Abraham Lincoln's 'Bank War'," Executive Intelligence Review (May 30, 1986).

2. "Abraham Lincoln," "Republican Party," "Whig Party," Wikipedia.

3. Ibid.; the Adelphi Organization, "Profiles of Famous Brothers," adelphi.com.

4. Patrick Carmack, Bill Still, The Money Masters: How International Bankers Gained Control of America (video, 1998), text at http://users.cyberone.com.au/myers/money-masters.html.

5. Vernon Parrington, Vol. 3, Bk. I, Chap. III, "Changing Theory: Henry Carey," Main Currents in American Thought (1927).

6. Anton Chaitkin, "The 'American System' in Russia, China, Germany and Japan: How Henry Carey and the American Nationalists Built the Modern World," American Almanac (May 1997).

7. Irwin Unger, The Greenback Era (Princeton University Press, 1964), quoted in Stephen Zarlenga, The Lost Science of Money (Valatie, New York: American Monetary Institute, 2002, page 464.

8. J. G. Randall, The Civil War and Reconstruction (Boston: Heath & Co., 1937, 2d edition 1961), pages 3-11, quoted in S. Zarlenga, op. cit.

9. S. Zarlenga, op. cit., pages 455-66.

10. Bob Blain, "The Other Way to Deal with the National Debt," The Progressive Review (June 1994).

## Chapter 9

1. Quoted by Conrad Siem writing about Bismarck in La Vieille France 216:13-16 (March 17-24, 1921); see G. Edward Griffin, The Creature from Jekyll Island (Westlake Village, California: American Media, 1998), page 374; Patrick Carmack, Bill Still, The Money Masters: How International Bankers Gained Control of America (video, 1998), text at http://users.cyberone.com.au/myers/money-masters.html.

2. "Hazard Circular," 1862, quoted in Charles Lindburgh, Banking and Currency and the Money Trust (Washington D.C.: National Capital Press, 1913), page 102.

3. Quoted in Rob Kirby, "Dead Presidents' Society," financialsense.com (February 6, 2007), and many other sources.

4. Quoted in Robert Owen, National Economy and the Banking System (Washington D.C.: U.S. Government Printing Office, 1939).

5. Samuel P. Chase, "National Banking System," Gilder Lehrman Institute of American History, Document Number: GLC1574.01 (1863), gilderlehrman.org; S. Zarlenga, op. cit., pages 467-71; G. E. Griffin, op. cit., pages 386-88.

6. Stephen Zarlenga, The Lost Science of Money (Valatie, New York: American Monetary Institute, 2002), page 469, quoting Davis Rich Dewey, Financial History of the United States (New York: Longmans Green, 1903).

7. Sarah Emery, Seven Financial Conspiracies Which Have Enslaved the American People (Lansing, Michigan: R. Smith, revised edition 1894), chapter X.

8. David Rivera, Final Warning (1997), republished at silverbearcafe.com.

9. Texas State Historical Association, "Greenback Party," The Handbook of Texas Online (December 4, 2002).

## Chapter 10

1. Vernon Parrington, Vol. 3, Bk. 2, "The Old and New: Storm Clouds," Main Currents in American Thought (Harbinger, 1958; originally published in1927).

2. Henry C. K. Liu, "Banking Bunkum, Part 1: Monetary Theology," Asia Times (November 2, 2002).

3. Keith Bradsher, "From the Silk Road to the Superhighway, All Coin Leads to China," The New York Times (February 26, 2006).

4. Bob Blain, "The Other Way to Deal with the National Debt," Progressive Review (June 1994).

5. David Kidd, "How Money Is Created in Australia," http://dkd.net/davekidd/politics/money.html (2001); Michael Rowbotham, Goodbye America! Globalisation, Debt and the Dollar Empire (Charlbury, England: Jon Carpenter Publishing, 2000), pages188-89.

6. Eleazar Lord, National Currency: A Review of the National Banking Law (New York: 1863), page 8.

7. Thomas Greco Jr., Money and Debt: A Solution to the Global Debt Crisis (Tucson, Arizona, 1990), page 5.

8. Letter to Col. William F. Elkins, November 21, 1864, The Lincoln Encyclopedia (New York: Macmillan, 1950).

9. Thomas DiLorenzo, "Fake Lincoln Quotes," lewrockwell.com (2002).

10. Professor James Petras, "Who Rules America?", Global Research (January 13, 2007).

## Chapter 11

1. Quoted in The Federal Observer 4:172 (June 21, 2004), federalobserver.org.

2. Arundhati Roy, "Public Power in the Age of Empire," address to the American Sociological Association in San Francisco, democracynow.org (August 16, 2004).

3. Joe Lockard, et al., "Bad Subjects Interviews Howard Zinn," Bad Subjects: Political Education for Everyday Life , http://eserver.org/editors/2001-1-31.html (January 31, 2001).

4. Carlos Schwantes, Coxey's Army (Moscow, Idaho: University of Idaho Press, 1994), page 37.

5. "In Our Own Image: Teaching Iraq How to Deal with Protest," pressaction.com (October 3, 2003).

6. Lucy Barber, Marching on Washington: The Forging of an American Political Tradition (University of California Press, 2004).

7. Jacob Coxey, "'Address of Protest' on the Steps of the Capitol," from The Congressional Record, 53rd Congress, 2nd Session (May 9, 1894), page 4512.

8. L. Barber, op. cit., chapter 1.

9. "Militia Threatens March on Washington!", geocities.com/Athens/Forum/3807/features/hogan.html; "Coxey's Army," Reader's Companion to American History, college.hmco.com.

10. "In Our Own Image," op. cit.

11. Benjamin Dangl, "Lawyers, Guns and Money: IMF/World Bank Celebrate 60 Years of Infamy," Indymedia (April 28,2004).

12. Russ John, "Monte Ne," Arkansas Travelogue (February 1, 2002).

13. John Ascher, "Remembering President William McKinley," schillerinstitute.org (September 2001); Marcia Merry-Baker, et al., "Henry Carey and William McKinley," American Almanac (1995); Sherman Skolnick, "What Happened to America's Goldenboy?", skolnickreport.com.

14. Murray Rothbard, Wall Street, Banks, and American Foreign Policy (Center for Libertarian Studies, 1995).

## Chapter 12

1. "Woodrow Wilson: The Visionary President," http://home.att.net/~jrhsc/wilson.html.

2. "Daniel Inouye," Wikipedia (November 2004).

3. Quoted in Peaceful Revolutionary Network, "The History of Money Part 3," xat.org (August 2003).

4. Matthew Josephson, The Robber Barons (New York: Harcourt Brace & Co., 1934).

5. Steve Kangas, "Monopolies," Liberalism Resurgent, http://mirrors.korpios.org/resurgent/L-ausmon.htm (1996); Ron Chernow, Titan: The Life of John D. Rockefeller Sr. (Random House, 1998).

6. Steve Kangas, "Myth: The Gold Standard Is a Better Monetary System," The Long FAQ on Liberalism, huppi.com/kangaroo/L-gold.htm (1996).

7. Steve Kangas, "Monopolies," op. cit.; Donald Miller, "Capital and Labor: John Pierpont Morgan and the American Corporation," A Biography of America, learner.org; John Moody, The Truth about the Trusts (New York: Moody Publishing, 1904); Carroll Quigley, Tragedy and Hope (New York: MacMillan Company, 1966).

8. Sam Natapoff, "Rogue Whale," The American Prospect vol. 15, issue 3 (March 1, 2004).

9. "Federal Reserve," Liberty Nation, libertynation.org (2002).

10. G. Edward Griffin, The Creature from Jekyll Island (Westlake Village, California: American Media, 1998), pages 408-17, quoting George Wheeler, Pierpont Morgan and Friends: The Anatomy of a Myth (Englewood Cliffs, New Jersey: Prentice Hall, 1973).

11. David Rivera, Final Warning (1997), republished at silverbearcafe.com.

12. Leon Kilkenny, "Rome, Rockefeller, the U.S., and Standard Oil," reformation.org/rockefeller.html (April 5, 2003).

13. Dr. Peter Lindemann, "Where in the World Is All the Free Energy?" Nexus Magazine (vol. 8, no. 4), June-July 2001.

14. Quoted in Marc Seifer, "Confessions of a Tesla Nerd," netsense.net/tesla/article2.html (Feb. 1, 1997).

## Chapter 13

1. Frank Vanderlip, From Farm Boy to Financier, quoted in "The Great U.$. Fraud," iresist.com (August 8, 2002).

2. "The Roadshow of Deception," World Newsstand, wealth4freedom.com (1999).

3. "Who Was Philander Knox?", worldnewsstand.net/history/PhilanderKnox.htm. (1999).

4. Patrick Carmack, Bill Still, The Money Masters: How International Bankers Gained Control of America (video, 1998), text at http://users.cyberone.com.au/myers/money-masters.html.

5. Jon Christian Ryter, "When the Invisible Power Chooses to be Seen," NewsWithViews.com (August 16, 2006); Murray Rothbard, Wall Street, Banks, and American Foreign Policy (Center for Libertarian Studies, 1995); G. Edward Griffin, The Creature from Jekyll Island (Westlake Village, California: American Media, 1998), pages 239-40.

6. G. E. Griffin, op. cit., pages 465-68.

7. E. Germain, "Truth in History — World War I," Southern Heritage, johnnyreb 22553.tripod.com/southernheritage/id45.html; O. Skinner, "Who Worded the 16th Amendment?", The Best Kept Secret, ottoskinner.com.(2002).

8. Congressman McFadden on the Federal Reserve Corporation, Remarks in Congress, 1934 (Boston: Forum Publishing Co.), including excerpts from Congressional Record 1932, pages 12595-96.

9. See Lewis v. United States, 680 F.2d 1239 (1982), in which a federal circuit court so held.

10. Sam Natapoff, "Rogue Whale," The American Prospect, vol. 15, issue 3 (March 1, 2004).

11. Stephen Zarlenga, The Lost Science of Money (Valatie, New York: American Monetary Institute, 2002), page 536; G. E. Griffin, op. cit., page 423.

12. Edward Flaherty, "Myth #5: The Federal Reserve Is Owned and Controlled by Foreigners," geocities.com/CapitolHill/Senate/3616/flaherty5.html.

13. Hans Schicht, "Financial Spider Webbing," gold-eagle.com (February 27, 2004).

14. Ibid.; Hans Schicht, "From a Different Perspective," gold-eagle.com (July 7, 2003); Hans Schicht, "The Merchants of Debt," gold-eagle.com (July 25, 2001).

15. See Eric Samuelson, J.D., "The U.S. Council on Foreign Relations," sweetliberty.org (2001).

16. Jim Cornwell, "The New World Order," chapter 7, The Alpha and the Omega (1995), mazzaroth.com.

17. Pepe Escobar, "The Masters of the Universe," Asia Times (May 22, 2003).

18. Congressional Record, Second Session, Sixty-Fourth Congress, Volume LIV, page 2947, "Remarks," Oscar Callaway (February 9, 1917).

19. Norman Solomon, "Break up Microsoft? . . . Then How About the Media 'Big Six?,'" The Free Press (April 27, 2000).

20. John Taylor Gatto, The Underground History of American Education (Oxford, New York: Oxford Village Press, 2000-2001).

21. Joe Lockard, et al., "Bad Subjects Interviews Howard Zinn," Bad Subjects: Political Education for Everyday Life , http://eserver.org/editors/2001-1-31.html (January 31, 2001).

22. "Who Was Philander Knox?", op. cit.

## Chapter 14

1. "A Fairy Tale of Taxation," American Patriot Network, civil-liberties.com/pages/taxationtale.htm (June 24, 2000); see Kevin Bonsor, "How Income Taxes Work: Establishing a Federal Income Tax," http://money.howstuffworks.com/income-tax1.htm.

2. Citizens for Tax Justice, "Less Than Zero: Enron's Income Tax Payments, 1996-2000," ctj.org (January 17, 2002).

3. "Origins of the Income Tax," fairtax.org; Sen. Richard Lugar, "My Plan to End the Income Tax," remarks delivered April 5, 1995, CATO Money Report, cato.org.

4. Brushaber v. Union Pacific Railroad, 240 U.S. 1, 7 (1916).

5. "A Fairy Tale of Taxation," op. cit.

6. Ibid.

7. Congressman John Linder, "Become a Voluntary Taxpayer," Americans for Fair Taxation, fairtaxvolunteer.org (June 2, 2001).

8. Bill Benson, "The Law That Never Was – The Fraud of Income and Social Security Tax," thelawthatneverwas.com; Bill Branscum, "Marvin D. Miller's 'Reliance' on Benson (1989)," fraudsandscams.com (2003).

9. "Who Was Philander Knox?", worldnewsstand.net/history/PhilanderKnox.htm. (1999).

10. National Debt Awareness Center, "Federal Budget Spending and the National Debt," federalbudget.com (October 20, 2005); Joint Statement . . . on Budget Results for Fiscal Year 2005," treas.gov (October 14, 2005).

11. President's Private Sector Survey on Cost Control: A Report to the President (vol. 1), approved by the Executive Committee at its meeting on January 15, 1984; reprinted at uhuh.com/taxstuff/gracecom.htm.

## Chapter 15

1. Stanley Schultz, "Crashing Hopes: The Great Depression," American History 102: Civil War to the Present (University of Wisconsin 1999), http://us.history.wisc.edu/hist102/lectures/lecture18.html.

2. Albert Burns, "Born Under a Bad Sign: The Roots of the 'Great Depression,'" sianews.com (October 14, 2003).

3. Lester Chandler, Benjamin Strong, Central Banker (Washington: Brookings, 1958), quoted in Stephen

Zarlenga, The Lost Science of Money (Valatie, New York: American Monetary Institute, 2002), page 541.

4. Carroll Quigley, Tragedy and Hope: A History of the World in our Time (New York: Macmillan Company, 1966), page 326, quoted in G. Edward Griffin, The Creature from Jekyll Island (Westlake Village, California: American Media, 1998), page 424.

5. G. E. Griffin, op. cit., pages 423-26, 502-03.

6. S. Zarlenga, op. cit., pages 546-48.

7. G. E. Griffin, op. cit., pages 49-50.

8. "On the Side of Golden Angels," gold-eagle.com (September 8, 1977).

9. Congressman McFadden on the Federal Reserve Corporation, Remarks in Congress, 1934 (Boston: Forum Publishing Co.), including excerpts from Congressional Record 1932, pages 12595-96.

10. Quoted in The Federal Observer 4:172 (June 21, 2004), federalobserver.org. See "The Bankers' Manifesto and Sustainable Development," afn.org/~govern/safe.html (June 9, 1998).

11. "Profile of the Farmer-Labor Party," Buttons and Ballots (July 1997), reprinted at msys.net.

12. "Massillon's J.S. Coxey Led First March on D.C.," The Enquirer (Cincinnati), April 16, 2003; "Jacob Coxey," spartacus.schoolnet.co.uk.

13. Lucy Barber, Marching on Washington: The Forging of an American Political Tradition (University of California Press, 2004); "Jacob Coxey," spartacus.schoolnet.co.uk.

14. Russ John, "Monte Ne," Arkansas Travelogue (February 1, 2002).

## Chapter 16

1. Lyndon LaRouche, "Economics: The End of a Delusion (Leesburg, Virginia, April 2002).

2. Stephen Zarlenga, The Lost Science of Money (Valatie, New York: American Monetary Institute, 2002), page 554.

3. G. Edward Griffin, The Creature from Jekyll Island (Westlake Village, California: American Media, 1998), page 142, citing Murray Rothbard, What Has Government Done to Our Money? (Larkspur, Colorado: Pine Tree Press, 1964), page 13.

4. "John Maynard Keynes," Time (March 29,1999); Steve Kangas, "A Brief Review of Keynesian Theory," Liberalism Resurgent, http://home.att.net/~Resurgence/L-chikeynes.htm.

5. Henry C. K. Liu, "Banking Bunkum, Part 1: Monetary Theology," Asia Times (November 6, 2002), citing John Maynard Keynes, General Theory (1936).

6. "Roosevelt, the Deficit and the New Deal," Land and Freedom (resources for high school teachers), landandfreedom.org; Jim Powell "How FDR's New Deal Harmed Millions of Poor People," The Cato Institute, cato.org (December 29, 2003).

7. Federal Reserve Statistical Release (October 23, 2003), federalreserve. gov/releases/H6/hist/h6hist1.txt; Jonathan Nicholson, "U.S. National Debt Tops $7 Trillion for First Time," Reuters (February 18, 2004).

8. Cliff Potts, "The American Dollar," USAFWZ (radio), geocities.com/usafwz/dollar.html (November 1, 2003).

9. Robert Hemphill, "Sound Money" (March 17, 1934), quoted by Louis

McFadden in "A Call for Impeachment" presented to Congress May 23, 1933, quoted in James Montgomery, A Country Defeated in Victory, Part III," biblebelievers.org.au.

10. Quoted in J. Montgomery, ibid.

11. S. Zarlenga, op. cit., pages 560-61.

12. Ed Steer, "Who Owns the Federal Reserve?", financialsense.com (October 14, 2004).

13. Dr. Edwin Vieira, "A New Gold Seizure: Possibility or Paranoia?", newswithviews.com (March 2, 2006).

14. Bill O'Rahilly, "Goodbye, Yellow Brick Road," Financial Times (August 5, 2003).

15. Congressman McFadden on the Federal Reserve Corporation, Remarks in Congress, 1934 (Boston: Forum Publishing Co.), including excerpts from Congressional Record 1932, pages 12595-96.

16. Jackson Lears, "A History of the World According to Wall Street: The Magicians of Money," New Republic Online (June 20, 2005).

17. Smedley Butler, War Is a Racket (Los Angeles: Feral House, 1939, 2003); The History Channel, "America's Hidden History: The Plot to Overthrow FDR," informationclearinghouse.info; Lonnie Wolfe, "The Morgan-British Fascist Coup Against FDR," American Almanac (February 1999).

18. S. Zarlenga, op. cit., page 561.

19. R. Edmondson, "Attacks on McFadden's Life Reported," Pelley's Weekly (October 14, 1936).

## Chapter 17

1. Book review of Wright Patman: Populism, Liberalism, and the American Dream by Nancy Young (Southern Methodist University Press, 2000) in Journal of American History 90:1, historycooperative.org.

2. Ibid.

3. Quoted in Archibald Roberts, The Most Secret Science (Fort Collins, Colorado: Betsy Ross Press, 1984).

4. Edward Flaherty, "Myth #7: The Federal Reserve Charges Interest on the Currency We Use," geocities.com/CapitolHill/Senate/3616/flaherty7.html.

5. Wright Patman, A Primer on Money (Government Printing Office, prepared for the Sub-committee on Domestic Finance, House of Representatives, Committee on Banking and Currency, 88th Congress, 2nd session, 1964), chapter 3.

6. Jerry Voorhis, The Strange Case of Richard Milhous Nixon (New York: S. Erikson Inc., 1972).

7. Peter White, "The Power of Money," National Geographic (January 1993), pages 83-86.

8. J. Voorhis, op. cit.

9. E. Flaherty, op. cit.

10. Murray Rothbard, The Case Against the Fed (1994). See also Chapter 2.

11. "United States Debt," Wikipedia.

12. G. Edward Griffin, The Creature from Jekyll Island (Westlake Village, California: American Media, 1998), pages 192-93.

13. Federal Reserve Bank of New York, "Reserve Requirements," ny.frb.org/aboutthefed/fedpoint/fed45.html (June 2004).

14. "Savings Account," Wikipedia.

15. E. Flaherty, op. cit.

16. Board of Governors of the Federal Reserve System, Annual Report; see E. Flaherty, op. cit.

17. The Federal Banking Agency Audit Act of 1978.

18. Wright Patman, "Money Facts," Supplement to a Primer on Money

(88th Congress, 2nd Session 1964); Stephen Zarlenga, The Lost Science of Money (Valatie, New York: American Monetary Institute, 2002), page 673.

## Chapter 18

1. Chicago Federal Reserve, Modern Money Mechanics (1963), originally produced and distributed free by the Public Information Center of the Federal Reserve Bank of Chicago, Chicago, Illinois, now available on the Internet at http://landru.i-link-2.net/monques/mmm2.html.

2. William Hummel, "The Myth of the Money Multiplier," in Money: What It Is, How It Works, http://wfhummel.net (March 17, 2004).

3. W. Hummel, "Bank Lending and Reserves," ibid. (June 23, 2004).

4. Murray Rothbard, "Fractional Reserve Banking," The Freeman (October 1995), reprinted on lewrockwell.com.

5. Carmen Pirritano, "Money & Myths" (May 1993), http://69.69.245.68/money/debate06.htm.

6. Kevin LaRoche, "Investment Banks and Commercial Banks Are Analogous to Oil and Water: They Just Do Not Mix," Boston University, bu.edu/econ/faculty.

7. Emily Thornton, "Inside Wall Street's Culture of Risk: Investment Banks Are Placing Bigger Bets than Ever and Beating the Odds – at Least for Now," BusinessWeek.com (June12, 2006).

8. Sean Corrigan, "Speculation in the Late Empire," LewRockwell.com (January 14, 2006).

9. Barry's Bulls Newsletter, "Those Bond Bums," Barron's Online (June 30, 2006).

## Chapter 19

1. Richard Geist, "New Short Selling Regulations," Bull & Bear Financial Report (March 4, 2004).

2. David Knight, "Short Selling = Counterfeiting?", www.marketocracy.com (2005).

3. Bob Drummond, "Corporate Voting Charade," Bloomberg Markets (April 2006).

4. Daniel Kadlec, "Watch Out, They Bite! How Hedge Funds Tied to Embattled Broker Refco Used 'Naked Short Selling' to Plunder Small Companies," Time (November 6, 2005).

5. Judith Burns, "SEC Proposes Barring Restrictions on Stock Transfers," Dow Jones Newswires (May 26, 2004).

6. "Short Selling," Wikipedia (August 31, 2006).

7. In Karl Thiel, "The Naked Truth on Illegal Shorting," The Motley Fool, fool.com (March 24, 2005).

8. "Stockgate: DTCC Sued Again," Investors Business Daily, investors.com (July 28, 2004).

9. Mark Faulk, "Faulking Truth Recommends Abolishing the SEC," faulkingtruth.com (April 27, 2006).

10. Patrick Byrne, "The Darkside of the Looking Glass: The Corruption of Our Capital Markets," businessjive.com/nss/darkside.html (2004-05).

11. Warren Buffett, "Avoiding a 'Mega-catastrophe': Derivatives Are Financial Weapons of Mass Destruction," Fortune (March 3, 2003).

## Chapter 20

1. Bob Chapman, "The Derivatives Mess," International Forecaster (November 11, 1998), reprinted in usagold.com (November 2005)

(editor's note).

2. Robert Milroy, Standard & Poor's Guide to Offshore Investment Funds 28 (2000); David Chapman, "Derivatives Disaster, Hedge Fund Monsters?", gold-eagle.com (November 11, 2005).

3. Richard Freeman, "London's Cayman Islands: The Empire of the Hedge Funds," Executive Intelligence Review (March 9, 2007).

4. Christopher White, "How to Bring the Cancerous Derivatives Market Under Control," American Almanac (September 6, 1993); R. Colt Bagley III, "Update: Record Derivatives Growth Ups System Risk," moneyfiles.org/specialgata04.html (July 29,2004), reprinted from LeMetropoleCafe.

5. See Gary Novak, "Derivatives Creating Global Economic Collapse," http://nov55.com/economy.html (June 30, 2006).

6. Interview of John Hoefle, "Hedge Fund Rescue, and What to Do with the Blow Out of the Bubble?," EIR Talks (October 2, 1998).

7. Martin Weiss, Global Vesuvius: $285 Trillion in Very High-risk Debts and Bets!," Safe Money Report (November 2006).

8. Thomas Kostigen, "Sophisticated Investor: Derivative Danger," MarketWatch (September 26, 2006). See also Ari Weinberg, "The Great Derivatives Smackdown," forbes.com (May 9, 2003); Michael Edward, "Cooking the Books Part II – US $71 Trillion Casino Banks," rense.com (March 27, 2004).

9. G. Novak, op. cit.

10. Christopher White, Testimony Submitted on April 13, 1994 to the House Committee on Banking, Finance and Urban Affairs, "The Monetary System Is Collapsing," The New Federalist (May 30, 1994).

11. Martin Weiss, "Global Vesuvius," Safe Money Report (November 2006).

12. C. White, op. cit.

13. IMF Research Department Staff, "Capital Flow Sustainability and Speculative Currency Attacks," worldbank.org (November 12, 1997).

14. "A Hitchhiker's Guide to Hedge Funds," The Economist (June 13, 1998).

15. George Soros, The Crisis of Global Capitalism, excerpted in Newsweek International (February 1, 1999).

16. "Credit Derivatives Led by Too Few Banks, Fitch Says," Bloomberg.com (November 18, 2005).

17. John Hoefle, "EIR Testimony Scored Scorched-Earth Looters," Executive Intelligence Review (May 27, 2005).

18. Michael Rowbotham, "How to Cancel Third World Debt," in Goodbye America! Globalisation, Debt and the Dollar Empire (Charlbury, England: Jon Carpenter Publishing, 2000). See also G. Edward Griffin, The Creature from Jekyll Island (Westlake Village, California: American Media, 1998), page 27.

19. See Chapter 31.

20. Sean Corrigan, "Speculation in the Late Empire," LewRockwell.com (January 14, 2006).

21. Quoted in "History of Money," www.xat.org.

22. See Introduction.

## Chapter 21

1. Donald Gibson, Battling Wall Street: The Kennedy Presidency (New York: Sheridan Square Press, 1994), pages 41 and 79, and chapter 6.

2. Compare Melvin Sickler, "Abraham Lincoln and John F. Kennedy: Two

Great Presidents Assassinated for the Cause of Justice," prolognet.qc.ca/clyde/pres.htm; and G. Edward Griffin, "Updates to Creature: The JFK Myth," realityzone.com/creatup.html (2000).

3. "What Is the History of Gold and Silver Use?," jaredstory.com; Kelley Ross, "Six Kinds of United States Paper Currency," friesian.com/notes.htm#us (1997).

4. See, e.g., "JFK Assassination," geocities.com/northstarzone.JFK.html; M. Sickler, op. cit.

5. David Ruppe, "Book: U.S. Military Drafted Plans to Terrorize U.S. Cities to Provoke War With Cuba," ABC News (November 7, 2001), abcnews.com, reviewing Friendly Fire by James Bramford; see also "JFK Assassination," op. cit.

6. William Engdahl, "A New American Century? Iraq and the Hidden Euro-dollar Wars," Current Concerns (November 1, 2003).

7. Henry C K Liu, "The Wages of Neo-Liberalism, Part 1: Core Contradictions," Asia Times (March 22, 2006); Stephen Zarlenga, The Lost Science of Money (Valatie, New York: American Monetary Institute, 2002), chapter 22.

8. Hans Schicht, "Financial Spider Webbing," gold-eagle.com (February 25, 2004).

9. William Engdahl, A Century of War (New York: Paul & Co., 1993); Antal Fekete, "Where Friedman Went Wrong," lemetropolecafe.com (December 1, 2006).

10. Antal Fekete, "Dollar, My Foot," Asia Times (May 28, 2005).

11. Joan Veon, "Does the Global Economy Need a Global Currency?," NewsWithViews.com (August 16, 2003).

12. M. Rowbotham, op. cit., pages 77-84; Bernard Lietaer, "The Terra TRC White Paper," terratrc.org.

13. John Perkins, Confessions of an Economic Hit Man, (San Francisco: Berrett-Koehler Publishers, Inc., 2004), page 91; W. Engdahl, A Century of War, op. cit., pages 135-39.

14. Michael Rowbothan, Goodbye America! Globalisation, Debt and the Dollar Empire (Charlbury, England: Jon Carpenter Publishing, 2000), pages 79-80.

15. Bernard Lietaer, The Future of Money: Creating New Wealth, Work, and a Wiser World (Century, 2001).

16. Robert Schenk, "Fixed Exchange Rates," Cyber-Economics, ingrimayne.com (April 2006).

17. Henry C. K. Liu, "China, Part 2: Tequila Trap Beckons China," Asia Times (November 6, 2004).

18. G. Edward Griffin, The Creature from Jekyll Island (Westlake Village, California: American Media, 1998), page 107; Michael Rowbotham, "How Third World Debt Is Created and How It Can Be Cancelled," Sovereignty (May 2002), sovereignty.org.uk.

19. Vincent Ferraro, et al., "Global Debt and Third World Development," in Michael Klare et al., eds., World Security: Challenges for a New Century (New York: St. Martin's Press, 1994), pages 332-35.

20. William Engdahl, "Why Iran's Oil Bourse Can't Break the Buck," Energy Bulletin (March 12, 2006).

21. John Mueller, "Reserve Currency Problems Need Golden Solutions," Financial Times (August 20, 2004); Chris Gaffney, "Waiting on the Numbers," Daily Reckoning (August 11, 2006).

## Chapter 22

1. William Engdahl, <u>A Century of War</u> Insurance Corporation, <u>History of the 80s</u>, Volume I, Chapter 5, "The LDC Crisis," fdic.gov (2000).

2. W. L. Hoskins, et al., "Mexico: Policy Failure, Moral Hazard, and Market Solutions," <u>Cato Policy Analysis</u>, cato.org (October 10, 1995); "Mexican Populism: 1970 to 1982," http//:daphne.palomar.edu (1996).

3. Henry C. K. Liu, "China, Part 2: Tequila Trap Beckons China," <u>Asia Times</u> (November 6, 2004).

4. W. Engdahl, <u>op. cit.</u>

5. Jane Ingraham, "A Fistful of . . . Pesos?", <u>New American</u> (February 20, 1995).

6. H. C. K. Liu, <u>op. cit.</u>

7. Achin Vanaik, "Cancel Third World Debt," <u>The Hindu</u>, hindu.com. (August 18, 2001).

8. J. N. Tlaga, "Euro and Gold Price Manipulation," gold-eagle.com (December 22, 2000).

9. Eqbal Ahmad, "The Reconquest of Mexico," tni.org (March 1995).

10. Bill Murphy, "Blueprint for a GATA Victory," gata.org (August 6, 2000).

11. J. Ingraham, <u>op. cit.</u>

12. Joseph Stiglitz, "The Broken Promise of NAFTA," <u>New York Times</u> (January 6, 2004).

13. David Peterson, "Militant Capitalism," <u>ZMagazine</u> (February 1996).

14. Christopher Whalen, "Robert Rubin's Shell Game," eco.utexas.edu (October 10, 1995); Jim Callis, "What NAFTA Has Brought to Mexicans," cooperativeindividualism.org (March 1998).

15. H.C. K. Liu, <u>op. cit.</u>

16. Michel Chossudovsky, "The Curse of Economic Globalization," <u>Monetary Reform On-line</u> (fall/winter 1998-99).

## Chapter 23

1. Rachel Douglas, et al., "The Fight to Bring the American System to 19th Century Russia," <u>Executive Intelligence Review</u> (January 1992).

2. Anton Chaitkin, "The 'American System' in Russia, China, Germany and Japan: How Henry Carey and the American Nationalists Built the Modern World," <u>American Almanac</u> (May 1997).

3. G. Edward Griffin, <u>The Creature from Jekyll Island</u> (Westlake Village, California: American Media, 1998), chapter 13.

4. Rachel Douglas, et al., "The Fight to Bring the American System to 19th Century Russia," <u>Executive Intelligence Review</u> (January 3, 1992).

5. "History: Bank of Russia," www.cbr.ru (2005).

6. G. E. Griffin, <u>op. cit.</u>, chapter 13; Robert Wilton, <u>Russia's Agony</u> (1918) and <u>the Last Days of the Romanovs</u> (1920).

7. G. E. Griffin, <u>op. cit.</u>, pages 287-88.

8. "History: Bank of Russia," <u>op. cit.</u>

9. G. E. Griffin, <u>op. cit.</u>, pages 292-93.

10. Srdja Trifkovic, "Neoconservatism, Where Trotsky Meets Stalin and Hitler," <u>Chronicles</u> (July 23, 2003); Martin Kelly, "NeoCons and the Blue Bolsheviks," <u>Washington Dispatch</u> (September 24, 2004); "Alex Jones Interviews Jude Wanniski," prisonplanet.tv (February 2, 2005).

11. S. Trifkovic, <u>op. cit.</u>

12. "History: Bank of Russia," <u>op. cit.</u>

13. "Alex Jones Interviews Jude Wanniski," prisonplanet.tv (February 2, 2005).

14. Wayne Ellwood, "The Great Privatization Grab," <u>New Internationalist Magazine</u> (April 2003).

15. Mark Weisbrot, "Testimony Before the House of Representatives Committee on Banking and Financial Services on the International Monetary Fund and Its Operations in Russia," http://financialservices.house.gov/banking/91098ppp.htm (September 10, 1998).

## Chapter 24

1. John Weitz, Hitler's Banker (Great Britain: Warner Books, 1999).

2. Matt Koehl, "The Good Society?", rense.com (January 13, 2005); Stephen Zarlenga, The Lost Science of Money (Valatie, New York: American Monetary Institute, 2002), pages 590-600.

3. S. Zarlenga, op. cit., page 590.

4. Ibid., pages 591, 595-96.

5. Henry Makow, "Hitler Did Not Want War," savethemales.com (March 21, 2004).

6. Henry C. K. Liu, "Nazism and the German Economic Miracle," Asia Times (May 24, 2005).

7. Stephen Zarlenga, "Germany's 1923 Hyperinflation: A 'Private' Affair," Barnes Review (July-August 1999); David Kidd, "How Money Is Created in Australia," http://dkd.net/davekidd/politics/money.html (2001).

8. S. Zarlenga, "Germany's 1923 Hyperinflation," op. cit.

## Chapter 25

1. William Engdahl, A Century of War (New York: Paul & Co., 1993), page 235.

2. Professor Thayer Watkins, San Jose State University Economics Department, "What Happens When a Paper Currency Fails?", www.2.sjsu.edu.

3. W. Engdahl, op. cit., pages 239-41.

4. Ibid., page 236.

5. Albero Benegas Lynch, "The Argentine Inflation," libertyhaven.com (1972).

6. Carlos Escud , "From Captive to Failed State: Argentina Under Systemic Populism, 1975-2006," The Fletcher Forum of World Affairs (Tufts University, Summer 2006).

7. Dennis Small, "Argentina Proves," Executive Intelligence Review (February 8, 2002).

8. Larry Rohter, "Argentina's Economic Rally Defies Forecasts," New York Times (December 23, 2004).

9. "Argentine Peso," Answers.com; "Banco Central de la Republica Argentina," Wikipedia.org; "Tucking in to the Good Times," Economist.com (December 19, 2006).

10. "Tucking in to the Good Times," ibid.

11. Jorge Altamira, "The Payment to the IMF Is Embezzlement Committed Against Argentina," Prensa Obrera no. 929 (2005).

12. Ibid.; Cynthia Rush, "Argentina, Brazil Pay Off Debt to IMF," Executive Intelligence Review (December 30, 2005); Dennis Small, "'Vulture Funds' Descend on Dying Third World Economies," Executive Intelligence Review (October 10, 2003).

13. "Bags of Bricks: Zimbabweans Get New Money – for What It's Worth," The Economist (August 24, 2006); Thomas Homes, "IMF Contributes to Zimbabwe's Hyperinflation," newzimbabwe.com (March 5, 2006).

14. Henry C. K. Liu, "China, Part 2: Tequila Trap Beckons China," Asia Times (November 6, 2004).

### Chapter 26

1. Kathy Wolfe, "Hamilton's Ghost Haunts Washington from Tokyo – Excerpts from the Leaders of the Meiji Restoration," Executive Intelligence Review (January 1992).

2. Ibid.

3. Chalmers Johnson, "On the Japanese Threat," Multinational Monitor (November 1989).

4. William Engdahl, A Century of War (New York: Paul & Co., 1993), page 229.

5. Ibid.

6. Chalmers Johnson, "How America's Crony Capitalists Ruined Their Rivals," Los Angeles Times (May 7, 1999).

7. Mark Weisbrot, "Testimony Before the House of Representatives Committee on Banking and Financial Services on the International Monetary Fund and Its Operations in Russia," http://financialservices.house.gov/banking/91098ppp.htm (September 10, 1998).

8. Michel Chossudovsky, "The Curse of Economic Globalization," Monetary Reform On-line (fall/winter 1998-99).

9. Ibid.

10. Martin Khor, "Malaysia Institutes Radical Exchange, Capital Controls," Third World Network, www.twnside.org.

11. "World Bank Reverses Position on Financial Controls and on Malaysia," Global Intelligence Update Weekly Analysis (September 20, 1999).

### Chapter 27

1. Bill Ridley, "China and the Final War for Resources," gold-eagle.com/editorials (February 9, 2005).

2. Lee Siu Hin, "Journey to My Home – Hong Kong and China: Rediscovering the Meaning of Labor Activism, Being Chinese and Chinese Nationalism," actionla.org (April 2004).

3. Michael Billington, "Hamilton Influenced Sun Yat-Sen's Founding of the Chinese Republic," Executive Intelligence Review (January 1992); "Sun Yat-Sen," reference.com (2005).

4. Jiawen Yang, et al., The Chinese Currency: Background and the Current Debate (GW Center for the Study of Globalization, George Washington University).

5. "The People's Bank of China: Rules and Regulations," www.pbc.gov.cn (December 27, 2003); "Japan Nationalizes, While China Privatizes," RIETI, rieti.go.jp/en/miyakodayori/072.html (June 25, 2003); Chi Hung Kwan, "Will China's Four Major Banks Succeed in Going Public?," China in Transition, rieti.go.jp/en/china (August 31, 2004); Henry C K Liu, "The Wages of Neoliberalism, Part III: China's Internal Debt Problem," Asia Times (May 28, 2006).

6. C. H. Kwan, op. cit.; "Central Bank," Wikipedia.

7. Henry C K Liu, "Banking Bunkum, Part 1: Monetary Theology," Asia Times (November 2, 2002).

8. Henry C K Liu, "The Wages of Neo-Liberalism, Part 1: Core Contradictions," Asia Times (March 22, 2006).

9. Greg Grillot, "The Mystery of Mr. Wu," The Daily Reckoning (May 10, 2005).

10. Henry C. K. Liu, "The Global Economy in Transition," Asia Times (September 16, 2003).

11. John Mauldin, "The Yield Curve," gold-eagle.com (January 7, 2006).

12. Gary Dorsch, "The Commodity 'Super Cycle' Goes into Extra Innings," financialsense.com (April

24, 2006).

13. William Buckler, "The Week the Bottom Fell Out," The Privateer (March 2006); Gary Dorsch, "The Commodity 'Super Cycle,'" financialsense.com (January 30, 2006); Stephen Poloz, "China's Trillion Dollar Nest Egg," Export Development Canada , www.edc.ca (April 4, 2007).

14. Keith Bradsher, "From the Silk Road to the Superhighway, All Coin Leads to China," The New York Times (February 26, 2006).

15. Henry C. K. Liu, "China, Part 2: Tequila Trap Beckons China," Asia Times (November 6, 2004).

16. Henry C. K. Liu, "Nazism and the German Economic Miracle," Asia Times (May 24, 2005).

17. Henry C. K. Liu, "Crippling Debt and Bankrupt Solutions," Asia Times (September 28, 2002).

18. David Fuller, "Taking the Bull by the Horns," The Daily Reckoning (October 4, 2005).

19. B. Ridley, op. cit.

**Chapter 28**

1. "Commanding Heights: The Battle for the World Economy," pbs.org (2002).

2. William Engdahl, A Century of War (New York: Paul & Co., 1993), pages 140, 161.

3. The Research Unit for Political Economy, "India as 'Global Power,'" Aspects of India's Global Economy , rupe-india.org (December 2005).

4. Wayne Ellwood, "The Great Privatization Grab," New Internationalist Magazine (April 2003).

5. Vincent Ferraro, et al., "Global Debt and Third World Development," in Michael Klare et al., eds., World Security: Challenges for a New Century (New York: St. Martin's

Press, 1994), pages 332-35.

6. H. Caldicott, "First World Greed and Third World Debt," in If You Love This Planet (New York: W.W. Norton, 1992).

7. Henry C K Liu, "How the U.S. Will Play China in the New Cold War," Asia Times (April 18, 2002).

8. Achin Vanaik, "Cancel Third World Debt," The Hindu, hindu.com (August 18, 2001).

9. Christian Weller, Adam Hersh, "Free Markets and Poverty," American Prospect (January 1, 2002).

10. "Indian Banking – Introduction," asiatradehub.com (2006).

11. "State Bank of India Ranks Highest in Consumer Satisfaction," J.D. Power Asia Pacific Reports (2001).

12. Greg Palast, "French Fried Friedman," The Nouvelle Globalizer (June 5, 2005).

13. Caroline Lucas MEP, Vandana Shiva, Colin Hines, "The Consequence of the UK Government's Damaging Approach to Global Trade," Sustainable Economics (April 2005).

14. Radio interview of Vendana Shiva, democracynow.org (December 13, 2006).

15. C. Lucas, et al., op. cit.

16. Bob Djurdjevic, "Wall Street's Financial Terrorism," Chronicles (March 1998).

**Chapter 29**

1. Al Martin, "Bushonomics II (Part 1): The End Game," almartinraw.com (April 11, 2005); Speech by Global Exchange founder Kevin Danaher, "Indymedia," KPFK (Los Angeles), March 15, 2004.

2. A. Martin, op. cit.

3. M. Whitney,"Coming Sooner Than You Think: The Economic Tsunami,"

counterpunch.com (April 8, 2005).

4. Catherine Austin Fitts, "The American Tapeworm – Debt Up, Equity Down & Out," Scoop, scoop.co.nz (May 1, 2003); Chris Sanders, "Where Is the Collateral?", scoop.co.nz (October 28, 2003).

5. Citizens for Tax Justice, "New Data Show Growing Wealth Inequality," ctj.org (May 12, 2006).

6. Jeff Gates, "Ten Ways That Neoliberals Redistribute Wealth Worldwide," Radar (July 2001); Ralph Nader interviewed by George Noory, coasttocoastam.com (September 24, 2004).

7. Barbara Whilehan, "Bankruptcy Bill Bad for Debtors," bankrate.com (March 23, 2005

8. Jeffrey Steinberg, "We Can Beat Rohatyn and the Synarchists," White Paper from EIR Seminar in Berlin (June 27, 2006).

9. "Figures Show States Falling Deeper into Deficit," The Business Journal (Tampa Bay), January 7, 2003.

10. Paul Krugman, "The Debt-Peonage Society," New York Times (March 8, 2005).

11. Elizabeth Warren, Amelia Warren Tyagi, The Two-Income Trap: Why Middle-Class Mothers and Fathers Are Going Broke (New York: Basic Books, 2003).

12. Nicole Colson, "Drowning in Debt," Socialist Worker Online (February 13, 2004).

13. Chicago Federal Reserve, "Modern Money Mechanics" (1963), originally produced and distributed free by the Public Information Center of the Federal Reserve Bank of Chicago, Chicago, Illinois, now available on the Internet at http://landru.i-link-2.net/monques/mmm2.html, page 6.

14. "The Facts About Credit Cards," worldnewsstand.net/money/

credit_cards.htm.

## Chapter 30

1. Christian Weller, "For Middle-class Families, Dream of Own House Drowns in Sea of Debt," Center for American Progress, americanprogress.org (May 2005).

2. U.S. Department of Housing and Urban Development (HUD), "Large Percentage of Properties Are Owned Free and Clear," hud.gov (October 12, 2005).

3. C. Weller, op. cit.; HUD, op.cit.; Mike Whitney, "The Fed's Role in the Housing Crash of '07," Dissident Voice, dissidentvoice.org (January 9, 2007); Martin Weiss, "Final Stage of the Real Estate Bubble," Safe Money Report (June 2005).

4. William Buckler, "The Week the Bottom Fell Out," The Privateer (March 2006); Gracchus, "A New America," rense.com (February 19, 2003).

5. Comptroller of the Currency, "Comptroller Dugan Expresses Concern about Negative Amortization," occ.gov (December 1, 2005).

6. See bankrate.com.

7. Craig Harris, "The Real Estate Bubble," 321gold.com/editorials (March 11, 2004).

8. Gary North, "Surreal Estate on the San Andreas Fault," Reality Check (November 22, 2005).

9. Annys Shin, "House Passes Bill on Fannie and Freddie Oversight," Washington Post (October 27, 2005); "Alan Greenspan is Worried about the Mortgage Lending Agencies," The Economist, economist.com (February 18, 2005).

10. M. Whitney, op. cit.; Richard Freeman, "Fannie and Freddie Were Lenders: U.S. Real Estate Bubble Near Its End," Executive Intelligence

Review (June 21, 2002).

11. M. Whitney, op. cit.

## Chapter 31

1. Al Martin, "Bullish Shillism," almartinraw.com (June 20, 2005). See also Dana Milbank, "Almost Unnoticed, Bipartisan Budget Anxiety," Washington Post (May 18, 2005).

2. Adam Hamilton, "Real Rates and Gold 6," ZEAL, zealllc.com (2004).

3. Al Martin, op. cit.

4. Ibid., citing testimony by Federal Reserve Chairman Alan Greenspan before the Joint Economic Committee in June 2005. See also Kurt Richebacher, "Mr. Ponzi Salutes," The Richebacher Letter (June 2005).

5. Richard Freeman, "Fannie and Freddie Were Lenders: U.S. Real Estate Bubble Near Its End," Executive Intelligence Review (June 21, 2002).

6. "U.S. Financial Systemic Risk: Fannie Mae & Freddie Mac," http://seattlebubble.blogspot.com (August 11, 2006).

## Chapter 32

1. R. Colt Bagley III, "Update: Record Derivatives Growth Ups System Risk," moneyfiles.org/specialgata04.html (July 29, 2004), reprinted in LeMetropoleCafe.

2. C. White, "How to Bring the Cancerous Derivatives Market Under Control," American Almanac (September 6, 1993).

3. Martin Weiss, Global Vesuvius: $285 Trillion in Very High-risk Debts and Bets!," Safe Money Report (November 2006).

4. See Chapter 20.

5. M. Weiss, op. cit.

6. Gary Novak, "Derivatives Creating Global Economic Collapse," http://nov55.com/economy.html (June 30, 2006).

7. "Slipping on Derivative Banana Peels," http://worldvisionportal.org (February 9, 2004).

8. Lothar Komp, "'Hedge Fund' Blowout Threatens World Markets," Executive Intelligence Review (May 27, 2005).

9. Ibid.

10. Nelson Hultberg, "Cornered Rats and the PPT," gold-eagle.com/editorials (March 26, 2003).

11. Captain Hook, "A Few Thoughts on Recently Announced Reporting Changes at the Fed," Treasure Chests, November 14, 2005, reprinted on safehaven.com (November 18, 2005).

12. The Mogambo Guru (Richard Daughty), "The 'Two Trill in Cash' Plan," The Daily Reckoning (April 10, 2006).

13. "Petro-Euro: A Reality or Distant Nightmare for U.S.?", aljazeera.com (April 30, 2006).

14. Rob Kirby, "The Grand Illusion," financialsense.com (December 13, 2005).

15. R. Daughty, op.cit.

16. "America's Black Budget and the Manipulation of Mortgage and Financial Markets," interview with Catherine Austin Fitts, Financial Sense Newshour, netcastdaily.com (May 22, 2004).

17. M. Whitney,"Coming Sooner Than You Think: The Economic Tsunami," counterpunch.com (April 8, 2005); Gregory Palast, "The Globalizer Who Came in from the Cold," The London Observer (October 10, 2001).

18. See, e.g., Bob Chapman, The International Forecaster (September 3, 2003), goldseek.com/news/InternationalForecaster/1062763200.php.

19. Jeremy Scahill, "Blackwater Down," The Nation (October 10, 2005).

20. Henry Kissinger, Speech at Bilderberg Conference in Evians-Les-Bains, France, May 1992, "Quotations Attributed to Henry Kissinger," rense.com (December 1, 2002).

21. Al Martin, "FEMA, CILFs and State Security: Shocking Updates," almartinraw.com (November 28, 2005).

22. Ibid.; Michael Meurer, "Greenspan Testimony Highlights Bush Plan for Deliberate Federal Bankruptcy," truthout.org (March 2, 2004).

23. Henry C K Liu, "The Global Economy in Transition," Asia Times (September 16, 2003).

24. See Richard Hoskins, War Cycles, Peace Cycles (Lynchburg, Virginia: Virginia Publishing Company, 1985).

25. John Crudele, "Paulson's Other Job as Wall St. Plunge Protector," New York Post (June 9, 2006).

## Chapter 33

1. Michael Bolser, "Cartel Capitulation Watch," Midas, lemetropolecafe.com (April 18, 2004).

2. Bill Murphy, "Consolidation Day Before Gold and Silver Resume Move Higher," Midas, lemetropolecafe.com (Oct. 2, 2005).

3. John Crudele, "George Let Plunge Slip," New York Post (June 27, 2006).

4. Executive Order 12631 of March 18, 1988, 53 FR, 3 CFR, 1988 Comp., page 559.

5. Michael Bolser, "Enough Is Enough," Midas, lemetropolecafe.com (January 26, 2004). See his chart site at pbase.com/gmbolser/interventional_analysis.

6. John Emry, Not Free, Not Fair: The Long-term Manipulation of the Gold Price (Toronto: Sprott Asset Management, August 24, 2004), reprinted at fallstreet.com.

7. John Embry, Andrew Hepburn, "US Stocks: The Visible Hand of Uncle Sam," introduction by Japan Focus, Asia Times (October 19, 2005).

8. Chuck Augustin, "Plunge Protection or Enormous Hidden Tax Revenues," lemetropolecafe.com (June 30, 2006).

9. Jim Sinclair, "Cartel Blatantly Hammers Gold," jsmineset.com (November 21, 2003).

10. The John Brimelow Report, "Goldman Sach's 'Partner'," Midas, lemetropolecafe.com (March 24, 2004), quoting Bianco Research report.

11. The Prowler, "Raid on the Treasury," The American Spectator (October 12, 2006).

12. Bill Murphy, "Moral Hazard," LeMetropoleCafe.com (September 8, 2006), reposted at gata.org/node/4361 (September 9, 2006), quoting Joe Stocks at siliconinvestor.com/readmsg.aspx?msgid=22789705.

13. Ibid., citing federalreserve.gov/boarddocs/speeches/2002/200209252/default.htm.

14. Ibid., citing crmpolicygroup.org/docs/CRMPG-II.pdf.

15. M. Bolser, op. cit.

16. Alex Wallenwein, "The Dollar, the Crash, and the FTAA," financialsense.com (April 21, 2004).

17. Addison Wiggin, The Demise of the Dollar ( Hoboken, New Jersey: John Wiley & Sons, 2005), page 63.

18. Hans Schicht, "From a Different Perspective, " gold-eagle.com (July 7, 2003).

19. Richard Freeman, "London's Cayman Islands: The Empire of the Hedge Funds, <u>Executive Intelligence Review</u> (March 9, 2007).

## Chapter 34

1. "The Coming Storm," <u>The Economist</u> (London), February 17, 2004, quoted in "New Bretton Woods Advances as Dollar Faces 'The Coming Storm,'" <u>Executive Intelligence Review</u> (March 5, 2004).

2. John Hoefle, "Mergers, Derivatives Losses Reveal Bankruptcy of the U.S. Banking System," <u>Executive Intelligence Review</u> (November 1, 2002).

3. Michael Edward, "Cooking the Books: U.S. Banks Are Giant Casinos," http://worldvisionportalorg (February 2, 2004).

4. Robert Guttman, <u>How Credit-Money Shapes the Economy</u> (Armonk, New York: M. E. Sharpe, 1994), Sections 11, 11.1.

5. <u>Ibid.</u>, Sections 10 and 11.

6. The Boston Consulting Group, "Growing Profits Under Pressure: Integrating Corporate and Investment Banking," bcg.com (2002).

7. "Wall Street v Wall Street," <u>The Economist</u> (June 29, 2006).

8. William Hummel, "Money Center Banks," in <u>Money: What It Is, How It Works</u> http://wfhummel.net (January 8, 2004).

9. Radio interviews of Patrick Byrne on <u>Christian Financial Network</u>, November 11, 2006; and on <u>Financial Sense Online</u>, March 31, 2007.

10. Liz Moyer, "Naked Shorts," <u>Forbes.com</u> (April 13, 2006). See also Liz Moyer, "Crying Foul in Short-selling Land," <u>Forbes.com</u> (June 21, 2006).

11. Dave Lewis, "Too Big to Bail (Out): A Case of Humpty Dumpty Finance," http://dharmajoint.blogspot.com/2007/03/too-big-to-bail-out-case-of-humpty.html (March 9, 2007).

12. Murray Rothbard, "Fractional Reserve Banking," <u>The Freeman</u> (October 1995), reprinted on lewrockwell.com.

13. See, e.g., Addison Wiggin, <u>The Demise of the Dollar</u> ( Hoboken, New Jersey: John Wiley & Sons, 2005), chapter 8; Martin Weiss, safemoneyreport.com; J. Taylor, miningstocks.com; Bill Bonner, dailyreckoning.com.

## Chapter 35

1. David Parker, "The Rise and Fall of The Wonderful Wizard of Oz as a 'Parable on Populism,'" <u>Journal of the Georgia Association of Historians</u> 15:49-63 (1994).

2. Dr. Peter Lindemann, "Where in the World Is All the Free Energy?" <u>Nexus Magazine</u> (vol. 8, no. 4), June-July 2001.

3. Ron Paul questioning Ben Bernanke before the Joint Economic Committee on March 28, 2006, C-SPAN.

4. Board of Governors of the Federal Reserve, "M3 Money Stock (discontinued series)," http://research.stlouisfed.org/fred2/data/M3SL.txt.

5. Richard Russell, "I Believe the Dollar Is Doomed," <u>The Russell Report</u> (August 23, 2006).

6. Y. Trofimov, "Conspiracy Theory Gains Currency, Thanks to Town's Professor Auriti," <u>Wall Street Journal</u> (October 7, 2000), page 34.

7. NORFED, norfed.org.

8. Barbara Hagenbaugh, "Feds Lower Boom on Alternative Money," <u>USA Today</u> (September 15, 2006)

9. GoldMoney, goldmoney.com.

8.  "Impact of the Grameen Bank on Local Society," rdc.com.au/ grameen/Impact.html.

10.  Michael Strong, "Forget the World Bank, Try Wal-Mart," TCS Daily (August 22, 2006).

## Chapter 36

1.  Stephen DeMeulenaere, "A Pictorial History of Community Currency Systems," appropriate-economics.org (2000).

2.  Thomas Greco Jr., New Money for Healthy Communities (Tucson, Arizona, 1994), pages 17-21, quoting "A Public Service Economy: An Interview with Edgar S. Cahn," Multinational Monitor (April 1989).

3.  T. Greco, op. cit.

4.  Ravi Dykema, "An Interview with Bernard Lietaer," Nexus (July/ August 2003).

5.  David Johnston, Bernard Lietaer, "ECO2 Carbon Credit Card Project" (Draft Proposal, January 31, 2007).

6.  James Taris, "Travelling the World Without Money," lets-linkup.com.

7.  Thomas Greco Jr., Money and Debt: A Solution to the Global Debt Crisis (Tucson, Arizona, 1990), page 42.

8.  Stephen Zarlenga, The Lost Science of Money (Valatie, New York: American Monetary Institute, 2002), page 660.

## Chapter 37

1.  Gretchen Ritter, Goldbugs and Greenbacks: The Antimonopoly Tradition and the Politics of Finance in America, 1865-1896 (New York: University of Cambridge, 1997).

2.  Vernon Parrington,"The Old and New: Storm Clouds," Vol. 3, Bk. 2, Main Currents in American Thought (1927).

3.  Stephen Zarlenga, The Lost Science

of Money (Valatie, New York: American Monetary Institute, 2002), page 604.

4.  Hon. Ron Paul of Texas before the U.S. House of Representatives, "The End of Dollar Hegemony", lewrockwell.com/paul/paul303.html (February 15, 2006).

5.  Hon. Ron Paul of Texas, Speech before the U.S. House of Representatives, "Abolish the Federal Reserve," house.gov (September 10, 2002).

6.  Tuoi Tre, Ho Chi Minh City, Vietnam, via VietNamBridge.net (November 26, 2005).

7.  S. Zarlenga, op. cit., page 658.

8.  Hugo Price, "How to Introduce the One Ounce Silver 'Libertad' Coin into Circulation in Mexico," gold-eagle.com (June 11, 2003).

9.  G. Edward Griffin, The Creature from Jekyll Island (Westlake Village, California: American Media, 1998), page 142.

10. Harvey Barnard, The National Economic Stabilization and Recovery Act, http://nesara.org.

## Chapter 38

1.  National Press Club speech by David Walker in Washington on September 17, 2003.

2.  Al Martin, "Bushonomics II (Part 1): The End Game," almartinraw.com (April 11, 2005).

3.  John Pilger, "Iran: The Next War," New Statesman, newstatesman.com (February 13, 2006).

4.  Mike Whitney,"Coming Sooner Than You Think: The Economic Tsunami," counterpunch.com (April 8, 2005).

6.  Rob Kirby, "Pirates of the Caribbean," financialsense.com (March 18, 2005).

6. Rob Kirby, "Currency Conundrums," financialsense.com (November 21, 2005).

7. Robert McHugh, "What's the Fed Up to with the Money Supply?", safehaven.com (December 23, 2005); Ed Haas, "Iran, Bourse and the U.S. Dollar," NewsWithViews.com (January 28, 2006); "The Dollar May Fall This March," Pravda (January 14, 2006); Martin Walker, "Iran's Really Big Weapon," globalresearch.ca (January 23, 2006); and see Chapter 32.

8. See "Ponzi Scheme," You Be the Judge and Jury, chapter 3, maxexchange.com/ybj/chapter3.htm.

9. Department of the Treasury, "Public Debt News," Bureau of the Public Debt, Washington, D.C. 20239 (January 15, 2004).

10. "U.S. Treasury Defaults on 30 Year Bond Holders," rense.com (January 20, 2004).

11. Jerry Voorhis, The Strange Case of Richard Milhous Nixon (New York: S. Erikson Inc., 1972).

12. American Monetary Institute, "The American Monetary Act" (September 2006), "Proposed Legislation," www.monetary.org.

## Chapter 39

1. William Hummel, "Zeroing the National Debt," Money: What It Is, How It Works, http://wfhummel.net (March 3, 2002).

2. "Broad Liquidity," investopedia.com (2006).

3. "National Debt Clocks: National Debt by the Second," http://zfacts.com/p/461.html (March 4, 2005).

4. March 2005 radio interview of Mark Weisbrot, co-author of Social Security: The Phony Crisis (Chicago: University of Chicago Press, 1999).

5. Treasury Bulletin, fms.treas.gov/bulletin/b44ofs.doc (December 2004).

6. "U.S. Public Debt," Wikipedia, citing figures from The Analytical Perspectives of the 2006 U.S. Budget, page 257.

7. Robert Bell, "The Invisible Hand (of the U.S. Government) in Financial Markets," financialsense.com (April 3, 2005).

8. "The Dow Jones Wilshire 5000 Composite Index, Fundamental Characteristics Month Ending 12/30/2005," wilshire.com/Indexes/Broad/Wilshire5000/Characteristics.html.

9. "S&P 500 Index," yahoo.com.

10. Stanley Schultz, "Crashing Hopes: The Great Depression," American History 102: Civil War to the Present (University of Wisconsin 1999).

## Chapter 40

1. Richard Russell, "I Believe the Dollar Is Doomed," The Russell Report (August 23, 2006).

2. Ben Bernanke, "Deflation: Making Sure 'It' Doesn't Happen Here," Remarks Before the National Economists Club, Washington, D.C. (November 21, 2002).

3. Ben Bernanke, "Some Thoughts on Monetary Policy in Japan" (May 2003), quoted in Richard Duncan, "How Japan Financed Global Reflation," John Mauldin's Outside the Box, reprinted in gold-eagle.com (May 16, 2005).

4. "Bank of Japan Law," globaledge.msu.edu (December 15, 1998); "Japan Nationalizes, While China Privatizes," RIETI, rieti.go.jp/en/miyakodayori/072.html (June 25, 2003).

5. Richard Duncan, "Japan's Monetary Alchemy May Not Yield Gold," Financial Times (February 10, 2004).

6. R. Duncan, "How Japan Financed Global Reflation," op. cit.

7. Ibid.

8. Joseph Stroupe, "Speaking Freely: Crisis Towers Over the Dollar," Asia Times (November 25, 2004).

9. Rob Kirby, "Pirates of the Caribbean," financialsense.com (March 18, 2005). See Chapter 33.

10. Robert McHugh, "What's the Fed Up to with the Money Supply?", safehaven.com (December 23, 2005).

## Chapter 41

1. See Chapter 2.

2. William Hummel, "Non-banks Versus Banks," in Money: What It Is, How It Works, http://wfhummel.net (May 17, 2002).

3. Gerry Rough, "A Bank of England Conspiracy?", floodlight.org (1997).

4. James Robertson, John Bunzl, Monetary Reform: Making It Happen (2003), jamesrobertson.com, page 26.

5. Ibid., pages 41- 42.

6. Stephen Zarlenga, The Lost Science of Money (Valatie, New York: American Monetary Institute, 2002), pages 671-73.

7. Robert de Fremery, Rights Vs. Privileges (San Anselmo, California: Provocative Press 1997), pages 84-85.

8. American Monetary Institute, "The American Monetary Act" (September 2006), "Proposed Legislation," www.monetary.org.

9. "Monetary Reform Act," themoneymasters.com (2006).

10. Table B-72, "Bank Credit of All Commercial Banks, 1959-2005," http://a257.g.akamaitech.net/7/257/2422/15feb20061000/www.gpoaccess.gov/eop/2006/B72.xls.

11. William Hummel, "A Plan for Monetary Reform," Money: What It Is, How It Works, http://wfhummel.net (December 7, 2006).

12. Ibid.

13. Robert Guttman, How Credit-Money Shapes the Economy (Armonk, New York: M. E. Sharpe, 1994).

14. "History of the U.S. Postal Service, 1775-1993," usps.com.

15. W. Hummel, op. cit.

## Chapter 42

1. Roger Langrick, "A Monetary System for the New Millennium," worldtrans.org/whole/monetarysystem.html.

2. Haitham Al-Haddad and Tarek El-Diwany, "The Islamic Mortgage: Paradigm Shift or Trojan Horse?", islamic-finance.com (November 2006).

3. Betty Reid Mandell, "Privatization of Everything," New Politics 9(1-2) (2002).

4. See Chapter 28.

5. David Kidd, "How Money is Created in Australia," http://dkd.net/davekidd/politics/money.html (2001).

6. Lyndon LaRouche, "Economics: The End of a Delusion (Leesburg, Virginia, April 2002), page 88.

7. B. Mandell, op. cit.

8. See Harvey Wasserman, "California's Deregulation Disaster," The Nation (February 12, 2001).

9. Catherine Austin Fitts, "How the Money Works," SRA Quarterly, London (November 2001).

10. See Chapter 29.

## Chapter 43

1. Richard Russell, "The Takeover of U.S. Money Creation," Dow Theory Letter (April 2005).

2. Hans Schicht, "The Death of Banking and Macro Politics," 321gold.com/editorials (February 9, 2005).

3. Insurance Information Institute, Financial Services Fact Book (2005), http://financialservicefacts.org/financial2/banking/commercial/content.print.

4. William Hummel, "Deposit Insurance and Bank Failures," in Money: What It Is, How It Works, http://wfhummel.net (April 15, 2000).

5. G. Edward Griffin, The Creature from Jekyll Island (Westlake Village, California: American Media, 1998), pages 63, 65.

6. Emily Thornton, Mike France, "For Enron's Bankers, a 'Get Out of Jail Free' Card," businessweek.com (August 11, 2003).

7. Martin Weiss, "Global Vesuvius," Safe Money Report (November 2006).

8. John Hoefle, "The Federal Reserve Vs. The United States," Executive Intellligence Review, April 12, 2002.

9. Dean Baker, "Effective Currency Transaction Taxes: The Need to Tax Derivatives," Center for Economic and Policy Research, cepr.net (June 19, 2001).

10. Dean Baker, "Taxing Financial Speculation: Shifting the Tax Burden from Wages to Wagers," cepr.net (February 2000).

**Chapter 44**

1. "Federal Budget Spending and the National Debt," federalbudget.com (October 20, 2005).

2. Federal Reserve, "Assets and Liabilities of Commercial Banks in the United States," federalreserve.gov/releases/h8/Current/ (December 30, 2005).

3. John Williams, "Monthly Commentary," Shadow Government Statistics, shadowstats.com/cgi-bin/sgs/archives (August 2006).

4. See Chapter 38.

5. Bill Fleckenstein, "The Numbers Behind the Lies," MSN Money, http://moneycentral.msn.com (March 6, 2006).

6. Jan Vandermoortele, Are the MDGs Feasible? (New York: United Development Program Bureau for Development Policy, July 2002).

7. Harry Magdoff, et al., "The New Face of Capitalism: Slow Growth, Excess Capital, and a Mountain of Debt," Monthly Review (April 2002).

8. Michael Hodges, "America's Total Debt Report," http://mwhodges.home.att.net (March 2006).

9. American Monetary Institute, "The American Monetary Act" (September 2006), "Proposed Legislation," www.monetary.org.

10. "CAFRs: The Biggest Secret," rense.com (June 30, 2000); Tom Valentine, "Media Watchdogs Won't Expose Hidden Slush," American Free Press, americanfreepress.net.

11. "Debate Continues on Alaska Oil Drilling," CNNfyi.com (March 23, 2001).

12. Roger Langrick, "A Monetary System for the New Millennium," worldtrans.org/whole/monetarysystem.html.

**Chapter 45**

1. Martin Khor, "IMF: Bailing Out Countries or Foreign Banks?", Third World Network (February 18, 2005).

2. Abraham McLaughlin, "Debt Forgiveness Gathers Steam,"

Christian Science Monitor (September 30, 2004).

3. Michael Rowbotham, "How Third World Debt Is Created and How It Can Be Cancelled," Sovereignty (May 2002), sovereignty.org.uk, excerpted from M. Rowbotham, "The Invalidity of Third World Debt" (1998), pages 14-17, and M. Rowbotham, Goodbye America! (Charlbury, England: Jon Carpenter Publishing, 2000), pages 135-36 and 140-43.

4. See Chapter 25.

5. Andrew Berg, et al., "The Dollarization Debate," Finance Development (March 2000); "Mixed Blessing: Can Dollarized Ecuador Avoid the Argentine Trap?", Financial Times (January 24, 2002); "El Salvador Learns to Love the Greenback," Economist (September 26, 2002); Marcia Towers, "The Socioeconomic Implications of Dollarization in El Salvador," Latin American Politics and Society (fall 2004).

**Chapter 46**

1. Michael Rowbotham, "An Indispensable Key to a Just World Economy," Prosperity, prosperityuk.com (October 2001).

2. Thomas Greco, "New Money: A Creative Opportunity for Business," The Global Development Research Center, www.gdrc.org.

3. Bernard Lietaer, "A 'Green' Convertible Currency," www.transaction.net.

4. Frederick Mann, "Economic Means to Freedom – Part V," buildfreedom.com (October 2, 1998).

5. Doug Gillespie, "'Core' Inflation Doesn't Work in Either Your Stomach or Your Gas Tank!",

PrudentBear.com (May 26, 2005); Tim Iacono, "Home Ownership Costs and Core Inflation," http:// themessthatgreenspanmade.blogspot.com (October 17, 2005).

6. Lyndon LaRouche Political Action Committee, "A New Bretton Woods Now!", larouchepac.com (April 29, 2005).

7. Lyndon LaRouche, "Trade Without Currency," schillerinstitute.org (2000).

8. "Dr. Mahathir Mohamad," aljazeera.com (August 12, 2004).

9. "Gold Dinar Coins," taxfreegold.co.uk/golddinar.html.

10. Tarek El Diwany, "Third World Debt," presentation at Cambridge University's "One World Week" in February 2002, citing UNDP Human Development Report (1997), page 93.

11. Tarek El Diwany, "A Debate on Money," islamic-banking.com (July 2001).

**Chapter 47**

1. George Friedman, "Global Market Brief: China's Engineered Drop," worldnewstrust.com (March 1, 2007); Mike Whitney, "Tuesday's Market Meltdown," counterpunch.org (March 1, 2007).

2. See, e.g., "The James Joyce Table," lemetropolecafe.com (February 28, 2007); and see Chapter 33.

3. M. Whitney, op. cit.

# Index

# G

# H

LaVergne, TN USA
10 December 2009

166632LV00007B/48/A

9 780979 560804